DIGITAL ECONOMICS

*How Information Technology
Has Transformed Business Thinking*

RICHARD B. MCKENZIE

PRAEGER

**Westport, Connecticut
London**

Library of Congress Cataloging-in-Publication Data

McKenzie, Richard B.
   Digital economics : how information technology has transformed business thinking /
   Richard B. McKenzie.
      p. cm.
   Includes bibliographical references and index.
   ISBN 1-56720-644-1 (alk. paper)
      1. Information technology—Economic aspects.   2. Economics.   3. Business planning.
   I. Title
   HC79.I55 M369   2003
   338.5—dc21   2002028308

British Library Cataloguing in Publication Data is available.

Library of Congress Catalog Card Number: 2002028308
ISBN: 1-56720-644-1

First published in 2003

Praeger Publishers, 88 Post Road West, Westport, CT 06881
An imprint of Greenwood Publishing Group, Inc.
www.praeger.com

Printed in the United States of America

The paper used in this book complies with the
Permanent Paper Standard issued by the National
Information Standards Organization (Z39.48-1984).

10   9   8   7   6   5   4   3   2   1

Contents

1

The Spread of 1's and 0's in the World

These words were born digitally, that is, as strings of 1's and 0's. I say that because the words were typed into computers, and computers (no matter how many gigahertz of processor speed or gigabytes of hard drive space) are too dumb to be able to deal with anything other than 1's and 0's. "Dumbness" is a defining characteristic of most information technology. The great paradox of our age is how so much brilliant work can be done with innately dumb technology. What is even more paradoxical is how in large and small ways dumb informational technology is forcing economists and managers alike to change the way they think about how the world works. This book is about the transformation in thinking based at times on "big ideas"—those ideas that are remarkably simple but yet spawn whole new mental constructions of the economy, meaning they engineer theoretical "paradigm shifts"—and at other times on "small ideas"—those that merely force revisions or extensions of established thinking within given theoretical paradigms.

In the digital scheme of things, letters, numbers, and special symbols typed on computer keyboards are represented by binary code, or sequences of 1's and 0's. For example, the letter A is represented by the combination 10100001 (under the ASCII coding scheme, and there are other coding schemes), while B is represented by 10100010. The number 1 is represented by 01010001, and the number 2 by 01010010. Hence, to write out something as simple as the word *digit* in binary code requires this string of 1's and 0's: 011001001010100110100111110 010100110110100. You can imagine that this paragraph (which has only 196 words) could easily take up five or more pages in this book if the letters (and spaces and other punctuation marks) were converted back to 1's and 0's, an observation that highlights a deficiency of code and the efficiency of the printed word. What computers lack in the way of brevity of the code on which they rely, however, they more than make up for by their speed, and by the ease with which changes can be made in the strings of 1's and 0's, which explains why these words had virtual births, so to speak.

More than three decades ago, when I started writing from my academic post, the economics of writing books was much different. My words were born as ink smudges on yellow pages, which had the feel of newsprint. Revisions of my typed words were arduous and time-consuming. I literally had to cut and paste my way through new drafts, a process few people under thirty today remember anyone ever doing (my current students have no idea what Liquid Paper or White Out is). Three decades ago, I suspect that I could have found a mainframe computer (personal computers were not available until the late 1970s) that I could have used to type my manuscripts, but I did not do it for a good and time-honored economic reason: the cost was prohibitive, reaching into the thousands of dollars per hour.

Digital drafts and redrafts of manuscripts can now be made with ease, and economically as well, given the near evaporation of the cost of computer power and time. Consequently, as I go through this book, I expect my pages will be under constant revision. If I find a new relevant fact or come up with a new argument after a chapter has been "finalized," no problem. Changes will be made without much hesitation on computers that are far more powerful than I realistically need but that I bought anyway because the excess power, which I just might use, is dirt cheap.

I start this book with a recognition of the digital births of the words in it as my way of highlighting a critical aspect of the digital economy that will be a focus of the book: There is an economics to "digital goods," meaning a cost–benefit explanation for why 1's and 0's are used. As we will see, economic theory may not have changed fundamentally with the advent of the digital economy, but the conditions of the economy have changed radically with the passing years. Digital goods—by which I mean things we produce, such as this book in its original form, that can be reduced to 1's and 0's—are materially different from other goods, mainly in that they are material-less and have economic lives of their own. Once born, they need not be reborn. When I completed the typing, and cutting and pasting, on my earlier book manuscripts, the words had to once again be retyped—or born again—at the printers. The only way to get copies of the books was to run the presses, causing more than a few trees to be felled in the process. If revisions needed to be made in following editions of the books, the typing and retyping (and the cutting and pasting) would start all over again. If books needed to be sold, they had to be shipped by truck or train, driving up their retail price.

Of course, this book is about far more than the exact medium by which it was created. It is about the radical change in the nature of goods when they can be digitized. The costs of production are different, but so are their costs of distribution, given the weightless nature of digits, as well as the fact that the speed limit on electronic distribution networks is nothing short of the speed of light. The book is also about how the creation of what Microsoft founder Bill Gates now likes to call a firm's "digital nervous systems," made up of their digitized data resources and communication systems (like E-mail), has done much more than lowered the cost of record keeping and communications within firms. For some firms, their digital nervous systems have done nothing more novel than contributed another productivity improvement, or cost reduction, and have affected their scale of operations, much like the telephone, the intercom, and mainframe computers did decades in our past. For other firms, their digital nervous systems have had a far more substantial impact. They have literally changed the way firms are, and must be, managed. They have changed the intensity, if not nature, of their interfirm competition. As we will see, the digitization of goods unsettles many long-standing economic and management principles.

However, the impact of digital goods extends far beyond the bounds of firms. Governments—what they can and cannot do, how they must be managed, and what policies they must adopt—have also been affected. This is because digital goods—the real capital and jobs they represent—are so mobile, able not only "to leap tall buildings in a single bound" (as Superman could do), but to bounce about the globe at little cost, crossing national borders at will, and taking their economic value with them. As Dwight Lee and I have explained in another book, because of the advent of the digitized world economy, businesses must now compete on a global scale as never before.[1] The same is true for governments; they must also compete in terms of the policies they choose to adopt just to keep all those digits working within their jurisdictions.

More important than the particulars of the topics we take up, this book seeks to provide a way of thinking about the digital economy. Once we have an organized way of thinking about digitized goods—what I call "digital economics"—we can then explore a number of new public policy issues that have emerged along with the digital sector, not the least of which are consumer and employee privacy, piracy of digital goods, and antitrust enforcement.

For more than two decades, a host of new concepts has been developed that have fueled and activated economic thinking, changing the way economists and policy makers look at the world. These concepts go by the terms *network effects, network externalities, lagged demands, tipping, path dependency, feedback effects, switching costs,* and *lock-ins.* While many of these concepts were developed with nondigital goods in mind, interest in them at both the academic and policy level of analysis has been greatly encouraged by the development and spreading use of digital goods. As we will see, these concepts are readily integrated into digital economics, turning much economic thinking on its head. In no small way, this book seeks to be a management and policy manual for the new economic era, unimaginable two centuries ago, that is at our doorstep.

FLOWS OF THE ECONOMY, PAST AND PRESENT

At the turn of the nineteenth century, the most important "flow" in the economy of the United States, or any other country for that matter, was water, composed, as every schoolchild knows, of one part hydrogen and two parts oxygen. Water was important because the economy was largely agrarian, and, of course, crops cannot grow without water. More than 90 percent of the U.S. labor force was engaged in farming, which meant the livelihoods of Americans, as well as the citizens of every other country, were dependent on water. Moreover, way back then, farming was so unproductive that few people could do much of anything other than work to put food on the table. Services (whether in finance or trade) were a trivial part of the economic activity. Self-sufficiency was far more the order of this earlier era than now.

Because cross-country roads were few and literally far between, the river ways of the country were critically important to long-distance transportation of both people and goods. Understandably, many of the public works projects of the day were canals that extended the ability of people to move themselves and goods over long distances, which meant, at most, one-third of the way across the country. In this early era, much intrastate commercial traffic moved across oceans at the speed and whim of the air currents, or moved through the countryside at the leisurely speed of the Mississippi or the Hudson Rivers. The rest of the traffic was more time-consuming and arduous, by foot or horseback.

At the turn of the twentieth century, perhaps the most important economic flow was rail traffic. Although still slow, trains moved far more goods and people farther and faster, and more efficiently, than could have been dreamed a century earlier, at times breaking 50 miles an hour. In 1900, close to 40 percent of the labor force still worked on farms. Nearly 20 percent worked in manufacturing. Less than one-tenth of the labor force was involved in wholesale and retail trade. Only 5 or 6 percent of the labor force was involved in finance and services. Less than 5 percent of the labor force worked in transportation, meaning, by and large, ocean and railway traffic. The automobile industry was in its infancy. In these "good old days," as one author put it, life bordered on being "terrible" (by today's standards).[2] In many urban areas, the air was thick with coal dust. As late as 1882, only 2 percent of the houses in New York had inside water sources. Pigs were allowed to roam the streets because they cleaned up the garbage strewn about, but then they, like the horses that provided much of the transportation, left their droppings everywhere. People still wore boots, and for good reason, given the dung in the streets.

Back then, most economic activity was local, restricted to drawing on nearby resources, using local labor and local (often proprietor-provided) capital, with the shipment of goods largely contained within the same regions of the country, if not the same communities. Sure, some goods were traded internationally, but not many. Transnational and transoceanic shipments were expensive, not to mention uncertain and dangerous. Some very wealthy people traveled abroad, but most people did not stray far from home during their lives. Few people had a chance to talk, much less work, with people in foreign countries. Talk was then not cheap and was largely face to face. Mail? Well, it was inexpensive (because it was heavily subsidized by the government) but dreadfully slow, like so much else.

Goods in these earlier eras were, in the main, made from "real resources"— natural or man-made materials of one sort or another—that, in turn, were transformed into "real things" such as clothes, foods, buggy whips, and a few primitive automobiles scattered about the country. In no small way, gross domestic product carried "weight." The more that was produced, the heavier the total output was and the more things people had that they could touch and feel, as well as use. Indeed, the use of goods back then was almost totally tied to the senses: touch, taste, smell, sound, and sight.

In no small way, people at the turn of the twentieth century, as well as the nineteenth century, could hold to the rule "If you can touch it, it's real" and its corollary "If you can't touch it, it isn't real." One hundred years ago, even the unreal stuff of commerce associated with electricity—telegraph, telephone, and lighting—contributed little economic value, although the influence of electricity was certainly growing. Information, as an input into production and as an output, was hardly unknown, but the country and world were, by today's standards, information poor, and most information was tied to some material form, mainly ink and paper. Few books were published in the United States at the turn of the nineteenth century. Indeed, only forty-five hundred books were published in 1900. Even education was not a particularly important activity as late as the turn of the twentieth century. A mere 6 percent of 17-year-olds graduated from high school (which then generally meant the eleventh grade). Only .02 percent of twenty-three year-olds had college degrees. For most people, education was elementary, as in "elementary school." In these earlier eras, understandably, the horse-drawn plows and belching factory smokestacks, all worked by low-skilled laborers (many of whom were illiterate), were the icons of economic activity.

As we move into the twenty-first century, the economy of the country and world has changed, and is changing, remarkably. Less than one-sixth of the labor force is now involved in the manufacturing of real goods (after staying above one-third of the labor force through the 1950s), with the physical weight of the goods produced falling with each dollar rise in value. More than three-quarters of the labor force is employed in public or private services, which have no weight to speak of. The flow of traffic along waterways and railways has retreated substantially in economic importance with the growing influence of the movement of people and goods by cars, trucks, and planes. The speed limits even on some city streets are higher than trains could move a century ago.

The most important flow of our age, however, is one that while it might not yet be the dominant, most consequential economic flow, it is surely heavily influencing the future direction of the twenty-first-century economy. At the same time, this flow lacks the real physical substance and weight of flows on the nation's waterways and railways: As noted at the start of the book, it is the flow of digits—that is, 1's and 0's—that are going in all directions via phone calls, faxes, E-mails, and the Internet through the airways, through cables under the seas, and through an ever-expanding array of land-based wires whose capacity for carrying digits is enormous and continues to mount faster than the actual flow of digitized information (which explains the rapidly falling prices of transmissions).

At present, the flow of digits around the world remains constrained by "bandwidth," or the carrying capacity of the wires, especially the last mile of copper wires that go into people's homes and businesses. The bandwidth constraint shows up in Internet user complaints that "www" stands for, "world wide wait," given the time people spend staring at their computer screens as the graphics of Web pages are filled in. With the widespread installation of fiber optics, the problem might be an abundance of carrying capacity that could mean that the cost of transmissions might be so low that pricing Internet services by the use could be prohibitively costly. Then how should usage be priced, if at all? If there is no price, how should the service be provided? Would there be sufficient incentives for private firms to be in the Internet business, or any other business when the marginal cost of use might approximate zero? Might we not have to rethink the economic consequences of "monopoly" and "entry barriers," given firms' need to recover their upfront investments in the face of a zero marginal cost of production? Those are surely intriguing questions to which we will return.

Then again, we say the flow is of "digits" not because 1's and 0's literally flow anywhere—they cannot and do not—but because that is the most concrete way we have to represent the essence of the flow of words on this page. Nevertheless, those two digits—which, fortunately, can be arranged in an infinite number of sequences to represent letters, numbers, or numbers of pixels on a screen—can be converted to electrons that can then be sent along wires and through the airways at no less than the speed of light.

The economic flows of the past were substantial, in the sense that there was substance—material—to them. The modern flows of digits lack substance but only in the sense that the flows are nonmaterial, meaning they do not have weight and mass, and flows of electrons are about as close to nothing as anything can get. You cannot taste, smell, feel, or even see them, not directly at least. On this point, management guru Tom Peters recalls an executive once telling him, "Welcome to a world where, in the words of one executive I know, 'If you can touch it, it's not real.' I don't know about you, but that's a tough concept for an old (me) civil engineer (me, again) to get."[3]

But then, there is nothing new, fundamentally at least, about this ongoing modern transformation of economic activity, at least not in one sense. Futurist and technology guru George Gilder has noted, "The displacement of materials with ideas is the essence of all real economic progress."[4]

The modern flows of digits, like the past flows of barges on rivers and trains on tracks, have enhanced economic value, surely running into the hundreds of billions of dollars (with projections for the economic value of the flows to rise rapidly into the trillions of dollars within the first decade of the new century). Their value does not come from intrinsic sources—electrons are just that, electrons—and not from their appeal to the senses—they cannot be sensed. Instead, their value comes from what they represent and what they can be reconverted into once they have been transmitted, which can be a lot. The flows can be data, or numbers that are useful for evaluating companies' market worth. They can be text, meaning books and letters. They can be notes, that is, songs. They can be conversations, as in telephone calls. The flows can be blueprints for buildings or machines, and they can be pictures, individual snapshots, or whole videos or movies for replaying on computer or television screens.

The most important thing to note about the new economy is that collections of digits are goods and services and, as such, represent a modern-day sector of the economy worthy of study partly because of the volume and value of the goods and services produced in the sector. The digital sector of the economy is also worthy of study because of its importance to so much else that goes on in the national and global economy. At the onset of earlier centuries, much economic activity would have come to a screeching halt without, first, water and then trains. The same could be said today about the flow of digits. In no small way, businesses rely on digits to manage their production processes, keep their books, and fuel their sales. Consumers also have come to rely on digits to keep in contact with friends and family members, to search for shopping deals, and to maintain their household records.

The digital sector of the national economy is worthy of study for another, perhaps more important, reason: Digital goods and services are fundamentally different from other goods. As noted, they are, in important respects, material-less. As such, they do not always face the production constraints of material-based goods. How does the absence of material affect their economics, meaning, in the main, production and consumption decisions?

Sure, there are costs to producing digital goods—for example, software, books, videos, or music. Someone has to write out the strings of digits that make up digital goods and services (or write out strings of digits that make up computer programs that, in turn, convert sights and sounds to strings of digits). Such a feat requires some equipment (a computer) and some facility (an office). To use the digital good, the buyer also has to incur costs, not the least of which might be a computer that uses the software; an electronic reader used to read digitized books; or an MP3 player that plays digitized music. But Jim Clark, Netscape founder, makes an important point about the production of software that can be extended to other digital goods, "In comparison [to industrial age goods], the manufacture of software is no big deal. The idea, the design, and the engineering are all done in the same place, by the same people. The basic materials are laughably cheap. No spot-welding robots need apply. All you need is a good brain and an okay computer (though some people have managed surprisingly well by reversing those adjectives)."[5] Might not the full-blown emergence of digital goods and services require new ways of evaluating and thinking about economic activity? Might not economic theory now be out of date, in need of revisions, if not a reshaping of fundamental theorems and models of how the economy (or a major growth sector of it) is conceived and works?

What is really different about digital goods and services is that, once a master has been developed, the cost of reproducing copies is about as close to zero as such costs can get. This is because there is little, if any, material involved and the time required to reproduce digital goods is unbelievably short, given the speed of the now blazingly fast computers used to reproduce them. Similarly, music lovers can easily, and at little cost, copy music files from Web sites and each other.

In no small way, while overall production costs may be lower for many goods with the advent of digitization, a heavier share of costs in the digital sector have been shifted forward, to be captured by upfront development costs. There are two implications of that fact to keep in mind. First, with all production costs absorbed at the time they are developed, the nature of competition among digital goods firms should be expected to change significantly, most notably in terms of the intensity of price competition. Second, the low—close to zero—cost of reproducing digital goods makes for a different type of production economics, given that actual reproduction costs can be largely ignored. Pricing should be expected to be geared more to how much consumers value the product. At the same time, copies of digital goods need never die and, what's more, they can themselves be reproduced in the same way that Dell's master copy of Windows can be reproduced. This means that "digital pirates" can do what both Dell and college students can do, copy what others have produced with no payment—and no upfront development costs of their own. Software pirates can then distribute multiple copies of their copies to many buyers more or less simultaneously via the Internet at about the same cost of their reproduction, close to zero, setting off a cascade of piracy around the world. Surely, piracy should be expected to be a greater problem in the production of digital goods than in the production of conventional, material-based, nondigital goods. Are these production prospects not another reason for a separate digital economics that accommodates the economics of piracy?

Traditional economic analysis is founded on the proposition that all goods are scarce in supply and that the more scarce a good is, the more valuable it is. With the economies of scale in production that are inherent in the zero cost of reproducing digital goods, certainly such goods are likely to be less scarce than are more conventional, nondigital goods. This, no doubt, affects prices and profits of digital goods producers, as well as their motivation to go into the production of digital goods. In addition, many digital goods, such as operating systems for personal computers, are said to exhibit "economies of scale in demand," or so-called network effects. That is to say, the more abundant the digital good is, the more valuable it is. For example, if more people buy a given operating system, which is inherently a digital good, then developers of computer applications will write more applications for the operating system. The more applications there are for any given operating system, the more valuable the operating system is and the more copies of the operating system will be bought, which can, in turn, spawn the development of even more applications and even more operating system sales. Similarly, more goods will be listed for auction on eBay when there are more potential buyers, but the greater array of goods will attract more buyers, which, in turn, can attract even more goods for sale.

Granted, as we will see later in the book, the sales of a number of many nondigital goods (for example, movies on film form and books in print form) exhibit network effects (or feedback effects). But might not digital goods be more inclined to exhibit network effects since they are born digitally and can be transmitted widely through networks? If so, should not the prevalence of network effects change, at least somewhat (in emphasis, if not fundamental theorems), the underlying economics of the digital sector of the economy and hence unsettle many conventional conclusions about how the economy works and how it might evolve as more and more economic activity goes digital? First, before we address that question, we need to have some sense of the size and form of what I call the "digital economy."

THE SIZE OF THE DIGITAL FLOWS

How large is the digital sector of the economy? The size actually depends on what is measured and how the measurement is made. For starters, we might measure the amount of information generated in the world, given that a sizable chunk of all information is, like this book, born digitally. The rest of the available information is potentially subject to digitization.

According to one study released in late 2000 from the University of California–Berkeley, if all of the information in various forms—books, office documents, movies, photographs, music, X rays, newspapers, periodicals (journals and magazines), videos, E-mails, and Web pages—were digitized (as many of the forms already are), there exists in the world today a stock of unique information (meaning copies are excluded) that equals about 12 exabytes, with an exabyte equal to one billion gigabytes (which equals one thousand megabytes). Furthermore, people around the world now generate approximately 1.5 exabytes of unique information (again, copies excluded) each year, which amounts to approximately 250 megabytes (or one thousand kilobytes) of information for every man, woman, and child on the planet (many of whom are in the Third World and produce little or no digitizable information).[6]

How much information is that? A gigabyte is one thousand megabytes, which, in turn, equals one thousand bytes (with a byte usually having 8 bits and each bit, or binary digit, being the proverbial 1 or 0). Figuring that a 250-page book can be converted to less than one megabyte of data, 1.5 exabytes of data is the equivalent of approximately 6 billion unique books, one-quarter or more of which originate in the United States.[7] Of course, if we were to add in the copies of the books, recordings, and so on that are produced each year in digital and nondigital forms, the count of exabytes would skyrocket. How much? The Berkeley researchers did not even try to estimate the volume.

The Berkeley researchers also found that only about .003 percent of all available unique information is stored in printed form. Published books alone constituted only 8 terabytes of information (with a terabyte equaling one thousand gigabytes). Approximately one-third of the volume of printed information comes in the form of newspapers and two-thirds comes in magazines and journals. But the researchers cautioned, "This doesn't imply that print is insignificant. Quite the contrary: it simply means that the written word is an extremely efficient way to convey information."[8]

The information available on the 2.1 billion Web pages in 2000 was phenomenal (about 21 terabytes of static HTML pages), but still, some 610 billion (and perhaps as many as 1.1 trillion) E-mails sent that year constituted more than 500 more bytes of information than all of the existing Web pages (and six times the number of pieces of paper mail, whether first-class letters or circulars, delivered by the U.S. Postal Service). Digitizable information in the form of cinema, music CDs, data CDs, and DVD-video constituted 45 terabytes. Published office documents (not those produced and stored exclusively on our personal computers), by far the largest form of information, constituted 195 terabytes of information.[9]

Perhaps more important, the Berkeley researchers found that technology had led to the "democratization of data," and the amount of information produced by individuals (in the form of photographs, home videos, X rays, and everything stored on the hard drives of personal computers) in 2000 was six hundred times the amount of published information.[10] In addition, the researchers found that when all information in all its various forms was converted to its digital (terabyte) equivalent (with movies, videos, photographs, and sounds being terabyte intensive), 93 percent of all of the information created in 2000 was, like this book, created digitally, meaning no digital conversion was necessary in order for the information to be stored and transmitted electronically.

Finally, in their survey of the country's "digital future," a set of researchers at the University of California–Los Angeles found that the carrying capacity of the Internet is doubling every one hundred days, which must be the case, given the growth of the Internet and its use.[11] Few people knew what the Internet was in 1993. By 1997, there were 19 million American users. By April 2001, Neilsen/NetRatings placed the count of Internet users in U.S. households at 103 million, up 25 percent from a year earlier.[12] Between the beginning of 2000 and mid-2001, 555 dot-com companies failed, many of which were sizable ventures (Pets.com, Eve.com, Utility.com, Z.com, Synge.com, Mothernature.com, Smartkids.com, Furniture.com, Earlychildhood.com, and Living.com, just to name a few); 330 dot-coms ceased operations in the first half of 2001 alone.[13] Nevertheless, during this period 3.2 million Web pages and 715,000 images were being added to the U.S. stock of Web-based images *every day*.[14] (And it should be remembered that there were 7,000–10,000 Internet companies still alive in late 2001.)

Now, two-thirds of Americans have some kind of access to the Internet, with Internet usage highly correlated with education.[15] One-third of the remaining one-third of Americans who are non-Internet users claim to be "not interested" in gaining access to the Web,[16] while 67 percent of American Internet users consider the Internet an "important" or "extremely important" source of information, one-half of whom ranked the Internet with television as a source of information.[17] All of these Americans who have access to computers and the Web are capable of adding to the world's stock of information.

Understandably, with that kind of growth in the Internet, the Berkeley researchers found that the aggregate amount of information being generated per person in the world could be expected to double each year for the foreseeable future. This means that by the end of 2003, the world's stock of information will have doubled from what it was in 2000, which means it will take the world three years to produce as much information as it did in the first three hundred thousand years of human existence.[18] And no one should be surprised if the world's stock of information doubles every few years repeatedly for the next decade or more, meaning that the peak growth in information measured by terabytes, with practically all of the new information totally digital, is surely years, if not decades, away.

Admittedly, the data on the rise of the digitized sector of the economy is mind-boggling. An exabyte of information is hard to imagine just in terms of the zeros involved, much less to comprehend what the number means. However, that is the point of reciting the numbers. A problem people already face is how to manage the gigabytes and terabytes of information to which they can already access. That problem can only be aggravated by the flood of terabytes of information coming in the future.

A core problem people face, whether they are acting alone or as members of businesses and other organizations, is that their brains, meaning their biological capacities to productively handle information, do not appear to have changed materially in some time, if not for eons, leading to the potential problem of information overload. People's "consumption" of information may have changed somewhat, given the adoption of new ways of using the brainpower they have, but surely their consumption has not changed as much as the supply of information has increased. People have been able to ease the problem of consuming information by storing gigabytes of data not immediately needed, at rapidly shrinking costs, on their computer's hard drives in retrievable form.

Still, the potential information overload problem can only get worse with the onslaught of terabytes of information that will flow their way in the future, and the mounting gigabytes they store on their ever-expanding hard drives. Understandably, given all the attention focused on computers in the digital economy, analysts have shifted from emphasizing "market share," as a measure of business success, to stressing "mind share" (or "eyeball share") as a now more fundamental, critical measure of success. To a growing extent, in the digital economy market share follows from mind share, which I suspect elevates the importance of determinants of people's attention spans in plotting corporate strategies.

Fortunately, many of the bytes of information that are available on the Web (for example, pictures of various children's birthday parties) and that are transmitted over wires and through the air (for example, jokes) are, for most people, nothing more than digital trash, stuff to be ignored or quickly discarded if ever downloaded. Then, many terabytes of information in all forms amount to gross duplication. In a search of Google.com, there were, at this writing, 201,000 hits for "birthday party," with the first several pages of hits taken up with companies (for example, "Birthday Party Ideas" and "Billy Bear's Birthday Party") providing many of the same party supplies and services. There were more than 2.5 million sites when the search was made for "jokes" (for example, "Joke of the Day," "Joke Post," and "Joke Zone").

Nevertheless, the information overload will not go away no matter how we cut the data. What are the implications of having so much information? First, it is clear that people will need to actively manage, somehow and in some way, the information in digital and nondigital forms that they confront. Management of resources is an old problem, of course. However, much management in the past has been geared toward managing resources that are scarce in supply. The management task has been one of getting more of the scarce resources at, often, ever-higher prices.

On the other hand, the management problem in information, for both individuals and businesses, is one of plentitude, basically how to cull the good information from the worthless information without devoting too many (scarce) resources to the culling process. There are, no doubt, in the information dilemma new management problems, as well as opportunities. Those people and firms that are able to do the culling more efficiently than others will find their market fortunes enhanced. And as information grows in importance, much competition will move toward finding ways of more efficiently culling the good from the bad information.

Second, it is very unlikely that there will be a full technological fix for the problem of information abundance. Granted, larger, more powerful computers with less expensive hard drives will certainly help us absorb and utilize more information. Web search engines, such as Google.com, have and will continue to help with the culling. However, we should not be sanguine about technological fixes. A basic problem is that, as already noted, a growing number of people around the world are hooking up to computer networks and are adding to the information flow, which has its own derivative information flows. As more people work together in person and via the Internet, the opportunities to generate more information will likely escalate, perhaps geometrically.

More efficient search engines can mean, as it has already meant, that we have a problem of figuring out which of the growing array of hits are useful. As the production and use of information becomes more efficient with falling real prices for computing hardware and software, the national economy is bound to expand along with the digital sector, giving rise to more digital goods and services, and a greater problem of information abundance.

Make no mistake, the problem of information abundance will necessarily spawn nontechnological fixes. There will be growth in demand for people (digital librarians?) who develop the specific skills necessary to sort through information sources and to organize and store information so that it can be efficiently retrieved. The information flows will require more people to become more educated, but the flows will also demand a reorganization of education toward handling information. The demand for educators (people in consulting firms, as well as people in colleges and universities) who can provide the requisite search-and-sort-and-store skills will likely rise relatively, as will their incomes.

To bring their information problems to manageable proportions, people will likely continue to do what they have been doing for the past two hundred years, and more: become ever more specialized in the production of ever more narrowly conceived nondigital, as well as digital, goods and services. Specialization will permit them to focus on, and deal effectively with, a subset of the available information, thereby reducing the information they must handle to within manageable proportions.

Ironically, the growth of available information, and the spawned specialization, will naturally mean that people will gradually become progressively more ignorant of the full range of information. Their relatively growing ignorance will cause people to become progressively more dependent on others who access available information that they do not access. This does not mean that the complexity of what is produced is limited by the information they can handle individually. On the contrary, the linkages among people via the Internet and other means will mean that the complexity of what can and will be produced will increase, given that the interactions will be synergized by the added brainpower bound together, much like personal computers and servers are made more powerful by the addition of microprocessors working in conjunction with one another. Technologist George Gilder posits the "law of the telecosm" (a revision of Robert Metcalfe's law of networks), which "ordains that the value of a network rises by the square of the collective *power* of computers compatibly attached to it" (emphasis in original).[19] The "power" will come from two sources: the added computers and the brainpower working the computers. Perhaps there should be a "law of markets" that adds that the power of markets to achieve complex outcomes rises by the square of the value of networks.

Inevitably, the flood of available information being transmitted around the world by broadband fiber optic systems, means that people will have to rely more and more on markets in the exchange of information and the goods and services that are produced with the information that is exchanged. The volume of information distributed throughout markets will be so great that it is unlikely that would-be government regulators will be able to intervene to good effect. They just will not be able to understand very well what is going on and, consequently, will not be able to regulate very effectively, a point that the late economist and philosopher Friedrich Hayek posited six decades ago when information was far more sparse.[20]

But technology, specialization, and markets will not likely amount to a total panacea for the information overload problem. People will surely need a mental means of cutting through the clutter of information that will abound everywhere. Theory—which is nothing more than a mental means of dealing with complexity—of one sort or another, from one discipline or another, will thereby grow in demand simply because theory is a tried-and-true means of structuring thought, of reducing the information considered to manageable proportion. The late economist Kenneth Boulding made my point here best when he observed prophetically in the early 1970s, "It is a very fundamental principle indeed that knowledge is always gained by the orderly loss of information; that is, by condensing and abstracting and indexing the great buzzing confusion of information that comes from the world around us into a form we can appreciate and comprehend."[21] Given the research findings from Berkeley and Los Angeles, as well as elsewhere, we cannot help but believe that the "great buzzing confusion of information" has become all the more confusing since Boulding wrote those words and should lead to a growing prominence not of data collectors and manipulators (statistician types), but of the even more scarce skilled and creative theoreticians. Theory will be in short supply, and, I might add, very likely highly rewarded. Like it or not, people—in business and government, not to mention homes—will demand more theory, which is one reason I wrote this book.

THE PRIMORDIAL DIGITAL SOUP

In the course of a few years, the digital sector of the economy has taken quite a roller-coaster ride, initially running up unbelievable heights of optimism, given that venture capital seemed to freely flow to any firm that had ".com" after its name. In the mid- and late 1990s, the Internet was a virtual "Field of Dreams" in terms of a central business philosophy underlying the development of many Internet companies: "Build it, and they will come!" And the stock market seemed to endorse common expectations, that businesses and consumers were ready for digital dealing, no matter what the product or service, virtual or real, might be, just so long at it was provided, in one way or another or to one extent or another, via the Internet. Through the first quarter of 2000, newly minted dot-com companies' price–earnings ratios often exceeded 400 (at a time when many banks and old-world manufacturing giants could barely break price–earnings ratios of 12). Of course, the price–earnings ratios of many dot-com firms, including the retail titan of the Web, Amazon.com, could not be calculated at all, given the red ink that flowed on their books. After the first quarter of 2000, the fate of dot-coms changed dramatically. Venture capital for many virtually dried up, resulting in a spate of closures, meaning many promising dot-coms became "dot-bombs" practically overnight. Total dot-com job losses during 2000 were more than forty-one thousand, with only five thousand of those job losses coming in the first half of the year and with the losses mounting every month during the last half of the year. The only glimmer of hope one newspaper report could find in the job-loss data was that the increase in job losses was moderating slightly as the year came to an end.[22]

Does the reversal of the fortunes of many dot-com companies imply an end, or just a contraction, of the digital economy as some commentators have speculated? Contraction, maybe. End, not very likely. Forrester Research, which tracks electronic commerce, sees continued growth in the digital economy, especially in business-to-business E-commerce. In 2000, Forrester Research estimated that electronic commerce sales in the United States (business-to-business and business-to-consumer) amounted to $509 billion. By 2004, Forrester expects electronic commerce sales to expand nearly sevenfold to just under $3.5 trillion, at which time they would be nearly 13 percent of total U.S. sales.[23]

Frankly, while Forrester may have overestimated the growth of E-commerce, since its projections were made based on data collected on Web growth in 1999 and before, it seems to me that the efficiency gains to be had by digitizing many (but certainly nowhere near all) goods and services appear far too strong to expect much more than a reduction in the expected growth over the next few years, along with the ongoing rationalization of investment funds among dot-com companies and between dot-coms and their brick-and-mortar counterparts. It simply makes a lot of sense for many orders for some fairly standardized consumer goods, such as personal computers and books, to be taken over the Internet, as Dell has shown. No telephone operator is needed, and the sellers' paperwork is reduced. The orders themselves, plus all the information the sellers collect on the buyers, become an integral part of the sellers' digital nervous system, reducing the cost not only of order taking but also of supply-chain and inventory management. In addition, it makes sense to sell many goods—especially purely digital goods such as books and music—over the Internet, and then distribute some of them—for example, digitized music, books, and software—over the same lines on which the orders were placed.

The fact that the dot-com world appears to have been operating irrationally over the past few years, as measured by the many handsomely funded dot-com failures, does not mean that there was anything "irrational" about the weaning process. The Internet is a relatively new technology, at least as far as its widespread use by general business, and when any mode of doing business is new, it is hard to know, in advance, what can be done with the technology. This is especially true of technologies that, like the Internet, can be used in so many different and original ways, a few of which will likely prove to be successful but also many of which, in hindsight, will appear brainless.

It would be nice to know in advance exactly which of the many Internet opportunities would eventually prove successful, but few entrepreneurs and investors have that level or luxury of foresight. One of the problems is there is often no way to fully assess the market value of an idea other than trying it in the market. Another problem is that the success of many ideas depends on how the firm that is created to execute the idea actually executes it and the accompanying business model. Success also depends on how other players in the market—competitors, suppliers, and buyers, for example—develop and react to one another.

In the mid-1990s, few really had a good understanding of the effectiveness of banner advertising on Web sites. As did so many other dot-coms, Synge.com, which, before its demise, prided itself on being the portal of choice for young adults (much like MTV is frequently the television channel of choice for many young adults), assumed that a part of the cost of developing content could be covered with banner ads and consumer referrals—if they were able to attract a sufficient number of daily hits, which could be possible if other firms did not try the same idea. On many Web sites, banner ads have proven to be not very effective for the advertisers, which caused Synge's revenue from that source to plunge. As a consequence, Synge shifted its business model from relying on advertising revenue and product referrals to doing that which was at the core of its site, producing interesting, sexy, slightly irreverent content targeted for young audiences and then selling the content to other content providers, for example, iSyndicate and Screaming Media. But even that shift in business strategy could not save the firm when its venture capital dried up in the dot-com crunch of 2001.

Before Amazon.com set up its Internet shop, few people knew much about the economics of selling something as simple and uniform as books. For example, no one knew in 1995 how responsive Web-based book buyers would be to price changes, or if they would be willing to pay extra for the convenience of ordering from the Amazon site. Before Amazon, no one really knew how to secure credit card information that was released on the Web, or how consumers would fear the loss of privacy when their buying habits could be tracked by the information they provide sellers when they fill out orders or just by visiting a site (with "cookies" implanted in their computers by every site they visit).

Who would have imagined that Amazon would be able to lose hundreds of millions annually as late as 2001, in spite of having more than $1 billion in annual sales? For that matter, who would have imagined that eBay, which provides what amounts to an ongoing online garage sale, would be a more profitable net venture than Amazon? If eBay could make it, why couldn't Furniture.com?

Sure, we might now think, with the arrogance of hindsight, that it should have been obvious to the founders of Furniture.com that people would want to sit on sofas and chairs before they buy them. However, there just might be enough people who hate shopping in congested furniture stores or who live in remote areas without furniture stores nearby and who would be willing to take the risk of buying sofas without first testing them. Similarly, perhaps it should have been obvious to venture capitalists that Pet.com would prove unsuccessful, given that pet food is bulky and costly to ship per dollar of pet food sales, but then maybe pet food buyers, at least the high-income ones, would be willing to pay the shipping costs to avoid their even higher time cost of going to brick-and-mortar pet food stores and carting the bags of food home themselves.

It is important to remember that the Internet in the late 1990s was in its "primordial soup" stage of development. It was not then clear which companies would win the Darwinian struggle to achieve sufficient market share to be successful by adjusting and readjusting their business strategies in response to the adjustments and readjustments of others operating both online and offline.

The Internet primordial soup, involving many failures, is nothing really new. There was a primordial soup in gold prospecting after the precious metal was discovered in California at Sutter's Mill in January 1848. An estimated one hundred thousand people, mainly men, in the East and Midwest, as well as other parts of the world, eagerly left their safe agricultural and industry jobs and lives to head for the California hills in the hopes of finding a fortune. They knew that gold would be found in the High Sierras, but they had little knowledge of exactly where. With little more than a mule, a pick, and a hunch, they headed for the hills. Very few got wealthy. Some found a little gold, but most went bust. An estimated ten thousand of the forty-niners died from accidents and dysentery and other diseases.

The railway and automobile industries experienced their own short-lived "gold rushes" in their own formative years. More miles of railway track were laid in the 1880s than in any other ten-year stretch in the history of the country, and during the following decade, the 1890s, there were more railroad companies that filed for bankruptcy than in any other decade since. Between 1904 and 1908, 240 firms started producing automobiles in the United States. Most of these firms, many of which formerly built bicycles and buggies, did not last past 1910.

My point here is that what has happened in the dot-com digital world—boom and bust—might have been expected. So much is necessarily unknown at the dawn of any industry because so little is known about what does and does not work in the industry. The restaurant industry has been around for a long time, but even in that industry, because of the complexity of doing business, the failure rate remains very high. We might expect the failure rate of dot-coms to be higher (and no one knows if it is higher because the subject has not been studied). It is hard to know at the primordial-soup stage of development how the market will eventually turn out. Firms starting out must and will adjust to the billions, if not trillions, of evolving business decisions made by others, and make no mistake about it, the development of any industry is an evolutionary process, the end of which can hardly be known by anyone at the start.

And it should never be forgotten that some firms fail not because of anything they may have done wrong, but because market forces turned against them. For example, very well-designed businesses in one sector of the economy might fail because of the growth of other firms in the same sector or in other sectors of the economy that, because of their expansion, increase the demand for some critical resource (like programmers or Internet engineers), drive up the resource's price, and drive out of business firms that cannot pay the higher resource price. Which firms in which sectors will be the relatively more productive and be best able to pay top dollar for the resources they need is a question that is hard to answer absent the playing out of the market forces.

Nevertheless, as heady dot-com'ers have over the past decade packed up their laptops and programming languages and ventured into the unknown "Internet hills," the resulting failures have been instructive. They have added to our stock of collective and individual knowledge of what will not and will likely work—and, hence, where resources should be more productively and profitably devoted in the future. We know now better than ever that many dot-com entrepreneurs went off half-cocked in hot pursuit of their Internet fantasies, not stopping to think carefully about the nature of the markets they were entering. We now know entrepreneurs need to understand the nature of the market they are in and need to think more carefully about what they plan to do, before they seek venture capital and put their plans into operation. This brings us back to a central point of the book: people need an improved way of thinking about the digital economy. I cannot hope to provide a complete way of thinking through the myriad of dot-com, or digital, world problems, but I can offer a way of thinking through many of the problems.

CONCLUDING COMMENTS

The digital economy—encompassing computers, telecommunications, and all of their technological trappings, as well as all the goods and services that can be reduced to 1's and 0's—has been the subject of a great deal of media hype coming from a number of quarters, not the least of which have been dot-com companies themselves who have an understandable interest in hyping their products and influence on the rest of the world. However, much hype has come from academics and other commentators who are convinced that the digital economy will revolutionize—meaning totally remake—the world economy as no other technological advancement has done in the past, not even the advancements that were made two centuries ago during the Industrial Revolution.

While I would be the first to agree that digital technology has affected, if not transformed, much work and leisure-time activity over the past half century, I would also be the first to caution against excessive claims and expectations about where the "digital revolution" has led and might lead. As discussed in the next chapter, you will see I share University of Chicago economist Robert Gordon's hesitation in accepting often repeated claims that the "new economy" of the 1990s, founded on computer and telecommunication technology, has advanced human welfare at a rate faster than the rate of advancement during the Second Industrial Revolution (1860–1900) and the subsequent Golden Age (1913–1972) that was founded on a sequence of so-called golden inventions—electricity, telegraph, telephone, motor transportation, air transportation, radio, computers, space travel, atomic energy, television, motion pictures, and indoor plumbing, just to name a few.[24] I endorse Federal Reserve Board chairman Alan Greenspan's assessment that financial markets did exhibit a measure of "irrational exuberance" during the last half of the 1990s, especially toward untested dot-com business models. How else can the prices of some high-tech stocks be explained, given the company's growing histories of losses? Perceptively, one online financial analyst commented in mid-1999 that the only way Yahoo!'s stock price could be justified at that time was for the Yahoo! site to be visited four times a day everyday by every man, woman, and child on the planet, most of whom do not have access to computers (for a total of 24 billion page views a day).[25]

In short, the Internet has been touted as the latest and greatest "disruptive technology." It has, and will continue to be, disruptive, but probably not as disruptive was imagined years ago. Contrary to the hype about what should have happened by now, first-class mail and telephones are still being used. People continue to have face-to-face conversations, although research is beginning to show that time spent on computers at home and work has reduced the time people spend with family, friends, and colleagues.[26] People still work together and share office buildings. Telecommuting has grown as a form of work arrangement, but there were signs at the start of this century that employers were confronting problems of monitoring their employees who work at home and elsewhere, causing some employers to make plans for phasing out their telecommuting work option.[27] "Virtual meetings" happen, but I do not suspect they affect more than a small share of the way people interact. The overwhelming majority of university courses continue to be conducted in lecture halls, with online courses making, to date, only a marginal impact on how higher education is provided. Indeed, even people who are pressing the digital revolution forward still meet in nice resort locations to have professional conferences, in contrast to the past talk about how chat rooms would supplant the need for conventions.

There is a good reason many, if not most, face-to-face meetings will be hard to displace by computer/telecommunication technology: Meetings are an efficient means of transmitting terabytes of information. Indeed, much information obtained in meetings cannot be transmitted with known technology. This is because in face-to-face meetings, virtually all of the senses—sound, taste, smell, sight, and touch—can be employed at once and in various combinations. In meetings, we can pick up on the way other people look, act, and dress from head to toe, on the twitches in their faces, the inflections in their voices, and their smells, all of which can literally speak volumes about the other people. Then, exactly how the other people interact, or fail to interact, with one another adds information and value to the meetings. Even touch is important when handshakes and hugs are involved, with the particulars of exactly how and under what circumstances they occur adding to their meaning.

Granted, some of the information gathered at meetings might be efficiently reduced to 1's and 0's and transmitted through telecommunication systems, as is done regularly via E-mail systems. However, much information obtained at meetings would never be reduced to 1's and 0's because, even if it were possible, it would run into the exabytes of data and would likely be very expensive to transmit—or, more to the point, it would be more expensive to convey via computer/telecommunication technology than through good old-fashioned person-to-person meetings.

Location remains important in business (albeit perhaps less important than in the past), as evident from the number of firms that choose to run their businesses from the epicenters of the digital revolution: the Silicon Valley in California, Route 128 outside of Boston, and the Research Triangle Park in North Carolina. If location no longer mattered, as some "digital hypesters" have argued (given that business can now be done anywhere), why are people crawling over one another to buy houses at inflated prices in San Jose and surrounding communities?

Brick-and-mortar stores have obviously not collapsed from the competition from supposedly cheaper online stores. Online shopping will likely make inroads in terms of market shares of business and retail sales, but I suspect that offline stores will continue to sell people a substantial share of what they buy. Shopping remains an end in itself for many consumers.

I am also convinced that the digitization of goods and services is affecting more than how or where sales are rung up. The ongoing digitization process is having a significant impact on how people do business, but so did the advent of the printing press, the steam engine, electricity, trains, telephones, and planes. We cannot be so sure which of several technological revolutions over the past two centuries has had the greater, longest-lasting impact on the course of human development. But that debate is of little consequence for what I propose to do in this book.

What we do know is that the digitization process is lowering production costs and changing the nature of a wide array of goods and services. While I would be the last to argue that the digital revolution has made conventional economics obsolete, I still recognize that the economy has changed sufficiently to warrant significant adjustments in the way economic theory is developed. If nothing else, we need to understand better why the digital age has had the sizable impact that it has on people lives, but also why it has not had a greater impact. Those required adjustments are all we need to press for the development of digital economics, which I begin in the next chapter.

NOTES

1. Richard B. McKenzie and Dwight R. Lee, *Quicksilver Capital: How the Rapid Movement of Wealth Has Changed the World* (New York: Free Press, 1991).

2. Otto L. Bettmann, *The Good Old Days—They Were Terrible!* (New York: Random House, 1974).

3. Tom Peters, *Tom Peters Seminar: Crazy Times Call for Crazy Organizations* (New York: Vintage Books, 1994), 13.

4. George Gilder, *Microcosm: The Quantum Revolution in Economics and Technology* (New York: Simon & Schuster, 1989), 63.

5. Jim Clark, with Owen Edwards, *Netscape Time: The Making of the Billion-Dollar Start-Up That Took on Microsoft* (New York: St. Martin's, 1999), 83.

6. Peter Lyman, Hal Varian et. al., *How Much Information?* Working Paper (Berkeley, Calif.: School of Information Management and Systems at the University of California–Berkeley, November 2000), as found at http://www.sims.berkeley.edu/how-much-info/.

7. The United States accounts for 35 percent of all printed material, 40 percent of all images, and 50 percent of all digitally stored material produced in the world (Lyman, Varian et al., *How Much Information?*), 3.

8. Ibid.

9. Ibid., 5–7.

10. Ibid.

11. Jeffrey I. Cole et. al, *The UCLA Internet Report: Surveying the Digital Future* (Los Angeles: Center for Communication Policy, University of California–Los Angeles, November 2000), as found at http://ccp.ucla.edu/ucla-internet.pdf.

12. As reported by Michael J. Miller, "Forward Thinking: The E-Business Revolution Continues," *PC Magazine*, July 2001, 7.

13. "330 Dot-Coms Closed in First Half of Year," Los Angeles Times, 4 July 2001, p. C3. Hoovers Online maintains a running list of the more prominent dead and dying dot-coms (http://www.hoovers.com/). Another, later report from Webmergers.com found that there were 537 dot-com deaths in 2001, more than double its count of dot-com deaths of 225 for 2000 ("Report Says Dot-Com Deaths Doubled in 2001," *Los Angeles Times*, 28 December 2001, p. C3.

14. Miller, "Forward Thinking," 7.

15. Only 31 percent of Americans eighteen years of age or older with less than a high school education were Internet users in 2000. High school graduates had a 53 percent usage rate. Americans, with college degrees and advanced degrees, had usage rates of 86 percent. Americans with less than $15,000 of annual income had usage rates of 41 percent (Miller, "Forward Thinking," 11). The usage rate escalates with income to just under 89 percent for Americans with over $100,000 of annual income (p. 12). According to another report, in 2001, 54 percent of U.S. households had Internet access, with 9 percent having some form of broadband access (in the main, via cable or DSL modems). By 2005, 71 percent of U.S. households will have Internet access, with 29 percent having access by way of broadband ("Reality Bytes," *Wall Street Journal*, 23 April 2001, p. B3).

16. Ibid., 22.

17. Ibid., 10, 33.

18. As reported in "New Study Finds Explosive Growth of World's Information Is Only Beginning: 12 Exabytes of Existing 'Unique' Information Will Be Dwarfed by New Data, Expected to Nearly Double Annually," Press Release (EMC, October 24, 2000), as found at http://biz.yahoo.com/bw/001024/ma_emc.html.

19. George Gilder, *Telecosm: How Infinite Bandwidth Will Revolutionize Our World* (New York: Free Press, 2000), 151.

20. Hayek observed, "Knowledge exists only as the knowledge of individuals. It is not much better than a metaphor to speak of the knowledge of society as a whole. The sum of the knowledge of all the individuals exists nowhere as an integrated whole." Hayek reckoned that the "great problem" of society is how to benefit from the totality of knowledge that "exists only dispersed as the separate, partial, and sometimes conflicting beliefs of all men" (F. A. Hayek, *The Constitution of Liberty* [Chicago: University of Chicago Press, 1960], 24–25). He added a point that is surely more rel-

evant today: "The more men know, the smaller the share of all that knowledge becomes that any one mind can absorb. The more civilized we become, the more relatively ignorant must each individual be of the facts on which the working of his civilization depends. The very division of knowledge increases the necessary ignorance of the individual of most of this knowledge" (p. 26).

21. Kenneth E. Boulding, *Economics as a Science* (New York: McGraw-Hill, 1970), 2.

22. Monee Fields-White, "Dot-Com Job Losses Increase 19%," *Los Angeles Times*, 28 December 2000, p. C7.

23. Forrester Research estimated that worldwide electronic commerce sales were $657 billion, making U.S electronic sales then 77 percent. By 2004, worldwide electronic commerce sales were expected to expand more than tenfold to $6.8 trillion, at which time U.S. sales would be down to a 50 percent share (Forrester Research, Inc., December 15, 2000, as found at http://www.forrester.com/ER/Press/ForrFind/0,1768,0,FF.html).

24. Robert J. Gordon, "Does the 'New Economy' Measure Up to the Great Inventions of the Past?" Working Paper 7833 (Cambridge, Mass.: National Bureau of Economic Research, August 2000), as found at www.nber.org/papers/w7833. Also published in *Journal of Economic Perspective* 14 (Fall 2000): 49–74).

25. As reported by Hal R. Varian, "Economic Scene: Comparing the NASDAQ Bubble to Tulipmania Is Unfair to the Flowers," *New York Times*, 8 February 2001, p. C2.

26. In a survey of more than six thousand respondents between the ages of eighteen and sixty-four, researchers at Stanford University and Free University of Berlin found that after adjusting for a number of variables (age, gender, and so forth), for each minute of time spent on the Internet at home during the day before the survey was conducted, the respondents spent one-third minute less interacting with family and friends. For every minute spent on the Internet at work, the respondents spent 7 seconds less interacting with family and friends and 11 seconds less spent interacting with colleagues: "Thus, Internet use subtracts an additional 18 minutes a day, almost an hour a week, in active participation with others in both work and play." See Norman H. Nie, D. Sunshine Hillygus, and Lutz Erbring, "Internet Use, Interpersonal Relations and Sociability: Findings from a Detailed Time Diary Study" in *The Internet in Everyday Life*, ed. Barry Wellman and Caroline Haythornthwaite (Oxford: Blackwell, 2002), 431–463. This study is hardly conclusive, given that there is the competing hypothesis that time spent on the Internet at work increases the efficiency of work and thereby leaves more time for friends and family that also has some, albeit more limited, empirical support from researchers at the University of California–Los Angeles (UCLA Internet Report, "Surveying the Digital Future" [October, 2000]).

27. The American Management Association found at the end of 2000 that 62 percent of the 648 firms they surveyed planned to hire fewer "teleworkers," and 21 percent of the employers planned to phase out telecommuting (Bonnie Harris, "Companies Turning Cool to Telecommuting Trend," *Los Angeles Times*, 28 December 2000, p. A1).

2

The Productivity Paradox

The so-called computer revolution appears self-evident in high-tech industries, mainly because of the ever-growing complexity, power, and cheapness of computing. The count of transistors on microprocessors has doubled every eighteen to twenty-four months since the early 1960s (more or less as Gordon Moore, one of Intel's founders, said it would back in 1965[1]). The storage capacity of hard disks has been growing even faster than the power of microprocessors, that is, doubling every nine months, with the price of the storage space declining. A megabyte of storage space dropped in terms of price (inflation adjusted) from $16.25 in 1988 to $.02 in 1999.[2]

As a consequence of the growing abundance in computing power and storage capacity, there was an acceleration in the decline in the price of computers during the 1990s: an annual average of 12.1 percent between 1987 and the third quarter of 1994. Between the fourth quarter of 1994 and the end of 1999, the annual price decline of computers more than doubled from the 1987–1994 period, averaging 26.2 percent in the later period.[3] Perhaps expectedly, business investment in computers and software grew rapidly with the declining real prices. The growth in the real dollar value of sales of computers, communications equipment, and semiconductors surged from an average annual increase of 11.8 percent between 1990 and 1993 to 39.2 percent between 1994 and 1999.[4]

With the precipitous decline in the price of computing power, work has progressively become dependent on the productivity of 1's and 0's, and the hardware and software that can manipulate those 1's and 0's. Sales of desktop computers in the United States went from practically nothing in 1980 to more than 8 million units in 1990, and then to just under 30 million units in 2000.

eTForecast, a firm that tracks industry trends, projects that desktop sales will increase by nearly half again by 2005, when unit sales are expected to exceed 43 million.[5] Server and mobile computer sales have followed a similar, albeit more recent, sales growth pattern. Server sales were nonexistent in 1990; however, they are projected to be 3.5 million in 2005. Mobile personal computers, which include laptops and handheld personal assistants, grew from slightly more than 1 million in 1990 to nearly 11 million in 2000, with unit sales expected to reach nearly 18 million in 2005.[6] With the growing sales of computers, the percent of American households with personal computers has jumped from 11 percent in 1990 to 62 percent in 2000, a growth in the penetration of the potential market that is on par with the market penetration of electricity in the 1910s and 1920s.

The expansion of the Internet has been even more dramatic. In 1992, there were only 700,000 Internet hosts, or servers, that had unique Internet addresses. Over the next year, the increase in the count of hosts was 600,000, putting the total count of Internet hosts at 1.3 million. In the six years between 1993 and 1999, Internet hosts grew by more than 40 million. However, it is important to note that the pace of increase was quickening, and substantially, over that six-year period. In one year, between 1999 and 2000, the count of hosts grew by nearly 30 million to more than 72 million, as reported by Internet Software Consortium.[7]

eMarketer found the count of U.S. households that had been online in the thirty days prior to a survey was over 14 million, or 14.5 percent of households, in 1997. By 2000, eMarketer conservatively estimated that the count of online households had more than doubled, to nearly 33 million, or nearly one-third of households.[8] The Employment Policy Institute more aggressively estimated that 43.5 percent of American households were online in 2000, and projected that 66.9 percent of households would be online by the end of 2002.[9]

Largely because of the growing value of the Internet along with the declining prices of computers, modems, and Internet services, computer and Internet use has and will continue to spread among all income groups, with lower-income groups catching up somewhat with higher-income groups in their computer and Internet usage. Jupiter Communications estimates that by 2005, 45 percent of low-income Americans (those with household incomes under $15,000 a year) will be online (up from 15 percent in 1999). At that time, 93 percent of households with more than $75,000 in annual income will be online (up from 73 percent in 1999).[10] (The Employment Policy Foundation estimates that the spread of computer and Internet usage within low- and high-income groups will be even more rapid than Jupiter figures it will be.[11]) This means that in the very early 2000s, the overwhelming majority of Americans who want computers and Internet access will have it.

By the start of the new millennium, surely there was no large U.S. business that did not use computers in one way or another (and most in many different ways) and did not have some form of Internet access for its workers. The Internet tracking company International Data Corporation found that 85 percent of the 7.5 million small businesses in the country were computer equipped. Nearly 60 percent of small businesses had access to the Internet, more than one-fourth had a home page, and one out of eight was engaged in some form of electronic commerce.[12] The consulting firm Accenture (formerly Arthur Anderson) found in a survey of small- and medium-size businesses, 71 percent used the Internet for E-mail, 60 percent for research, 40 percent for the purchasing of goods and services, 23 percent for selling goods and services, and 8 percent for recruiting employees.[13]

Between 1998 and 2000, the count of Americans who were online buyers (not just surfers) rose from 19 million to 29 million, or by more than 50 percent, according to Jupiter Communications.[14] Estimates of online sales by businesses directly to consumers—dubbed "B2C"—in 1999 ranged from a low of $15 billion to a high of $24 billion, with even the highest online sales representing a tiny percentage of all retail sales in the $10-trillion U.S. economy (and at most one-quarter of the sales of the country's fast-food industry). Nevertheless, all organizations tracking B2C online sales project such sales rising by factors of between three and seven times in the three years between 1999 and 2003.[15]

All industry analysts seem to think that the real action in electronic commerce is, and will remain, in the business-to-business (B2B) sector, although estimates of the size of the sector differ widely. According to eMarketer, B2B online sales around the world were $75.6 billion in 1999.[16] Goldman Sachs's estimate of the size of the B2B sector in the United States alone in 1999 was twice that of eMarketer's estimate of B2B sales for the world. Still, such sales represented only a small fraction of domestic economic activity at the start of the new millennium.

However, in spite of the dot-com bust beginning in 2000, online sales between businesses are expected to jump by 2003, with projected sales in the United States for that year ranging from $1 trillion to $2 trillion, and a growing share of B2B sales shifting from partnering businesses to unconnected businesses (with direct trade between partners falling from 87 percent of B2B sales in 2000 to 53 percent, according to Forrester Research).[17] By 2003, over half of B2B sales are expected to be outside the United States.

The growth in the so-called new economy is self-evident in a variety of other statistics. For example, the count of unique visitors to the top-fifteen U.S. Web sites (Yahoo!, AOL, eBay, Amazon, Netscape, and so on.) more than doubled from just under 200,000 in July 1999 to 410,000 a year later.[18] The count of cellular phones grew from 4.4 million in 1990 to 76.3 million in 1999.[19] The number of subscribers to Internet services with DSL and cable modem hookups more than doubled between 1999 and 2000, from 1.5 million to 3.4 million, with the count projected to reach 19.4 million in 2004.[20] The ongoing substitution of fiber-optic cable for twisted-wire permits a dramatic increase in the volume and speed of voice and data communications. And between 1993 and 1998, the miles of fiber-optic cable deployed in the country rose from 7.7 million to 19.2 million, an increase of two and one-half times.[21] The sum of all income earned in the information technology sector of the economy rose from $335 billion in 1990 to $815 billion in 2000, an increase of 143 percent, according to the U.S. Department of Commerce.[22]

Concurrent with the accelerating growth in computer power and sales and the takeoff in Internet traffic and telecommunication during the first half of the 1990s, there was (apparently) an acceleration in labor productivity growth starting around the middle of the decade. Between 1972 and 1995, labor productivity (measured as dollar output per hour of work) grew an average of 1.4 percent per year (below the annual average of 2.9 percent for the 1947–1972 period). However, between 1995 and 1999, labor productivity doubled to 2.8 percent a year.[23]

From all these statistics, it might seem reasonable to conclude that, independent of other forces, the "computer revolution" has indeed wrought a national "revolution" of sizable proportions, one that is incontrovertible, supported by a transparent substantial improvement in Americans' economic well-being. No such luck. As we will see in this chapter, the exact impact of the computer revolution on the non-high-technology sectors of the economy remains a contentious issue, although, as years go by and new data become available, it does appear that at long last the economic power of computing may have begun to show up in national economic data. However, the exact size of the impact remains subject to debate. There are a number of good conceptual reasons why the economic impact of computers has not been more transparent.

THE MATTER OF EVIDENCE

Back in 1987, two business professors at the University of California–Berkeley, Stephen Cohen and John Zysman, published a book entitled

Manufacturing Matters, which amounted to a defense of the manufacturing industry in the United States. At the time, manufacturing appeared to many analysts to be in serious decline. The term *deindustrialization* was widely used in the 1980s to describe a supposed downward economic trend in the production of manufactured goods (although, as a matter of fact, the real value of manufactured goods and the productivity of the manufacturing sector were actually rising for most of the 1980s; only employment in manufacturing was in decline[24]). Cohen and Zysman insisted in their book that manufacturing must forever remain an integral part of the national economy and, hence, should be nurtured by government through an array of "industrial policies."[25]

The authors were fortunate to have their book chosen for review in the *New York Times Book Review*, but they were unfortunate in the luck of the draw of reviewers. Robert Solow, an MIT economist and Nobel laureate, who was asked to review the book, did not much like it (although he had a few nice things to say), mainly because he felt that the book "only appears to be saying something."[26]

More important, he faulted the authors for having observed, "We do not need to show that the new technologies [mainly in telecommunications and computers] produce a break with past patterns of productivity growth. . . . [That] would depend not just on the possibilities the technologies represent, but rather on how effectively they are used."[27] Solow then provided his own translation of what he thought the authors were really saying and, in the process, sparked an academic debate that continues to this day under the rubric of the "Solow Paradox": "What this means," Solow wrote, "is that they, like everyone else, are somewhat embarrassed by the fact that what everyone feels to have been a technological revolution, a drastic change in our productive lives, has been accompanied everywhere, including Japan, by a slowing down of productivity growth, not by a step up. You can see the computer revolution everywhere but in the productivity statistics."[28]

In effect, Solow cautioned that Cohen and Zysman (and, by implication, others who had made similar arguments over the years) could not simply assume that the technological revolution had the intended and expected effect. He admonished researchers to prove it in the good old-fashioned way, with data, a charge that proved to be much more difficult than many observers would have thought.

Research continued into the early 1990s (and according to one study that will be reviewed later, into the late 1990s) to show what Solow had surmised earlier, that there had been a marked slowdown in productivity long after the introduction of the semiconductor. After adjusting for quality changes, researchers found that the rate of growth in total factor productivity (including both capital and labor inputs) remained close to the productivity growth rate of 1.4 percent per year for the 1890–1966 period, which was also close to the productivity growth rate for the 1929–1966 period, 1.45 percent. However, in the 1966–1989 period, the total factor productivity growth rate plunged to .04 percent.[29] Nevertheless, claims about the economic power of the presumed modern-day technological revolution have, since Solow's book review, continued unabated. In a publication for the Semiconductor Industry Association, Kenneth Flamm observed, "The invention of the semiconductor transistor set in motion a technological revolution that is arguably even more impressive and pervasive than that of the Great Industrial Revolution of the last century."[30] Federal Reserve Board chairman Alan Greenspan, who is renowned for measuring his words very carefully, added credence to the optimistic view of the computer's economic impact when he observed, "We are living through one of those rare, perhaps once-in-a-century events. . . . The advent of the transistor and the integrated circuit and, as a consequence, the emergence of the modern computer, telecommunication and satellite technologies have fundamentally changed the structure of the American economy."[31]

However, throughout the late 1980s and the first half of the 1990s, economists have repeatedly tried to find evidence of an improvement in U.S. productivity from the growing investments businesses were making in computer systems. After all, they had strong observations and logical arguments on their side. Computers were becoming ubiquitous, at home and at work. If there had truly been a technological revolution underway since at least the development of the semiconductor chip, productivity should have risen. Moreover, why would businesses buy so many computers and software packages if they did not expect a productivity improvement? The added capital expense could only be justified with an increase in their productivity. If firms could not show a productivity improvement for their capital investment, their competitive positions in their product markets could be expected to falter because of the cost structures that would be inflated by their purchases of computers and related equipment. The firms' errant investment policies would be punished by a reduction in their stock prices. Detecting that investment errors were being made, astute investors could buy managing control of the firms at the deflated stock prices, change the firms' investment strategies, and sell their stock at a capital gain.

Of course, not all firms would have to be bought out for corrections to be made. Feeling the product and financial pressures, managers could, sooner or later, get the message that they must adjust their investment strategies, relying less on computers.

A true revolution should imply more than an increase in productivity over time; it should imply an acceleration in the increase of productivity. This is because productivity has indeed trended upward for a long time due to a host of forces, and could have been expected to march onward and upward even without the introduction of semiconductors, or, more broadly, the emergence of the so-called new economy. If a revolution were underway, it should be seen in an increase in productivity that would not have been expected from past trends, meaning there should have been an upward divergence from the past trend, or an increase in the rate of productivity improvement, that could be expected to be sustained over a long period of time. Stated differently, this means that we might expect to observe an increase in output that is disproportionately greater than the increase in capital (for example, computers) and greater than was generated from an increase in capital in the past.

However, between 1973 and the middle of the 1990s, there was no apparent revolutionary change in labor productivity, defined as the output per hour of labor time in the nonfarm business sector of the economy. Productivity growth has historically faltered during recessions, as it did in the four recessions during the period. However, outside of those recessions, productivity growth during the 1980s and early 1990s appears to be on, or close to, the upward trend charted in the 1970s. From this information alone, it is understandable why Solow made his comment and why so many researchers in the early 1990s were hard-pressed to find an impact of the computer revolution on productivity. For example, Federal Reserve Board economist Daniel Sichel found that between 1960 and 1973, labor productivity grew at an annual rate of 3 percent, only to plunge to 1.1 percent in the 1973–1995 period.[32]

Even Oxford University economist Paul David, who, as we will see later, believed that the impact of the computer revolution would eventually show up in the data, deduced:

The productivity growth rate's deviation below the trend that had prevailed during the 1950–1972 "golden age" of post–World War II growth became even more pronounced during the late 1980s and early 1990s, instead of becoming less marked as the oil shock and inflationary disturbances of the 1970s and the recession of the early 1980s passed into history. Measured labor productivity rose during 1988–1996 at only .83 percent per annum, half a percentage point *less* rapidly than the average pace maintained during 1972–1988, and thus fully 2.25 percentage points below the average pace during 1950–1972. (emphasis in original)[33]

Then, it must be stressed that some of the measured rise in labor productivity during the years covered by David's study might actually be attributed to the fact that more capital (computers) was being used, not to the prospect that the capital or labor was being made more productive (or that more output was being obtained from each additional unit of input). As late as 1997, Princeton University economists Alan Blinder and Richard Quandt found some evidence that computers raised labor productivity, but only scant evidence that the productivity of all factors of production, including capital, taken together had been raised. They worried that the surge in business investments might pay off in the future, but it appeared to them that "we may be condemned to an extended period of transition in which growing pains change in nature, but don't go away."[34]

Similarly, Federal Reserve Board economist Daniel Sichel, writing in 1997 (and reporting on his econometric work with fellow Federal Reserve Board economist Stephen Oliner) concluded that

> Computer hardware has made a small contribution to growth. Between 1970 and 1992 output growth averaged 2.8 percent. Of this growth, computers contributed only 0.15 percentage point annually to the growth of business output. . . . In the more recent period, 1980 to 1992, the contribution of computers is more than double that in the preceding decade [the 1970s], but still is only 0.20 percentage point a year. Although an extra couple of tenths of a percentage point of growth a year would accumulate substantially over many years, it remains quite small compared with the productivity slowdown of about one and one-half percentage points in the 1970s.[35]

More recently, Northwestern University economist Robert Gordon continued the flow of pessimistic assessments of the impact of the new economy, by which he means "the Internet and the accompanying acceleration of technical change in computers and telecommunications," on overall productivity in the country.[36] He concluded in 2000 that "outside the 12 percent of the economy engaged in manufacturing durable goods, the new economy's effects on productivity growth are surprisingly absent, and capital deepening has been remarkably unproductive" (p. 4).

Gordon did find an increase in the growth of output in the economy during the last half of the 1990s. The growth rate for output, according to his methods, was 2.75 percent for the 1972–1995 period and 4.90 percent for the 1995–1999 period (table 1). However, he attributes much of the acceleration in productivity growth to the greater use of the existing capital base as the recovery, which started in the early 1990s, progressed (something that has always happened in recoveries and might be expected when the unemployment rate dips below 4 percent as it did at the end of the decade). He also found that the impact of the new economy showed up in an accelerated growth in high-tech industries. However, when the computer hardware industry, which constitutes only 4 percent of national production, is excluded from the productivity estimates and when adjustments are made to account for the expected improvement in output attributable to the recovery and to "capital deepening," due to more computers being bought, he found, unexpectedly, that during the 1995–1999 period the productivity of all factors of production (what he calls the "multi-factor productivity") declined by .09 percent a year. If the analysis is further restricted to the productivity improvement in the national economy outside of the durable goods manufacturing sector, the overall annual productivity growth rate in 1995–1999 declined even more, by .28 percent per year (table 2).

Gordon goes on to argue that the response of consumer purchases of computer equipment to a reduction in the price was greater before 1987 than after 1987, and the response was even lower after computer prices began to accelerate downward after 1995. As a consequence, he surmised that "the speed at which diminishing returns have taken hold makes it likely that the greatest benefits of computers lie a decade or more in the past, not in the future (p. 5). Finally, he deduces what might be dubbed the "Gordon Paradox": "The 'New Economy' is alive and well, but only within computer manufacturing and the remainder of the manufacturing durable sector" (p. 16).

IN SEARCH OF EXPLANATIONS

Given the thrust of the statistical findings from an array of studies, economists have spilled a great deal of ink trying to explain the absence of a substantial impact of the supposed modern-day technological revolution on productivity. There are several prominent explanations that have been put forward.

The Mismeasurement Problem

Many economic analysts are convinced that much economic activity within key sectors of the economy is no longer measured very accurately.[37] Manufacturing output, such as cars and watches or even computers, can be counted with relative ease, or so it is generally thought. A car is a car. A watch is a watch. How many cars and watches are produced can be determined by a count, and their quality improvements can, with reasonable accuracy, be appraised by their prices.

On the other hand, services, such as medical care or education, are not so easily identified, given the difficulty of specifying the boundaries of the units that are measured and given the importance of quality in the selection of service providers. For example, it is hard to say what constitutes comparable operations done by surgeons. Moreover, operations differ, and people select surgeons often because of their experience and reputations. Even when the count (or dollar value) of operations has not risen, the productivity of surgeons could have risen, given that the operations could be better (as measured by the success rate of the operations or by the patients' degree of satisfaction with what was done to them and how much pain they feel afterward). Hence, it is thought that services may be more poorly counted in government statistics than are manufactured goods.

For many decades, the economy has been shifting from goods-based to services-based. This means that measuring what is produced, and doing so accurately, could have become progressively more problematic for government bean counters, with the result being more undermeasurement. This argument basically reduces to the proposition that the productivity increase is really there, only we cannot see it in the available, imperfect government data.

Perhaps productivity is undermeasured because consumers may be taking the productivity gains in a way that is not thought of as additional output, that is, through quality improvements and greater choice of products. That is certainly a debatable proposition. Researchers point out that the telegraph may have done more to speed up communications than has the Internet, simply because communications were so slow at the time the telegraph was invented (1844)[38] and that the quality improvement in the automobile was greater during the first decade of the twentieth century than in the last decade of that century.[39]

Other researchers have found that while there are far more products available today than at any other time in history that does not mean that the rate of increase of new products is higher. For example, in 1994, there were twice as many products in the typical grocery store as there were in 1972. However, the rate of increase in new products on grocery store shelves in the 1948–1972 period (figured as a percent of the count of existing products) was more than four times the rate of increase in the 1972–1994 period.[40] Still, it could be that, as one study found, the use of computers and related equipment has tended to lead to an increase in product variety over and above what would have otherwise been the case.[41]

Indeed, it could in fact be true that output statistics have progressively understated total production, which means that the "productivity" (a ratio that has production in the numerator and labor or some other input in the denominator) could be further and further removed from the "correct" and, presumably, higher figure. Proponents of this explanation have taken some solace in the findings of a commission set up in the mid-1990s, and headed by Stanford University economist Michael Boskin, to appraise the accuracy of the consumer price index. If the price index is inaccurate, then measures of real, inflation-adjusted output can be distorted, as can productivity, which must use the distorted output figures. The Boskin Commission did find in 1996 that at least since the late 1970s, the consumer price index has overstated inflation by an average of 1.1 percent a year, which suggests that official estimates of real output levels have been understated. Accordingly, productivity improvements have been understated.[42]

While there might be a measure of truth in this undermeasurement argument, the problem of inaccurate national output statistics has been around for a very long time.[43] Quality improvements in even manufactured goods are not always easy to assess, and the quality of manufactured goods has improved substantially over the decades. It is not at all clear that the mismeasurement of the quality improvements in manufactured goods has become progressively less of a problem than the mismeasurement of quality improvements in services, mainly because many manufactured goods have been made more reliable (meaning they need fewer repair services) and other manufactured goods come with more services (for example, many manufacturers help control their resellers' inventories).[44]

In addition, the overstatement in the consumer price index did not likely start in the late 1970s. This mismeasurement of prices was considered way back in 1961 by a task force organized by the National Bureau of Economic Research and headed by the late Nobel laureate in economics George Stigler. Like the Boskin Commission, the Stigler Task Force found a measurement gap in real output resulting from problems in the price statistics, but it did not find that the gap was increasing over time.[45] And the slowdown in productivity increase in the 1970s, 1980s, and early 1990s could only be attributed to a measurement problem if the output were to a greater and greater degree undermeasured.

Sichel has tried to quantitatively assess the impact of the shift in the economy from goods production to services production. He found that the shift accounts for one-sixth of the slowdown in productivity during the 1980s and 1990s. He concluded that "the interaction of the mismeasurement gap and a higher service share is an unlikely explanation for the sluggish pace of output and productivity growth over the past two decades."[46]

Furthermore, there may have been an understatement (and perhaps a growing understatement) of the count of units of computers and related equipment, given that computers have become far more powerful with the passing years. That is, a computer today may be the equivalent of several computers bought at higher prices in the past. If so, this means there could have been a growing understatement of the growth in use of computer power and a growing overstatement of productivity improvements of all factors of production.

No doubt the debate over the exact nature of the measurement problems in output data will continue. What appears fairly clear now is that the whole of the productivity paradox cannot be dismissed simply as a mismeasurement problem.

Diminishing Returns to Computer Uses

When computers are first introduced in business, we should expect firms to deploy them where they can contribute the most value. This goes for all other modern low- or high-technology equipment, such as drill presses, printers, and cell phones. If everything stays constant, when the use of computers is extended, the remaining uses will, by definition, be less valuable. With any new technology, there is the prospect that the technology will be used to exploit what are, before the fact, believed to be profitable opportunities, but turn out to be technological blind alleys. Initially, all investment avenues might be construed as "blind alleys," given how little is known about the market potential for products using the technology. Many mistakes may be made, in other words. As more is learned about the dimensions of the market, the avenues with high probabilities of success might be exploited, leaving risky avenues to be exploited later.

Hence, it can be argued that we might anticipate some decline in the contribution of additional computers to firm output, meaning diminishing returns can be expected. The diminishing returns can translate into a slowdown in productivity growth, a point that has been made by several economists.[47]

Furthermore, as the price of computers has declined, firms have a progressively greater incentive to use computers in ways that add less and less to firm output, and thereby to firm productivity. Indeed, computers can be substituted for other progressively less productive factors of production. For example, when computer prices are high, they might be used to supplant high-skilled labor. When the prices fall, they can be used to supplant low-skilled labor. As the substitution is extended over less productive factors, the additional computers can be expected to add less and less to output, because the resources they replace add less and less to output. With lower computing prices, firms might justify buying more computing power for workers than they really need on the argument that they might be able to use the added power in the future. This means that firms can even rationally take chances that the computing power will be wasted. After all, the firms simply do not have to earn as much on their smaller investments in computers.[48]

Again, there is surely a measure of truth in this argument. However, there are two problems with it in explaining the slowdown in productivity growth with the emergence of the computer revolution. First, the argument assumes that everything else remains the same. I noted earlier in the book that network effects should be prevalent in high-tech industries—if not in computer hardware, then surely in software. Network effects necessarily imply that everything else does not remain the same. Computers can become more valuable as they can do more and more, and as more and more people use them to coordinate their work with each other (say, through the Internet). As a consequence, the demand for computers can rise along with their marginal contributions to firm output.

Second, while it is certainly true that the price of computing power has fallen rapidly over the past half century, and perhaps especially rapidly in the 1990s, the cost of using computers includes far more than the price of the hardware and the software. The total cost of computer services includes the time people spend upgrading their hardware and software, learning new programs, seeking help when error messages arise, working out conflicts between software and hardware, and repairing broken computer systems. The total cost also includes the time workers spend not doing anything while their computers (and/or networks) are down for repairs. These costs have been increasing.[49] If firms have correctly judged these costs (and that is a big "if"), the rising costs should have led to higher valued uses of computers, fewer uses of computers, and rising productivity from the continuing computerization of the workplace.

The Lag Effect

Paul David has reasoned that the productivity impact will likely show up in the data, but perhaps with a long delay, or what he calls an "extended transition."[50] He argues that many new technologies, like electricity, have spread slowly throughout history. All of the necessary elements for the successful commercialization of electricity, according to David, were available as early as 1880. By 1899, only 5 percent of the total mechanical drives for manufacturing were electrified. However, five years later 11 percent of the mechanical drives were electrified. By the 1920s, 50 percent of mechanical drives in manufacturing were electric, a diffusion level for electrified manufacturing that led to a surge in manufacturing productivity. Before people could use electricity productively, they not only needed electricity, they needed reliable sources of electricity, and they also needed to have their cities, workplaces, and houses wired. In addition, there needed to be sales networks for electrical appliances and for their repair. People also had to get over their fear of electricity, since it could be deadly.

Similarly, the fax machine was invented in 1843 and first used commercially in 1963. Newspapers began using fax machines to send pictures between branch offices in the early twentieth century. However, fax machines were not in widespread business and personal use, and able to contribute markedly to overall productivity, until the 1980s (if they had any measurable effect then).

For similar reasons, measured productivity improvements from the use of computers should be expected to show up with a long delay. People have had to learn how to use computers and software (and sometimes they have had to reeducate themselves with each new advance in hardware and software). Perhaps more important, they have had to become comfortable with them. Systems for computer purchases, repair, and replacement had to be established.

There may also have been a need for a critical mass of computers before computers could productively be networked and used in a coordinated and synergetic manner in business. If orders are taken over the phone and put into a computer in the sales department, the value of the computers in the sales department might not be fully realized until the digitized orders can be sent to production (or to outside suppliers). And the value of the computers in sales may be limited until all in the firm have computers and the need for a dual communication system—one digital and one paper—is eliminated. As MIT management professor Erik Brynjolfsson and Wharton School management professor Lorin Hitt argue, the impact of information technology is dependent not just on the purchase of machines, but on a "large number of complementary changes," including, often, a wholesale redesign—or "reengineering"—of management and production systems.[51] For example, informational technology may change pay schemes, the size of firms, the extent to which key decisions are made by higher managers or line employees, and the extent to which components are made in-house or are outsourced. The company's "culture" may have to be reoriented, and such a change can be time-consuming and can require a multitude of complementary investments as well as the creation of intangible business assets that are not normally thought of as capital (for example, business processes for taking orders and servicing customer needs). Moreover, when such changes are introduced, albeit gradually, firm productivity can fall off, only to be recouped later, perhaps much later when all required components of the new system are in place.[52]

Surely, the argument has validity, but must be viewed with some caution. As Robert Gordon has argued, the computerization of businesses is not a process that began with the advent of the IBM-compatible personal computer in the early 1980s. Personal computers were only another step in the computerization process that may date back to the turn of the century when punch-card systems were introduced to automate some business systems. Of course, the mainframe computer spread rapidly in large businesses in the 1950s and 1960s. And all the while, the price of computing power (or what Gordon calls "characteristics" of computers that take into account computer speed, memory, capacity of hard drive, presence and type of CD-ROM reader, and other factors) was declining, and that decline began long before the advent of the personal computers in the 1970s. Given the way he measured computing power, the price decline was more or less steady during the 1980s and 1990s, practically on the same downward straight-line trend established in the 1960s. This price decline of computer characteristics averaged 19.4 percent per year during the 1960–1999 period.[53]

Gordon in effect argues that four decades seems long enough for the expected lag in productivity to end, if a productivity increase can really be expected to show up. He is doubtful, given the constant prospects of diminishing returns coming out in a multitude of ways:

> Many of the industries that are the heaviest users of computer technology, e.g., airlines, banks, and insurance companies, began in the 1960s and 1970s with mainframe technology and still perform the most computation-intensive activities on mainframes, often using PCs as smart terminals to access the mainframe data base. In this sense computers have been around for almost 50 years, not just a decade or so, and the "waiting for Godot" hypothesis of David and others loses further credibility. (p. 31)

Furthermore, Gordon argues that many of the enhancements made to computers and software have been more on the order of refinements, not revolutionary improvements in the way people work. For example, he suggests that computerized word processing greatly enhanced his ability to write papers in the early 1980s, given that he could then alter his writing without having to retype the manuscripts. Gordon adds:

> The productivity enhancement of WYSIWYG [for "what you see is what you get"] was minor in comparison [to the initial ability of computer users to edit their papers], and what was contributed by the final step to the latest version of Word for Windows, beyond the ease of training for novice users, escapes me. As the computer industry has developed, the steady decline in the prices of computer characteristics has fueled the development of increasingly complex software with high requirements for speed and memory required by graphical point-and-click interfaces that yield increasingly small increments of true functionality. The race between hardware capability and software requirements has been aptly summed up in the phrase, "What Intel giveth, Microsoft taketh away." (p. 30)

Perhaps the problem has been best characterized by Nathan Myhrvold, vice president for applications and content at Microsoft, who suggests that software is like a gas that "expands to fill its container."[54]

Computers as "Small Potatoes" in the Economy

Daniel Sichel argues that perhaps no one should have expected computers (and peripheral equipment) in the 1970s and 1980s to have had a major impact on the productivity statistics for the national economy. The reason is simple: Computers (and peripheral equipment) have been "small potatoes" in the economy; that is, they have represented a small share of business investment and an even smaller share of the national capital stock. In both 1970 and 1980, computers in nominal dollar terms represented only 2.6 percent of business investment in nonresidential equipment and structures, and a meager 0.9 percent of the net capital stock (net of depreciation). By 1993, after years of growth in computer purchases, computers represented only 7.6 percent of business investment and 1.8 percent of the capital stock of businesses. Even when we correct for the rapid fall in the prices of computers (using 1987 as the base year), business purchases of computers amounted to only 17.8 percent of total investment and 4.7 percent of the capital stock[55] (but then Sichel shows that these real shares are influenced by the base year selected for computing the real value; the use of 1992 as the base year lowers the real share of computers in business investment and capital stock).[56]

How can computers make up such a small share of investment and the capital stock? Sichel argues, "A key reason is that computers become obsolete so rapidly. Much new spending on computers [more than half in the 1980s] goes to replacing and updating older equipment. . . . Put another way, while computers are coming in the front door at a good clip, they are going out the back door at a hefty pace."[57]

The small impact of computers' share of capital on their potential contribution to productivity is compounded by the fact that the real growth in computer purchases in the 1950–1993 period occurred in the service sector. By 1993, more than three-quarters of computers (and peripheral equipment) bought were used in services, up from one-half in 1950.[58] The problem is that many services remain bound to the involvement of people, which necessarily limits the contributions of computers to productivity. As Gordon notes:

> Commercial aircraft, large and small alike, will always need two human pilots, no matter how advanced the avionics in the cockpit. Trucks will always need at least one driver. In manufacturing, some critical functions have proven to be resistant to automation, such as the connecting of tubes and wires when an auto chassis is "married" to the body. No matter how powerful the computer hardware and how user-friendly the software, most functions provided by personal computers, including word-processing, spreadsheets, and data-base management, still require hands-on human contact through a keyboard and mouse to be productive.[59]

Of course, computers could have been a force in the relative expansion of the service sector. If that were the case, then they would have contributed to the growth in that sector of the economy relatively more bound by the need to have human involvement. However, as we have seen, the emergence of the service sector does not appear to explain a substantial falloff in the productivity growth, at least through the mid-1990s. At the same time, as Brynjolfsson and Hitt stress, statistics on productivity changes in key service industries do not seem to square with commonsense observations: "According to official government statistics, a bank today is only 80 percent as productive as a bank in 1977; a health care facility is only 70 percent as productive and a lawyer only 65 percent as productive as they were in 1977."[60] This is after the banking industry has installed 139,000 ATM machines; medical records have been computerized and hospital stays have shortened; and lawyers have been able to employ a variety of software packages that speed up the writing of wills and contracts and have extended their legal research with services such as LexisNexis.

The Limitations of the Human Mind

In assessing the human condition, one fact stands out: People will be fully employed at all times until the day they die. They will be doing something every minute, even if something is nothing more than sleeping or gazing off into space. The only real, unrelenting issue people face is what they will be doing. Similarly, people will at all times be using their brains on one thing or another. Granted, they can use their brains more or less intensely, but they cannot avoid running up against their mental limits to do things, and they must face the fact that, as research has shown, more intense use of the brain's mental capacity does not always lead to improved mental output.[61] Indeed, researchers have found that as the brain is taxed more and more heavily with greater computational demands, diminishing returns eventually set in. Given the limits of the brain, people must often substitute one mental activity for another.

So it may be with computers. Computers can augment people's ability to undertake complex computations, and they can increase the ability to store and retrieve information. They can encourage, if not force, people to use their brains more intensely, but again, beyond some point, diminishing returns can set in, meaning that the addition of computing power (or the addition of whole computers) can progressively add to the ability of people to use the additional computer power productively in terms of more and better output, whether measured in decisions or in manuscript pages.

In other words, it may very well be the case that more powerful computers can increase the array of software programs that a person can use in the office and the speed with which various tasks can be accomplished. In that regard, the potential contribution to labor productivity may increase with each new computer model (with more speed and storage capacity) and each new software version. However, the limiting factor may be people's capacity to utilize computers, not what the machines can potentially do. People may only be able to exploit a smaller and smaller percent of the additional computing power.[62] Part of the explanation can be that as they butt up against their mental capacities, they become confused, if not overtaxed, which, again, can lead to diminishing returns. From this perspective, there should be no wonder why I found in a survey of 152 computer-savvy M.B.A. students that one-fifth reported using no more than the six programs in Microsoft Office and 84 percent used a dozen or fewer programs (including games)—in spite of the fact that there may have been thousands of programs they could have used.[63]

Great Technological Inventions in History

Robert Gordon's favorite explanation for the productivity paradox is that the modern-day computer revolution simply does not come close to measuring the impact of technological revolutions of the past on the human condition (a conclusion shared by others[64]). To appreciate his point, you must understand that life today is a far cry from what it was one or two hundred years ago, meaning there was a century or more ago much room for improvement in human welfare. Gordon prominently cites an economic history book the title of which, *The Good Old Days—They Were Terrible!*, conveys his essential message, documented with references to living conditions.[65] Gordon paints a gruesome picture:

> The urban streets of the 1870s and 1880s were full not just of horses but pigs, which roamed the streets and were tolerated because they ate garbage. In Kansas City, the confusion and stench of patrolling hogs were so penetrating that Oscar Wilde observed, "They made granite eyes weep." The steadily increasing production of animal waste caused the more pessimistic observers to fear that American cities would disappear like Pompeii—but not under ashes. Added to that was acrid industrial smog, sidewalks piled high with kitchen slops, coal dust, and dumped merchandise, which became stirred together in slime after a rain. All of this was made worse in the summer, which was almost as unbearable outdoors as inside, especially with the heavy clothes of the day. Rudyard Kipling said of Chicago, "Having seen it, I desire urgently never to see it again. Its air is dirt." Added to putrid air was the danger of spoiled food—imagine unrefrigerated meat and poultry hung unrefrigerated for days, spoiled fruit, bacteria-infected milk, and virtually all types of food were suspected of adulteration. Epidemics included yellow fever, scarlet fever, and smallpox. The pain and lack of sanitation in surgery were endemic, and many hospitals were deathtraps.[66]

In the late 1890s, the principal mode of transportation was still horseback. Railways were in use but far less safe than they are today. Only 2 percent of the houses in New York City had running water, with "middle-class apartment buildings little more than glorified tenements."[67] Work was dangerous and lasted as long as sunlight allowed it.

In this context, new technologies could easily improve living conditions, and Gordon cites five "clusters" of inventions that very likely had a greater impact than the semiconductor:

1. Electricity;
2. Internal combustion engine;

3. Petroleum, natural gas, and "various processes that 'rearrange molecules,' including chemicals, plastics, and pharmaceuticals";
4. Entertainment and communications, including the telegraph (1844), telephone (1876), phonograph (1877), photography (1880s and 1890s), radio (1899), motion pictures (1881 to 1888), and television (1911);
5. Running water, indoor plumbing, and an urban sanitation infrastructure.[68]

He points out that his list of "Great Inventions" lines up well with the list of the "Greatest [Twenty] Achievements of the 20th Century" developed by the National Academy of Engineering.[69] In the list, computers rank eighth in importance, with the Internet coming in at thirteenth.[70] He suggests that it might be too much to expect computers and related equipment, which amount to a new cluster of inventions, to supercede the impact of indoor plumbing, much less the impact of electricity that has underpinned so many derivative technologies, including computers. It is just darn hard for any technology like computers to make a significant improvement when the living standard is so high and when computers account for such a small part of the economy's capital stock. Then again, Gordon's argument may amount to a supposition, not grounded in what might ultimately turn out to be the facts of the computer revolution's impact on living standards.

THE BEGINNINGS OF A NEW ECONOMY?

In its last *Economic Report to the President*, distributed just before President Bill Clinton left office in January 2001, the Council of Economic Advisors gloated over finding strong evidence of the emergence of a new economy in government statistics during the Clinton years in office: "In the 1990s, after two decades of disappointing performance, the economy enjoyed one of the most prosperous periods ever."[71] The Council members added, "Since the beginning of 1993, output per hour in the nonfarm business sector has grown at an average rate of 2.3 percent per year, compared with an average of 1.4 percent for the previous 20 years. Even more remarkably, since the fourth quarter of 1995 productivity growth has averaged 3 percent a year. This acceleration in productivity has produced higher incomes and greater wealth" (p. 20). They attribute the resurgence of growth to the interplay of "advances in technologies, business practices, and economic policies" (p. 23).

The economic policies that they thought were instrumental in the economic revival included, naturally, anything (and perhaps everything) their boss had instituted. The policy accomplishments they cited included progress in freeing international trade from import barriers, the greater federal focus on education, welfare reform, and the shift in the federal budget from a substantial deficit balance that the Clinton administration inherited from the (older) Bush administration to a substantial surplus balance that they left the incoming (younger) Bush administration (with the shift in budget balance, according to the Clinton Council, helping to bring down real interest rates).

One of the advances in business practices the Council cites is businesses' concern for improving firm productivity and profits through "supply-chain management," which has resulted in a continuation of the transparent long-term downward trend in business inventories as a percent of sales. In 1982, firms, on average, had inventories to cover upward of 1.7 months of sales. By 2000, the inventory-to-sales ratio was down 25 percent, with enough inventories to cover, on average, approximately 1.3 months of sales. There was also a sharp decline in the sales-to-inventory-to-sales ratio in 1998 and 1999, with an uptick in the ratio in 2000. The Council economists also attributed some of the renewed economic growth to the financial contributions of venture capitalists to entrepreneurship; the efforts of firms to form partnerships and alliances; the greater research and development efforts of small- and medium-size firms and their growing tendency to locate near research universities; and the greater tendency of large firms to tap the entrepreneurial energies of smaller firms through alliances, buyouts, and mergers (which grew fourfold over the decade of the 1990s (p. 41, chart 1-8)

However, the Council members were clear on one point, that the productivity acceleration, and the underlying organizational changes in American business, could be, to a substantial degree, attributable to the long-awaited impact of technological advances relating to computers and related devices and telecommunications. These advances were, according to the Council members, fueled during the Clinton years by a 50 percent increase in R&D spending, a greater than 40 percent jump in patents granted annually, and an acceleration in the annual decline in computer prices from approximately 5 percent in 1994 to more than 25 percent in 1998. These economic forces resulted in a fourteenfold increase in the production of information goods and a doubling of information technology jobs during the 1990s (p. 35, chart 1-5).

More important, the Council of Economic Advisors drew a conclusion about productivity improvements in the late 1990s that stands in sharp contrast to the conclusions of the economists cited in earlier sections of this chapter: "Updated, sector-specific data on productivity gains indicate that those sectors that have invested heavily in information technology—wholesale trade and finance, among others—experienced some of the greatest gains during the 1990s" (p. 21).

The Council members make their case, in the main, with reference to the findings in Table 2.1. This table shows that labor productivity growth accelerated from 1.39 percent per year, on average, between 1973 and 1995 to 3.01 percent per year between 1995 and 2000, leaving a net growth rate improvement between the two periods of 1.69 percentage points (or an increase of 117 percent).

More important for the purposes of this chapter, the Council members decomposed the accelerated growth rate into contributions made by various determinants of labor productivity growth. As noted earlier, the economic recovery, which was still underway in the late 1990s, may have been responsible for a significant share of the accelerated growth, as Robert Gordon stressed was likely. However, in contrast to Gordon's findings, the Council members found that the business cycle effect (third line down in Table 2.1) played a trivial role, explaining a meager .04 percentage points (second column) of the 1.63 percentage point increase in the productivity growth rate. The Council members also found that the additional use of information capital services (what I called earlier "capital deepening") played on balance a modest role, explaining a .62 percentage point of the growth rate increase (fifth line down, third column). This means that capital deepening explains nearly two-fifths of the accelerated growth. Labor quality rose during the 1995–2000 period, but at a substantially reduced growth rate. Accordingly, the Council members found that total factor productivity (TFP in the table), which is labor productivity minus the positive contributions of capital services and negative contributions of labor quality, explains 1.00 percentage point. This means that TFP outside of the computer-producing sector explains approximately 63 percent of the 1.63 percentage points acceleration in the labor productivity growth rate. The members conclude, "This implies that improvements in the ways capital and labor are used throughout the economy are central to the recent acceleration in productivity. Some of these gains have likely resulted as firms learn to apply innovative information technology to their particular business and production methods" (p. 30).

Has the long-awaited impact of the computer revolution finally shown its head? Might it be that the economy is now, finally, on the other side of Paul David's "extended transition" to a new economic order based more heavily on computer technology? Maybe so. Other researchers believe that the productivity paradox may have disappeared as early as 1991.[72] But then, maybe not.

One explanation for the Council members' more rosy assessment of technology's impact as compared with, say, Gordon's assessment, could be that the members had a political motivation to find a strong impact. Such an

Table 2.1
Accounting for the Productivity Acceleration in the 1990s

Item	1973 to 1995	1995 to 2000	Change (percentage points)
Labor Productivity Growth Rate (percent)	1.39	3.01	1.63
Percentage Point Contributions			
Less: Business Cycle Effect	.00	.04	.04
Equals: Structural Labor Productivity	1.39	2.97	1.56
Less: Capital Services	.70	1.09	.38
Information Capital Services	.41	1.03	.62
Other Capital Services	.30	.06	−.23
Labor Quality	.27	.27	.00
Equals: Structural TFP	.40	1.59	1.19
Less: Computer Sector TFP	.18	.36	.18
Equals: TFP Excluding Computer Sector TFP	.22	1.22	1.00

Sources: Department of Commence (Bureau of Economic Analysis) for output and computer prices. Department of Labor (Bureau of Labor Statistics) for hours and for capital services and labor quality through 1998; and Council of Economic Advisors for the business cycle effect and for capital services and labor quality for 1995 and 2000, as reported by Council of Economic Advisors, Office of the President, *Economic Report of the President 2001* (Washington, D.C.: U.S. Government Printing Office, January 2001), 28.

Notes: Labor productivity is the average of income and product-side measures of output per hour worked. Total factor productivity (TFP) is labor productivity less the contributions of capital services per hour (capital deepenings and labor quality). Productivity for 2000 is inferred from the first three quarters. Detail may not add to totals because of spending.

explanation might be construed as an effort by the Council members to make their boss' terms in office look good with econometric analysis (which is subject to manipulation by appropriate selection of years and included variables). On the other hand, if the Council members could not attribute as much of the spurt in economic growth, income, and wealth in the late 1990s to technological advances, they could have given more direct credit to the Clinton policies as the force for positive change. Hence, a political argument for the measured improvement could cut both ways.

The Council of Economic Advisors' positive assessment might be due to their analysis covering 1995 through 2000, whereas the analyses undertaken by Gordon and others went no further than 1999. The inclusion of the year

2000 raised the average productivity growth rate from 2.90 percent for 1995–1999, computed for the Council's 2000 *Economic Report*, to 3.01 for 1995–2000, computed for its 2001 *Economic Report*.[73] If Gordon had access to the same data range, perhaps his conclusions would have been modified. We will just have to see how his recalculations turn out. Plus, we will have to follow an honorable tradition in policy disputes, wait and see what other researchers find. As it is, the research findings of others seem to be coming down on the Council's side.[74]

Very much like the Council of Economic Advisors, Federal Reserve Board economists Stephen Oliner and Daniel Sichel estimate that the introduction of computer technology accounts for two-thirds of the acceleration in labor productivity growth. Accordingly, in answer to the question Is information technology the whole story in explaining the resurgence in productivity growth? they say firmly, yes! It is important to note that Oliner and Sichel's data goes only through 1999, not 2000. A number of firm-based studies undertaken since the first half of the 1990s have found evidence of a positive productivity impact of computers, or more generally information technology. Goldman Sachs has estimated that when computerized procurement systems are introduced, the cost of purchases fall by 10 to 40 percent.[75] Dell's Web-based ordering system has given it a 10 percent cost advantage over its rivals in computer sales.[76] By giving its customers the ability to track their deliveries by the Internet, UPS has reduced the cost of seven hundred thousand tracking inquiries from $2 to $.10.[77]

In a study of three hundred firms, Brynjolfsson and Hitt found a definite positive relationship between a firm's investment in information technology and firm productivity, albeit with much variation in outcomes.[78] The positive effects of information technology on firm productivity appear to be showing up in stock market evaluations of firms. For example, Brynjolfsson and Shunkyu Yang found that when a Fortune 1000 firm invested $1 in "ordinary [noninformation technology] capital" during the 1987–1994 period, the company market value went up by $1. When the firm invested the $1 in information technology, its stock market evaluation rose by $10, suggesting that in the process of buying the information technology capital, it also increased its intangible assets, in the form of new business processes, by $9, further evidence that the impact of computers and related equipment may be partially obscured by how business operations are being changed in terms of the delegation of decision making, size, and reliance on outsourcing.[79]

Still, while these studies might be comforting to proponents of the view that computers have contributed to productivity, we cannot be totally confident that the extended transition has ended. There are always short-run blips in data series, and the upward tilt in the productivity trend line in the last half of the 1990s may be spurious or subject to reversal in the next few years, leaving researchers to once again scratch their heads. Even the Council members caution, "We could be observing [in Table 2.1] not a long-run shift to a faster productivity growth rate but simply a shift to a higher level of productivity, with faster growth for a while followed by a return to the pre-1995 trend. Or we may be witnessing the opportunity for faster trend growth over a longer time span."[80] Indeed, both the Congressional Budget Office and the Office of Management and Budget have projected labor productivity to fall to the 2 percent annual growth range by 2010.[81]

Nevertheless, there are several reasons, apart from computer advances, for agreeing with the Council that the economy may be on a productivity growth rate path that is higher than the path the economy was on before 1995:

- The world has become more globalized and competitive, and the ongoing growth in the competitiveness of markets (to the extent that it continues) can force businesses to eek out ever-greater productivity from their labor and capital inputs.
- It is a little-known fact that under Bill Clinton, federal government expenditures fell as a percentage of gross domestic product.[82] If that trend continues, more and more resources will be available for use by the private sector to spur productivity.
- There may be something to Alan Greenspan's view that productivity growth and inflation are inversely related.[83] When prices are more stable and predictable, firms can pay more attention to how best to squeeze more production out of their resources because they do not have to devote as many resources to figuring out the movement of prices in the economy generally.
- As evident from the dying off of a host of dot-com companies, beginning in 2000, much of the investment in information technology was for lost, and unproductive, causes. (Perhaps some undefined portion was a total waste.) The entrepreneurial excesses of the 1990s may very well be curbed in years ahead as funding sources, including venture capitalists, demand that proposed business models demonstrate the profitability of the funded firms. In other words, the country has learned much from the business failures of the past, and the knowledge gained from the failures can lead to more productive use of resources in the future.
- The Internet just might be providing a whole new technology for linking up computers with a resulting growth in economic synergy among businesses. These linkages might allow firms to more efficiently—that is, more productively—exploit the computing power at their disposal to tap and coordinate the brainpower and specialized knowledge of more and more people around

the globe, all of which can fuel business competitiveness that, in turn, can spur additional productive technological advances. The result can be several sources of cost savings for both business and government.[84]

However, some caution is in order. The dot-com boom of the late 1990s may have exaggerated the rate of productivity growth, given that a lot of the output may have been on wasted ventures or should not have been made, and would not have been made absent the stock market bubble of the late 1990s. Moreover, in mid-2001, the Commerce Department adjusted its estimate of the annual growth rate in real gross domestic product for 1996–2000 downward from 5 percent to 4.1 percent, very close to the average annual growth rate of 4 percent for the 1948–1973 period (but still above the average annual growth rate of 2.8 percent for 1974–1995).[85]

Finally, economists at the McKinsey Global Institute have issued a report that effectively says that the productivity growth rate did surge in the late 1990s, but the causes are far more complex than other researchers have assumed, and more related to what transpired in old-economy sectors than many observers have realized.[86] Information technology did play a role, but mainly in terms of how it was applied for competitive advantages in six sectors, representing only 30 percent of the economy in terms of output. Of the 1.32 percentage point acceleration in the productivity growth rate from the 1987–1995 period (.99 percent) to the 1995–1999 period (2.32 percent), six key industries made the following contributions:

Wholesale Trade	.37 percent
Retail Trade	.34 percent
Securities and Commodity Trading	.25 percent
Electronic and Electric Equipment (primarily semiconductors)	.17 percent
Industrial Machinery and Equipment (primarily computers)	.12 percent
Telecom Services	.07 percent[87]

All of the remaining 53 sectors, representing the remaining 70 percent of the economy, on balance added a meager .01 percent to the annual productivity growth rate (with many sectors experiencing a deceleration in their productivity growth rate). Surprisingly, given conventional wisdom about the impact of the Internet, the advent of the Internet also contributed only .01 percent to the acceleration in the growth rate, according to the McKinsey researchers. This means that retail and wholesale trade had 71 times the impact of the rest of the economy and of the Internet.

The researchers also drew three other notable conclusions. First, much of the productivity growth in the retail sector can be attributed to one firm, Wal-Mart. Second, much of the productivity growth in the retail sector can be attributed to the application of relatively simple technologies (barcodes, scanners, picking machines, and inventory control software), all of which were developed prior to 1995. Third, much of the improvement in productivity growth in the six sectors can be chalked up to the upswing in aggregate demand with the boom in the stock market and to growing competitive pressures from firms such as Wal-Mart that were innovating and driving their costs down and causing other firms to do likewise.[88]

CONCLUDING COMMENTS

The real world is often a messy place, full of conflicting forces and facts, making life difficult and disappointing for people who seek nice, neat answers to questions such as What has the computerization of the world done to productivity growth? Unfortunately, the available studies, along with the data they employ, are all imperfect, beset with a myriad of measurement problems. They have afforded us only a muddled answer to the above question, at least to date. Perhaps the statistical debate will be resolved in the not-too-distant future with more data points and more studies. But, then, these are complicated issues that might take some time to settle with any reasonable degree of confidence. (Many economists are still debating the causes of the Great Depression.)

What I have done in this chapter is to take note of the competing arguments. They can give a sense of dimension and completeness to the complexity of the question as posed. When the facts and econometric studies do not provide the nice, neat, clear answers because they appear to be in conflict, we must look to the soundness of the underlying economic logic. Frankly, in the case of the productivity debate, I am prone to believe that modern technological advances must be doing something to productivity. Otherwise, why would businesses be devoting an ever-growing percentage of their resources to information technology capital? Sure, businesses can make mistakes in their investments, but there are good reasons for doubting that markets would allow for systemic investment mistakes to continue and to escalate with time for as long as they have, perhaps two or three decades. After all, as explained in this chapter, mistakes give rise to powerful market incentives for investors to correct mistaken firm strategies that are systemic in nature.

Furthermore, human welfare does tend to be improved when some new, cheap, and available resource is discovered and utilized. Computers themselves soak up real resources when they are manufactured and used, but they also allow people everywhere to produce a wide array of goods and services that tap an abundant resource, 1's and 0's. Surely, many good things have come from that fact alone. Hence, I am inclined to side with the Council of Economic Advisors' assessment that the computer revolution has been productive.

Having said that, I hasten to add that concurrence with the Council's assessment does not mean that we should dismiss Robert Gordon's most basic criticism, that, contrary to the claims of computer enthusiasts, the computer revolution has not measured up to the Industrial Revolution (or even just the electricity revolution). Paul David might also be correct, that computers have had a positive impact on productivity; the problem is that the full impact cannot yet be indisputably documented, meaning it might show up more clearly in the future once the statistical smoke from the "extended transition" has been blown away with time.

Clearly, the computer revolution is not yet over, despite popular claims that the PC is dead. At this writing, while personal computer sales were on the wane, the world stock of computing power was still on the rise. The Internet remains in its primordial stage. Perhaps the computer revolution will, eventually, ape or even surpass the Industrial Revolution in terms of its impact on human welfare. Perhaps not. There is no need to rush to judgment on a matter that requires time for a multitude of technological forces to play out.

NOTES

1. Gordon Moore's observation about the exponential growth of microprocessors has since been dubbed "Moore's Law." See "What Is Moore's Law" at http://intel.com/intel/museum/25anniv/hof/moore.htm.

2. As reported by the staff of the Economics and Statistics Administration, Office of Policy Development, U.S. Department of Commerce, *Digital Economy 2000* (Washington, D.C.: U.S. Electronic Policy), as found at http://www.esa.doc.gov/de2000.pdf, 2.

3. Ibid., 3.

4. Ibid.

5. As compiled by Jeffrey Eisenach, Thomas Lenard, and Stephen McGonegal, *The Digital Economy Fact Book: Second Edition, 2000* (Washington, D.C.: Progress and Freedom Foundation, 2000), 25.

6. Ibid.

7. Ibid., 3.

8. Ibid., 9.

9. "Computer Ownership and Internet Access: Opportunities for Workforce Development and Job Flexibility," in *Technology Forecast* (Washington, D.C.: Employment Policy Foundation, January 11, 2001), 2.

10. Ibid., 13.

11. The Employment Policy Institute projects that as early as 2002, 41.2 percent of households with the lowest quartile of weekly wages will have computers and be on-line. For households in the highest quartile of weekly earnings, 80.7 percent will have computers and Internet connections ("Computer Ownership and Internet Access," 2).

12. Eisenach, Lenard, and McGonegal, *The Digital Economy Fact Book*, 11.

13. Ibid., 11.

14. Ibid., 61.

15. Ibid., 63.

16. Ibid., 65.

17. See Stacy Lawrence, "Behind the Numbers: The Mystery of B-to-B Forecasts Revealed," *The Industry Standard*, February 21, 2000, as found at http://www.thestandard.com/research/metrics/display/0,2799,11300,00.html.

18. Eisenach, Lenard, and McGonegal, *The Digital Economy Fact Book*, 17.

19. Ibid., 35.

20. Ibid., 39.

21. Ibid., 43.

22. Ibid., 79.

23. Economics and Statistics Administration, *Digital Economy 2000*, 1.

24. I have written extensively on various aspects of the supposed "deindustrialization" of the country. See Richard B. McKenzie, *What Went Right in the 1980s* (San Francisco: Pacific Research Institute, 1994).

25. Stephen S. Cohen and John Zysman, *Manufacturing Matters: The Myth of the Post-Industrial Economy* (New York: Basic Books, 1987).

26. Robert M. Solow, "We'd Better Watch Out," *New York Times Book Review*, 12 July 1987, 36.

27. Ibid.

28. Ibid.

29. See Moses Ambramovitz and Paul A. David, "Reinterpreting Economic Growth: Parables and Realities," *American Economic Review* 63, no. 2 (1973); and Moses Ambramovitz and Paul A. David, "American Macroeconomic Growth in the Era of Knowledge-Based Progress: The Long-Run Perspective," Discussion Paper Series (Stanford, Calif.: Institute for Economic Policy Research, December 1999).

30. Kenneth Flamm, *More for Less: The Economic Impact of Semiconductors* (Washington, D.C.: Semiconductor Industry Association, December 1997), 1.

31. Testimony of Alan Greenspan before the House of Representatives Committee on Banking and Financial Services, July 23, 1996.

32. Daniel E. Sichel, *The Computer Revolution: An Economic Perspective* (Washington, D.C.: Brookings Institution, 1997), p. 7 fig. 1.4.

33. Paul A. David, "Understanding Digital Technology's Evolution and the Path of Measured Productivity Growth: Present and Future in the Mirror of the Past," in *Understanding the Digital Economy: Data, Tools, and Research* (Cambridge: MIT Press, 2000), 52.

34. Alan S. Blinder and Richard E. Quandt, "Waiting for Godot: Information Technology and the Productivity Miracle," Working Paper (Princeton, N.J.: Economics Department, Princeton University, May 1997).

35. Sichel, *The Computer Revolution*, 77–78. See, also, Stephen D. Oliner and Daniel E. Sichel, "Computers and Output Growth Revisited, How Big Is the Puzzle?" *Brookings Papers on Economic Activity* 2 (1994): 273–317.

36. Robert J. Gordon, "Does the 'New Economy' Measure Up to the Great Inventions of the Past?" Working Paper 7833 (Cambridge, Mass.: National Bureau of Economic Research, August 2000), as found at http://www.nber.org/papers/w7833, p. 1 of abstract. Also published in *Journal of Economic Perspective* 14 (Fall 2000): p. 49–74.

37. For example, see Martin Baily and James Brian Quinn, "Information Technology: The Key to Service Productivity," *Brookings Review* 12 (Summer 1994): 37–41; Erik Brynjolfsson, "The Productivity Paradox of Information Technology," *Communications of the Association of Computing Machinery*, December 1996, 66–77; and Zvi Griliches, "Productivity, R&D, the Data Constraints," *American Economic Review* (March 1994): 1–23.

38. Joel Mokyr, "Are We Living in the Middle of an Industrial Revolution?" *Federal Reserve Bank of Kansas City Economic Review* 82, no. 2 (1997): 31-43.

39. Daniel M. G. Raff and Manuel Trajtenberg, "Quality-Adjusted Prices for the American Automobile Industry: 1906–1940," in *The Economics of New Goods*, ed. Timothy F. Bresnahan and Robert J. Gordon (Chicago: University of Chicago Press, 1997): 77–108.

40. See W. Erwin Diewert and Kevin Fox, "Can Measurement Error Explain the Productivity Paradox?" in Jack E. Triplett, "The Solow Productivity Paradox: What Do Computers Do to Productivity?" *Canadian Journal of Economics* 32 (April 1999): 309–334.

41. G. M. Brooke, "The Economics of Information Technology: Explaining the Productivity Paradox," Working Paper 238 (Cambridge: Center for Information Systems Research, Sloan School of Management, MIT, April 1992).

42. Michael Boskin et al., Advisory Commission to Study the Consumer Price Index, *Toward a More Accurate Measure of the Cost of Living*, Final Report to the Senate Finance Committee, December 4, 1996.

43. MIT economist William Nordhaus found that measures of the growth in the price of lighting have been overstated since the Industrial Revolution, meaning real output growth in lighting has been understated by official statistics since then. See William D. Nordhaus, "Do Real Output and Real Wage Measures Capture Reality, The History of Lighting Suggests Not," Discussion Paper 1078 (New Haven, Conn.: Cowles Foundation for Research in Economics, 1994).

44. Economists Martin Baily and Robert Gordon did find that measures of business and financial service and airline sectors substantially understate the output in those sectors and that the undermeasurement likely grew in the years prior to the release of their study, which was 1988. See Martin Neil Baily and Robert J. Gordon, "The Productivity Slowdown, Measurement Issues, and the Explosion of Computer Power," *Brookings Papers on Economic Activity* 2 (1988): 347–420.

45. George J. Stigler, et al., *The Price Statistics of the Federal Government: Review, Appraisal, and Recommendations* (Cambridge, Mass.: National Bureau of Economic Research, 1961): 23–49. Donald Siegel found that the measurement error in the producer price index was the same in both the 1972–1977 and 1977–1982 periods he studied. See Donald Siegel, "Errors in Output Deflators Revisited: Unit Values and the Producer Price Index," *Economic Inquiry* 32 (January 1994): 11–32.

46. Sichel, *The Computer Revolution*, 99.

47. For example, see Erik Brynjolfsson, "The Contribution of Information Technology to Consumer Welfare," *Information Systems Research* 7 (September 1996): 290; Robert J. Gordon, *The Measurement of Durable Goods Prices* (Chicago: University of Chicago Press for the National Bureau of Economic Research, 1990), 46; and Sichel, *The Computer Revolution*, 17.

48. According to Sichel, because of the declining prices of computers and software, firms may have underestimated the total cost of computing services, given that the hardware and software are a minor part of the total cost, which has been estimated in 1995 at $3,830 per year per computer. Thus, firms may have bought computers that contribute less to firm output than to firm costs (Sichel, *The Computer Revolution*: 33–34).

49. Ibid.

50. Paul A. David, "The Dynamo and the Computer: An Historical Perspective on the Modern Productivity Paradox," *American Economic Review* 80, no. 2 (1990): 355–361; and "Computer and Dynamo: The Modern Productivity Paradox in a Not-Too-Distant Mirror," in *Technology and Productivity: The Challenge for Economic Policy* (Paris: Organisation for Economic Co-operation and Development, 1991): 315–348.

51. Erik Brynjolfsson and Lorin M. Hitt, "Beyond Computation: Information Technology, Organizational Transformation, and Business Performance," *Journal of Economic Perspectives* 14 (Fall 2000): 23–48.

52. See Erik Brynjolfsson, Amy A. Renshaw, and Marshall Van Alstyne, "The Matrix of Change," *Sloan Management Review* 38 (Winter 1997): 37–54.

53. Gordon, "Does the 'New Economy' Measure Up?" 26.

54. As reported by W. Wayt Gibbs, "Taking Computers to Task," *Scientific American*, July 1997, 82–90, as found at http://www.sciam.com/0797issue/0797trends.html. Myhrvold also mused with an audience, "After all, if we hadn't brought your processor to its knees, why else would you get a new one?" (ibid.).

55. Sichel, *The Computer Revolution*, p. 41, table 3.1. See also Dale W. Jorgenson and Kevin Stiroh, "Computers and Growth," *Economics of Innovation and New Technology* 3 (1995): 295–316. These authors found that computing equipment accounted for 0.5 percent of business capital stock in 1994.

56. Oliner and Sichel, "Computers and Output Growth Revisited."

57. Sichel, *The Computer Revolution*, p. 42–43.

58. Ibid., p. 44, table 3.2.

59. Gordon, "Does the 'New Economy' Measure Up?" 32–33.

60. Brynjolfsson and Hitt, "Beyond Computation," 42.

61. See Richard J. Haier, Benjamin V. Siegel, Keith H. Nuechterlein, Erin Hazlett et. al., "Cortical Glucose Metabolic Rate Correlates of Abstract Reasoning and Attention Studied with Positron Emission Tomography," *Intelligence* 12 (April–June, 1988): 199–217.

62. See Paul McCarthy, "Computer Prices: How Good Is the Quality Adjustment?" paper presented at a conference on capital stock organized by the Organisation of Economic Co-operation and Development, March 10–14, 1997, as found at http://www.oecd.org/std/capstock97/oecd3.pdf.

63. Richard B. McKenzie, "Microsoft's 'Applications Barrier to Entry': The Missing 70,000 Programs," *Policy Report*, no. 380 (Washington, D.C.: Cato Institute, August 31, 2000), 9–10, as found at http://www.cato.org/pubs/pas/pa380.pdf.

64. See Mokyr, "Are We Living in the Middle of an Industrial Revolution?"

65. Otto L. Bettmann, *The Good Old Days—They Were Terrible!* (New York: Random House, 1974).

66. Gordon, "Does the 'New Economy' Measure Up?" 17–18.

67. Ibid., 19.

68. Ibid., 21–23.

69. Ibid., table 3.

70. The list of "Greatest Engineering Achievements of the 20th Century" is as follows in order of importance as determined by the National Academy of Engineering: (1) electricity, (2) the automobile, (3) the airplane, (4) water supply and distribution, (5) electronics, (6) radio and television, (7) agricultural mechanization, (8) computers, (9) the telephone, (10) air-conditioning and refrigeration, (11) highways, (12) spacecraft, (13) the Internet, (14) imaging, (15) household appliances, (16) health technologies, (17) petroleum and petrochemical technologies, (18) laser and fiber optics, (19) nuclear technologies, and (20) high-performance materials (as found at www.greatestachievement.org).

71. Council of Economic Advisors, Office of the President, *Economic Report of the President 2001* (Washington, D.C.: U.S. Government Printing Office, January 2001), 19.

72. Erik Brynjolfsson and Lorin Hitt, "Paradox Lost? Firm-Level Evidence on the Returns to Information Systems Spending," *Management Science* 42 (April 1996): 541–558.

73. Council of Economic Advisors, Office of the President, *Economic Report of the President 2000* (Washington, D.C.: U.S. Government Printing Office, January 2000), 83; and *Economic Report of the President 2001*, 28.

74. Alan S. Blinder, "The Internet and the New Economy," *Briefing the President* (Washington, D.C.: Internet Policy Institute, January 2000), as found at www.

internetpolicyinst.org/briefing/1_00_sum.html; and Robert E. Litan and Alice M. Rivlin, "The Economy and the Internet: What Lies Ahead," *Conference Report* (Washington, D.C.: Brookings Institution, December 2000), as found at www.brook.edu/comm/conferencereport/cr4/cr4.htm.

75. Goldman Sachs, "B2B: To Be or Not to 2B?" High Technology Group Whitepaper, November 1999.

76. V. Kasturi Rangan and Marie Bell, "Dell Online," *Harvard Business School Case Study*, 9-598-116 (Cambridge: Harvard Business School Press, 1998).

77. Patricia Seybold and Ronni Marshak, *Customers.com: How to Create a Profitable Business Strategy for the Internet and Beyond* (New York: Times Books, 1998).

78. Erik Brynjolfsson and Lorin M. Hitt, "Information Technology as Factor of Production: The Role of Differences among Firms," *Economics of Innovation and New Technology* 3, no. 4 (1995): 183–200; and "Paradox Lost?"

79. Erik Brynjolfsson and Shunkyu Yang, "The Intangible Benefits and Costs of Computer Investments: Evidence from Financial Markets," Working Paper (Cambridge: Sloan School of Management, MIT, December 1999). Of course, these authors' findings may have been distorted by what appears to have been, from the perspective of 2001 (the time of this writing), a stock market "bubble" in technology stocks during the last half of the 1990s.

80. Council of Economic Advisors, *Economic Report of the President 2001*, 29–30

81. As reported by Litan and Rivlin, "The Economy and the Internet," 2.

82. Federal outlays as a percent of gross domestic product fell 22.2 in the 1990–1993 period to 21.1 in the 1994–1997 period. See Richard B. McKenzie, "Clinton Confidential," *Reason*, November 1996, 40–43.

83. Testimony of Alan Greenspan before the House of Representatives Committee on Banking and Financial Services, July 23, 1996.

84. Princeton University economist Alan Blinder has concluded that information technology investments may finally be producing dividends, primarily because of the advent of the Internet (Blinder, "The Internet and the New Economy." Litan and Rivlin ("The Economy and the Internet") deduced from the findings reported at a conference sponsored by the Brookings Institution and the Internet Policy Institute that productivity improvements can come from

[s]ignificantly reducing the cost of many transactions necessary to produce and distribute goods and services; increasing management efficiency, especially by enabling firms to manage their supply chains more effectively and communicate more easily both within the firm and with customers and partners; increasing competition, making prices more transparent, and broadening markets for buyers and sellers; increasing the effectiveness of marketing and pricing; and increasing consumer choice, convenience and satisfaction in a variety of ways. (p. 3)

85. As reported by Greg Ip, "Did Greenspan Push High-Tech Optimism on Growth Too Far," *Wall Street Journal*, 28 December 2001, p. A1.

86. McKinsey Global Institute, *U.S. Productivity Growth, 1995–2000*, as found on March 1, 2002, at http://www.mckinsey.com/knowledge/mgi/reports/productivity.asp. For a concise review of the report, see Virginia Postrel, "Lessons in Keeping Business Humming, Courtesy of Wal-Mart," *New York Times*, 28 February 2002, p. C2.

87. Based on McKinsey Global Institute, *U.S. Productivity Growth, 1995–2000*, exh. 2. Martin Baily and Robert Lawrence also found that information technology favored productivity growth in the retail and services sectors. See Martin Neil Baily and Robert Z. Lawrence, "Do We Have a New E-conomy?" Working Paper 8243 (Cambridge, Mass.: National Bureau for Economic Research, April 2001).

88. McKinsey Global Institute, *U.S. Productivity Growth, 1995–2000*. See the executive summary at http://www.mckinsey.com/knowledge/mgi/reports/pdfs/Productivity/ExecutiveSummary.pdf.

3

Digital Costs and Production Choices

T he concepts of supply and demand have played an honorable role in economic theorizing. They have been two very big ideas in the history of economic thought. This is because they capture in a simple and elegant way most competitive market forces. They can also reveal how changes in market forces can affect output and prices in competitive markets. Economists have built careers out of manipulating those two curves in a multitude of ways.

This chapter builds on my discussion of the impact of computers and related equipment on productivity in Chapter 2, mainly because productivity feeds into firms' calculations of their production costs that, in turn, feed into market supply. In this chapter, however, I focus on the impact of the digitization of business processes (for example, accounting and communication systems) and the digitization of goods and services (for example, E-books and E-music) and how this can affect expected market outcomes. Assuming competitive markets, we can begin to explore the differential impact of the digitization of business processes and of the digitization of the goods themselves. I start with a review of how computers and telecommunications have affected firm costs, because costs will affect market supply. I take up demand for digital goods (with network effects) in some detail in the next chapter. (Readers unfamiliar with supply and demand analytics that are subsumed in my analysis in this chapter should consult any standard microeconomics textbook.[1])

THE DIGITIZATION OF BUSINESS PROCESSES

The advent of the digital era has had major impacts on many old economy firms. Indeed, probably few old economy firms will be able to long survive without adapting their production facilities and array of products and services to the potential for the digitization of business processes. For example, the sixty-six-year-old Handleman Company, which is based in Troy, Michigan, reinvented itself in recent years as a distributor of CD titles, including Britney Spears and U2, to such mass-market retailers as Kmart and Wal-Mart, shipping 130 million CDs in 2000. The company improved its bottom line by 50 percent in one year by moving to high-tech distribution centers, which allowed their retail customers to order CDs over the Internet. They have also set up kiosks in major retailers that allow music lovers to order from among fifty thousand titles and have their purchases delivered either to the store or their home addresses. In 2001 the company was experimenting with on-demand manufacturing, meaning CDs would be burned as they are ordered.[2]

In 1999, Bethlehem Steel acquired MetalSite, a Web-based firm that allowed for online sales of steel. Before it bought MetalSite, Bethlehem would fax lists of excess steel products to potential buyers and receive their orders back by fax and telephone. With MetalSite, Bethlehem can simply post its excess products on the MetalSite Web site, allowing buyers to bid for the available products. In the eighteen months since it bought MetalSite, Bethlehem's sales of excess metal have increased thirtyfold.[3]

Because of the terrorist toppling of the twin towers of New York City's World Trade Center on September 11, 2001, with commandeered airplanes, air travel plunged in the United States and around the world, causing many airlines to see red on their books. Like other airlines, Delta almost immediately began laying off workers, including its telephone reservationists. The airline also began to devote even more resources to the development of its Web-based frequent-flyer reservation system as a means of doing more with less, mainly because frequent-flyer reservations via phone were taking an average of 45 minutes, more time than any reservation resulting in payment.[4]

Many other firms in other industries have devised similar exchanges that resulted in production efficiencies. These efficiencies have allowed some firms such as Handleman to improve their profit positions, at least for a time. They have enabled other firms such as Bethlehem and Delta from seeing their profits fall or losses mount as much as otherwise.

For firms that simply use computers to digitize their internal and external communications, produce and disseminate financial and other reports, and take and place orders—that is, create a firm-based digital nervous system—

I hasten to add that the impact of the technology on production decisions is not always an improvement in competitive positions. The exact impact will depend on the net effect of the greater expenditures firms make on information technology and the improvement in firm productivity. Generally, if productivity goes up, we might expect cost per unit produced of any good to fall, but only *if* firm costs remain the same. That "if" is a very big one. A given technology could very well significantly increase productivity, measured by, say, output per worker hour, but the added expenditures incurred from introducing the technology can rise, negating the productivity benefits of the new equipment and business systems. In other words, some technologies may be beneficial in terms of added output but not worth adopting because of their added cost. The reverse can be true of other technologies.

It would appear that the introduction of computers into a business is a no brainer, given that a reasonably equipped desktop computer now costs as little as $600—or $200 per year, assuming the computer can last for three years— and that office computers, especially when they can be linked together, have the potential of reducing the hours that workers might otherwise spend on any number of routine business tasks. However, few firms buy the cheapest machines they can find, and the cost of the machine, whatever it is and taken by itself, is hardly all that must be considered in computerizing offices. Firms need to worry about the machine's TCO (total cost of ownership).

According to the Gartner Group, in 1999, a firm could buy a typical computer and printer for approximately $3,000 ($2,000 for the computer and $1,000 for the printer), which could be predicted to last for, at most, four years with little salvage value at the end of that time. Assuming the computer is used only for three years, the annual direct equipment cost is only $1,000 per year.[5] However, the total annual cost of ownership for the desktop computer is much higher, just under $13,000, mainly because of all of the auxiliary costs that must be incurred. The Gartner Group estimates that a firm will spend approximately $1,710 per year on software for each computer, and it will provide another $3,510 per year in technical support services for the desktop machines themselves and another $1,170 per year on network support.

Finally, the Gartner Group estimates that each employee will spend time "futzing" with the computers, that is, trying to correct problems and learning new things that can be done with computers. Even then, Gartner may be understating the amount of employee futzing. SBT Accounting Systems, a San Rafael, California, firm, found from a survey of six thousand workers that each spends an average of 5.1 hours per week, or nearly 13 percent of their workweek, futzing with their computers, resulting in $100 billion in lost worker productivity each year. An Australian think tank, the Nolan Norton

Institute in Melbourne, estimates that workers on average spend 4–10 percent of their time helping coworkers solve their computer problems, which, if correct, would hike the total cost of ownership from an average of $13,000 per year to $23,000 per year.[6]

Whatever their costs, the costs of computers and networks must be set against their contribution to firm output. The Gartner Group also figures that the local area network for any thirty computer users would reduce secretarial work by one-third. The system would also reduce the cost of materials (mainly paper and photocopies), improve firm efficiency by reducing the time wasted on document sharing, and increase firm output. The Gartner Group concludes that the firm can expect to earn, on average, a net rate of return on the firm's network investment of 104 percent.[1] Such a high rate of return, however, does not consider how the firm's market conditions might change if all firms in the industry adopt the technology that, as a consequence, leads to an increase in market supply. The increase in market supply, in turn, can lower the prices all firms can charge for their products, causing much of the calculated high rate of return on the computer investment to evaporate.

Presumably, every firm in the market has access to the same computers and networking systems, and each firm would have two reasons for employing the technology, one offensive and the other defensive. The offensive reason would be to achieve the 104 percent net return on investment, which could be expected to add to the market value of the firm's stock. The defensive reason would be the firm's effort to control its cost structure in light of the fact that every other firm would be seeking to garner the extra profits from adopting the efficiency-enhancing technology. The firms would, in effect, be anticipating that the industry-wide adoption of the computer/network technology would increase the supply of the product on the market. With the increase in the market supply of the product, the price of the product would fall. If any one firm fails to adopt the computer/network technology while others do, that firm will face a lower market price with a higher cost structure.

In short, there is no reason to believe that firms will achieve the 104 percent rate of return on their technology investment, simply because much of the benefits of the efficiency improvement will be transferred to consumers in the form of a lower product price (a point that helps explain the difficulty of finding productivity gains from technology, as discussed in Chapter 2). Perhaps those who institute the technology first might gain disproportionately to others who make the changes later. However, as time passes, the price can be expected to fall. Also, as time passes and more firms adopt the technology, the growing demand for the technology will give rise to higher market prices for some employees, such as network administrators, and these higher resource costs can offset some of the cost advantage to instituting the technology.

Understandably, people in high-tech circles often talk about the "first-mover advantage," because there can be such an advantage in terms of the price that can be charged. But the first-mover advantage may be overrated in management discussions for two reasons: First, the advantage might not be long lasting, given the rapidity with which technology can spread through an industry both because the technology itself speeds up the spread (computers and networks can be used to reduce the cost of ordering computers and networks), and because the high rate of return for first movers can accelerate the speed with which they are willing to adopt the technology. Second, first movers can often be "wrong movers," since, by definition, they do not have the benefit of their own and other movers' experience with the new technology. Mistakes that show up in added costs can abound.

Still, with the passage of time, much of the efficiency gains for firms from the introduction of computer and network technology should be expected to be competed away and garnered not so much by producers as by consumers in the form of "consumer surplus" (or the area under the demand curve and above the price). It follows that the greater and more rapidly the spread of the technology is expected to be within the industry, the stronger the incentive firms will have to adopt the technology for defensive reasons (to make sure they do not get left behind with a high-cost structure when the market price falls), and the faster the productivity gains will be competed away. Furthermore, the lower the cost of the technology relative to the potential gains to be had from being a first mover, the greater the expected speed of adoption of the technology. Firms will simply have a greater incentive to adopt the technology early.

The decline in the price of computers over time has been fueled by competition among firms such as Dell, IBM, Gateway, Hewlett-Packard, Toshiba, Micron, and any number of other personal computer makers who no longer exist. All of these firms have all along the way earnestly sought to lower their own costs to obtain more profits and to protect themselves from the ensuing price competition. They have also fueled greater competition among a host of other firms that do not produce computers but that adopt computer and network technology. The competition among these technology-using firms no doubt prevents the prices of the computer and network equipment from falling as much as or as fast as they otherwise would fall, mainly because the competition among technology-using firms increases the demand for computers.

A key point to remember from our supply-and-demand-curve analysis is that many discussions of developments within high technology/Internet markets have contained an internal contradiction. On the one hand, high-tech/

Internet enthusiasts have pointed to all the costs savings that can be had from firms employing modern technologies, implying that magnificent profits are to be had for the taking. These high-tech boosters have also pointed out how cheap it is to set up business, especially on the Internet: All you have to do is create a Web site and sales will flow in twenty-four hours a day, seven days a week, with all the transactions automated. But it does not take a degree in rocket science—or economics—to see the folly in the claims. Businesses that are easy to start up and cheap to develop are likely to be inundated with entrants, resulting in the vast profit potential being competed away and transferred to consumers.

DIGITAL GOODS: ZERO MARGINAL COSTS

My analysis of costs to this point has been restricted to how technologies that use 1's and 0's can affect market output and firms' efficiency, organization, and reliance on markets for inputs. However, as stressed from the start of this book, these same modern technologies can affect the nature of some goods. Goods such as books, music, and movies can now be at least partially, if not totally, reproduced time and again with 1's and 0's, and these goods can be distributed and used as such. Indeed, pure digital goods, such as electronic books, are made solely from 1's and 0's, a resource that is unlimited in supply around the globe. The cost of arranging the 1's and 0's into sequences that make sense and can be used, reproduced, and distributed might be substantial. Microsoft reports that it spends hundreds of millions of dollars annually to develop new versions of Windows, and it also spends nearly $4 billion a year on R&D across all of the company's product lines. Some of its R&D expenditures are for new versions of Windows, for example, Windows XP.

However, after a new version of Windows has been developed, the costs of reproduction and distribution are few. Microsoft might spend a couple of dollars per copy shrink-wrapping and distributing the copies of Windows sold in retail outlets such as CompUSA and Circuit City, but few copies of Windows are sold by Microsoft at retail. The overwhelming majority of Windows copies—upward of 90 percent—are sold with new computers manufactured by firms such as Gateway, Dell, Micron, Toshiba, and IBM. A relatively small percentage of computer users upgrade their operating systems before they replace their old computers. In 1999, only 16 percent of all Windows users were using Windows 98, the then latest version of Windows.

For copies of Windows sold with new computers, Microsoft's reproduction costs are, for all intents and purposes, very close to zero, if not zero. The reason is that Microsoft sends a master copy of Windows to each computer manufacturer, which the manufacturer then copies onto the hard drives of each computer sent down its assembly line. Dell can, with one master copy of Windows that it licenses from Microsoft, transfer a copy in less than two minutes (at a transfer rate of upward of 200 megabytes a minute) from its mainframe computer to each personal computer that it produces with little in the way of labor involved. The cost of the transferal, to the extent that it is worth mentioning, is incurred directly by the computer maker, not by Microsoft. In addition, as a part of its contracts, Microsoft requires the computer makers to take the service support calls on Windows.[8]

Similarly, content providers such as Mightywords.com and BarnesandNoble.com post articles and books written by well-known and not-so-well-known authors on their Web sites for downloading electronically by paying customers. These E-tailers may have been expensive to develop and some of the articles and books available for sale may have been relatively expensive for Mightywords.com and BarnesandNoble.com to buy. However, the downloaded copies cost the firms practically nothing since the customers do all the work and there are no materials involved in the downloads. Again, the E-tailers' marginal cost of production must be close to zero, if not zero.

The same is true of downloads of music recordings into MP3 files. Indeed, every downloaded copy can become something of a master copy that the buyers can use to reproduce copies for distribution through private listings or through organizations such as Napster.com (which in early 2001 was found guilty of facilitating the infringement of record companies' and artists' copyrights[9]).

From the nature of the cost structure of purely digital products, it follows that for a software firm such as Microsoft (or IBM or Nortel or Sun), the marginal cost of producing the first copy, that is, the master, can be quite substantial—equal to the upfront development costs. However, the marginal production cost for the second and every following unit can be zero (or close to zero), and constant at zero, given that the 1's and 0's involved can be created literally from thin air (or electrons) and have no real, substantive cost. Furthermore, there is no real reason to expect the law of diminishing returns to set in as more copies are produced. Copies can be reproduced endlessly without any loss in productivity or added cost.

A software firm can decide how sophisticated and complex its programs will be, which will determine its development costs, and the marginal cost of the first unit, but once the dimensions of the program are determined, the marginal cost of the second and all additional units falls to zero. The average cost of production declines, much as happens in the case of the conventional "natural monopolist" market model that economists have taught in their classes for decades.[10] However, the decline in average costs for our software/digital firm for the producer of the digital good is even more rapid than for a natural-monopoly producer of a nondigital good. If the digital firm spends $100 million on the development of its software product, the average cost of the first copy is the same as the marginal cost, $100 million. If two copies are produced, the marginal cost of the second unit is zero, and the average cost of the two units is $50 million. The average cost at three units is $33.3 million, and so on. The average cost of production will approach zero for very large units but will never, of course, reach zero (given that average cost equals the ratio, total cost/quantity, which must always have a positive value).

Given this cost structure, a software firm such as Microsoft has a strong incentive to spread the development costs over a large number of sales. However, it does not follow that the firm will want to sell an unlimited number of copies or as many copies as it can. This is because the firm's sales goal will be constrained by a more important consideration, firm profits, and firm profits will be constrained by the market demand, which will require the firm to lower its price to sell more copies. As a consequence, the firm will understandably pull up short of selling an unlimited number of copies or as many as it can because, beyond some point, the additional sales can be expected to lower revenues and profits.

This leads to an important observation: For digital goods, which have zero marginal costs of reproduction, the goal of profit maximization can be achieved by maximizing firm revenues. In other words, the firm will want to choose the price/quantity combination that yields maximum revenue. The reason revenue maximization equals profit maximization is that marginal cost is zero. Given its revenue maximizing price/quantity combination, if the firm lowers or raises its price, the revenues must fall. If marginal cost is zero, its total costs remain fixed at the level of development costs, which means its profits must also fall.

Under such cost conditions, competition among several producers of the same software product is likely to be intense because the reproduction cost of the product is zero, and each firm understands that only one firm will likely end up being the sole supplier. If there is more than one supplier—say, four—each producer's average cost of production will be greater than four times what the average cost would be for a firm selling to the entire market. Even when there are only two producers, the average cost of each will be more than twice the average cost of one firm supplying the entire market. Hence, with more than one producer, each producer can be expected to try to gain market share and lower its costs by underpricing the other producers. The result is that no more than one producer, if any, can survive the price competition.

If there are initially several competitors in the market, all of whom have incurred the development costs, and if the initial price is high, or rather above average cost (meaning profits are being made by all producers), the several competitors can be expected to push the price down. And there is no reason for them to hold the price to where they break even, or where price is equal to average cost. Each producer can figure that he can improve his profitability (do better than break even) by lowering his price a little with a resulting increase in revenues and profits, assuming no one else follows suit. However each competitor can reason that other competitors are thinking the same thing, which means that each can reason that he needs to lower his price to protect against the price reductions of the other competitors. The resulting price competition can result in each producer incurring losses, meaning that none of the competitors will survive in the long run. Indeed, the price will tend to be driven to zero (as long as consumers can switch freely among available products at little or no cost, a point that puts "switching costs," a topic I take up in Chapter 7, in a better light). Any price above zero would mean that the producer could incur lower losses than if it withdraws. A price of zero would mean that it would be no better—or no worse—off than if it withdrew from the market. The best that each competitor can hope for is that the other competitors have opportunity costs that cause them to withdraw and do something else.

There is one additional important difference between digital and nondigital markets: In nondigital markets, the firm that ultimately beats the competition to become the sole producer can expect its past competitors to withdraw from the market, closing up their plants and selling them and their locations to other producers. They do not have to constantly worry about competitors always being there with them in their markets. Digital markets are not always like that. The firm that beats the competition to become the sole producer must understand that it is not always completely alone in the market in any meaningful sense. The other firms with which the sole digital producer was originally competing have not faded into oblivion. Their programs (or other digitized goods) remain extant. They are highly durable and easily stored electronically at little cost; they still exist on some hard drive; and they can be retrieved, copied, and distributed easily.

In short, the cost of reentry into the market is minimal because the programs do not have to be developed. If the sole producer chooses to restrict sales to charge a higher price, then the other producers can restart the competition, and they can easily replicate their program at the same cost the sole producer can, zero, and replace the sales not made by the sole producer when it tries to restrict market sales to raise its price. Granted, customers might incur some switching cost in shifting to another program vendor, but those costs will have to be weighed against the "staying cost" (measured by the consumer surplus extracted by the monopoly price) in not shifting to one of the other producers.

When all is said and done, the so-called natural monopoly in a digital goods market is in a particularly poor market position to extract monopoly profits, mainly because of the very low marginal cost of reproduction. In addition, as I will argue in the next chapter, many firms that produce digital goods will face a highly elastic demand (meaning consumers will likely be highly responsive to price increases), which will further constrain their ability to charge prices above competitive levels.

THE IMPACT OF COMPLEMENTARY GOODS ON COST AND PRICE

Both Microsoft and Netscape have given away their browsers. RealAudio gives away a version of its computer audio player software. RealAge.com gives away information on how long visitors to its Web site can be expected to live, given their lifestyles. BigCharts.com lets users of its Web sites track their stock portfolios

How can firms charge zero and negative prices? University of California–Los Angeles economist Benjamin Klein has a relatively simple explanation: The producers sell goods that complement the product that carries a zero or negative price. RealAge.com and BigCharts.com earn incomes from advertisements on their Web sites. Their ads go with their Web site visits. The greater the number of site visitors they have, the greater their ad revenues. RealAudio expects to sell enhanced versions of its audio player by giving away its basic version.

Microsoft sells operating systems and other productivity applications along with Internet Explorer. When it increases the sales of Internet Explorer, it increases the demand for and sales of Windows and Office. In all of these cases, the firms have an added incentive to lower their prices. The revenue lost from the lower prices of some products can be recouped by a higher demand and higher prices and sales on their other complementary products. The tie-in between the sales of the products can be so strong that the firms, even if they are monopolist in their product categories, can justify giving away one of their products, or even paying people to take it, which is where the negative prices come in. Any revenue lost on Windows can be offset by greater sales and revenues from Office. Given that the marginal cost of producing both Windows and Office is close to zero, if not zero, then how far down Microsoft pushes the price of Windows depends on the revenue tradeoff between the two products. That is, Microsoft should be expected to lower the price of Windows as long as the revenue lost on Windows is more than offset by greater revenues from Office.

In dealing with nondigital goods, economists always make sure that the product's demand curve is in the northeast quadrant, and does not cut the horizontal axis. This is because it is not very likely that producers will charge negative prices, or would ever pay consumers to take their products. The reason is that by charging negative prices for a product, the producer might sell more of that product and its complement, but it is unlikely that doing so would be profitable. This is because both the nondigital good and its complement can be expected to have positive and rising marginal costs of production. Hence, the firm would not only have to make the payments to consumers to take the extra units, they would also have to incur added production costs. It might sell more of the complementary good and gain more profits, but it would also incur added production costs of that good.

In addition, in nondigital markets, the market for the complement is likely to be fragmented among several producers because of the rising marginal cost of production that restricts how much of the market can be served by any producer. If one producer lowers its price, it will increase the sales of its own complementary good, but also the sales of complementary goods produced by other firms. Hence, any one producer will not get the full benefit of its lower priced product.

For the digital firm, there is no (or little) marginal cost of production that can constrain sales, which means that all the digital firm has to do is maximize sales on its product and the complement. In addition, with zero marginal cost, there is likely to be only one dominant producer. When that dominant producer lowers the price of its product (for example, Windows), it gets the full (or nearly full) benefits of greater sales of the complementary product (for example, Office).

Hence, in digital markets, the demand curve can be drawn through the horizontal axis. This is because it can be profitable for digital firms to pay their consumers to buy their digital goods. Understandably, zero and negative prices are rarely observed in nondigital markets. They are much more common in digital markets, given the prospects of greater sales of complements. Indeed, because of this line of analysis, we should expect digital firms to develop complementary products: They can give away one product (or pay people to take it) in the hopes of stimulating sales of their other products. Basic versions of one product are often given away in the hope that the give-away will increase consumers' demand for the standard, professional, and premium versions that are, of course, sold at positive prices.

Alternately, a firm such as Microsoft can develop a complementary prod-uct such as Office. Increases in the number of copies of Windows in use can lead to an increase in the sales of Office.

As will be argued later in the chapter on antitrust enforcement in the digi-tal age (Chapter 11), the economics of digital markets should cause antitrust enforcers to tread carefully when they are contemplating charging digital firms with predation when they charge zero prices or even pay consumers to take their products (the Justice Department charged Microsoft with preda-tion in 1998 because Microsoft gave away its browser).

CONCLUDING COMMENTS

Costs matter. They matter a great deal in explaining why firms do what they do and do not do. One of the tasks of economists is to ferret out hidden costs to explain people's and firms' behavior. For example, flat-panel moni-tors are expensive, perhaps three or four times the cost of CRT monitors. Many people may buy flat-panel monitors because they prefer their looks. However, economists might add that other people can be expected to buy flat-panel monitors because they are "cheaper"—given that they take up less desk space and, accordingly, can be less costly than CRTs when space is scarce and expensive. Alternatively, the more expensive the floor and desk space or the greater the number of screens that are needed, the more likely flat-panel monitors will be bought.

More important, I have stressed in this chapter, and the last one, that the structure of firms' costs matters a great deal because the cost structure will af-fect a firm's output and pricing decisions. The structure will also affect the na-ture of the competitive struggle and outcome among firms. I have noted that competition among digital firms and among nondigital firms can be expected to differ for one key reason: The marginal cost of production for digital goods is likely to be close to zero, if not zero. There are, in other words, sub-stantial economies of scale in the production of digital goods. That simple ob-servation may leave fundamental economic precepts intact, but, as we will see throughout this book, it changes the nature of firms' production and pricing calculations. For one, the economies of scale in production should be expected to lead digital firms to price their product with only the product's demand in mind. Digital firms, in other words, should seek only to maximize revenues, and when they produce more than one complementary digital product they should price their products with a view toward maximizing net revenues across all of their products. This is an important but counterintuitive conclusion because it means that a firm's upfront development costs for a digital good—such as a software program, E-book, or E-music—should have no bearing on its price. I say net revenues because some digital firms will find that giving away, or even paying customers to take, one or more of their digital products can increase firm revenues, on balance. However, as will be seen in later chapters, the pricing decisions of digital firms are greatly complicated by two economic concepts that can be at work in digital (and nondigital) markets, network effects and switching costs.

But then, digital firms (like their nondigital counterparts) can reason that they can get more revenues—and garner more profits—if they can charge different consumers different prices. The ability of digital firms to price discriminate is both facilitated and discouraged by the nature of digital goods. To price discriminate, firms need to be able to segment their markets, charging different groups of consumers with different demands different prices, and one way markets can be segmented is for the good to be tailored to fit different consumers' needs. Automobile manufacturers such as General Motors have segmented their markets by creating different models of cars. However, this form of market segmentation can be very expensive, given the need to design and produce different models on different assembly lines, all constrained by the law of diminishing returns and diseconomies of scale.

Digital firms are not nearly so constrained in their efforts to create different versions of their products, mainly because the required material resources are limited, given the reliance on 1's and 0's at the core of the products. A firm such as Microsoft can develop an array of productivity applications, combine them into various suite packages—standard, deluxe, and premium—at little additional cost, and then sell the packages to different market segments at different prices. At the same time, so-called product versioning with the intent to price discriminate is also circumscribed by the fact that digital products are made of 1's and 0's. This is because price discrimination can encourage piracy, given that pirates can use their purchased (or pirated) copies of the good as masters and go into the business of selling pirated copies to those consumers who would otherwise be willing to pay an inflated price. Nevertheless, we should not be surprised that digital markets are unusually marked by versioning, price discrimination, and widespread piracy. I take up piracy in Chapter 10.

NOTES

1. For example, see Edgar K. Browning and Mark A. Zupan, *Microeconomics: Theory and Applications* (New York: Wiley, 2002), chap. 2.

2. See Sarah L. Roberts-Witt, "They May be Old, But They're Acting Like Start-Ups," *PC Magazine*, June 12, 2001, 9.

3. Ibid., 14.

4. Saul Hansell, "The Elusive Search for Efficiency," *New York Times*, 5 November 2001, F1.

5. David Armstrong, "Computers and Business Technology: Hidden Costs of Owning a PC," *The Press*, 26 January 1999, sec. 2, p. 19.

6. Ibid.

7. Dennis Berman, "Return to Spender: Do You Get the Biggest Bang for Your Tech Buck?" *Business Week*, January 31, 2000, F16.

8. When a software/digital firm such as Microsoft is able to pass off service calls for its software to resellers such as Dell or IBM, it does not follow that Microsoft does not bear a cost for the service support incurred by computer makers. With every increase in the service costs borne by the computer makers, Microsoft suffers a reduction (albeit small) in the demand for Windows from the computer makers and must offset their costs with a reduction in the price it charges for Windows. The higher the installation and support costs, the lower the price for Windows. This is the case even if Microsoft were a monopolist charging maximum monopoly prices. There is only so much the computer makers would be willing to pay for Windows, either in terms of the price paid to Microsoft or in terms of costs incurred in support. When the maximum price is being charged and support costs go up, it stands to reason that the price must fall.

9. Lee Gnomes, "Federal Court Orders Napster to Stop Copyright Infringement," *Wall Street Journal*, 21 February 2001, as found at http://interactive.wsj.com/pages/techmain.htm.

10. Browning and Zupan, *Microeconomics*, chap. 15.

4

Firm Size and Disruptive Technologies

How large should a firm become? What should the scope of its products be? These are old questions in economics that have been given renewed relevance in the digital age, primarily because of the many direct and indirect ways digitized communication systems and products can affect a firm's size and scope. I cannot, and will not, pretend to offer an answer for a particular firm, such as General Motors or Oracle. What I can do is offer a method for thinking through such questions and for assessing the impact of the digital age on firm size and scope.

TRANSACTION COSTS

For a couple of hundred years and more, the conventional short answer to the question of firm size from economists has been economies of scale, which is grounded in technology. This explanation rests not on theory, but a claim that for some production processes, as all factors of production are expanded, the nature of production can be changed in such beneficial ways that output rises disproportionately to inputs, resulting in falling marginal and average costs. For example, at some scale of operation, an assembly line can be introduced that allows two things to happen: First, production can flow from start to finish much more smoothly with fewer movements on the part of workers to get parts and change tools. Second, the assembly line has the added advantage of regulating the pace and dedication of the workers, making them more productive by requiring that they remain attentive to the flow of the work before them. Slackers can be easily detected and penalized.

Where economies of scale are available, firms in competitive markets must expand their scales of operations, or else be run out of their markets by other firms that expand. The firms that expand can increase the supply of the good on markets and drive down the price (below the costs of the firms that do not expand). Sooner or later, however, scale economies can run out, leading to "diseconomies of scale," cost increases relating to the limited ability of managers to communicate with and control ever larger enterprises.

Can we say more about what firms should or should not do? Back in the 1930s, Ronald Coase, another Nobel laureate in economics, gave a more complete and perhaps satisfying yet stunningly simple answer in the form of what has been widely recognized as one of the bigger ideas in economics in the twentieth century.[1] In so doing, he articulated a framework for thinking about management control issues that permits an exploration of how technology can impact firm size and scope. He argued that an answer must emerge from the reason firms exist in the first place, and he then added that firms arise because they allow their owners to get some things done more cost effectively, and profitably, than they could be done through market transactions.

Conceivably, complex goods could be produced using only competitive markets at each stage of product development. Competitive markets can keep buyers and sellers on their toes, forcing sellers to minimize their costs and charge competitive prices, and forcing buyers to pay market prices. Each maker of each part of a drill press could buy on the open market the steel (or whatever) needed to make the part. The assembler of some larger part of the drill press maker could buy the parts made by several parts makers. The drill press assembler could then buy the larger parts from the assemblers, and combine them into drill presses that are then sold to drill press users.

Such a production sequence (with every stage of production conceivably taking place in a given area or even a given building) offers the advantage of the sales being made at competitive market prices, which can force efficient production within each stage of production. However, as Coase observed, the market transactions themselves can be costly, mainly because at each stage of production, alternative sources of supply must be found (to ensure truly competitive bids), contracts have to be negotiated, and then the buyers at every stage have to monitor the suppliers' compliance with the contracts.

Seeing this point, Coase then was able to conclude that firms arise because they cut out some of these transaction costs, meaning production within firms could be more efficient, and profitable, than competitive markets alone. Indeed, if firms, as agglomerations of suppliers and buyers, were not able to produce goods more cost effectively than could be done through buy-and-sell sequences, the firms would not be able to sell what they produce to consumers. Consumers would buy what they want more cheaply from sources other than firms.

How much should firms do? How big should they get? Before Coase, as noted, the best answer economists could give was that it depends on how extensive the economies of scale are (which are grounded in the technology of production). The greater the scale economies, the larger the firms can be expected to be within any industry.

Coase offered a better answer by noting that there are diminishing returns to management, which force up the costs of organizing more and more production (or a greater and greater variety of products) within a given firm. This means that how large a firm gets depends on the relative costs, on the margin, of transferring activities from being completed in markets to being completed within a firm. If the marginal cost of completing another activity within a firm is lower than the marginal cost of completing it in markets, then the activity will be moved inside the firm. Hence, Coase concluded (following the marginal logic that James Buchanan found endemic to all good economic analysis) that "a firm will tend to expand until the costs of organizing an extra transaction within the firm become equal to the costs of carrying out the same transaction by means of an exchange on the open market or the costs of organizing in another firm."[2] Moreover, the scope of the products produced will involve a similar logic, with the firm weighing off the costs of organizing greater production of a given product with the costs of organizing production of other products. At some point, the firm can be better off by expanding its scope than by expanding its size in any given product line.

Coase illustrates his organizing principle with a set of concentric circles. The circles represent a community with the industries gathered around the center of town, with each circle further removed from the center—A, B, and C—representing a different industry.[3] One can imagine a firm in industry B expanding around point X (in the second circle from the center). It can expand its production of B or it can expand into the production of C or A. As the firm expands in one line (B), "the cost of organizing increases until at some point," Coase writes, "it becomes equal to that of a dissimilar product which is nearer [in industries A or C, or in the adjacent circles]."[4] Hence, Coase was able to argue that contrary to prevailing economic wisdom at the time, the size of a firm was not limited strictly by an upward sloping marginal cost curve. It had to be limited by some other factor, namely, the relative cost of doing business via a firm and doing business via markets.

INTERNAL AND EXTERNAL COORDINATING COSTS

Vijay Gurbaxani and Seungjin Whang have improved on Coase's explanation for why firms do what they do by noting that at all times firms face two types of costs for organizing activities outside and inside the firms (both of which are implicit in Coase's work).[5] The first is the cost of organizing production within markets, or what Gurbaxani and Whang call "external coordinating costs." When heavy reliance is made on markets, meaning little is done inside firms, firms incur heavy costs of finding alternative sources of supply, contracting, and monitoring outside suppliers—Coase's transaction costs. The external coordinating costs will likely fall as the firm does more inside, that is, becomes larger. In panel A of Figure 4.1, the drop in external coordinating cost is depicted by the curve that slopes downward from the upper left to the lower right.

However, at all times, firms also face what have been called "principal/agent problems," as Gurbaxani and Whang suggest. The principals, or the owners, of firms cannot do everything they want the firm to do. Hence, they have to hire agents, or managers and line workers, to do their work for them. The principals and agents very likely share a common objective, to maximize their own personal well-being. However, their shared goals can often be in conflict. The principals want the agents to do what they were hired to do—maximize the wealth of the firm and thereby the wealth of the principals—but the agents want to maximize their own wealth as best they can. This can mean that they look for as much payment as they can get from the principals—and then use their discretion over firm resources to add to their own gains, at the expense of the principals, of course. The agents can simply shirk on the job, that is, not work as hard as they are supposed to work or misuse their work time for personal chores (calling and E-mailing friends or paying their household expenses or even running their own businesses). Agents can simply goof off in an unlimited number of ways. Agents can also steal from the firm or can give favorable treatment to their friends and family members. The more discretion agents have over firm resources, the more they can misuse or abuse their discretion.

As a consequence, to minimize the misuse of resources, the principals will have to monitor their agents or come up with payment methods that impose costs on agents who misuse their discretion. For example, they may be paid by commission (or by piece rate, or how much the agents produce) or they might be given stock options. The more discretion the agents have, the more closely they will need to be monitored or have their pay tied to some measure of sales or production.[6]

Figure 4.1. External and Internal Coordinating Costs and Firm Size

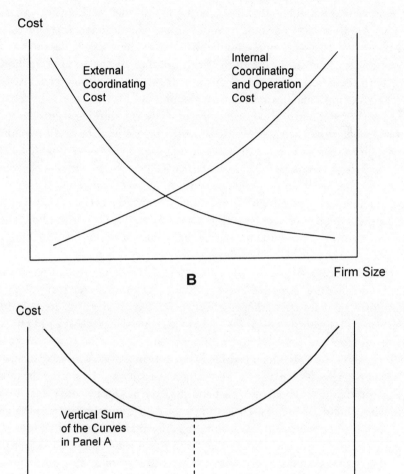

Source: Vijay Gurbaxani and Seungjin Whang, "The Impact of Information Systems on Organization and Markets," *Communications of the ACM* 34 (January 1991): 59–73. Copyright © 1991 ACM Inc. Reprinted by permission.

As the firm grows, monitoring of agents can become more difficult, and more costly, given that there will be more people to monitor and each agent very likely has less of an incentive to work for the betterment of the firm. In a small firm, it may be easy for the principal to detect who is not doing the jobs as he or she should—that is, who may be shirking (meaning not working as hard or efficiently as he or she should or misusing firm resources). Also, in small firms, each agent can reason that what he or she does or does not do can significantly affect the health of the firm, and thereby the agent's livelihood. For both reasons, agents have some incentive to do what they were hired to do, and not shirk and not misuse firm resources.

However, as the firm grows, detection of wayward, shirking agents becomes more problematic. Each agent has less incentive to do what he or she was hired to do, given that what he or she does or does not do is less detectable by the principals because the contributions of each agent get fused with the contributions of other agents. Simply put, the contributions of individual agents have less of an impact on the health of the firm, and also the agent's livelihood. To offset the tendency of agents to shirk as the firm grows, more and more resources must be devoted to monitoring the agents (or finding ways of curbing the need for monitoring such as developing new pay schemes).[7]

Hence, Gurbaxani and Whang reason that as the firm grows in size, its internal coordinating costs are likely to grow, given the known technology of monitoring and compensating employees. The expected rising internal coordinating and operation cost is depicted by the curve in panel A of Figure 4.1 that rises from the lower left to the upper right.

Firm size—or how much is done inside a firm and how much reliance is placed on markets—can be determined, conceptually, by the sum of the internal coordinating and operation cost and the external coordinating cost, or by the vertical sum of the two curves in panel A of Figure 4.1. When the two curves are added vertically, the combined coordinating costs of various size firms are shown by the U-shaped curve in panel B of Figure 4.1. The combined cost of coordination is minimized at a firm size of S_1. If the firm adopts a larger size, then its costs of monitoring inside agents to undertake certain additional activities (such as develop parts or provide accounting services) exceed the transaction costs of having those activities performed by outside firms.

What makes this graphical analysis useful in this book is that it provides a framework for thinking about changes in the relative costs of doing things inside and outside firms. Coase notes almost in passing, "Inventions which tend to bring factors of production nearer together, by lessening spatial distribution, tend to increase the size of the firm. Changes like the telephone and the telegraph, which tend to reduce the cost of organizing spatially, will tend to increase the size of the firm. All changes that improve management technique will tend to increase the size of the firm."[8] In terms of Figure 4.1, any reduction in the spatial distribution of factors or improved management technique can have the effect of lessening the internal coordinating cost and causing the curve for internal coordinating cost to drop in panel A, which causes the U-shaped curve in panel B to shift to the right, meaning that the cost-minimizing firm size can be expected to increase.

COMPUTER/TELECOMMUNICATION TECHNOLOGY AND FIRM SIZE

Supply-and-demand analysis is helpful in understanding how markets might adjust to the introduction of new technologies like computers and the Internet, but there is, naturally (given the inherent simplicity of supply and demand graphs), a lot of detail about exactly how firms adjust that is side-stepped by the analysis. For example, when cost-reducing technologies are introduced into a given market, supply-and-demand analysis predicts that market output rises as the market price falls. These are useful insights, but a couple of questions are left unaddressed: Does the rise in market output mean that the firms in the market can be expected to get larger, as measured, say, by the count of employees and/or sales? Should employees and sales move in the same or opposite directions?

Because they lower firm production costs, computers and networks (and related equipment) could take away the scale advantages that existing larger firms have and could, at the same time, lower the cost of market entry by new and smaller firms. For example, with a few relatively cheap computers and a couple of word-processing and desktop publishing programs, whole newspapers and magazines can now be designed for small or niche markets and can be produced by one or two people. Hence, the greater industry sales could be made by more firms with each firm having fewer sales and disproportionately smaller counts of employees than did the firms in the market before the advent of the new technologies. On the other hand, the greater sales could be made by the same or even a smaller number of firms, each of which grows larger due to the scale economies the new technologies bring to production.

The new technologies can also affect firm sizes by changing the extent to which the firms rely on internal production for the components of the products they produce, or on external sources of supply (so-called outsourcing). For example, Dell could produce its own hard drives and microprocessors for its computers (as IBM does), or it could buy the parts from outside vendors such as Western Digital and Intel. Dell could be an assembler (not a producer) of computers, and conceivably it could contract with another firm to assemble the computers, making Dell the proverbial "hollow corporation." If the technologies increase firms' reliance on internal production, then the firms can be expected to grow in terms of sales and employees. If the technologies cause firms to rely more on external sources of supply, then firm sizes can be expected to rise in terms of sales but fall in terms of the count of employees. Many smaller firms would be producing the needed parts and then would be linked together in a supply chain that would have to be managed just as internal production would have to be managed.

As management information professors Vijay Gurbaxani and Seungjin Whang stress, modern information technology, like computers and the Internet, can affect the firm's internal coordinating cost curves in Figure 4.1 in several ways.[9] First, they can add to production scale economies. Gurbaxani and Whang point out that CAD/CAM (computer-aided design/computer-aided manufacturing) and CIM (computer-integrated manufacturing) programs, robotics, and optical scanners linked to computers and inventory programs can lower production costs for any given scale of operations.[10]

Second, information technology has also increased firms' flexibility, enabling many firms, such as Dell, to engage in what has been called "mass customization" of their products. Greater flexibility in production can translate not only into greater benefits for buyers but also a reduction in labor costs for firms.

Third, information technology—from optical barcode scanners to automatic teller machines to reservation systems—has lowered the costs firms incur in taking inventory and in dealing with customers. Most chain stores now use cash registers that automatically send sales data back to the headquarters periodically, if not continually, throughout the workday.

Fourth, information technology can also be used to monitor workers, hence cutting down on shirking. The optical scanners used at checkout counters in grocery stores are frequently used to assess the speed with which clerks are checking through customers (and then determine employee-of-the-month awards for clerks with high checkout speeds).[11] From the handheld computers that Frito-Lay gives its salespeople to take and transmit orders, the company is able to determine when salespeople begin their workdays and how long they take to make the trips between sales stops. Of course, UPS and FedEx are renowned for using handheld computers, plus global positioning satellites, to monitor the whereabouts and speed of their delivery people.

Fifth, information technology can ease decision making. Computerized accounting and financial systems can increase the accuracy and speed of communications within firms and reduce mistakes. E-mail exchanges and videoconferencing can obviate the need for meetings, which in turn can reduce travel costs. Accordingly, firms can spread out their operations across the country or the world, ensuring that as the firm grows, the greater demand for resources, especially labor, does not have to be concentrated in one location where wages might be pressed upward by the firms' expansion.

In all these ways, the internal coordinating and production costs that firms confront can be lowered by information technology. As a consequence, the technology can cause the internal coordinating cost curve in Figure 4.1 (panel A) to shift downward and to the right. By itself, such a shift would be expected to lead to an increase in firm size, in scale as well as scope of products, given that the low point of the two curves combined would shift to the right in the figure.

However, information technology can also be expected to lower external coordinating cost in several ways. First, the Internet can be used to locate alternative sources of supply, as well as obtain competitive bids from suppliers. Firms needing trucking services can post notices of deliveries needed and can get back bids by trucking firms.

Second, information technology can facilitate the development of contracts, given that various drafts can be transmitted and retransmitted to the law offices of the various parties via E-mail. With the passage of the Electronic Signatures in Global and National Commerce Act in 2000, many contracts can now be finalized with the electronic signatures of the parties involved.

Third, the progress of outside vendors in filling orders can be monitored with information technology, given that the buyers can tap into their suppliers' own internal computerized tracking systems much as FedEx patrons can track the progress of their orders from the sellers to the patrons' doorsteps.

Fourth, a major problem firms face in dealing with each other is the potential for what economists tag "opportunistic behavior" on the part of one or both. For example, the supplier of a part might have to invest in a specific piece of machinery to supply a part requested by the buyer. If the machinery has no use other than to produce the requested part, the machine piece has no resale value. In such a situation, the supplier might hesitate in making the required investment, fearing that the buyer will not live up to the contract (or the buyer might fail during the period of the contract), or will try to engage in what is called a "holdup." That is, the buyer might try to take advantage of its position (in much the same way as a mugger does), seeking to get more cash at the supplier's expense. It might propose a lower price, knowing that the supplier cannot do anything else with the piece of machinery designed for the specific use.

To the extent that information technology permits the development of more flexible machinery, the threat of a holdup, and the costs of preventing holdups, can be abated.[12] This is the case because if the buyer of the requested parts threatens to pull its orders unless price concessions are made the supplier can reconfigure the machinery to be used on other orders.

These cost savings can be expected to cause the external coordinating cost curve in Figure 4.1 (panel A) to move down and to the left. Such a shift by itself can be expected to lead to smaller firm sizes, given that the firms can buy more of their components at lower transaction costs from outside vendors.

The downward shifts in the two curves combined lead to an ambiguous result, given that the impact of information technology on firm size depends on the relative magnitude of the two forms of cost savings. If information technology lowers internal coordinating cost by more than it lowers external coordinating cost, then firm size can be expected to rise, given that the low point of the two curves will shift to the right. On the other hand, if the technology lowers the external coordinating cost by more than it lowers internal coordinating cost, then firm size can be expected to fall, as firms will then secure more of their components at lower relative cost from outside sources. In other words, firms will expand their outsourcing.

Obviously, given the offsetting theoretical considerations, the issue of how information technology affects firm size must be determined empirically. And, unfortunately, raw employment data by firm size does not clarify the issue. During the 1970s and 1980s, reports began surfacing that showed that almost all of the employment growth in the United States was in small firms, those with fewer than one hundred workers, the result of which was that average firm size in terms of employment began to shrink from about 1970 onward.[13] Researchers also found a precipitous drop-off in manufacturing firm size in the late 1970s and early 1980s.[14] However, between 1990 and 1996, employment in firms with fewer than one hundred workers rose by 5 million workers, whereas employment in firms with one thousand or more workers grew by 800,000. Given that in both 1990 and 1996 there were approximately six times as many workers in firms with fewer than one hundred workers, it follows that the percentage growth of employment in both categories of firm size over the 1990–1996 period was comparable.

The problem of assessing the impact of information technology on firm size is made more complicated by the fact that economic forces other than information technology are, during any period, at work on firm size. For example, changes in firm size across the economy could also be influenced by the growth of the service sector relative to the growth of the manufacturing sector, given that service firms tend to be smaller in both sales and workers than manufacturing firms. Greater foreign competition could have forced firms to become more efficient, which could have led to smaller firms. Similarly, the freeing of international commerce from import duties could have led firms to expand into foreign markets and/or tap foreign sources of supply of parts. Again, the economic forces at work on firm size are working in all directions.

Fortunately, there has been a study by researchers at MIT and the University of California–Irvine that tries to sort out the effects of information technology from all the other variables at work on firm size.[15] These researchers found that at least from the late 1970s through the 1980s, information technology expenditures by firms in the United States led to unmistakable reductions in the average number of employees in companies and in their establishments (office buildings or plants, for example). Indeed, they found that a 1 percent increase in information technology spending in real-dollar terms led to a decrease in average employment at firms of .14 percent and at establishments of .13 percent. Because of the large increase in information technology spending during the period covered by the research (1977–1989), they figured that information technology spending accounted for 20 percent of the decline in the average size of firms. Finally, the researchers found that the doubling of the information technology capital stock during the period led to a reduction in firms' sales of 13 percent and a reduction in firms' value added (sales minus the cost of inputs) of 12 percent (pp. 1638–1640). They conclude, understandably, that information technology "is facilitating the 'decoupling' of existing vertically integrated firms and the supplanting of existing firms by value-adding networks of new, smaller firms" (p. 1640).

In terms of Figure 4.1, this means that information technology seems to be decreasing firms' external coordinating cost more than their internal coordinating cost, causing them to rely more on markets for their needed parts and services. The authors add, "One implication of our findings is that the current downsizing of firms, the popularity of outsourcing, and the rise of value-adding partnerships is not simply a management fad, but rather may have a technology and theoretical basis" (p. 1642).

Does this mean that information technology will always lead to smaller firm size? That is doubtful. Different technological developments can have different effects. The spread of personal computers in the 1980s may have lowered average firm size because it reduced laborious duplications of effort that went with, for example, typing and retyping reports. The spread and price reduction of various telecommunication technologies—fiber optics, cell phones, and the Internet—in the 1990s may have increased firm size because they enabled firms to communicate more effectively across borders and establishment locations, and may help explain the growth of large firms and the merger wave of the late 1990s.

Accordingly, it would not be surprising if there are periods of time in which firms contract in size and other periods of time in which they expand. And it is probably true that information technology is simultaneously increasing the sizes of some firms in some industries (for example, banking and fast food), while shrinking the sizes of firms in others (for example, book publishing and accounting services).

The main points to draw from this discussion are not so much factual; the facts of the impact of technologies on firm size are in dispute and will likely remain so for some time. The main points are conceptual in nature, or rather how to think about the ways technologies can affect firms' make-or-buy decisions. As widely recognized, technologies can affect firm cost directly, resulting in a lower market price and greater industry sales. However, that does not mean that firms will necessarily grow larger. Technologies that draw on 1's and 0's as key resources can also affect the ease with which firms can make market-based, outside-the-firm transactions. As a consequence of technological developments, firms can rely more on markets for their parts not because they have become less efficient at producing parts (indeed, they may have become more efficient at producing them), but rather because market transactions have been facilitated even more than internal production by the technologies. It is sometimes simply cheaper for firms to incur the transaction cost of buying what they need in markets than to incur the agency cost of having what they need produced internally.

One reason firms have a proclivity for relying on external markets for their needs is that people who work inside firms often begin to see themselves—especially when firms never consider outside sources of supply—as monopoly suppliers with an attendant ability to charge above-competitive prices for what they supply their own firms. Market purchases of parts have the advantage of permitting competitive bidding among alternative suppliers. Even if firms never take advantage of market sources of supply that technologies afford them, the mere fact that they could buy what they need at lower transaction cost, because of new technologies, can have feedback effects on internal firm efficiencies. This is because the greater ease with which internal supply sources can be supplanted by external sources will put the internal supply sources on notice that they now have greater competition and must lower their charges to their firms for what they do. And note that with the advent of the Internet and modern communication technologies, the external sources of competition can come from more places, both local and remote. This is to say that with the introduction of technologies that lower transactions cost, firms might want to outsource some of their activities partly to take advantage of the lower external cost, but also just to put their internal people on notice that they have to compete with outside sources of supply and the firm is willing to outsource.

In Figure 4.1, it may appear that because the two curves are separate, external and internal coordinating costs are not linked, but the lesson of the last few paragraphs is that they are. A reduction in external coordinating cost, and a drop in the curve to the left, can give rise to greater internal firm efficiency and a drop in internal coordinating cost.

In short, technologies that lower transactions costs in markets can also be expected to lower agency cost inside firms. To the extent that agency cost are lowered within a range of firms, then firms have all the more reason to deal with one another in market transactions. Firms that adopt the new technologies but are unable to lower their agency cost can be expected to have trouble holding onto their market share, and perhaps surviving, given that they will likely have higher cost structures than their competitors. Financial markets will, of course, add pressure on firms to control their agency cost. If they are not able to control their agency costs, their stock prices can be expected to fall, giving rise to a firm buyout and a replacement of the management team with people who pay more attention to agency costs. Then again, as we will soon see, under some market conditions, control of agency cost can have downsides not commonly recognized. This can happen when market exploration is warranted.

THE PROBLEM OF DISRUPTIVE TECHNOLOGIES

As the analysis to this point suggests, the greater use of computer and network (and related management information) technologies can result, to the extent they reduce net cost, in lower prices and greater sales. Does that mean that the firms that survive the ensuing competition will be the firms that were in the industry before the advent of the new technologies? Not necessarily, because the firms in the market before the introduction of the new technologies could be slow to adopt them, which means they could be replaced by new entrants with lower cost structures. Indeed, there could be a largely new cast of producers in the industry after the cost and price competition has played out. With its heavy use of computer-based inventory controls and its Web-based order system, Dell was instrumental in running a number of old-line computer makers—for example, Wang and NEC—out of the personal computer market.

Clearly, many firms fail for all the reasons conventionally given in management books:

- A lack of attention to their cost;
- Excessive contentment with their market position;
- Being stuck in their ways with established bureaucratic rules and regulations;
- Reliance on command-and-control, top-down administrations;
- A lack of imagination and foresight.

I do not mean to discount the importance of these explanations. I simply want to add another reason, that, ironically, is a part of the problem that many old-line, incumbent producers face in meeting new competitive threats from new entrants with new technologies, whether incorporated in new products or new business practices that may be spawned by management information hardware and software. My explanation for many firms' market failure is that the incumbents, by the fact that they are the incumbents, have usually been successful at producing and selling old-line goods with established business practices and corporate cultures that have worked for them.[19] In addition, these incumbents have become, in varying degrees, proficient at tweaking successive quality improvements and cost savings out of their products and business practices, leading them to ever-higher profits and industry respect.

Understandably, from the path they have followed in the past, the incumbents can often project even more improvements and more profitability from their products and practices for the future, partially because they have fine-tuned company incentives to ensure that the tweaking process will continue. The point is that their past and projected successes with old products and practices can be a source of their undoing, as it has been for a number of established U.S. firms.

Sears became the country's largest retailer by pioneering supply-chain management practices and catalog sales often bought with a Sears credit card (a retail innovation in its own right). How did Sears do it? *Fortune* magazine reporter John McDonald asked in 1964. McDonald answered his own question, "In a way, the most arresting aspect of its story is that there was no gimmick. Sears opened no big bag of tricks, shot off no skyrockets. Instead, it looked as though in its organization it simply did the right thing, easily and naturally. And their accumulative effect was to create an extraordinary powerhouse of a company."[17]

Clayton Christensen, Harvard business professor and author of *The Innovator's Dilemma*, points out:

> It is striking to note that Sears received its accolades at exactly the time—in the mid-1960s—when it was ignoring the rise of discount retailers and home centers, the lower-cost formats for marketing name-brand hard goods that ultimately

stripped Sears of its core franchise. Sears was praised as one of the best-managed companies in the world at the very time it let Visa and MasterCard usurp the enormous lead it had established in the use of credit cards in retailing.[18]

Sears is hardly alone in missing out on new directions for business and ultimately losing the competitive struggle with new entrants. Woolworth and Montgomery Ward are also classic examples of U.S. firms that developed relatively rapidly to dominant positions in the retail industries, only to fold under the competitive pressures from other retailers, most notably Wal-Mart. General Motors has followed a similar pattern of development, first growing rapidly to market dominance, only to start losing market share. Although General Motors is far from folding, it did expand rapidly in the first half of the twentieth century to become the dominant American automobile firm, only to lose market share thereafter largely to foreign competitors. Similarly, in the1990s newly appointed IBM chief executive officer Lou Gerstner made it clear that IBM had lost a measure of its prominence in the computer industry because the company was trapped by its corporate cultures (which, in part, made jobs there a worker entitlement, something workers could count on holding for their careers). Its culture made the company unable to respond effectively to the rapidly emerging personal computer industry.[19]

Indeed, the truly long-term survivability of firms, as originally organized, appears to be a rarity in American business. When firms avoid failure or absorption by other firms, their leadership roles within industry are often highly unstable. Researchers have observed a considerable change of leadership in the electronics industry over four decades, mainly because of the evolutionary and revolutionary changes in technology and the inability or unwillingness of early leaders to adapt and hold their leadership roles.[20] For example, none of the top producers of vacuum tubes (including such household names as RCA, Sylvania, and General Electric) in 1955 was among the top-ten producers of semiconductors in the middle 1990s.[21]

Many other established firms appear to tempt their own demise, when faced with new competitive threats from so-called disruptive technologies, before they reengineer themselves, shucking many of their old products and businesses practices, and return to profitability. In other words, management scholars have found that many firms tend to evolve gradually through long stretches of time that are characterized by relative stability in performance (equilibrium periods), and then change abruptly and dramatically (revolutionary periods), after which the firms have established substantially new missions and begin another relatively stable period of equilibrium. That is to say, firms tend to follow development patterns of discontinuous change, or "punctuated equilibria," that are similar to the developmental processes found in nature.[22] The idea may prove in time to be a consequential one because it seems to be widely descriptive of the life patterns of many firms.

According to case studies, it is apparent that AT&T, General Radio, Citibank, and Prime Computers are good examples of firms that have grown their way through punctuated equilibria. That is to say, they have periodically reinvented themselves, with long periods of time with consistent organizational structures and strategies, followed by periods of substantial change during which new missions for the firms were developed.[23]

Does it follow that Sears, Woolworth, and Montgomery Ward did something wrong, like not see the advent of Wal-Mart and Visa? Not necessarily. Contrary to what Christensen suggests, these firms probably did take note of their emerging competition, as IBM very likely took note of the development of the first personal computer (it could not miss the massive count of articles on the nascent personal computing industry in the press), but IBM (and other similarly prominent firms) no doubt asked itself many times in the 1970s, if not before and after, "Why should we change? Things are going well. In addition, our customers are telling us to continue to do what we are doing. They want us to continue to keep our focus on our 'core competency' and improve our line of mainframe computers that they are using heavily."

Besides, the production of personal computers with the IBM imprimatur on them would simply encourage businesses to shift away from mainframes. That is to say, IBM had to worry that it would have to cannibalize its other product lines. Furthermore, at the time, IBM had a poor record of developing products and getting them to market in a timely manner. For example, in the 1970s, it took IBM seven years to develop a printer. When IBM did decide to develop a personal computer in the very early 1980s, it had to set up a whole new unit outside of the traditional IBM bureaucracy, but when that unit went to select the microprocessor for the first IBM personal computer, it chose Intel's 16-bit 8088 processor, not the faster 8086 chip, not only because it was slightly cheaper, but also because it made "the personal computer less threatening to IBM's minicomputers."[24]

New technologies that require new business practices and, perhaps, a new corporate culture are necessarily untried in comparison to established products and practices. A changeover can take time to institute and can be costly not only in terms of buying new equipment and providing new forms of training, but also in terms of undoing and rebuilding the companies' incentive structures.

Moreover, a changeover can disrupt the ability of the firms to mine profits from established technologies and business practices. Because many managers will have developed skills in working with old technologies and practices, there will be strong defenders (especially those nearing retirement) of the old products and practices within the firms, causing internal firm debates that can slow the established firms down in making switchovers. The result of this can be that the established firms' competitive position may be seriously weakened before the defenders of the old products and practice see the light and advocate adopting the new technologies and accompanying new business practices. Once the old products and practices are abandoned, or are relegated to a subsidiary interest of the firms, principal/agent problems (which were introduced in Chapter 2) can reemerge in new forms, which means the interests of the agents will once again have to be realigned so that the profit potential in the new products and practices can be exploited.

When Wilkinson Sword introduced its "Super Sword-Edge" razor blade in 1962, Gillette had known the technology for producing stainless-steel blades for years. However, according to Gerard Tellis and Peter Golder, Gillette held off introducing its own stainless-steel blade because the new blade would have made its relatively new productive capacity for making carbon-steel blades obsolete, increased its production cost, and reduced the number of blades each consumer bought, since stainless-steel blades provided more than three times the shaves before they had to be discarded. It was not until Gillette's market share for double-edged razor blades fell from 90 to 50 percent in 1964 that it introduced its own stainless-steel blade.[25]

A central problem established firms face is that when a new disruptive technology appears, managers cannot be certain that the technology will be truly disruptive until it has proven to be so, and the required proof can take time in coming. In the early 1970s, Wang dominated the market for dedicated word-processing machines. When personal computers started appearing in the 1970s, Wang remained committed to its word-processor format, giving its word-processing machines more computing power, but not turning them into personal computers with more than just a word-processing capability. As computing power became less expensive, people began developing a variety of uses for personal computers, making dedicated word-processor machines, as well as their word-processing programs, progressively obsolete.[26]

The Xerox story is even more telling. Chester Carlson, a patent attorney who had tired of copying his legal documents in the 1930s, learned that a Hungarian had developed a technique for copying images using powder and static electricity. Once he had improved the technique—called "xerography"—to where it could make crude images, he shopped the idea with IBM, Kodak, RCA, General Electric, Remington Rand, and fifteen other established firms, to no avail. It was not until Carlson approached Haloid, a small company that happened at the time to be seeking a new business venture to add diversification and growth, that he found a commercial sponsor. Even then, it took Haloid several failed attempts to produce a reasonably simple, cheap, and fast copier, and it was not until 1960 that the Xerox 914 took off and the company justifiably changed its name to the Xerox Corporation.[27]

Did IBM, Kodak, and the others make a mistake in turning Carlson down? In hindsight, clearly they did. But we can draw that conclusion only because we now know that the thirteen or fourteen years of product development actually paid off. Such was hardly known in the late 1940s.

Additionally, switchovers can be shunned because of the disparity in the timing of the gains and pains from switchover: The costs and lost profits from any firm adjustment to a new technology or set of business practices will likely be close at hand and largely known, while the gains to be had from a switchover will be uncertain and, if realized, distant in time. Therein lies the economic foundation of the "innovator's dilemma" (to use Christensen's phrase). Firms can be damned if they do, but also damned if they don't.

Indeed, one reason firms have business systems and cultures in place is to prevent themselves from chasing after every possible new business technology, because they know most new technologies that are touted as disruptive are not that at all. When technologies are truly disruptive, the profit potential often evaporates as people deploy them. Some established firms will not, because of their intact systems, try to make the switchover and others will take a wait-and-see approach, to allow some of the uncertainties to clear. When the personal computer was introduced in the 1970s, it was potentially—and only potentially—a disruptive technology. So was the Internet in the 1990s. Clearly, the value of not being among the first movers when disruptive technologies emerge could be seen at the start of the 2000s in the carnage of dot-com companies.

We know now, because of hindsight, that computers and the Internet were indeed disruptive technologies, but that is not to say that anyone could be assured of that fact at the time they were introduced, a perspective that helps to explain why IBM did not introduce its own personal computer until 1982. Similarly, Microsoft did not embrace the Internet and produce its own browser until 1995. And Barnes and Noble did not immediately follow the lead of Amazon and develop its Web-based book sales division until March 1997, after Amazon set up its E-bookstore in July 1995.

When markets are ill defined, there are always a lot of "perhaps's." Perhaps all three firms—IBM, Microsoft, and Barnes and Noble—should have embraced the new technologies earlier, but then maybe not. All three understandably wanted more evidence about market acceptance of the new technologies before they diverted corporate attention away from their profitable, established core products. In addition, they had reason to believe, given their market positions and firm resources, that they could take a wait-and-see approach and move when the new technology relevant to their core businesses showed signs of being truly disruptive, and then use their established reputations to beat the competition.

Perhaps even IBM should have thought longer about getting into the personal computer business. The personal computer division has rarely been a stellar performer for the company and has been a loss leader during many years. Perhaps Barnes and Noble should not have been so hasty in setting up its Web-based outlet to compete with Amazon. Barnes and Noble posted losses for the fourth quarter of 2000 of $138 million for its dot-com division (continuing an unbroken string of losses for the division since its inception) and had to lay off 16 percent of its more than two thousand workers.[28]

In Microsoft's case, chairman Bill Gates did not embrace the Internet as a force directing the company's product development (at least not openly and with vigor) until May 1995, a full year after Netscape had become a start-up company to dethrone the then king-of-the-Internet hill Mosaic, which had been developed in 1993. In a memorandum to his senior executives in which he laid a new direction for the company, Gates noted that he had gone "through several stages" of elevating the importance of the Internet in his own thinking, only to add, "Now I assign the Internet the highest level of importance. In this memo I want to make clear that our focus on the Internet is crucial to every part of our business. The Internet is the most important single development to come along since the IBM PC was introduced in 1981. It is even more important than the arrival of the graphical user interface."[29] Later, Gates conceded, showing his concern that Microsoft's operating systems might be displaced by Netscape's Navigator (a fact that was evident in his inability to find a single Word document on the Internet in the hours he spent surfing before he wrote his memorandum):

> A new competitor "born" on the Internet is Netscape. Their browser is dominant with 70% usage share, allowing them to determine which network extensions will catch on. They are pursuing a multi-platform strategy where they move the key API [application programmer interface] into the client to commoditize the underlying operating system. . . . We have to match and beat their offerings including working with MCI, newspapers, and others who are considering their products.[30]

Microsoft staved off the Netscape threat by developing its own browser, Internet Explorer; by having it available to be bundled with its operating system free of charge on new computers when Windows 95 was released three months later in August 1995; and by inducing a number of Web-based businesses such as AOL to offer Internet Explorer free of charge as their recommended browser—tactics that were highly successful (and that, ultimately, made Microsoft the object of an antitrust probe and trial, which will be covered in more detail in Chaper 11).

Should Microsoft have taken the lead in the development of browser technology? It is easier to answer yes now than in the late 1980s or early 1990s, when the use of the Internet was limited to universities and the defense establishment. However, even now it is not clear that Microsoft needed to take on the Internet any sooner than it did, mainly because Microsoft typically seeks to provide software to broad, not niche, markets. Before 1995, the browser market size may not have achieved the critical mass that Gates and others at Microsoft might find necessary for Microsoft's involvement in the market.[31] Then, Gates might have felt confident that he could turn his company on the proverbial dime and redirect its business if, or when, the critical mass in market size emerged—as he did indeed do.

Of course, when wait-and-see market strategies are broadly adopted by firms, it should be no surprise that some firms, such as Woolworth and Montgomery Ward, alter their business strategies too late. Many such firms can be expected to fade from the market, and perhaps their eventual demise might be construed as intentional. This is because at the time they are considering a switchover to a new technology path, and assessing the probabilities of successful switchovers, the present value of the new anticipated discounted profit path, appropriately discounted for risk and time, can be lower than the discounted value of the cost that the firms must incur to make the switchover. It may simply be in the best interests of some companies' stockholders for their managers to treat their firms as "cash cows," which should be "milked" for as long as they can. When the company cows are stripped clean, then and only then should they be closed, as perhaps planned. To do otherwise can mean a loss of firm value.

The fundamental long-term problem real-world firms face in dealing with new technologies is grounded in their lack of omniscience, or their inability to anticipate more than a narrow range of opportunities and developments over a relatively short period of time. They cannot know technological developments that are yet to be discovered or how newly discovered technologies can be tweaked for greater productivity and profits in the future. They also cannot know how other firms will deploy technological developments already known and those that emerge, and how firms will react to the deployment of technological developments of others (a line of argument that is central to the life's work of the late Friedrich Hayek[32]). To say that the long-term development of firms is a complex endeavor is an understatement. Markets that do not yet exist are very difficult, if not impossible, to analyze very well.

THE ADAPTIVE LANDSCAPE

We can imagine the developmental problem that wealth-maximizing firms face at any point in time as being similar to the problem mountain climbers would face when climbing in the dark or in dense fog and confronted with a broad mountain range. To maximize their gains, the climbers—that is, firms—would like to occupy the highest peak possible. The problem is that they cannot always see the full landscape ahead of them, and cannot expect ever to do so.

The climbers could be very intelligent. They might remember very well the history of their past climbs, they can compare notes with other climbers (and watch the climbs of others), and they can interpolate and extrapolate from past experiences. Nevertheless, much of the information they have at their disposal is very local; it concerns the way they came to their current position. In particular, they might know a lot about the mountaintops achieved earlier, because their progress stopped there for some significant period of time. However, much less is known about areas between the mountains that have not yet been climbed. Little may be known in advance about possibilities of whether other peaks in the range are actually higher than the one they are on, and the climbers may know little about crossing the wide valleys that lead to the slopes of some thought-to-be higher mountains until someone actually tries to do it and succeeds.

Even when we reduce the complexity of the climbers to only two hills, the climbers face a dilemma over what to do. (Imagine the two hills are side by side.) They know they are on the hillside of the left-hand mountain, and they know which way is up. They also know that across the way there is the right-hand mountain, but they cannot see its top. Even if they could, they might not be able to tell whether its peak is higher than the one they are on. Their dilemma is whether to climb the mountain they are on or go to the next one. Understandably, with so much unknown, many climbers will simply climb the hill they know best, the one they are on. But in an important sense, they may have to feel their way up the mountainsides, by way of trial and error.

Even then, our imagined two mountains might suggest that the climbers'—or innovators'—problems are simpler than they really are. This is because the mountains (technologies) are out there, in existence, whereas in fact it is far better to think in terms of the mountain range itself taking shape while it is being transversed. The range (or technological landscape) itself, in other words, cannot be known very well outside of the process by which it is explored. In such a setting, we might better understand why some climbers—firms—who have been moving up one technological mountainside might choose to continue their treks upward toward the peak of the mountain they are on and, when they reach it, stay where they are. It might be that they could go down the far side of their mountain and climb anew elsewhere in the range, but then they might climb a mountain with a peak that is lower than the one they are on, and they might not be successful in any ensuing competition with new climbers to reach the peak of the new mountain.

The problem of finding new and higher mountains to climb bedevils all firms, not just firms that produce high-tech or digital goods and services. However, there are good reasons for believing that the problem is especially acute for digital/high-tech firms. Such firms are rightfully recognized for being at the core of the so-called new economy. As such, the actual landscape that must be traversed is less known, less explored, and less developed than might be expected of the landscape facing firms that are established members of the old economy.

How steel or cars will evolve and be used over the next several years is not certain, but surely their evolutionary paths and uses are better known than how computers and the Internet will evolve and be used. No one can be sure whether buyers will ever be willing to substitute Internet appliances for their home desktops, or whether computer users will be willing to "rent" their applications on a per-use basis from application service providers over the Internet (as Microsoft and other software firms are now proposing). Similarly, when the Internet emerged in the mid-1990s, no one really knew whether or how consumers would be willing to pay for the convenience of buying goods—whether cat food, computers, cars, cosmetics, or books—from Internet vendors, or whether the vendors could achieve a cost advantage that could compensate them for the more intense price competition expected from the greater ease with which Internet buyers can compare prices, such as with the use of "shopping bots."

When considering the cost and benefits that can come with the introduction of new technologies such as computers and the Internet, it is tempting to assume that the market moves smoothly and quickly from the initial equilibrium price and quantity to the new equilibrium price and quantity. That might in fact happen, but in all likelihood we should expect most markets to grope their way to a new equilibrium in fits and starts, mainly because so much is new and unknown about how the technologies can and will be used.

That is to say, with producers not knowing what all other producers are doing, there might be a form of "irrational exuberance" in the market (to use Alan Greenspan's carefully chosen words to characterize the run-up in stock prices in the late 1990s).

Accordingly, the supply response to technological innovations might be excessive because individual producers know little about how many other producers are entering their markets, resulting in the market price falling to levels not anticipated by people adopting the technology and giving rise to firm failures. This is all the more reason some established firms with long histories might stay with their core businesses as they take wait-and-see stances and why, because of their hesitation, some will fail intentionally and others will fail unintentionally.

It is understandable that the firms with the established technologies will gradually grope their way up the left-hand hillside. This means that they can tweak greater profits out of their known technologies. Their corporate cultures can be so designed that experimentation and exploration with new technologies are discouraged, at least beyond some limits. After all, employee experimentation and exploration can take employee attention off the prize, enhancing their established core businesses and competencies, and many exploratory searches can lead to hillsides with lower peaks than the peak of the hill they are on. As a consequence, the firms with established technologies can do what IBM did with its mainframe technology, marching relentlessly up its technology hillside. In the process, other firms with less or nothing at stake in the known technology can do the experimentation and exploration, with the potential of one or more of the experimenters and explorers finding another hillside and exploiting it, perhaps to the detriment of the firms on the left-hand hillside.

Some of the firms on the left-hand hillside can be expected to rush to follow the lead of those firms that have found the saddle crossing to the next hillside. However, not all firms can be expected to follow suit, not immediately at least. This is because they may not yet have found the peak of the hill they are on. In addition, even if they were at the peak, they might not join the rush to the second hill. This is, again, because the shift to the new hillside—technology—can itself be disruptive, meaning costly to its own efforts to milk profits from its known technology, and uncertainties concerning the peak of the second hill—or profits from exploiting the new technology—will likely remain. Hence, it should be no surprise that firms like IBM hesitate before they shift their business focus, weakening their future profitability, if not survivability, in doing so. And it should be no surprise that some firms like Woolworth or DEC hesitate too long, sealing their eventual demise.

THE VALUE OF FIRM EXPLORATION AND "DEVIANCE"

The mountain construct can help us understand the value of exploration when it comes to the development of new technologies, new products, or new ways of producing old (or new) products and, hence, can help us understand that there is a distinct potential downside to the control of agency cost, contrary to what may be surmised from conventional principal/agent theory. If the right-side crossing is to be found, it will likely be found only by those agents (firms or individuals within firms) in the wings of the distribution, close to the crossing, who are inclined toward exploration (and creativity) and are willing to concede the immediate gains that can come with moving up the side of the hill they are on. Once one or more of these—should I say—"deviant" agents/firms find the crossing (to a new product or service or way of doing things), they can move rapidly up the second hillside, forcing many of the firms (and their agents) at the peak of the first hill to adjust radically. For those firms at the peak of the first hill, their delay in adjustment can translate into a drain on the firms' (that is, principals') equity, as profits fade and losses are endured. Some of the firms at the peak of the first hill will, of course, not be able to adjust with sufficient speed; they will fade and/or fold.

The hill-climbing discussion applies to multiple firms, taken as organizational units, seeking to maximize their wealth, given the actions of the other firms in moving up the hillside. We can think of competitive pressures pushing individual firms up the first hill, with those firms not able to devise the best strategies falling behind. However, the hill climbing can also describe the predicament of a firm with many employees who differ in their ability and inclination to climb the known hillside. The firm's control system seeks to corral worker efforts to replicate—or benchmark—the efforts of the fastest moving worker or firm further up the hillside. Once the peak is reached, the firm's goal can be interpreted as one of ensuring that all worker efforts are tightly bound toward staying at the peak, which can be interpreted to mean exploiting a given technology in the most efficient manner.

Restated, we might say that the first hillside is discovered, which causes a firm to organize its workers to exploit the newfound knowledge and to move quickly up the hillside, which is dependent on how well the firm is able to utilize the best information available and how well deviant efforts of workers are corralled and directed toward the goal of moving up the hillside. This can be interpreted to mean the speed with which the hillside is ascended depends on how well the firm is able to lower its agency cost, both in moving up the hillside and staying there. Of course, competitive pressures in the market will also influence the extent to which and speed with which firms will move up the hillside. However, note that any contraction in the extent of the deviance (or spread of the distribution of the clusters) will lower the chance of the firms discovering the next higher mountain and crossing the saddle between the two mountains.

Of course, a major reason the firm may have strategies in place that delay the discoveries is that the new crossing will not always lead to steeper hillsides and higher peaks. They can, and sometimes will, lead to lower peaks. Strategies, which include control systems on deviance, that restrict the crossing of hillsides may, accordingly, be cost effective, even in the long run. However, that is not the same as saying that the established firms will choose cost-effective strategies for long-term survival. Cost-effective strategies can still mean that higher peaks are left unexploited by established firms. The mere greater potential number of nonestablished firms can mean that some nonestablished firms will find the unexploited crossings to higher peaks.

In developing its strategies and control system, a firm has to look into the future with an understanding that whatever it does, there will be rewards and costs. The rewards will be the present value of the profits that can be had by exploiting known conditions (moving up the known hillside, appropriately discounted for risks of immediate misjudgments as to where the hillside will lead). The cost will be the future losses from opportunities for crossings to even higher hillsides that are missed because of the control of deviance within firms. Given that the discoveries of the crossings will be in the future and probabilities associated with finding the crossings and higher hillsides will likely be much lower than the probabilities of gains to be had from moving upward on the first hillside, the firm has reason to accept the immediate gains at the cost of future opportunities. In this regard, it leaves open the prospects of other entrants finding the crossings and moving up the higher hillsides. Accordingly, in the initial construction of its strategies and control systems, it can be anticipating its own eventual demise in the face of ongoing, evolving market forces. In short, taking advantage of any given hillside, and thereby operating as efficiently as possible in that context, it should plan or anticipate its own obsolescence, or demise. It cannot remain totally flexible and, at the same time, contain its agency costs.

The actual impact of management control systems on long-term profitability and survival will be dependent on the pace of prospective new discoveries, which, in the simulation, can be represented by the breadth of the crossing (and by the variety of crossings not shown). One can imagine the crossing as being so broad that the deviants are so far away from the crossing that they never manage to find the side of the higher hill. In this case, the control system would only be efficiency enhancing. It would cut the costs of operating on the peak of the first hill and would not impede, nor deny, the discovery of the second hill. Nothing would be lost. However, with a narrow crossing, a very effective control system could greatly narrow the range of the deviants, crimping the likelihood of the second hillside being there.

Put another way, it could very well be that an effective management control system that minimizes agency cost does much good and little harm by choking off deviants when the prospects of finding new ways of doing business and new things to do (other hillsides) are remote or rare, or when the advancement found has modest benefits (when the peak of any new hill found is not all that much higher than the known hill). However, when the pace of prospective change quickens for those firms on the hillside, the control systems in those firms far removed from the crossing (those at the peak of the first hill) can greatly undermine advancement, even the profitability and survivability of the firm. In this latter case, the firm may seek to abandon its control system in the interest of encouraging deviance among its agents, and the prospects of finding the new hillsides and higher peaks. Again, from this perspective, the modern tendency of firms to "flatten" their corporate hierarchies, to devolve decision making, can be seen as a way by which the firm can improve its chances of finding those new hillsides, or not leaving unexploited opportunities to be found by rivals outside the corporation's control.

IMPLICATIONS FOR
MANAGEMENT INFORMATION SYSTEMS

My points relating to the impact of control systems on long-run firm survival can be discussed with reference to management information systems. Management information systems within firms are supposed to reduce the cost and improve the quality of the information flow from principals to agents and back. Again, management information systems are designed to align the interests of the agents with the interests of the principals, ensuring that the goals of the principals are pursued partly by improving the monitoring of workers. That is, management information systems are designed to reduce the variance in the goals pursued by agents—to constrain the adaptive forces within and among the various levels of agents. They are, in other words, designed to reduce the incidence of deviance.

Cost-effective management information systems might be very productive for firms just after some crucial innovation—some qualitative shift or paradigm change—has taken place, meaning, in terms of our hill-climbing example, a saddle has been crossed. In the hill-climbing phase of the firm-based evolutionary process, the full range of benefits from the innovation can be exploited by extending the size or scope of the firm. The firm progresses by increasing the likelihood that the crucial innovation is more widely the focus of the agents' efforts. (The firm moves up the hillside.) However, once the full potential of the crucial innovation has been achieved—the hilltop has been reached—the entrenched management information system can hamper the future evolutionary development of the firm, mainly because the goals of the agents are too closely aligned with the previously conceived goals of the principals. A management system of any type, especially an efficient one, can choke off deviance, or the explorations of people in what might appear to be peripheral fields of opportunities for the firm. The principals, whose purview of business can be dominated and restricted by the view of the fully exploited peak, can be inclined to adopt any improvement in the management information system that further constrains deviance and further contracts opportunities for paradigm shifts from within the firm, especially when no new crucial innovation appears likely on the horizon. The improved management information system can simply force a further clustering of trials at the top of the current hill, lowering the probability that the saddle crossing will be found.

Of course, it might be that principals devise a firm structure that will allow or even encourage a calculated degree of deviance, or explorations by the agents. However, to the extent that management information systems are institutionalized during the hill-climbing phase, it can still be said that the system can retard or delay saddle crossings. They have proven their success and are in place, which implies institutionalized barriers to their being eliminated or made more flexible, once the hilltop has been reached. Furthermore, reductions in the cost of information flows, given the reliance on any institutionalized system, will likely mean a contraction of the range of deviance or explorations, ceteris paribus.

This view of management information systems leads to several central implications that are at odds with conventional wisdom:

- Management information systems may very well help firms develop and prosper, once a crucial innovation has appeared. However, those same systems can retard or delay the development of any further crucial innovations.
- Reduction in management information cost can add to the retardation of crucial innovations within established firms.
- Improvements in management information systems can cause a failure or breakup of established firms that are dependent on cost-effective management information systems. Established firms, bound by the restraints of the effective management information systems, may leave opportunities to

devise crucial innovations to other smaller, newer, deviant firms. These deviant firms can make the required saddle crossings and start up the next hillside, undercutting the market positions of the established firms. Other established firms, recognizing the constraining nature of management information systems, can break up, thus allowing for the development of crucial innovations.

- Conventional principal/agency analysis recognizes that separation of ownership and control and dispersion of ownership are sources of agency costs that can be alleviated by appropriate management information or other control systems. From the perspective of my hill-climbing simulation, it might be said that separation of ownership and control and dispersion of ownership can be an advantage, at least up to some point, by increasing the likelihood that crucial innovations can be forthcoming.

- A central problem with the development of crucial innovations is that the benefits are often externalized, captured by people who do not incur the cost of developing them. Accordingly, firms have an impaired incentive to devote resources to their development. Inefficient management information systems can permit what individual firms perceive as aberrant behavior within their own individual operations. However, a public good can be produced for all firms, as agents within a number (or multitude) of firms do engage in deviant behavior. A cost-effective management information system can choke off the production of the public good, and all can be worse off in the long run.

CONCLUDING COMMENTS

A standard presumption within conventional microeconomics is that a firm's size depends critically on the extent of the economies of scale that can be realized within any given industry. The more extensive scale economies are, the larger the firms. Firm size will ultimately be choked off by rising marginal costs. Ronald Coase has taken issue with the conventional view in two ways: First, he points out that a firm can grow even with upward sloping costs curves, simply by expanding its scope of operations. Second, he has argued that firm size can also be affected by an important factor external to a firm's industry, namely, transaction costs. If transaction costs, for example, are reduced, firm size can be expected to fall as firms outsource services and parts that they need.

Another standard presumption within organizational economics is that agency cost are always "bad." Their elimination with improved systems of monitoring and control is always "good" in the sense that greater firm profits can be had from lower agency costs. Reductions in agency costs can improve a firm's chances of long-term survival. That point may be well taken when technology is a given, and when a firm's main task is to exploit the known technology. The new point developed in this chapter is relatively simple but equally important because of its oversight: An effective control system can contribute to some firms' ultimate demise. Such monitoring/control systems can cause some firms to focus even more on exploiting known technologies, thus leaving the discovery of new and potentially superior technologies to be discovered by others, perhaps new market entrants.

NOTES

1. Coase's original article on "The Nature of the Firms" from *Economica* (November 1937) has been reprinted in R. H. Coase, *The Firm, the Market, and the Law* (Chicago: University of Chicago Press, 1988), 33–55.

2. Ibid., 44.

3. Ibid., 52, fig.

4. Ibid., 53.

5. Vijay Gurbaxani and Seungjin Whang, "The Impact of Information Systems on Organizations and Markets," *Communication of the ACM* 34 (January 1991): 59–73.

6. The principal/agent problem is developed at considerable length, and with many applications by Richard B. McKenzie and Dwight R. Lee, *Managing through Incentives: How to Develop a More Collaborative, Productive, and Profitable Organization* (New York: Oxford University Press, 1998).

7. For an excellent discussion of the impact of group size on member incentives to pursue the goals of the group, see Mancur Olson, *The Logic of Collective Action: Public Goods and the Theory of Groups* (Cambridge: Harvard University Press, 1965).

8. Coase, *The Firm, the Market, and the Law*, 46.

9. Gurbaxani and Whang, "The Impact of Information Systems on Organizations and Markets."

10. Ibid., 66.

11. Ibid., 67.

12. See Erik Brynjolfsson, "Information Assets, Technology, and Organization," *Management Science* 40, no. 12 (1994): 1645–1662.

13. Tjerk Huppes, *The Western Edge: Work and Management in the Information Age* (Dordrecht, Netherlands: Kluwer Academic Publishers, 1987).

14. Erik Brynjolfsson, Thomas W. Malone, Vijay Gurbaxani, and Ajit Kambil, "Does Information Technology Lead to Smaller Firm Size?" *Management Science* 40 (December 1994): 1630.

15. Ibid., 1628–1643.

16. See Richard B. McKenzie, "The Importance of Deviance in Intellectual Development," *The Production and Diffusion of Public Choice Theory*, ed. Douglas Eckel, Joseph C. Pitt, and Djavad Salehi-Isfahani (London: in Blackwell, forthcoming).

17. John McDonald, "Sears Makes It Look Easy," *Fortune*, May 1964, 120–121.

18. Clayton M. Christensen, *The Innovator's Dilemma: When New Technologies Cause Great Firms to Fail* (Cambridge: Harvard Business School Press, 1997), x.

19. Laurie Hays, "Gerstner Is Struggling as He Tries to Change Ingrained IBM Culture," *Wall Street Journal* 13 May 1994, p. A1.

20. Michael L. Tushman and Charles A. O'Reiley III, "The Ambidextrous Organization: Managing Evolutionary and Revolutionary Change," *California Management Review* 38 (Summer 1996): 1–23.

21. Ibid., 2. Tushman and O'Reilly cite and add to the work of Richard Foster, *Innovation: The Attacker's Advantage* (New York: Summit Books, 1986).

22. See Stephen Jay Gould and Niles Eldridge, "Punctuated Equilibria: The Tempo and Mode of Evolution Reconsidered," *Paleobiologist* 3 (1977): 115–151; and Thomas S. Kuhn, *The Structure of Scientific Revolution*, 2d ed. (Chicago: University of Chicago Press, 1962). For discussions of punctuated equilibria as a model for firm development, see Connie J. Gersick, "Revolutionary Change Theories: A Multilevel Exploration of the Punctuated Equilibrium Paradigm," *Academy of Management Review* 16 (1991): 10–36; Danny Miller and Peter H. Friesen, "Momentum and Revolution in Organizational Transition," *Academy of Management Journal* 23 (1980): 591–614; and Michael L. Tushman and Elaine Romanelli, "Organizational Evolution: A Metamorphosis Model of Convergence and Reorientation," in *Research in Organizational Behavior*, vol. 7, ed. L. L. Cummings and Barry M. Staw (Greenwich, Conn.: JAI Press, 1985), 171–222.

23. See Michael L. Tushman, William H. Newman, and Elaine Romanelli, "Convergence and Upheaval: Managing the Unsteady Pace of Organizational Evolution," *California Management Review* 29, no. 1 (1986): 1–16. These authors report that research shows that discontinuous change appears to be a profitable mode of development. Firms that have followed development patterns of punctuated equilibria perform better over their lives than other firms that resisted revolutionary transformation. Moreover, such firms are more common than might be supposed. Revolutionary transformations of firms (which followed major environmental and chief executive changes) outnumber nonrevolutionary transformations by more than six to one among the twenty-five firms studied in the minicomputer industry.

24. Gerard J. Tellis and Peter N. Golder, *Will and Vision: How Latecomers Grow to Dominate Markets* (New York: McGraw-Hill, 2002), 247.

25. Ibid., 141–143.

26. Ibid., 20–21.

27. Ibid., 117–123.

28. As reported in "BarnesandNoble.com Cuts Jobs," *Los Angeles Times*, 8 February 2001, p. C5.

29. Bill Gates, "The Internet Tidal Wave," memorandum, May 26, 1995, . 1, as found in one of the U.S. Department of Justice's exhibits in its antitrust case against Microsoft, government exhibit no. 20, http://www.usdoj.gov/atr/cases/ms_exhibits.htm.

30. Ibid., 4.

31. Gates explained the company's delay in directing company efforts with the Internet in mind with the comment given later in 1995: "In any phenomenon like this [the emergence of the Internet] you get long periods of time where people anticipate it, and yet there isn't critical mass. There's not enough users, so there isn't enough content; there's not enough content, so there isn't enough users" (Bill Gates, keynote address, popularly known as "The Pearl Harbor Day Address." Internet Strategy Workshop, December 7, 1995, p. 2). The clear implication was that he had decided that the requisite critical mass for Microsoft's involvement in the Internet was in place, or soon would be.

32. Friedrich A. Hayek, "The Use of Knowledge in Society," *American Economic Review* 35 (September 1945): 519–530.

5

Network Effects

The most cherished concept in economic theory is the law of demand, which posits that the price of a good and the quantity of the good consumers are willing and able to buy are inversely related. That is to say, given some good consumers know they want and thus are willing to buy, the lower the price, the greater the quantity consumers will purchase, and vice versa. The defined inverse relationship is always accompanied, implicitly or explicitly, by the qualifier, everything else held constant.

The quantity people buy is, of course, affected by many variables: weather, number of buyers and their incomes, prices of other goods, and consumer preferences, just to name a few. By adding the qualifier everything else held constant, economists do not mean to suggest that in the real world all variables other than the price of the good will ever, in actuality, be held constant. At all times many market variables are in flux, influencing people's actual purchasing decisions. Everything else held constant is simply economists' way of isolating from all other variables the presumed inverse relationship between the price of the good and the quantity sold, and thereby clarifying what the law of demand means, and does not mean.

When other variables in the real world change at the same time price falls, the law of demand simply means that regardless of the changes in other forces, the price reduction, in and of itself, will lead to more of the good sold than would otherwise be the case. If the good in question is ice cream and the weather turns cold at the same time that the price falls, it may be that consumers buy less ice cream. However, because of the law of demand, we know that, given the reduction in the price, consumers buy more ice cream, whatever the amount is, than if the price had not fallen. The greater the price reduction, the greater the expected increase in sales over what they would otherwise be.

However, just how much more consumers buy with any given reduction in the good's price can vary across goods. That is, various goods' demands exhibit different elasticities: The more responsive consumer purchases are to a given price change, the more elastic the demand is said to be.

It may be no understatement to say that adherence to the law of demand borders on religious devotion, or universal truth, for some economists, viewed as applicable to all goods and services—meaning all things people place a value on and can change the amount acquired and in some way consumed or used. Accordingly, sales of normal goods such as bicycles and computer games are believed to follow the law of demand. If sales do not rise with a reduction in the good's price tag, economists will suspect that the price tag does not capture the "full price," or the total cost consumers incur in purchasing the good. For instance, if the stated price of desktop computers falls, but sales stay the same or fall, then economists will suspect that the reduction in the stated price has been offset or more than offset by an increase in some other factor in the total cost of ownership (introduced in Chapter 3). For example, service support costs could have risen at the same time the stated price of the computers fell.

The law of demand is also believed to be applicable to such unusual "goods" as cheating on tests or voting. If the (full) price of these activities goes up, then less will be "bought" of them. Hence, if the penalty for being caught cheating goes up (while the probability of being caught remains constant), fewer students can be expected to cheat. Similarly, if the probability of being caught goes up (while the penalty stays constant), we should expect the same outcome, a reduction in cheating. This is because the expected price of cheating will rise with the probability of being caught. Similarly, if the time value of going to the polls goes down (because, say, the introduction of more polling places reduces voters' travel time), more people can be expected to vote.[1] Why? People have a demand for voting, and all demands exhibit an inverse relationship between the effective price paid and the quantity demanded.[2]

There are two good reasons for economists' faith in the law of demand: First, the law has been empirically supported in both casual and sophisticated ways. Everyday life is full of examples in which people respond to price changes just as the law of demand predicts. Clearly, the precipitous drop in the price of computers during the 1990s led to an increase in household ownership of computers. The ability of people to download their music files free of charge over Napster beginning in the late 1990s understandably led to tens of millions of music lovers downloading music files. When Napster was forced in 2001 to charge for the files that are traded, the number of files traded fell precipitously.

In addition to casual evidence of the law of demand in operation in daily business life, there are a host of econometric studies undertaken over the past half century that have found that price and quantity are negatively related. Indeed, there have been so many of these studies supporting the law of demand that economists understand they might have serious difficulty getting empirical studies published in professional journals if the price variable in their regression equations is not negative.

Second, the law of demand is firmly grounded in utility theory, which is based on the very general proposition that consumers will seek to improve their well-being (as they define their well-being) as best they can with their available income (or resources). If they do seek to do that, consumers can be expected to allocate their resources so that the last dollar spent on the last unit of each good purchased adds the same to their well-being, a condition called "consumer equilibrium." If that condition does not hold, consumers can be expected to reallocate their income, purchasing more of the good that yields a higher marginal value per dollar. The result of the reallocation will be an increase in their well-being. It follows that when consumers are in equilibrium, a price reduction in one good means that the consumer is then adding more to his or her well-being per dollar from the last unit of the good the price of which has fallen, than from the last unit of other goods. Therefore, the consumer will buy more of the good when its price falls, and vice versa, meaning the consumer will play out the law of demand in reallocating his or her purchases.

In discussing the law of demand in their introductory economics classes, economists are always insistent that students understand that the downward sloping demand curves they draw describe the law of demand.[3] They also insist that changes in variables other than price affect the location of the demand curve, either shifting the curve in or out in their figures, and that changes in price do not affect demand (or the location of the demand curve in the figure), mainly because the price–quantity relationship defines demand, meaning the curve itself. Accordingly, a change in the price can only change the quantity demanded, or how much consumers buy, not the demand. A change in the price is shown by a movement along the demand curve. The demand curve itself, now and in the future, remains stationary when the price, and only the price, changes. Any student who dares make the mistake of answering a test question with the argument that "a price increase (or decrease) leads to a decrease (increase) in demand" will be graded down for the answer. To be strictly correct, the student must say something to the effect that "a price increase (or decrease) leads to a decrease (increase) in the quantity demanded."

As argued in this chapter, digital economics does not require that economics professors throw out their introductory lectures on demand theory, but it certainly does require them to be more guarded in denying a connection between price changes and demand. As will be seen, the theory of network effects (sometimes called "bandwagon effects") does in fact lead to the conclusion that changes in the price of a good can lead to a change in demand (not just quantity demanded), maybe not immediately, but at least in the future. As we will also see, network effects can be so immediately realized that for all practical purposes price can be said to affect demand, not just quantity demanded. But then, over the past twenty years, economists have been postulating tie-ins between current consumption, which can be affected by current price, and future demand from a couple of other theoretical perspectives, notably under the rubrics of "lagged demand" and "rational addiction," also reviewed in this chapter. I review these theoretical modifications, along with the theory of network effects, not so much because they apply only to digital-era goods. They apply to a wide range of conventional, distinctly nondigital goods, not the least of which are drugs, telephones, and automobiles. I go through these modifications mainly because the emergence of the digital sector of the economy has elevated their importance and role in theoretical and policy analysis. All three theories bring to light different aspects of the same forces at work in markets, especially digital markets.

THE THEORIES OF EXPERIENCE AND LAGGED-DEMAND GOODS

In developing the law of demand, rarely is much mentioned about how the benefits received by any one, say, candy bar buyer in one time period will affect the benefits received in subsequent time periods, or, rather, how the consumption level today will affect the demand in the future. This is because many of the goods considered are like candy bars. Little or nothing will also be written about how the benefits (and demand) depend on how many other people have bought candy bars, all of which is understandable. The benefit that one person gets from eating a candy bar in one time period does not materially affect the benefits received from eating another bar later, and is also not materially affected by how many other people buy bars in the various time periods. People just buy and consume candy bars independent of one another, and could not care less about how much other people enjoy their candy bars.

This is not true for two special classes of goods that have much in common: The first class is often called "experience goods" or "lagged-demand goods." The other class, to be considered later in the chapter, is called "network goods." An experience good is a good (or service) the consumption of which is affected by buyers' knowledge of the good's value or usefulness. Before consuming the good, the buyer might have no knowledge of the good's value (or the buyer might attribute some low probability that the good will have value). Accordingly, today's consumption can affect consumption tomorrow (or in future time periods), mainly by increasing buyers' knowledge of the good's value (or by eliminating the risk and uncertainty surrounding the good's value). Granted, with some experience goods, current consumption can leave future demand unaffected, given that in consuming a good, we can learn that we do not like it. However, the more interesting class of goods is those where current consumption improves the assessed value of the good and, hence, leads to a greater future demand. Prime examples of experience goods where this might be the case include music, various foods, books, some computer programs, and even shopping on the Internet, given that such goods must be tried, or experienced, in one way or another (tasted, smelled, touched, heard), before consumers can accurately know their value.

Understandably, producers of new products, like a new cracker, will hire clerks in grocery stores to pass out free samples of their crackers with some spread on it. Music producers encourage radio stations to air their songs free of charge; others make their songs available on the Internet. Car dealers allow potential customers to test-drive their new and used cars. Bookstores allow patrons to browse their stacks, even sit and read, while some publishers (like the publisher of this book) permit readers to download one or more chapters of their books. Software developers often let potential buyers use their programs for a defined period of time. The concept of experience goods, while surely applicable to industrial-era goods, has special relevance to the emergence of the digital/Internet economy. This is because when any new economic sector emerges, people lack experience with many of the goods sold in the sector, as well as lack experience buying and selling in the new sector. Without much doubt, the growth of Internet shopping was substantial in the 1990s, but growth was impaired by people's lack of experience with shopping (or more generally, doing any kind of business) online. Consumers could not be sure that the sellers (who could not be seen) could be trusted to ship what was bought with a reasonable probability. Consumers also had to worry that their credit card information sent over the Internet would be secure.

All marketing strategies are used with one overriding expectation in mind, that once users experience the products, they will be more inclined to value them and, hence, buy them. This means that giveaways can increase future demand and lead to higher-than-otherwise future prices and sales. Another way of saying the same thing is that by pricing their products at zero (or close to zero) today, producers of experience goods can stimulate future demand for their products after which some positive price can be charged. For that matter, charging negative prices (which means the producers pay the customers to take the product) can be altogether rational strategies for producers of experience goods, at least for the short term.

However, producers' incentives to lower their current prices toward zero and beyond are often checked by the fact that producers other than the ones lowering their prices can experience an increase in demand when a given good is more widely experienced. For example, by lowering the prices of its books to encourage consumers to buy online, Amazon.com drew in many new online shoppers who, once they were experienced buying books online from Amazon, would buy other products online—from other vendors. Amazon's problem in setting its pricing strategy is that it could not charge for the gains of other vendors, which might explain why Amazon did not initially lower the prices of its books more than it did and why Amazon quickly began to expand its operations from that of online bookseller to an online department store. Still, Amazon might have lowered its prices initially even more if it could have captured more of the external benefits (or "spillover effects") of its own sales.

Of course, this line of argument suggests that firms producing experience goods will see their incentive to initially lower their prices rise with the extent of their current and expected market dominance or the extent to which they can entice their initial customers to become repeat customers. The more dominant the firm is, the more likely customers will make their purchases from the firm that lowers its price. This means that monopoly producers of experience goods can have a greater incentive to lower their prices than firms in competitive markets, and for two reasons: First, a monopoly producer can figure that its customers will have to return to it, given there is no one else for the customers to return to. Second, the monopolist can figure it can recover any initial lost revenues from the higher prices it can charge in the future because of the increased demand.

In developing their more general theory of lagged demand, which is similar to the theory of experience goods, Dwight Lee and David Kreutzer had in mind any good in which consumption in the future is critically tied, for any number of reasons, to consumption in the current time period.[4] A demand can be lagged, because of experience buyers currently have with the good. But the tie-in between current and future consumption can also be a function of the good's availability, which can be a function of technology, market open-ness, and investment, as well as the enforcement of property rights. From this perspective, a lagged-demand good is one in which the future good is a com-plement to the current good. That is, they go together, or the use of one leads to use of the other. According to Lee and Kreutzer,

> The crucial assumption behind our analysis is that lags exist in the demand for the resource; future demands are influenced by current availability. The demand for petroleum is clearly an example of such a lagged demand structure, with fu-ture demand for petroleum significantly influenced by investment decisions made in response to current availability.[5]

Hence, it follows that like all complements (and as in the case of experience goods), the future demand for a product depends on the current price for the same good. Behind such an obvious point are important insights that might otherwise go unrecognized from the usual view of demand (and, as will be seen, excise taxes and other policy issues).

As a consequence of the complementarity in consumption over time, firms faced with lagged demand have an incentive to lower their current price to stimulate future sales. They might even lower their price in spite of the fact that (when their current demand is inelastic, or consumers are relatively un-responsive to the price drop) they lose current revenues from doing so. They can figure they can stimulate a greater future demand, which will permit them to raise their future prices and which can lead to greater profits. Of course, firms will follow such a pricing strategy only as long as the producers' rights to exploit future profits are not threatened.

What is interesting about this perspective is that under normal demand theory conditions, a cartel of producers is usually formed with the intent of raising the market price by getting the participating firms to restrict their col-lective sales. The cartel will break apart as members begin cheating, trying to expand their market shares and profits by cutting their prices. Under condi-tions of lagged demand (and experience goods), a cartel may form not with the intent of raising the group's current price, but with the intent of lowering the current price and expanding demand, and profits, in the future. If there are several firms in the market, each, acting individually and competitively, may not be lowering its price enough to stimulate the maximum increase in the future demand in the product they sell. The reason is that each firm can figure that if it lowers its price, it can stimulate its current sales and the future demand for the product. But each firm can also see that some of the future sales can go to the other firms, which can dampen each firm's incentive to lower its price. They can overcome the collective problem of inadequate price reduction by forming a cartel with a current price reduction its primary goal, mainly because if all members lower their prices, they can all sell more currently but, more important, they all can face higher demands in the future. Just as interesting, if such a cartel is ever formed, it may also dissolve because of rampant cheating involving price increases, not price decreases, with all firms seeking to benefit from the greater demand stimulated by lower prices charged by other cartel members.

It needs to be noted that the conventional treatment of demand, under which the demand tomorrow is unrelated to the consumption level today, holds that the potential for future threats to the stability of property rights could lead to overproduction during the current time period. This is the case because if a firm—for example, an oil company—fears it will lose its property rights to its reserves, then it has an incentive to increase production and expand sales today. Never mind that the added supply of oil might depress the current price. The oil firm can reason that if it does not pump the oil out of the ground in the short term, it will not have rights to the oil in the future.

As Lee and Kreutzer point out, for goods subject to the lagged-demand phenomenon, any looming threat to property rights can cause some firms to do the exact opposite: reduce production of oil (or the exploitation of any other resource), hike the current price, and extract whatever profits remain. When its property rights are threatened, the firm no longer has an incentive to artificially suppress its current price to cultivate future demand.

THE THEORY OF RATIONAL ADDICTION

Two economists from the University of Chicago, Gary Becker and Kevin Murphy, have developed a line of argument that proceeds in much the same way as the experience-good and lagged-demand argument, as well as the network-effects argument to be considered, but with a different emphasis that leads to counterintuitive conclusions about the elasticity of demand. The major difference is that Becker and Murphy's purpose was primarily to develop an economic theory of addiction.[6] Unlike the experience good, in the case of the addictive good, the tie-in between current consumption and future demand is physical (or may be chemical), as in the case of cigarettes. However, Becker and Murphy posit that people approach the prospect of addiction, or tie-in in consumption, with the same cost–benefit calculus, or rationality, that they use for the purchase of other goods. They just have to be more forward-looking in the case of the addictive goods. This means they have to weigh the costs (appropriately discounted for their timing and likelihood of being in-curred) that can come with addiction; these additional costs might include the payments they make for the addictive goods, the loss of future income, med-ical expenditures, the loss of family and friends, and possible incarceration (when illegal drugs are involved).

In more concrete terms, Becker and Murphy posit that people's future de-mand for cigarettes can be tied to their current consumption simply because of the body's chemical dependency on the intake of nicotine. As in the case of lagged-demand goods, producers of addictive goods have an incentive to sup-press the current price of their good—cigarettes—to stimulate the future de-mand for it. The lower the current price, the greater the future demand and the greater the future consumption.

This complementarity in consumption over time for an addictive (and lagged-demand) good is illustrated in Figure 5.1. At price P_1 in the current time period, the consumption will be Q_1 in the current time period. However, because of that current consumption level, the demand in the future rises to D_2. If the price is lowered to P_2, current consumption rises to Q_2, but the fu-ture demand rises to D_3. You can imagine that at even a lower price, P_3, there will be some even higher demand curve, D_3, in the future time period. You can see in the illustration why firms have an incentive to lower the current price: the future demand rises. With other complement goods, if the price of one complement goes down and more of it is sold, then the demand for the other complement will go up, with its price rising. The same thing happens in this case. The only difference is that the complements are the same good but consumed in different time periods.

The current demand for one addictive good—cigarettes—might be highly inelastic, as is commonly presumed in policy discussions of taxing cigarettes, but this does not mean that the long-run demand is necessarily inelastic, meaning consumers are relatively unresponsive to price changes up or down.[7] As illustrated in Figure 5.1, the short-term demand curves (the dark lines) are each very inelastic, but the long-term demand curve (light line, LR_1) is rather elastic. Indeed, Becker and Murphy maintain that the more addictive the good, the more elastic the long-term demand will be.[8] This is the case because a reduction in the price in the *current* time period might not stimulate current sales very much. However, for highly addictive goods, current consumption can lead to an even greater increase in the future demand because the buyers need it more in the future, thus resulting in even more future consumption than would be the case for less addictive goods. Hence, it is altogether under-standable why cigarette firms decades ago (when I started teaching) would often have cigarette girls parading around campus in short skirts giving away

Figure 5.1. The Lagged-Demand Curve

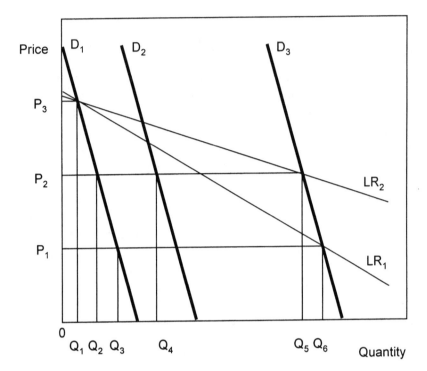

small packs of cigarettes, and why many drug dealers to this day eagerly give away the first hits to potential customers. Indeed, it seems reasonable to conclude from the Becker/Murphy line of argument, the more addictive the good, the lower the current price. This is because the more addictive the good, the higher the price the seller can charge in the future. We might not even be surprised that for some highly addictive goods, the producers "sell" their goods at below zero prices (or pay their customers to take the good). Again, this is because they can recover their current losses with higher sales at higher prices in the future.

As will be seen by pressing the development of network effects, the presumption of an interconnection between current consumption (and price) and future demand forces revisions in expected behaviors and policy proposals. In contrast to the theory of lagged demand, and following Becker and Murphy, this theory of rational addiction suggests explanations for a variety of behaviors, most notably, the observed differences in the consumption behavior of young and old, the tendency of overweight people to go on crash diets even when they may only want to lose a modest amount of weight, or alcoholics who become teetotalers when they decide to curtail their drinking. Old people may be less concerned about addictive behavior, everything else held constant, than the young. Old people simply have less to lose over time from addictions than younger people (given their shorter life expectancies). People who are addicted to food may rationally choose to drastically reduce their intake of food even though they may need to lose only a few pounds because their intake of food compels them to overconsume. Similarly, alcoholics may get on the wagon to temper their future demands for booze because even a modest consumption level can have a snowballing effect, with a little consumption leading to more drinks, which can lead to even more.

Standard excise-tax theory suggests that producers' opposition to excise taxes should be tempered by the fact that the tax can be extensively passed onto the consumers in the form of a price increase (that must always be less than the tax itself). The theory of lagged demand suggests otherwise: Producers of such goods have a substantial incentive to oppose the tax because of the elastic nature of their long-run demands. While they may be able to pass along a major share of the tax in the short run, they will not be able to do so in the long run. From standard economic theory, an excise tax imposed on the production of a good can be expected to have several effects: The supply of the good will be curbed; the price consumers pay will rise with the curtailment in supply; and the price received by producers after the tax will fall. The difference between the price paid by consumers and the price received by the producers equals the excise tax.

As you might imagine, the consequences of an excise tax for a good subject to a lagged demand or rational addiction are not exactly the same. The excise tax imposed on producers might, indeed, decrease the supply curve, as is conventionally thought. However, the impact on price and quantity sold will not likely be the same.[9] This is because of the incentive the producers have to suppress the current price to stimulate future demand. When the prospects of the excise tax being enacted are evident to producers, they can be expected to raise their prices currently (before the tax is enacted). This means that the prospects of an excise tax can lead to a higher current price being received by producers, as well as a lower quantity sold (even without the excise tax in effect). When the tax is imposed, the reduction in quantity sold can be from two forces: First, the price increase caused by the excise tax, and second, the price increase caused by the prospects of the tax and the fact that the tax might be raised in the future.

THE THEORY OF NETWORK EFFECTS

A network good is a product or service the value of which to consumers depends intrinsically on how many other people buy the good. A network good has one defining feature: The greater the number of buyers, the greater the benefits most, if not all, buyers receive (at least up to some point). These goods are said to exhibit network effects (or more generally, positive feedback effects), which have been appropriately described by one economist as "a phenomenon in which the attractiveness of a product to customers increases with the use of that product by others."[10]

As you can see, lagged demand and network goods have much in common—the interconnectedness of consumption, which has important implications for pricing strategy. The theory of network effects shares one key construct with the theories of lagged demand and rational addiction: the interconnectedness of demands. The interconnectedness in the theory of lagged demand and rational addiction is through time. The interconnectedness in the theory of network effects is across people and markets.

Some examples of network goods include fax machines, sidewalks, and telephones, as well as many computer programs.[11] There is no point in having a fax machine unless someone else has a fax machine, because without a second fax machine in existence, there would be no one to fax. The more fax machines, the greater the value of any one fax machine. Similarly, if one homeowner puts a sidewalk in front of his or her house, and no one else does, the one sidewalk segment is of limited value. However, if the neighbors follow suit, adding sidewalks in front of their houses, then all sidewalks can be connected up, and the sum of the value of the individual sidewalk segments escalates as people in the neighborhood can have more places to walk without having to worry about car traffic.

The details of the theory of network effects are best understood in terms of telephone systems that actually form networks, that is, are tied together with telephone lines (as well as microwave disks and satellites). No one would want to own a phone or buy telephone service if he or she were the only phone owner. There would be no one to call. However, if two people—A and B—buy phones then each person has someone to call, and there are two pairwise calls that can be made: A can call B, and B can also call A. As more and more people buy phones, the benefits of phone ownership escalate geometrically, given that there are progressively more people to call and even more possible pair-wise calls. If there are three phone owners—A, B, and C—then calls can be made in six pair-wise ways: A can call B or C, B can call A or C, and C can call A or B. If there are four phone owners, then there are

12 potential pair-wise calls; five phone owners, 20 potential pair-wise calls; twenty phone owners, 380, and so forth. If the network allows for conference calls, the count of the ways calls can be made quickly goes through the roof with the rise in the number of phone owners. It is important to remember that the benefits that buyers garner from others joining the network can rise just from the potential to call others; they need not ever call all of the additional joiners. No one need ever expect to call every business in the country, but each person can gain from having the opportunity to call any of the businesses that have phones. There is economic value to the opportunity to make calls because there is some probability, albeit a small one, that we will actually call people whom we do not now call.

Accordingly, the demand for phones can be expected to rise with phone ownership. That is to say, the benefits from ownership go up as more people join the network. There are in economics vernacular economies of scale in consumption or demand-side scale economies, which are one reason firms can be expected to stress at the start of their network development efforts the goal of achieving a large market share. Carrying forward with our phone example, as the count of users rises with market share, consumption benefits also rise concomitantly, which means consumers should be willing and able to pay more for phones as the count of phone owners goes up.

In passing, I note that networks and network goods, or those exhibiting network effects, tend to turn one basic economic proposition on its head. There is a canon in economic theory that has been stressed from the start: As any good becomes scarcer, it becomes more valuable. In the case of network goods, just the opposite is true: As the good becomes more abundant, its value goes up.[12]

"EXTERNALITIES" WITHIN A GIVEN NETWORK

Some of the network benefits of phone ownership are said to be "external"—dubbed "network externalities"—to the buyers of phones because people other than those who buy phones gain by the purchases. In more concrete terms, when one person—Hugo—buys a phone, then someone else—Renee—gains from Hugo's purchase—and Renee pays nothing for Hugo's purchase of his phone. For that matter, everyone who has a phone gains more opportunities to call as other people buy phones or as the network expands (at least up to some point). The gains that others receive from Hugo's or anyone else's purchase are external to Hugo, hence they are dubbed "external benefits" or, more to the point of this discussion, so-called network externalities.[13]

There are two basic problems that a phone company faces in building its network. First, the company has the initial problem of getting people to buy phones, given that at the start the benefits will be low. Second, if some of the benefits of buying a phone are external to buyers, then each buyer's willingness to buy a phone can be impaired. This is because the buyer cannot collect on the benefits provided others. In some cases, the inability of the buyers to collect on the benefits provided others could mean their benefits are not great enough for them to buy phones. Hence, the network will be more restricted than it should be and consumers get fewer benefits than they could get if buyers could collect on the benefits they provide others.

This dilemma has been described as a classic "prisoners' dilemma" for the buyers. All buyers would want everyone to buy into the network, in which case everyone could be better off, but each buyer may have an impaired incentive to buy in, meaning if the network development were left to the buyers, it would either not be formed or would be underdeveloped. The network externalities could lead (as externalities do when people pollute) to what economists cite as a "market failure," or an inefficiency in the market outcome. In the case of network externalities, too few units of the good would be produced (or the total added social value to everyone of some phone not bought, because some benefits are external to individual buyers, exceeds their added costs).[14] However, this need not be the case.

Fortunately, consumers are not left to their own devices. Not all benefits that are external to buyers are true externalities, as that term is normally used in economics with respect to topics like pollution. At least some, if not all, of the benefits are, or can be, internalized by the firms providing the good (or service). In short, some firms—called "network sponsors"—have the requisite incentive to build the network, given that the firms can charge higher prices if a sufficient number of buyers join the network. How might a firm help consumers overcome their prisoners' dilemma? One obvious solution is for the phone company to do what the producers in the theory of lagged demand and rational addiction do: underprice (or subsidize) their products—phones—or, at the extreme, give them away (or even pay people to install phones in their houses and offices).

The network effects in the software industry are similar but, of course, differ in detail from the network effects in the telephone industry. In the word-processing market, the developer might reason (as WordPerfect, no doubt, did back in the 1980s) that if it can get consumers to buy its word-processor program, then the demand for it will grow in the future. This is because people will want to have compatible word processors so they can help each other learn the program and can exchange documents with greater ease than if all used different word processors.

The potential network effects for an operating system are even greater than for a particular application, but that can mean the operating system developers have a two-sided prisoners' dilemma problem. The operating system developer—for example, Microsoft—must somehow get the computer users on one side of the market and application developers on the other side to join the network more or less together. The sponsor has a real "chicken-and-egg problem." Few people, other than computer geeks, are likely to buy an operating system without applications (for example, word-processing programs or games) being available. If a producer of an operating system is only able to get a few consumers to buy and use its product, the demand for the operating system can be highly restricted. This will be the case because few firms producing applications will write for an operating system with a very limited number of users, given the prospects of few sales for their applications. However, the applications written for the operating system can be expected to grow with the number of people using the system. Why? Because the potential sales for applications will grow with the expansion in the installed base of computers using the operating system. If more applications are written for the operating system, then more people will want to buy and use the operating system, which can lead to a snowball effect: more sales, more applications, and even more sales in an ever-expanding array of people connected to the operating system by way of the invisible network.

As in the case of telephones, some of the benefits of purchases of the operating system (and applications) are external to the people who buy them. People who join the operating system network increase the benefits of all previous joiners, given that they have more people with whom they can share computers or share data and manuscripts. All joiners have the additional benefit of knowing that a greater number of operating system users can increase the likelihood of more applications from which they can choose.

However, as in phone purchases, when the benefits are external, potential users have an impaired demand for buying into the network. They each simply cannot collect on the benefits their purchases provide each other. Despite each consumer getting benefits from the purchases of all other consumers, each consumer can still reason that his or her own purchases will have little impact on his or her own personal welfare. It follows that the greater the external benefits, the greater buying resistance (or willingness to cover the cost of the product).

At the same time, I hasten to add, again, that often the benefits that are external to consumers can and will be internal to the seller. That is to say, the producer can capture a portion, if not all, of the benefits of a larger network through larger sales made later, once the network is developed, with the later sales made possibly at higher prices. Of course, this means the producer can have the requisite incentive to find ways of overriding the consumers' impaired incentive to buy the product. One way the producer can do this is one already mentioned: lowering the upfront price, or even paying consumers to take the software product. The producer can justify charging zero or negative, below-cost, upfront prices, but only as long as it can anticipate charging higher prices in the future. This leads us to two observations on pricing strategy, which will be developed at greater length in later chapters:

- If a firm achieves market dominance through low upfront prices that give rise to network effects, and then begins to charge higher prices later, it does not necessarily follow that the dominant firm's higher prices are monopoly prices. This is because the upward adjustment in prices represents an increase from a price level that everyone, including the consumers, knew was being charged to spur the development of the network and could not be lasting.
- The consumers can be better off at the later higher price than at the lower upfront price. This is because of the network effects that develop and push the consumers' demand outward, increasing their consumer surplus. The loss in consumer welfare with the higher price is partially, if not totally, offset by the low upfront price.

The price is not the only variable the producer can manipulate. Upgrading the product subject to network effects without raising its price is another way to encourage consumers to buy in. The producer will understandably encourage the view that others are joining (regardless of whether they may be actually joining) and that the network will grow over time. Such perceptions can be self-realizing. In the case of an operating system, the producer can be expected to work hard at ensuring that applications developers write for the operating system.

The network may grow slowly at the start because people (both computer users and programmers) might be skeptical that any given product, especially an operating system, will be able to develop a sizable network (and provide the reciprocal external benefits that a large network can provide). However, as in the case of phones, abundance (not scarcity) can imply greater value for the software/operating system network.

EXTERNALITIES ACROSS NETWORKS

Some theorists have reasoned that the network externalities within networks can be internalized by the network sponsor, but that is not necessarily true across different and competing networks and their sponsors. Accordingly, markets beset with network effects can still fail to produce the optimum quantity of the network good. The argument might be developed in this way: When one network sponsor, such as Microsoft, lowers its price to expand its network, the sponsor can cause another competing network, such as Apple, to shrink, which means not only that the Apple network loses members, but the members who remain with Apple lose network benefits. The Apple network users suffer negative externalities because of Microsoft's pricing decisions. That is to say, the value of Apple network members staying with the Apple network declines, which is all the more reason for Apple members to move toward the Microsoft network.

Indeed, it might be said that a network sponsor, such as Microsoft, has an incentive to lower its prices precisely because of the expectation that the contraction of benefits going to the Apple network members will cause Apple members to move to Microsoft. The argument might be made that the lost benefits to the Apple members are on par with any other externality, such as the benefits that are lost by customers in a given shopping center when people throw trash about or when store owners allow the facades of their estabalishments to deteriorate. This implies that the network effects felt by Apple network members necessarily lead to a market failure, or an overexpansion of the Microsoft network (or the Apple network, depending on which potential sponsor were to take the pricing initiative).

Normal Market Externalities

However sound this line of argument seems, it is misleading and a misunderstanding of the type of externalities that lead to market inefficiency, that is, a so-called market failure. To see the error, consider the way a competitive market operates. Let us suppose there is a greater demand for beef. The resulting shortage of beef leads to consumers bidding up the beef price. Similarly, the greater the price of beef, the greater the demand by cattlemen for the resources (including cattle) that go into the production of beef and the greater the resource prices. In the resource market, the cattlemen impose externalities of a sort on each other by pushing up the resource prices. However, no one would construe these externalities of price increases as a form of market failure. On the contrary, they enhance market efficiency as resources are moved to their most highly valued uses. The cattlemen who pay the resulting market prices for the needed resources can use the resources more efficiently than those who are unwilling to pay the market prices. This means there can be more beef for consumers to buy than would be the case were resource prices not to rise and less efficient cattlemen got the resources. Thus, by having the most efficient cattlemen use the available resources, beef prices to consumers do not have to rise by as much as they would were the less efficient cattlemen to make use of the resources. Hence, not all externalities—or spillover effects—are necessarily bad for markets, a point that should not be forgotten when we turn to "cross-network externalities." Indeed, externalities that come from movements in competitive market prices add to market successes, not failures.[15]

Scale Economies on the Production Side

Also, consider the way "natural monopoly," or a single firm that comes to dominate the market because of economies of scale in supply, is usually treated in economics. If the initial market price in such a market is high and there are a number of competitors, because of supply-side scale economies, each competitor in the market has an incentive to lower its prices: By doing so, it can not only garner customers from other producers, it can also lower its marginal and average production costs, simply because such cost savings are inherent in the known technology of a larger production scale. By pressing price reductions to become the dominant producer, or a natural monopolist, the initial competitors harm one another. But no one has ever argued there is something inefficient about the reciprocal harm the competitors impose on one another.

Indeed, it is argued that the competitive price-cutting leads to greater market efficiency, because, with the elimination of competitors and the emergence of a single producer, production is then conducted on a larger and more efficient scale. That is to say, fewer resources are used in the production of the good than would otherwise be used to produce the higher output were a single producer not to emerge. While there may appear to be harm done with the reciprocal price-cutting of the initial competitors, there are actually gains, given that the resources that are released in producing the expanded output can be used to produce other goods that add to consumer welfare.

As has been argued, once the single producer/natural monopolist emerges, it might act like its namesake, a monopolist, and restrict output to raise its

price and profits. Hence, there is a potential inefficiency in the natural monopoly markets (as there is in all monopoly markets). I could take issue with
the claim that a natural monopolist will necessarily be able to act like a monopolist (after all, the natural monopolist does have to face the prospects of the
retry of old competitors and the entry of new ones when it restricts sales to
raise its price). However, note the difference in the use of resources in the case
of the monopoly action and in the case of the initial competitive price-cutting.
If the natural monopolist did act like a monopolist, the output restriction
would cause a reallocation of resources from a higher-valued use (in the monopolized market) to lower-valued uses in other markets, with a net welfare
loss resulting. When the initial competitors cut prices, the exact opposite happens: There is a net gain in output not only in the natural monopoly market
but elsewhere in the economy.

Economists have long argued that a natural monopolist (which is not able
to price discriminate) will fall short of producing the efficient output level,
mainly because if it produces the efficient output level (where marginal cost
and marginal benefit are equal), it will not be able to charge a price that will
allow the firm to cover all production costs.[16] Therefore, the efficient natural
monopolist would incur losses. To achieve the efficient output, economists
have historically recommended that the firm should be subsidized by the government for its losses. However, more recently, economists have recognized
the pitfall in such a solution: The subsidy will discourage cost control on the
firm's part (since their added costs will be offset by the subsidy), which suggests that the subsidy will not necessarily lead to greater efficiency. It could
have, and very likely will have, the exact opposite effect, especially since the
natural monopoly receiving the subsidy has an incentive to manipulate the political process so that it receives subsidies that are greater than its losses. In
short, a natural monopolist that produces an output short of the idealized efficient output level may be efficient in a more meaningful sense: Its output
level is as good as can be expected, given there are no clear policy options for
improving matters.

Scale Economies on the Demand Side

Economies of scale are economies of scale, and should be treated as such,
no matter which side of the market they emerge from. After all, scale
economies in production lead to cost savings, but since cost is nothing more
than the value of what else could be produced with the resources, those
product-side scale economies lead to the creation of greater value. So it is

with demand-side scale economies: The expansion of the consumer base within any given network leads to greater value for consumers. If that did not happen, then the expansion would be choked off, meaning people would not move to the expanding network.

Granted, Microsoft's network expansion causes a contraction of the Apple network. However, Apple could try to expand its network by the same methods that Microsoft uses, and Apple could counter Microsoft's moves with price cuts of its own (much as initial competitors in the previous discussions of the natural monopoly argument counter each other's price cuts). If Microsoft cuts prices and Apple does not, we must presume that Microsoft anticipates greater gains from the expansion of its network than Apple expects. Hence, the expansion of Microsoft's network at Apple's expense results in net welfare gains to those who make the switch. Those who stay with Apple must still expect that the network benefits are greater with Apple than with Microsoft (even though their benefits are undercut by Microsoft's expansion).

Alternately, the Apple network members who are willing to switch between networks can be seen as resources that can be used by either the Apple or Microsoft network to enhance overall consumer welfare (just as workers are viewed as resources that can be used to maximize gains of consumers). The Apple network members are, through Microsoft's pricing, moved to where they can, in effect, be employed to do the most good, meaning add the greater value to overall welfare. Acting as a proxy for its network members, Microsoft is induced to, effectively, outcompete Apple for a critical resource: network members. The network members are, in effect, moved from lower valued uses to higher valued uses, implying a net welfare gain from their use.

Of course, let us suppose that there is some market inefficiency because of network externalities, just for the sake of argument. The questions that naturally follow are, What do we do about the efficiency? Can an improvement be made? How do we orchestrate an improvement? Those are not easy questions that I can fully answer here. "Government regulation," in one form or another, is the usual answer. However, regulations that inspire greater efficiency do not fall from some truth function in the sky to which we can all defer. On the contrary, they emerge from political and bureaucratic processes that are noted for their own flaws. Such regulations can literally make markets more inefficient, given the way political and bureaucratic institutions are inclined to respond to private interest groups who are more concerned about their own welfare than improving the general welfare by forcing markets to work more efficiently.

In the case of the Microsoft/Apple example, do we prevent Apple users from moving to the Microsoft network? Do we restrict Microsoft's ability to lower its prices? Do we tax Microsoft users to compensate Apple users when Microsoft lowers its prices and expands its network? Unfortunately, all such policy options are a seedbed for inefficiencies of their own, as well recognized in economic literature.

The Extent of the Market

The usual presumption when talking about scale economies is to assume that the economies are inherently derived from the known technology. However, ever since the days of Adam Smith, economists have known that actual economies to be gained from resources are dependent on the extent of the market (not so much in geographical terms as in production terms).[17] In a classic article from 1928, Allyn Young took Smith's thesis one step further by observing that "the enlarging of the market for any one commodity, produced under conditions of increasing returns, generally has the net effect . . . of enlarging the market for other communities" that, following Smith's dictum, could be expected to lead to greater economies, meaning that potential economies of scale are not capped by a given known technology (although technology improvements can, in themselves, lead to greater economies, which can further extend the market).[18]

In appraising the impact of digital products, or the Internet, on human welfare, we cannot forget about the interplay of the size of the market and scale economies that can be realized. This is especially true when some digital products, such as a given computer operating system, can not only be produced efficiently on a very large scale, but because of the production economies realized from the extended use of personal computers, plus the network effects of the operating system and applications markets building on one another, but can greatly expand the extent of the market in ways that Smith and Young could hardly have imagined. And, of course, Smith and Young could not have dreamed of how the Internet would become a whole new medium for the conduct of commerce, which necessarily adds to the extent of the markets and scale economies realized far beyond the Internet. Once the potential from these scale economies is realized, any failure on the part of a natural monopolist, whether achieved because of supply- or demand-side consideration, to achieve supposed optimum efficiency pales in comparison from the welfare gains that infiltrate the entire economy because of scale economies of, say, an operating system or Internet, have been realized.

NETWORK NEGATIVES

Network effects are often discussed as though they are always positive. Hence, consumers are made progressively better off as a network expands. However, that is hardly the case, as can be seen with several telling examples.

Telemarketing

When telephone networks began to develop, it may have indeed been true that the network benefits were all positive. One reason may have been that the telemarketing business was yet to be developed, and the economics of telemarketing were against the industry's emergence: There were too few people whom the telemarketers could bother (at dinner hour!), meaning the costs of making sales pitches by phone were too high for the gains to be realized.

However, with the spread of the telephone network, the economics turned more favorable, giving rise to a host of telemarketing companies, each of which have geared up to interrupt telephone subscribers at the most likely time they will be home, the dinner hour. These negative consequences from the development of a network can restrict the extent to which the demand for the service can be expected to build on itself. As a consequence, these negative effects can undercut the net gains from the network expansion. They can, therefore, undercut the extent to which the short-run demand curves shift out in response to a current reduction in price. Hence, these negative effects can lower the elasticity of the long-run demand for the network service.

Indeed, in the case of telemarketing, the industry itself may, over the last decade, have overexpanded, giving rise to too many calls. The problem with telemarketing is that each firm can call as many telephone subscribers as it wishes. The costs they incur are restricted only to their out-of-pocket expenditures; they do not have to pay people for the inconvenience of being interrupted and the time spent listening to product pitches.[19] Therefore, each telemarketer can be expected to expand its calls until the value of the last call just covers that firm's out-of-pocket costs, which necessarily means that the total cost of the marginal call will exceed the expected gains from the call. The net result is some lost welfare for consumers and the telemarketers.

The losses to telephone subscribers might be obvious. The less obvious losses to the telemarketers can show up in the fact that subscribers, especially in demographically attractive urban and suburban areas, now get so many telemarketing calls that many of them have begun to turn down the calls as a matter of course, not listening to any of the pitches. Many subscribers are buying technological fixes, such as the "TeleZapper," to reduce their telemarketing calls.[20] No doubt, many subscribers figure that the cost incurred from listening to calls and seeking to sort out the attractive pitches from the bad ones exceeds the prospective gains. As a consequence, the telemarketers have to reduce the prices they can charge for the number of calls they promise to make.

The problem of excessive calls faced by the telemarketing industry also appears to be faced by Web sites that earn a major portion of their revenues from pop-up ads, those windows that appear automatically when people visit Web sites, with the ads often being tailored to the browsing history of the visitors. Viewers might be willing to tolerate, and respond to a few ads, but might be expected to tune out the ads when they are seen everywhere. Despite the fact that the ads might be viewed as bothersome by Web surfers, too many Web sites, which are dependent on ad revenue, continue to offer the ads. Indeed, with their declining effectiveness, given that everyone does it, the sites might try to increase the number of ads that pop up and increase their intrusiveness, just to override the browsers' heightened disregard for them.

The consequence can be that the ads can result in a decline in the count of "click-throughs" (or those people who click on the ads to learn more about the deals that the ads provide). In 1996, 2 percent of site visitors clicked on banner ads, according to Nielsen/NetRatings. By 2002, only 0.5 percent of visitors clicked on the ads.[21] This decline in click-throughs is understandable, given that by early 2002, 41 percent of Web browsers found the pop-up banner ads so annoying that they said that the ads themselves would make them less likely to return to the site, according to Media Metrix.[22] In addition, by 2002, consumers had the benefit of an array of software programs—such as Pop-Up Stopper, Pop-Up Killer, Pop Not, and Webwasher—that prevent the banner ads from ever appearing.[23]

An implication of this line of argument is that not all telemarketers and Web advertisers should necessarily be opposed to restrictions on calls and ads by firms within their industries. For example, Congress has legislated that telemarketers must delete from the directories they use the names of people who ask for their names to be deleted. Not all telemarketers should be expected to oppose such regulations. First, the deletions can reduce the number of worthless calls they make, thereby reducing their costs. Second, the telemarketers can presume that the people remaining on their list will be more receptive to their product pitches.

However, we must recognize that acknowledged inefficiencies in markets like those that appear self-evident in telemarketing and Web advertising industries—so-called market failures—do not, in and of themselves, suggest that the identified problems should be corrected, in spite of the consumer and producer harm that might be identified. The reason is that governments do not have a glowing record for regulating actual efficiency improvements, partly because governments often have a difficult time fine-tuning regulations and also partly because the regulations are political outcomes that can be manipulated by the industries that are regulated, themes that are taken up later in this book and at length by others.[24]

Cable Service Congestion

Cable-based provision of Internet services harbors the potential for positive network effects: As more people buy into the cable service, individual subscribers can have more people to E-mail and instant message. However, as more subscribers are added, beyond some point, the subscribers can, and do, face real-world problems of congestion, meaning that everyone's Internet connections can begin to slow down and that the benefits received by individual subscribers from the cable service can begin to drop.[25] In terms of Figure 5.2, which has the total cost and benefits on the vertical axis and the number of subscribers on the horizontal axis, the total benefits curve can initially rise, only to drop off after N_1.

On the other hand, the cost of the cable service might be prohibitively expensive for any one subscriber, if only that subscriber joined the service. However, as more subscribers join the service, the cost of the service to individual subscribers can fall continually, as is shown by the downward sloping cost curve in Figure 5.2. There need be no tragedy of the commons in the case of cable service, mainly because the cable company can act as the network sponsor, one that seeks to maximize its own gain from providing the service by optimizing the net gains to its subscribers—or, in terms of Figure 5.2, maximizing the gap between the total cost and benefits curves. Note that the gap is maximized at N_2, not at N_1, the point of maximum benefits to each subscriber. In effect, the cable service will seek N_2 subscribers, because that is where the subscribers would be willing to pay the most for the service.

Of course, the cable company may be prevented from seeking N_2 subscribers, mainly because of rules under which it must operate. For example, some regulatory body may set the company's rates, and the company might be told that it must take all comers. In such cases, the cable company might have more or fewer than N_2 subscribers.

Figure 5.2. Total Cost and Benefits from Expanding a Cable Network

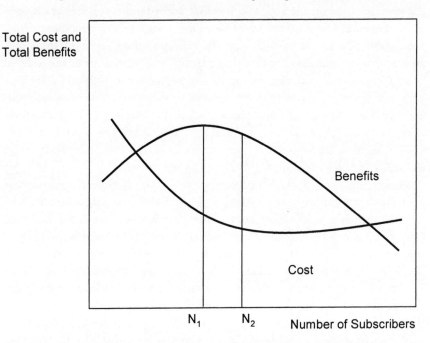

Source: Adapted from James M. Buchanan, "An Economic Theory of Clubs," *Economica* (February 1965): 1–14.

Hacking into Operating Systems

Any given operating system might have the potential for substantial positive network effects, as I have explained. However, the spread of the system's use does not always come without cost. When few people use a given operating system such as Windows, there may be little incentive for hackers to find and exploit the system's security flaws. When the system is ubiquitous, hackers can have more fun, and cause more mischief for others. It should be no surprise that hackers have focused their efforts on Windows because it is so widely used and have increased their efforts to implant more destructive viruses as more people have begun surfing the Internet at higher speeds (with the use of cable modems). And these efforts can be costly.

In 2001, two viruses—Code Red and Nimba—by themselves cost businesses an estimated $2 billion in damages.[26] But these viruses were simply the tip of a very large and growing security-breach iceberg. The CERT

Coordination Center at Carnegie-Mellon University, which gathers and disseminates information about Internet security threats, reports that in 1992 there were fewer than one thousand Internet security incidents of all kinds (which could involve a single site or any number of sites). However, by 1995, there were 2,412 reported incidents. By 2001, the count had jumped to 52,658 (more than double the count of reported incidents for 2000). While the growth in incidents may be attributable to greater awareness of the problem for computer users, and a greater inclination on the part of users to report potential problems, CERT had to issue thirty-seven advisories on serious security threats in 2001, two-thirds more than its count of advisories in 2000 and twice its count of advisories issued in 1995.[27]

As in the case of telemarketers, such growth in security threats will invariably check the spread of any software, precisely because those threats translate into prospective costs from using the software and the Internet. Specifically, such costs can foil market acceptance of Microsoft's new ".Net" strategy, under which it will provide an array of interactive and automated services (like software rentals) via the Internet. Understandably, after the revelation of a series of security flaws found in Outlook and Internet Explorer during 2001, Microsoft's Bill Gates declared enhancement of security a top priority for his company.[28]

As noted, many researchers argue that network effects amount to externalities, or spillover effects: When one person buys a phone, he or she provides benefits to all other network members, without their paying the phone buyer anything for the gains they garner. The presumption is that these external benefits will cause the market to underproduce the good. However, as already seen, as long as there is a network sponsor, the gains are not external; they are internalized by the sponsor who can adjust the price to properly align member incentives.

CONCLUDING COMMENTS

Market demands tend to be more elastic the longer the time period for purchases. That is because with more time, people have a greater chance to adjust their purchases to a price change, up or down. However, network effects add to the long-run elasticity of demand. The greater the (beneficial) network effects, the greater the long-run elasticity of demand. This is because, as explained in this chapter, future sales build on current sales. Producers of network goods have strong incentives for lowering their current prices. By lowering their current price, they can stimulate the building of the network and increase future demand. With a highly elastic demand, they can also bring in more revenue with lower prices than higher ones. If they are producing digital goods, like software, they incur little or no added cost by selling more units. Hence, their profits can be expected to rise. If they can raise their prices after network effects kick in, then producers have an even greater incentive to lower their upfront prices.

As we will see later in this book, the ability of producers to raise their future prices must mean that the network effects are not fully reversible. Otherwise, when they tried to raise their future prices, producers would face the elastic long-run demand, which means a price increase would result in lower sales and revenues as the network unraveled. However, this does not mean that prices of digital goods and services should not ever be expected to go up. In fact, as argued, network effects can cause producers to underprice their goods and services in the current time period with a view toward raising their prices in the future after network effects have begun to kick in. Such price increases should not be construed as the future pricing tactics of a monopolist. Indeed, they can be highly competitive, meaning beneficial, on balance, to consumers who might at some point have to pay higher prices but then will receive the benefits of a more fully developed network.

Moviefone.com is a firm that for a year after its inception in May 2000 did not charge a fee to visitors who purchased movie tickets online (although the company continued to charge, depending on the city, $1 to $1.50 per ticket purchased by phone). The company instituted a $1 charge for sales in May 2001 with the impact on sales uncertain, according to one report.[29] The telephone directory service 555.1212.com started business by providing its lookup service free, only to start charging $9.95 for one hundred lookups in May 2001. Its usage fell dramatically, from twenty thousand registered users when the lookup service was free to thirty-five hundred when the charge was instituted, a drop that can be attributable to the fact that Switchboard.com still provided free directory service, but also to the fact that 555.1212.com updates its directories every ninety days, while Switchboard.com updates its directories every twelve to fourteen months, again according to one report.[30]

Network effects do not necessarily tell the whole story of why many Web-based businesses began raising their prices in 2000 and thereafter. Some Web-based businesses rejected a revenue model for doing business and adopted an ad model because they, like newspapers and radio and television stations, expected that advertisement sales would cover their Web site development and maintenance costs, plus add a profit, at least eventually. The free service would simply be a way of attracting visitors and, thus, advertisers. When Web ads often proved ineffective after several years of experience, advertisers began pulling out their funding of the Web businesses, which caused the businesses to have to make up for their lost revenues with service charges to customers. Moreover, many dot-com companies lost their financial support from venture capitalists, which may explain why some dot-coms may have had to raise their prices earlier than they may have planned.

Nevertheless, network effects may be a partial explanation for why in late 2000 eVoice.com, a Web-based communications company that takes voice messages for people when their telephone lines are busy, started business by giving away its service, only to begin charging $7.95 per month when it built up a customer base. Similarly, PhotoPoint, a San Francisco–based firm that allowed its 1.6 million members to post and share photos online, began charging $19.95 to $29.95 per year for a service it had previously made available for free. eFax.com, a Web-based business that provides fax numbers and E-mail delivery of faxes, started by giving away its "basic" service to individuals. Once it had built its network, eFax began charging $9.95 per month for a "premium" set of fax services, including the ability to send (while still giving away its basic service).[31]

As I will argue later, the network effects for some products and services may not be fully reversible. That is to say, as some scholars have reasoned, the future prices on some products and services may be raised because of the existence of so-called switching costs. However, even when prices can be forced up because of switching costs, it does not always follow that consumers are worse off. Indeed, under certain market conditions, switching costs can lead to consumers being better off than they would have been in the absence of switching costs.

NOTES

1. For discussions of unusual applications of the law of demand, see Richard B. McKenzie and Gordon Tullock, *The New World of Economics*, 5th ed. (New York: McGraw-Hill, 1994); and Steven E. Landsburg, *The Armchair Economist: Economics and Everyday Life* (New York: Free Press, 1993).

2. As University of Chicago economist and Nobel laureate Gary Becker has observed:

Indeed I have come to the conclusion that the economic approach [founded in a major way on the law of demand] is a comprehensive one that is applicable to *all* human behavior, be it behavior involving money prices or imputed shadow prices, repeated or infrequent decisions, large or minor decisions, emotional or mechanical ends, rich or poor persons, adults or children, brilliant or stupid persons, patients or therapists, businessmen or politicians, teachers or students.

See Gary S. Becker, *The Economic Approach to Human Behavior* (Chicago: University of Chicago Press, 1976), 8.

3. For example, see Edgar K. Browning and Mark A. Zupan, *Microeconomics: Theory and Applications* (New York: Wiley, 2002), 16–17.

4. Dwight Lee and David Kreutzer, "Lagged Demand and a 'Perverse' Response to Threatened Property Rights," *Economic Inquiry* 20 (October 1982): 579–588.

5. Ibid, 580.

6. Gary S. Becker and Kevin M. Murphy, "A Theory of Rational Addiction," *Journal of Political Economy* 96 (August 1988): 675–700.

7. More formally, an inelastic demand is one in which the percentage change in the price is greater than the percentage change in the quantity consumers are willing and able to buy, meaning that a price increase will lead to an increase in revenues, and vice versa. An elastic demand is one in which the percentage change in the price is less than the percentage change in the quantity, meaning that a price increase will result in a reduction in revenues, and vice versa.

8. Becker and Murphy conclude, "Permanent changes in prices of addictive goods may have a modest short-run effect on the consumption of addictive goods. This could be the source of a general perception that addicts do not respond much to changes in price. However, we show that the long-run demand for addictive goods tends to be more elastic than the demand for non-addictive goods" ("A Theory of Rational Addiction," 695).

9. For a more complete discussion of the impact of excise taxes on addictive goods, see Richard B. McKenzie, "Rational Addiction, Lagged Demands, and the Efficiency of Excise Taxation: A Reconsideration of Conventional Tax Wisdom," *Public Choice* 77 (1991): 33–41.

10. Direct Testimony of Franklin M. Fisher, *United States v. Microsoft Corporation*, Civil Action No. 98-1233 (TPJ), filed October 14, 1998, p. 15, as downloaded from http://www.usdoj.gov/atr/cases/f2000/2057.pdf.

11. However, Brian Arthur, who did much of the fundamental theoretical work on network/feedback effects posits that network/feedback effects extend to goods such as clocks and typewriter keyboards that become the standard to which everyone defers. See W. Brian Arthur, *Increasing Returns and Path Dependence in the Economy* (Ann Arbor: University of Michigan Press, 1994). Once the good becomes a standard, people will adopt it because others understand and can use the product and will not have to incur switching costs to move to another standard (the subject of Chapter 6). In addition, Arthur sees feedback effects in the development of communities and whole cities. Because people move to a given location, others will move these also, and because services develop in a given location to meet the needs of the people already there, still more people will move there.

12. See Kevin Kelly, *New Rules for the New Economy* (New York: Viking/Penguin, 1998), chap. 3.

13. See Joseph Farrell and G. Saloner, "Standardization, Compatibility, and Innovation," *Rand Journal* 16 (1985): 70–83; and Michael L. Katz and Carl Shapiro, "Network Externalities, Competition, and Compatibility," *American Economic Review* 75 (1985): 424–440.

14. For more details of the inefficiency of externalities, both external benefits and costs, see Richard B. McKenzie and Dwight R. Lee, *Microeconomics for MBAs: Putting Economic Theory to Work in Understanding Markets and Managing Firms* (Irvine: Graduate School of Management, University of California, Irvine, 2001), chap. 7; http://www.gsm.uci.edu/~mckenzie/pdf_doc/Online%20book/Chapter%207%20Market%20Failures.pdf).

15. Such externalities that occur from competitive price movements are at best "pecuniary externalities," which have been shown to be efficiency enhancing for markets. The harmful forms of externalities, say, in the form of pollution, are called "technological externalities." Even then, not all technological externalities are, or should be, amenable to extra-market/governmental correction. This is when the cost of correction exceeds the efficiency gains from doing anything about the technological externalities. See James M. Buchanan and William C. Stubblebine, "Externalities," *Economica* 30 (November 1962): 371–384.

16. The problem is that with expansion of production scale and output, the natural monopolist's marginal and average costs are forever declining within the relevant range of the market demand, with the marginal cost always below the average cost. If the firm produces and prices where marginal cost equals marginal benefit, the price would be below the average cost (because marginal cost is below average cost). Hence, the firm's revenues (price times quantity sold) would not equal its total costs (the higher-than-price average cost times quantity). For a graphical exposition of this inefficiency argument, see McKenzie and Lee, *Microeconomics for MBAs*, chap. 12.

17. In Smith's words, "As it is the power of exchanging that gives occasion to the division of labor, so the extent of this division must always be limited by the extent of that power, or, in other words, by the extent of the market. When the market is very small, no person can have any encouragement to dedicate himself entirely to one employment." See Adam Smith, *An Inquiry into the Nature and Causes of the Wealth of Nations*, ed. R. H. Campbell and A. S. Skinner (1776; reprint, Indianapolis, Ind.: Liberty Classics, 1981), 1:31.

18. Allyn Young, "Increasing Returns and Economic Progress," *Economic Journal* 152 (December 1928): 527–540, as reprinted in James M. Buchanan and Yong J. Yoon, *The Return to Increasing Returns* (Ann Arbor: University of Michigan Press, 1994), 41. Young adds, "In this circumstance lies the possibility of economic progress, apart from the progress which comes as a result of the new knowledge which men are able to gain, whether in pursuit of their economic or noneconomic interests" (p. 44).

19. The logic followed can be much the same as the logic followed by polluters, with each polluter reasoning that his or her pollution is a trivial part of the overall

pollution problem and that not polluting would have little or no impact on the overall pollution problem. This outcome has been dubbed the "tragedy of the commons," suggesting that the core of the problem is that the property rights to whatever is being polluted (the waterways or airways, for example) have not been assigned. Ownership is said to be held in "common." We will return to the tragedy of the commons in the chapter (9) on intellectual property rights. The classic article on the subject is Garrett Hardin, "The Tragedy of the Commons," *Science* 162 (1968): 1243–1254.

20. TeleZapper, which in early 2002 sold at retail for $50, is a small electronic box that connects to a subscriber's phone. Before calls are allowed to get to the phone, the TeleZapper determines whether a call has been made by the automatic dialing equipment of telemarketers. Once the computerized call has been picked up by the subscriber, an actual person at the telemarketing firm takes over the call and makes the pitch. When a computerized call is detected, and before the telemarketing person takes over the call, TeleZapper sends a message to the telemarketer's computer, indicating that the number called is not a working number. Because telemarketers want to minimize their useless calls, they typically have their computers programmed to delete numbers from their directories that are determined to be nonvalid. Hence, TeleZapper fools the telemarketers' computers into deleting numbers from their databases, which reduces the likelihood of the deleted numbers being called again.

21. As reported by Dave Wilson, "Putting a Stop to Ads That Pop Up," *Los Angeles Times*, 17 January 2002, p. T1.

22. Ibid.

23. Ibid.

24. See Paul H. Rubin and Thomas M. Lenard, *Privacy and the Commercial Use of Personal Information* (Boston: Kluwer Academic Publishers, 2002).

25. This section is based on James M. Buchanan, "An Economic Theory of Clubs," *Economica* 32 (February 1965): 1–14.

26. As reported by Joseph Menn, "Security Flaws May Be Pitfall for Microsoft," *Los Angeles Times*, 14 January 2002, p. C1.

27. CERT Coordination Center, Software Engineering Institute, Carnegie-Mellon University, "CERT/CC Statistics 1988–2001," as found at http://us.f205.mail.yahoo.com/ym/login?.rand=9g7kg0a3dm2ki.

28. Gates wrote his employees:

In the past, we've made our software and services more compelling for users by adding new features and functionality, and by making our platform richly extensible. We've done a terrific job at that, but all those great features won't matter unless customers trust our software. So now, when we face a choice between adding features and resolving security issues, we need to choose security. Our products should emphasize security right out of the box, and we must constantly refine and improve that security as threats evolve.

Reported in Richard Morochove, "Gates Finds Religion Very, Very Late—His New Mantra Is Security Years after Chronic Problems Plague Products," *Toronto Star*, 21 January 2002, p. D2.

29. Susan Stellin, "E-Commerce Report: Internet Companies Brave the Transition from a Free Service to a Business That Charges," *New York Times*, 23 July 2001, p. C8.

30. Ibid.

31. Michael Liedtke, "Internet World No Longer Land of Free, Profits Lag, Firms Try to Lure Paying Customers," *Chicago Tribune*, 7 May 2001, p. A7.

6

Tipping and Path Dependency

The theory of network effects might suggest that they occur naturally, more or less as an initial chemical reaction might set off a series of subsequent reactions, or as a snowball might develop as it rolls down a hill. Some network effects may be natural, however, that is not necessarily always the case. Networks, as often as not, must be cultivated, mainly because of the startup, or chicken-and-egg, problems. As long as firms can influence the extent of the network effects, the network sponsor can be expected to work hard, and invest resources, as long as there are profits to be had from their network investments. Microsoft must figure that the several billions of dollars that it spends each year on helping applications developers write for Windows more than pays off in terms of network effects.

However, once market conditions have been appropriately developed, the shift of buyers to the product of a given network sponsor can, beyond some point, be self-reinforcing, that is, built on past shifts in consumer purchases of the product more or less automatically. That is to say, as the network for fax machines or a given productivity software like word processing develops, more and more people can begin to buy that product because everyone else is doing so. Moreover, consumers can begin to expect more and more people will join the network in the future, which, because of the compatibility benefits, can increase the expected consumer benefits from using the word processor. Hence, the fax machine's or word processor's current and future demand can increase, spurred ever onward with any real or expected additional price reductions.

When the market begins to shift in a self-generating manner toward, say, the word processor, the market is said to have reached its "tipping point." Once the market begins to tip toward a product, the producer may be able to back off somewhat, if not totally, in its network development efforts. Indeed, the prospects of the market tipping can encourage the producer to work hard up-front in developing network effects to hasten the arrival of the tipping point. As the old adage goes, time is money, a point that is fully applicable to market tipping. Firms should be expected to invest in the development of network effects and pushing forward the tipping point as long as the gains to be had after the market tips more than compensate them for the interest they pay on their investments to bring about the tipping. The greater the probability that the market will tip in its direction, the more the firm will invest to bring about the tipping point. The greater the likelihood that the firm's investment will speed up the tipping point, the greater the investment the firms will make. The more self-perpetuating the firm's market share becomes, once the tipping point has been reached, the harder the firm can be expected to work to reach the tipping point. Once the market has tipped in favor of one firm, there is a presumption that consumers become "locked in," with the net result that the producer of the network product can exert its market dominance, restrict sales, and garner monopoly profits, restricting market efficiency in the process.

In this chapter, I extend the analysis of network effects begun in the last chapter by taking up the market courses taken by products—fax machines, operating systems, picturephones, VCRs—that are presumed to exhibit network effects and to be subject to market tipping. I then take up the issue of path dependency, which suggests that markets subject to tipping can also be markets that fail in the sense that inferior product technologies can, from time to time, be expected to dominate. While the path dependency theory has a clear intellectual appeal, the available evidence raises doubts about its relevance.[1]

FAX MACHINES

Because fax machines spread rapidly among businesses, and even homes, in the 1980s and early 1990s, the presumption might be that the market for fax machines tipped rapidly once the machines were introduced. However, it actually took 150 years for fax machines to get to the point of tipping, mainly because all of the requisite conditions for tipping had to be put in place. The first fax machine was developed way back in 1843, with the first fax machine service for businesses inaugurated in 1865. For fax machines to become common, a number of technological improvements had to be made, including the invention of the photoelectric cell, which did not happen until the 1870s, and the development of the wirephoto technology in 1902, which was necessary to make fax service useful to newspapers.

Moreover, the spread of fax machines was checked by AT&T's ban on the attachment of non-Bell equipment to AT&T's telephone system, which was not ended until 1956 (with a court decision in the Hush-a-Phone case). Still, major manufacturers had to agree on technology standards for (group 3) fax machines, which they did not settle until 1979, and perhaps only then because, as Jeffrey Rohlfs notes, there was no dominant manufacturer that had a stake in ensuring that its technological edge was protected by the absence of agreement and, therefore, the absence of competition. With the emergence of competition in the fax machine market after the technology standards were adopted, fax machines rapidly improved, becoming faster, quieter, and far less expensive. The real price of fax machines (in 2001 dollars) fell by 93 percent, or from $4,236 in 1982 to $290 in 1987.[2]

OPERATING SYSTEMS

As with word processors, the market for operating systems can also tip toward one particular system, but with complications that enhance the reinforcing nature of the tipping process. As the market share for an operating system like Windows grows, more and more applications developers can be expected to want to write for Windows. As the count of applications rises, the benefits of using Windows can grow, leading to more consumers buying Windows and, in turn, more applications being written for Windows, which can fuel the further growth of Windows' market share. After the tipping point has been reached, the firm's eventual market dominance may be assured, which is all the more reason that an operating system firm may invest many resources in trying to get the market to tip its way.

Before the introduction of the IBM personal computer, Apple was the dominant personal computer, running the CP/M operating system.[3] However, IBM and Microsoft developed their respective operating systems (PC-DOS and MS-DOS, respectively) in 1981. At that time, 90 percent of programs ran under some version of CP/M.[4] CP/M's market dominance was likely undermined by two important factors: First, CP/M was selling at the time for $240 a copy; DOS was introduced at $40.[5] Second, the dominance of

IBM in the mainframe computer market could have indicated to many buyers that some version of DOS—most likely IBM's version—would eventually be the dominant operating system.

In addition, Apple refused to unbundle its computer system: It insisted on selling its own operating system with the Macintosh (and later generation models). There are two arguments for using the Apple approach. First, Apple could optimize its operating system for the components used in its personal computers. Second, it could restrict the availability of Apple computers and thereby hike their prices.

Microsoft took a radically different approach: It got IBM to agree to allow it to license its version of DOS—MS-DOS—to other manufacturers and then did just that to all comers, presumably in the expectation that the competition among computer manufacturers on price and other attributes would spread the use of personal computers—and, not incidentally, Microsoft's operating system. The expected abundance of MS-DOS systems led to an even greater demand for such systems, and to a lower demand for Apple systems. Many people started joining the Microsoft network, not always because they thought MS-DOS, followed by Windows, was a superior operating system to Apple's, but because any inferiority in the technical capabilities (if that were the case) would be offset by the benefits of the greater size network. Supposedly, as the network story might be told, there was a tipping point for Microsoft sometime in the late 1980s or early 1990s (possibly with the release of Windows 3.1) that caused sales of personal computers, and Windows, to take off, sending Apple into a market-share tailspin.

The tipping process might be started by low prices, even zero or below-zero prices. As noted, MS-DOS started with a price tag equal to one-sixth of the price for CP/M at a time when Apple and other operating system developers were charging much more. Microsoft continued its low-price/high-volume strategy with Windows. The tipping process, however, could have needed something other than a low price to get it going. This is because when Windows was introduced in 1983, it was not at all clear that it would dominate the operating system market as it has. At the time, there were few applications written for Windows. Applications developers could not be certain that the operating system market would tip toward Windows. It could have tipped toward Apple's Mac, given that PC-DOS and MS-DOS operating systems users might have unsettled the PC-DOS and MS-DOS networks, and given that users thinking about upgrading to a graphical user-interface operating system could have decided to move to the Apple's Mac or, later, to IBM's OS/2. Applications developers had to fear that their investment to adjust their programs to Windows would be a waste as the market could have tipped toward another operating system.

What better way for Microsoft to enlist the confidence of applications developers in writing for Windows than for Microsoft to develop the proverbial "killer application" (or set of applications) that came to be Office? With Office available, applications developers could set to work adding to the stock of Windows applications, which, through the heralded network effects (that were central to the government's antitrust suit arguments), could give rise to computer users switching to Windows. The greater number of users could be expected to give rise to more Windows applications, and greater benefits for computer users, and greater confidence that the market would indeed tip toward Windows.

The prospects of the market tipping toward one particular application or one operating system can also be a problem for the developer. Consumers have to worry that the application developer or operating system developer will see the network benefits as a restriction on the ability of users to switch to alternative programs and will, therefore, see its market dominance as a means of extorting monopoly profits from computer users. In the case of a dominant operating system, applications developers at all times must worry that an operating system firm like Microsoft that achieves market dominance will, at some future point, actually seek to impose its monopoly will on the operating system market. Microsoft's then restricted sales will result not only in fewer Windows sales but also in fewer applications sales, a prospect that would devalue developers' upfront investments. What better way to make its commitment to charge competitive prices credible than for Microsoft to develop its own applications, especially ones that dominate their product categories. If Microsoft then ever charges noncompetitive prices for Windows, it will hurt its own Office sales, thus making its competitive commitment self-enforcing and encouraging the development of applications by outside firms.

The pricing and market development strategies Microsoft used can also be the legal bane of firms that use them, as Microsoft found out, much to its regret. In 1998, the Justice Department took Microsoft to court for violation of the nation's antitrust laws. Among other charges, the Justice Department maintained that Microsoft was a monopolist, as evidenced by its dominant (90+ percent) market share in the operating system market, and that Microsoft was engaging in "predatory" pricing of its browser Internet Explorer. Microsoft had been giving away Internet Explorer with Windows 95 and had integrated Internet Explorer into Windows 98. The Justice Department claimed that the only reason Microsoft could possibly have had to offer Internet Explorer was to eliminate Netscape Navigator from the market. I cannot settle all of these issues here (antitrust is taken up in Chapter 11). But I can point out that the Justice Department starts its case against Microsoft with the claim that software markets are full of network effects. While it might be true that Microsoft may have been engaging in predatory pricing, it may also be true that Microsoft was responding to the dictates of network effects, underpricing its product to build its network and future demand. It had another reason to lower its price to levels that Netscape might not consider reasonable. If Microsoft lowers its price on Internet Explorer (or lowers its effective price for Windows by including Internet Explorer in Windows), then more computers could be sold, which means more copies of Windows would be sold and more copies of Microsoft's applications—Word, Excel, and so on—would be sold. This means that a lower price for Internet Explorer or Windows could give rise to higher sales, prices, and profits on the applications.

PICTUREPHONES

Of course, I must caution that any tipping of a market is never preordained, and hardly ever known with any clarity, which means that markets where tipping is expected might never tip, either because such markets never were meant to tip or because the producers failed to sufficiently solve the startup problems. Take the case of the Picturephone Service that the Bell system introduced in the early 1970s. From market research, AT&T found that the service could add value to people's communication experience and could, at the same time, provide face-to-face contact without the expense of travel, thereby, supposedly, justifying the $86.50 monthly fee for the service. However, the service never enlisted more than two hundred users in the Chicago test market, thus giving rise to the users' number one complaint: There was no one (or few people) to call. The service was aborted shortly thereafter.[6]

The reasons? Perhaps, the picturephone was introduced decades ahead of its time. Perhaps the price was too high, given the need at the start to increase usage so that subscribers would have a large (and expected larger) base of people to call and make use of the new form of communication. Then again, a part of the problem may have been that, as Rohlfs recounts, AT&T did not have the requisite incentive to overcome the startup, chicken-and-egg problems, given its regulatory constraints. If AT&T had developed the market for picturephones, and the market had tipped in the company's favor, its return on its investment would merely be the usual fair rate dictated by the company's regulators. On the other hand, if the service were unsuccessful, the costs associated with developing the technology and the market would likely not be counted as a part of its investment (thereby justifying higher returns for the company), as indeed they were not allowed when the service failed.[7] As Rohlfs notes, "To all appearances, AT&T introduced the bandwagon service, Picturephone, with no consideration of the start-up problem. The guiding principle appeared to be, 'Build it; they will come.' That principle does not work for bandwagon products. It has to be, 'Build it and reach a critical mass; the rest will follow.'"[8]

VCRs

When the VCR (or more properly the U-Matic VCR) was developed jointly, via a technology-sharing agreement between Sony and Matsushita in the early 1970s, network effects were not an important consideration.[9] This is because the two Japanese firms assumed that their VCRs would have a single purpose, the recording of television programs. When one person bought a VCR to record a television program, other buyers did not benefit. There was no network to develop (except to the limited extent that family and friends could share their recorded programs). As a consequence, there was no chicken-and-egg problem to solve and no particular need for the development of a single recording standard, which explains why, initially, the VHS and Beta recording standards emerged, which led to a market contest to which we will return later in the chapter.

The important point to note is that playing movies was not, initially, an expected use for VCRs. Indeed, the VCR manufacturers expected Hollywood production companies to protest the use of VCRs for recording and playing television programs, including movies, which Universal Studios did do in court in 1976, claiming that by producing and marketing VCRs, Sony was infringing on Universal's copyrights to television programs. Sony won the first legal round at the district court level, but in 1981, the Ninth Circuit Court of Appeals reversed the lower court. If that decision had not been taken up by the U.S. Supreme Court, VCRs might not have developed, legally, that is. Fortunately for consumers—and producers—the Supreme Court reversed the court of appeals decision in 1984, but only by a five-to-four decision, which means that the VCR and movie rental industry was able to develop by the thinnest of legal margins, one vote.

As the VCR industry developed (and as the copyright case made its way through the court system), Hollywood began to see the potential for movie rentals, which introduced network effects, and all of the attendant startup problems, including the need for choosing a recording/playing standard. The more VCRs that were sold, the more movies that producers would make available; the more movies there were, the more VCRs would be sold. Interestingly, Universal Studios, the plaintiff in the copyright case, had already begun licensing its movies for rental before the court of appeals ruled against Sony. And by 1986, Hollywood's revenues from video rentals exceeded its revenues at box offices.

All the while, the contest between the Beta and VHS formats continued, with VHS being the ultimate victor. The Beta format was introduced first, in 1975, but only one year ahead of the VHS format. However, by 1978, annual sales of videos recorded in the VHS format were nearly 48 percent higher than Beta sales. Beta sales continued to grow, but far more slowly than VHS sales, which led the market to clearly tip toward VHS in the early 1980s. After 1984, Beta sales began to diminish, not so much because Beta did not have some advantages over VHS, but because VHS had its own advantages, plus the advantage of market dominance (or 74 percent of all videos recorded in the two formats).[10]

PATH DEPENDENCY

The network effect argument has been extended and elevated in importance by contentions that the alternatives available to consumers through time can be path dependent. The path dependency claim is not only a factual assertion that network effects exist, and therefore today's choices are a function of choices made earlier, but also a claim that the evolutionary progress of thought-to-be choices are more or less predetermined, or are preset (which implies that as the evolutionary process develops, people's choices are seriously constricted by the path followed), at an early stage in the development of a new technology or product; that the critical and determining initial choices can be accidental or fortuitous and may, in themselves, be of little consequence; and that people cannot do much to get off the path they are on, even if a shift in paths makes good economic sense. Not only can demand swell as a technology or product is adopted, due to the positive feedback loop of network effects, but also production costs can fall with increasing returns to scale and as people learn by doing. As Brian Arthur developed the feedback loops on both the demand and supply side:

> Technologies typically improve as more people adopt them and firms gain experience that guides further development. This link is a positive feedback loop: the more people adopt the technology, the more it improves and the more attractive it is for further adoption. When two or more technologies (like two or more products) compete, positive feedbacks make the market for them unstable. If one pulls ahead in the market, perhaps by chance, its development may accelerate enough for it to corner the market. A technology that improves more rapidly as

more people adopt it stands a better chance of surviving—it has a "selectional advantage." Early superiority, however, is no guarantee of long-term fitness.[11]

Elsewhere, Arthur suggests there are six elements to his theory of path dependency:

1. The market is subject to instability; that is, it is self-perpetuating, or subject to tipping toward the product that takes the initial lead (which can give rise to a so-called "first-mover advantage").
2. The market is subject to multiple potential outcomes (or winning technologies or products), with the actual outcome dependent, not on its superiority, but on some initial event.
3. The actual outcome is unpredictable because so many variables are involved.
4. The market is subject to being "locked in" to a given technology or a given product.
5. The product that does come to dominate and lock up the market might be inferior to other possible technologies or products.
6. The winning firm can garner "fat profits."[12]

DOS Operating System

Arthur supports his theoretical arguments with a number of examples drawn from history, most notably, the eventual market dominance of the DOS operating system, the QWERTY typewriter keyboard, and the VHS format for videocassettes. In the case of the DOS operating system, he maintains that the competitive outcome between DOS and the Mac operating systems

> was not known in advance (before the IBM deal [made with Microsoft on the development of DOS]) which system would come to dominate. Once DOS/IBM got ahead, it locked in the market because it did not pay the users to switch. The dominant system was not the best: DOS was derided by computer professionals. And once DOS locked in the market, its sponsor, Microsoft, was able to spread its costs over a large base of users. The company enjoyed killer margins.[13]

QWERTY Keyboard

A great deal of ink has been spilled on the story of the QWERTY typewriter keyboard, so-called in reference to the order of letters beginning at the top left of the keyboard's second row. This particular arrangement of letters was supposedly introduced in the early days of typewriting as a way of solving a mechanical problem of keys overstriking one another and becoming physically jammed. According to the story, which Arthur repeats and which Paul David develops at length, a rival keyboard later invented by August Dvorak is vastly superior to the QWERTY keyboard, yet QWERTY was adopted for computer keyboards and remains in common use because typists and typewriter manufacturers cannot overcome path-dependent inertia: Typists do not train on the Dvorak keyboard because there are virtually none in existence, and virtually no Dvorak keyboards are manufactured because there are too few Dvorak typists. The QWERTY keyboard has the market locked up, in spite of the fact that it is inferior—supposedly.[14]

A carefully researched study of the evolution of typewriter keyboard standards, however, has shown that Dvorak's invention is not in fact markedly superior to QWERTY and, moreover, that "the continued use of QWERTY is efficient given the current understanding of keyboard design."[15] The accepted standard was not displaced in this case simply because the benefits of switching to the challenger were less than the costs. More generally, adherence to an inferior standard in the presence of a superior one is inconsistent with the normal workings of a freely functioning competitive marketplace, which creates profit opportunities for alert entrepreneurs who solve the coordination problem. Because switching to superior technologies increases the value to consumers of the products embodying them, manufacturers have strong incentives to see that they find a market. If the Dvorak keyboard had indeed been vastly superior to QWERTY, significantly raising the productivity of the typists who used it, then typewriter manufacturers could have sold more typewriters. They would then have had incentives to help users overcome the inertia of using the old standard by bearing some of the costs of switching, which they could do in a variety of ways, including offering discounts to early adopters of the new standard, providing guarantees of satisfaction, making the new products available on a rental basis, granting rebates to customers who exchange equipment embodying the old standard, or subsidizing training on the new equipment.[16] Some of the costs of switching will also be internalized by end users. While individual typists might be deterred from adopting the new technology because the costs to them personally are greater than the expected benefits, firms that employ large numbers of them would, if the Dvorak keyboard were in fact superior to QWERTY, have incentives to coordinate the technology choices of their employees to capture the productivity gains of adopting the new standard.

In short, a variety of market-based institutions exist that promote the displacement of obsolete technologies, including those beset by network externalities and superficially irresolvable coordination games. As a result, "observable instances in which a dramatically inferior standard prevails are likely to be short-lived, imposed by authority, or fictional."[17]

VHS Format

Fiction has likewise displaced fact in retellings of the second popular example of path dependence: the market's selection of VHS-formatted videocassette recorders over the now-obsolete Beta format. Claims of the
technological superiority of Beta over VHS are not only routinely overstated,
but VHS in fact has an edge on a dimension of product performance of great
value to consumers, namely, the length of the programs that can be recorded
on a single tape. VHS formatting made it possible to record a movie-length
program on one videocassette, an innovation that spawned a wholly new
home-entertainment industry. Such a development would not have been possible if Beta formatting, with its more limited recording time, had become the
industry standard. Hence, despite Beta's one-year head start over its rival, the
market apparently made the right technology choice.[18]

Arthur and others who argue by example that inferior technologies might
continue to dominate a market in spite of their inferiority point out that the inferior technologies are protected by switching costs (a subject that will be covered in greater detail in Chapter 7). They make a legitimate point when they
reason that a consumer will not switch to a superior technology unless the
value of the superiority is greater than the switching costs they must incur. At
the same time, they are wrong to suggest that the "inferior" technology should
be replaced by the "superior" one or that the market is not operating efficiently,
even when the switching costs are greater than the value added by the "superior" technology. The reason is simple: When switching costs are greater than
the value added, consumer welfare would fall if the switch were made. The
market would only be operating poorly if the switching costs were less than the
added value from switching to the superior technology. And Arthur and others
have never shown that superior technologies of that sort—ones that offer consumers more value than they add to all costs, including switching costs—have
ever failed to be adopted.[19] Indeed, it would be mystifying if such technologies
failed widespread adoption for the reasons already noted. There would be
profits to be made by firms who help consumers make the switch.

TIPPING AND GOVERNMENT POLICY

Nevertheless, when the QWERTY and VHS stories are accepted as valid, as
Arthur and others seem to do, it is all too easy to assume that their stories about
the evolution of the operating system market—that Microsoft, an inferior technology, has been able to lock up the operating system market—have some validity. The Justice Department has certainly bought Arthur's telling of the story

and, with little proof of its validity, has prosecuted Microsoft for antitrust violations. In its complaint against Microsoft in May 1998, Joel Klein, then assistant attorney general for antitrust at the Justice Department, reasoned:

> Microsoft has maintained a monopoly share (in excess of 80%) of the PC operating system market over an extended period of time. The durability of Microsoft's market power in part reflects the fact that the PC operating system market is characterized by certain economies of scale in production and by significant "network effects." In other words, the PC operating system for which there are the greatest number, variety, and quality of applications will be selected by the large majority of PC users, and in turn writers of applications will write their programs to work with the most commonly used operating system, in order to appeal to as many potential customers as possible. Economies of scale and network effects, which reinforce one another, result in high barriers to entry.[20]

However, it is questionable whether Microsoft can rely on consumer "lock-in" to continue to dominate the market for computer operating systems. If a superior alternative to Windows is written by a rival software developer that offers consumers more value than their switching costs, there is every reason to expect Windows will be displaced, just as CP/M was displaced. In the face of the threat of such potential competition, Microsoft's continued market dominance consequently depends on its ability to continuously improve its operating system by, among other things, making it more reliable and integrating more applications with it to reduce consumers' costs of searching for, purchasing, and installing compatible software products. In so doing, Microsoft has incentives to see that users of older versions of Windows upgrade to newer versions. To help solve the coordination problem and overcome consumer inertia, it offers discounts on software upgrades, allows users to experiment with (beta test) new software products before they are formally released, gives new applications away, makes programs "backward compatible" so that files created with obsolete versions can be read by newer versions, and enters into contracts with computer manufacturers requiring them to install the same operating system on all of the units they ship. Some of these actions may, in the eyes of Microsoft's rivals and the Justice Department, seem to be brutally competitive. Nonetheless, they are competitive responses to the market conditions.

"SUPERIOR" VERSUS "INFERIOR" TECHNOLOGIES

It is clear that the economy might be construed as operating with more efficiency if there were no switching costs, that is, if people could switch from an old technology to any new technology that proved to be "superior" in the slightest degree. However, that supposes a world that does not exist. Switching costs are like material costs; they exist and must be incurred. To assume the world would be better without switching costs is no more useful a statement than to assume away any cost category, say, materials or labor. In making statements about efficiency, we have to stay with the real world as we know it, and in that real world costs of all kinds cannot be assumed away.

It also might be thought that the economy would operate more efficiently if the truly "superior" technologies could be selected at all times at the start, before they begin their evolutionary developmental process. If that could happen, then no one would ever have to switch from an inferior to a superior technology. No one would then have to incur switching costs. Then people would, at all times, be able to garner the added benefits of the superior technology. However, again, always choosing the "superior" technology at the start is impossible to do: Because of the prospects of multiple developmental outcomes and because technologies improve through an evolutionary process of learning by doing, the eventual superior and dominant technology is simply not predictable in advance.[21] If it were, we would not need markets or any other social process in which unknowns could become knowns.

Once it is admitted that picking winning technologies is an impossible feat, because of our ignorance of what might eventually be proven true, then we have to set aside any notion that some other technology, like another keyboard or operating system, is indeed "superior" in any meaningful economic sense. This is because we cannot know that the supposed "superior" technology, which has not yet been adopted, will be superior to the supposed inferior technology in the future. The superior technology's superiority might be fleeting. Any attempt by government to correct market outcomes, based on what computer professionals say today, could be counterproductive.

Finally, it is all too easy to conclude when technology comes to dominate a market that the dominant technology is "not the best," as Arthur has claimed and backed up with an equally unsubstantiated assertion, "DOS was derided by computer professionals."[22] So what? They all may have derided other operating systems. Moreover, to dominate the operating system market, which means sell to a lot of people with different computing needs, an operating system developer is likely to make the operating system a bundle of features, not all of which will be used by everyone. Some people, for example, will never open the card game Solitaire that's in their operating system; others will not use Notepad. An operating system might operate more efficiently, or be "superior," if it were tailored to each user's particular needs. However, an operating system tailored to individuals' needs could be very costly. While it might be "superior" in a technical sense, it could nonetheless be judged "inferior" in terms of the willingness of computer users to buy it.

Moreover, it should be noted that computer professionals have different preferences for features (or the lack thereof) in their operating systems, and given that any operating system will be a bundle of features, at least some computer professionals can be expected to see some other bundle as "superior," which means that Arthur's comment that DOS was judged "inferior" by computer professionals does not add much to the discussion. If these computer professionals know of a truly better and more efficient (in the technical and economic senses) operating system, then they should give it a try in the market. If the consumer value of the greater efficiency exceeds the switching costs, there is really nothing stopping the switchover. Granted, the switching costs are an impediment, just as all production costs are, but then I return to a point that cannot be stressed enough: The gains from the superior technology can be used to override the switching costs.

THE MYTH OF THE FIRST-MOVER ADVANTAGE

One of the most widely believed tenets in management theory and practice, which is related to the theory of tipping, is the so-called first-mover advantage. That is, the first firm to market with a product will not only have the market to itself, but will be able to fend off all latecomers and dominate the market for some time to come. In one widely cited article in *Advertising Age*, published in 1983, researchers reported that nineteen of the twenty-five market leaders in their industries—from bacon to chewing gum to soup and toothpaste—in 1923 remained market leaders the year the article appeared.[23]

Why? Theory holds that the first mover will achieve name recognition, realize economies of scale, learn to develop even more economies from production experience, develop brand loyalty among buyers, and garner the benefits of network effects.[24] In addition, beyond some ill-defined point, the first mover can expect its market expansion to reach the tipping point, after which consumers will move to the dominant first mover simply because everyone else is moving in that direction. The first mover can expect to have its market locked up because consumers will be locked in, since consumers will face high switching costs to move to second and later comers. Hence, investors should flock to first movers because they will achieve a long-term stream of monopoly prices and profits.

Accordingly, former Intel chief executive officer Andrew Grove, in his book-length effort to explain why only "paranoid [managers] survive" in fast-paced competitive markets such as those for computer chips, admonishes managers, "Opportunity knocks when a technology break or other fundamental change comes your way. Grab it. The first mover and only the first mover, the company that acts while the others dither, has a true opportunity to gain time over its competitors—and time advantage, in this business, is the surest way to gain market share."[25]

Nice theory, but it is dead wrong—according to extensive research reported by marketing professors Gerald Tellis (University of Southern California) and Peter Golder (New York University) in their important new book, *Will and Vision: How Latecomers Grow to Dominate Markets*.[26] They offer many telling examples:

- Gillette is widely believed to have pioneered safety razors because it has dominated the safety razor market for so long. But the concept of safety razors was proposed a century before Gillette introduced its first razor. Moreover, several firms introduced safety razors two decades before Gillette did.

- Hewlett-Packard is assumed to have created the first laser printer, since it has a commanding share of laser printer sales. However, both Xerox and IBM commercialized laser printers years before HP's laser printers were built, using engines developed by Canon, not HP.

- Many people think Netscape produced the first Internet browser, and a few remember that Mosaic hit the browser market years before Netscape. However, computer geeks remember that Web browsers like Lynx, Viola, Erwise, and Midas, which were developed at various universities around the country, inspired the development of Mosaic at the University of Illinois. Even then, not one of these browsers was the true pioneer of browsing. That honor goes to a browser actually called the "worldwideweb," which was developed by Tim Berners-Lee, the creator of the protocol for the World Wide Web (pp. 150–151).

- Pampers now dominates the disposable diaper market, which is the reason many people think that Procter & Gamble was the first mover in that market in the mid-1960s. They have forgotten that Chux diapers, produced by Johnson and Johnson, were on the market as early as 1932.

- Apple Computer hardly dominates the personal computer market today (given its market share of no more than 5 percent in 2002), but there remains the presumption that Apple pioneered and then initially dominated the very early personal computing market because it created the product category. However, Micro Instrumentation and Telemetry Systems introduced its personal computer, Altair, in 1975. However, Xerox actually created the product category with the introduction of its Alto personal computer two years earlier (pp. 228–233). (Xerox also developed the mouse and graphical user interface but never was able to make those technological developments commercial successes of its own. It was left to Steve Jobs at Apple to see their market value.)

- The first-mover advantage was hardly an advantage for the CP/M personal computer operating system, nor for the Mac operating system, both of which, in their time, dominated the operating system market before Microsoft took over with MS-DOS and later Windows (ten years after the advent of CP/M).

The case against the first-mover advantage that Tellis and Golder make goes beyond a mountain of case histories that lead them to their central conclusion, which is that the first-mover advantage has never been the advantage it has been cracked up to be in any but six of the sixty-six industry groups they studied over the past decade (p. 44, table 3.2). Moreover, the failure rates of pioneers as of 2000 are quite high, 64 percent, for all industries studied. For the forty-two traditional industries studied, the failure rate was 71 percent; for high-tech industries, 50 percent (p. 43, table 3.1). And almost all pioneers dominated their markets when sales were well below mass-market proportions. In 2000, the first movers in the sixty-six industries had an average market share of only 6 percent (p. 44, table 3.2). All in all, Tellis and Golder conclude, "Market pioneers rarely endure as leaders. Most of them have low market share or fail completely. Actually, market pioneering is neither necessary nor sufficient for enduring success" (p. 41).

How did the first-mover advantage become the myth that it is? The answer is relatively simple. Many researchers did not do their historical homework. They often assumed that market leaders today developed their product's category because the dominant firms themselves now claim to be the pioneers, because pioneers did not see a potential mass market for their products (given their all-too-often initial high production costs), and because the first-mover failures have been lost to history that is all too rarely studied with the care that Tellis and Golder have taken.

What is the secret of market leadership if being the first mover is not it? Tellis and Golder draw an unsurprising old lesson that managers would be well advised to remember: "The real causes of enduring market leadership are *vision* and *will*. Enduring market leaders have a revolutionary and inspiring vision of the mass market, and they exhibit an indomitable will to realize that vision. They persist under adversity, innovate relentlessly, commit financial resources, and leverage assets to realize their vision" (p. 41; emphasis in original).

Ideas often matter beyond the walls of academe, and they certainly have mattered in guiding investments in the digital age. The widespread belief that markets invariably tip toward first movers is one unheralded reason for the digital gold rush of the late 1990s. Many venture capitalists presumed that if they did not exploit the Internet first, and do so quickly, in some product category, then the competitive race to riches would be over. Hence, the market rapidly filled with dot-comers, many of whom were trying to do the same thing: be the first mover in their product category. Of course, that gold rush led to a good old-fashioned competitive bloodbath.

THE REALITY OF SECOND-MOVER ADVANTAGES

Granted, the problem might be that while there are first-mover advantages, first movers do not seem to recognize the advantages or, if they recognize them, to exploit them. Then again, the problem might be, and very likely is, that there are substantial second-mover (and third-mover) advantages.

- The second mover does not have to invent the product category, nor does the second mover have to identify and develop the market from scratch. In moving into a new product market, first movers have two chores: They must develop consumer awareness of the product category—for example, disposable diapers—and of the brand itself—"Chux." Second movers can play to consumer recognition of the product category and focus on shifting consumer attention from one brand—"Chux"—to another—"Pampers."
- No products, especially untried new ones, are perfect; all products are subject to improvement. Second movers can spend their (limited) development resources taking apart—or reengineering—the products that are pioneers, always alert for how to improve the product, as well as to how the patent can be broken.
- First movers face risk costs that show up in their having to develop an array of new products, not knowing which ones will fail. Second movers can cherry-pick, going after the successes of others and, in the process, reducing risk costs. This means second movers can reduce their development costs or focus their resources on a more limited array of products.
- First movers that are able to develop brand loyalty all too often seek to exploit the loyalty by hiking their prices. Those prices that reflect a royalty premium open the market for second and later movers.
- First movers necessarily must organize a corporate bureaucracy and culture around a given product design. Those organizations can become very efficient at promoting the product as it has been developed and tweaking small product improvements that enhance firm profitability. However, the first

mover's business model can prevent it from seeking more revolutionary products (and production process redesign), as argued earlier in the discussion of disruptive technologies.

- As we have seen, network effects are not always the unmitigated benefit they have been made out to be to first movers (or just the movers that come to dominate their markets). A firm producing a word processor, for example, might be restrained in radically enhancing its product by the developments in the underlying operating system, as well as by the need to ensure that its users can continue to use the word processor to revise old documents. These restraints leave open the possibility that a new entrant can latch on to a new (and superior) operating system with a superior word processor. As a consequence, we should not be surprised that network markets are beset with serial monopolies, or one dominant producer after the other.

In short, first movers are not as protected from outside competitive assaults as has been supposed, which is why the Tellis/Golder findings should not have come as a big surprise.

CONCLUDING COMMENTS

Tipping is one of those concepts that should have been a core component of economic analysis long before its relatively recent inclusion. After all, network effects do exist, which are good reasons for consumers to gravitate toward a network that is either dominant or shows promise of becoming dominant. Market dominance can imply added consumer welfare for consumers who join the network.

However, the lesson of this chapter is straightforward: We must be careful not to exaggerate the economic consequences of the prospects of market tipping. Perhaps tipping can, from a strictly theoretical perspective, lead from time to time to "inferior" products or services being adopted, with the market choices exhibiting permanence. But then we have to ask, how often has this happened? How long has the inferior choice prevailed?

Examples of such perverse market outcomes favored by proponents of this kind of market failure—the QWERTY keyboard and VHS video format—are not convincing examples of inferior products being chosen, as Liebowitz and Margolis have shown. Claims that first movers in markets have market advantages that they can exploit are equally weak when tested against real-world experience, as Tellis and Golder have stressed. From the available evidence, dominant firms in markets that have tipped their way seem to be able to maintain their dominance by remaining competitive in both the pricing of their products and in technological innovation. The Tellis/Golder study teaches an old economic lesson: Firms that see market tipping, and the attendant economies of scale in demand, as newfangled forms of market protection and, accordingly, do not remain competitive are firms that are subject to replacement in the not-too-distant future.

Furthermore, the underlying argument for inferior market choices has its own flaws. It fails to adequately appreciate the fact that a choice that is truly inferior to a significant (not just trivial or minor) degree means that there are consumer and producer gains to be had from the market moving to the superior technology. To assume that consumers will remain locked into an inferior market choice, when there is a materially better option available, fails to recognize that producers—network sponsors—have an incentive to find ways to move consumers from the inferior to the superior network. Those who argue that inferior market outcomes are possible, if not likely, often point to the existence of switching costs that prevent network sponsors from shifting the market to the new, superior network. As will be seen in the next chapters, even this argument has its own limitations.

NOTES

1. Dwight Lee and I have taken up the more technical issues surrounding the prospects of consumer lock-ins, implied in the tipping and path dependency theories, in a journal article and conclude, with the help of a mathematical model, that lock-ins are not necessarily bad for consumers. See Dwight R. Lee and Richard B. McKenzie, "A Case for Letting a Firm Take Advantage of 'Locked-In' Consumers," *Hastings Law Journal* 52 (April 2001): 795–812.

2. Jeffrey H. Rohlfs, *Bandwagon Effects in High Technology Industries* (Cambridge: MIT Press, 2001), chap. 6.

3. David S. Evans, Albert Nichols, and Bernard Reddy, "The Rise and Fall of Leaders in Personal Computer Software" (Cambridge, Mass.: National Economic Research Associates, January 7, 1999), 4.

4. Ibid.

5. Ibid.

6. Rohlfs, *Bandwagon Effects*, chap. 8.

7. Ibid., 86.

8. Ibid.

9. This section is based on Rohlfs, *Bandwagon Effects*, chap. 10.

10. For details on VHS and Beta sales during the 1970s and 1980s, see Michael A. Cusumano, Yiorgos Mylonadis, and Richard S. Rosenbloom, "Strategic Maneuvering

and Mass-Market Dynamics: The Triumph of VHS over Beta," *Business History Review* 66 (Spring 1992): 51–94.

11. W. Brian Arthur, *Increasing Returns and Path Dependence in the Economy* (Ann Arbor: University of Michigan Press, 1994), 10.

12. W. Brian Arthur, "Increasing Returns and the New World of Business," *Harvard Business Review* 74 (July–August 1996): 102.

13. Ibid.

14. Arthur, *Increasing Returns*, xvii; and Paul A. David, "Clio and the Economics of QWERTY," *American Economic Review* 75, no. 2 (1985): 332–337.

15. Stan J. Liebowitz and Stephen E. Margolis, "The Fable of the Keys," *Journal of Law and Economics* 33 (April 1990): 2.

16. Ibid., 4–5. Indeed, according to Liebowitz and Margolis, "[T]ypewriter manufacturers were an important source of trained typists for at least the first fifty years of that technology" (p. 5).

17. Ibid., 4.

18. Stan J. Liebowitz, *Re-Thinking the Network Economy* (New York: American Management Association, 2002), 157–158.

19. See Stan J. Liebowitz and Stephen E. Margolis, "Network Externality: An Uncommon Tragedy," *Journal of Economic Perspectives* 8 (Spring 1994): 133–150.

20. Joel I. Klein et al., *United States v. Microsoft Corporation*, Complaint, First District Court, Civil Action No. 98-1232, May, 20, 1998, as found at ¶58, http://www.usdoj.gov/atr/cases/f1700/1763.htm.

21. Arthur details the evolutionary history of the operating system, in much the same way that has been done, noting that the DOS/IBM combination came to dominate the market, but then he concedes, "It was not predictable in advance" ("Increasing Returns," 102).

22. Ibid.

23. "Study: Majority of 25 Leaders in 1923 Still on Top," *Advertising Age* (1983): 32.

24. See Gregory S. Carpenter and Kent Nakamoto, "Consumer Preference Formation and Pioneering Advantage," *Journal of Marketing Research* 26 (August 1989): 285–298; Joseph S. Bain, *Barriers to New Competition* (Cambridge: Harvard University Press, 1956); Frank M. Bass and Thomas L. Pilon, "A Stochastic Brand Choice Framework for Econometric Modeling of Time Series Market Share Behavior," *Journal of Marketing Research* 17 (November 1980): 486–497; and Rajiv Lal and Paddy Padmanabhan, "Competitive Response and Equilibria," *Marketing Science* 14, no. 3 (1995): G101–G108.

25. Andrew S. Grove, *Only the Paranoid Survive: How to Exploit the Crisis Points That Challenge Every Company* (New York: Doubleday, 1996), 51.

26. Gerald J. Tellis and Peter N. Golder, *Will and Vision: How Latecomers Grow to Dominate Markets* (New York: McGraw-Hill, 2002).

7

Switching Costs

The costs that consumers must incur to switch from one product to another—or switching costs—are widely viewed as sources of monopoly power, a form of entry barrier on par with brand loyalty,
exclusive franchises, patents, and copyrights, that should everywhere and always be expected to lead to market inefficiency. Switching costs in computer
markets, for example, can include the expenditures computer users must
make for new hardware and software, as well as the time spent searching out
alternative products and then retraining on the new products, when they
move from one computer platform to another. These switching costs reduce,
presumably, the sensitivity of computer users to price increases for the platform they are currently using, which should be expected to result in higher-
than-competitive prices. IBM-compatible personal computer owners who
use Windows might endure a price for Windows above the price of an alternative operating system, say, Apple's Mac, because the cost of staying with
Windows could still be less than the costs of switching. When switching costs
make switching prohibitive, consumers are said to be "locked in."

Economists Alan Beggs and Paul Klemperer write that "switching costs
give firms a degree of monopoly power over their customers and so make current market shares an important determinant of future profits."[1] These switching costs are believed to protect producers on both the supply and the demand
sides of the market. Management professor Michael Porter reasons that firms
are protected on the supply side because "a barrier to entry is created by

switching costs."[2] Joseph Farrell and Carl Shapiro see the protection coming from the demand side:

> The relationship-specific assets [associated with finding and establishing a working tie with a new supplier] create *switching costs* for a buyer changing from one supplier to another. Evidently, such brand loyalty gives the seller some monopoly power: in the absence of effective long-term contracts a buyer is open to exploitation by an opportunistic seller who could raise the price above competitors' by an amount almost equal to the buyer's switching costs (emphasis in original).[3]

Presumably, switching costs should be associated with increased earnings, a relationship that researchers found in the case of Norwegian banking.[4]

Switching costs are no longer a matter of interest only to theoreticians, mainly because of the prominent role switching costs came to play in the Microsoft antitrust suit. In its original complaint filed in May 1998 against Microsoft, the Justice Department argued that Microsoft was fully aware of the monopoly role switching costs could play in its attempt to destroy Netscape's Internet browser, Navigator. This awareness was self-evident, according to the Justice Department, in the communications of Microsoft executives:

> Microsoft's Megan Bliss and Rob Bennett recognized that designing Windows 95 "to win the browser battle" required "a very substantial set of trade-offs." Nevertheless, they concluded the "key factors to keep in mind" were, first, the need to increase browser share and, second, that the way to do that was: "Leveraging our strong share on the desktop will make switching costs high (if they get our technology by default on every desk then they'll be less inclined to purchase a competitive solution)."[5]

In his testimony for the government in the Microsoft case, MIT economist Frederick Warren-Boulton provided a more complete explanation of the underlying theory:

> A second barrier both to entry [in addition to the barrier created by the development costs of a new operating system] and to expansion by an existing competitor is that users tend to become "locked in" to a particular operating systems [*sic*]. . . . [U]sers are reluctant to switch from Windows to another operating system, even another PC operating system, because to do so requires them to replace application software, to convert files, and to learn how to operate the new software. Often, switching operating systems also means re-

placing or modifying hardware. Businesses can face even greater switching costs, as they must integrate PCs using the new operating systems and application software within their PC networks and train their employees to use the new software. Accordingly, both personal and corporate consumers are extremely reluctant to change PC operating systems. The software "lock-in" phenomenon creates a barrier to entry for new PC operating systems to the extent that consumers' estimate of the switching costs is large relative to the perceived incremental value of the new operating system.

Additional switching costs arise from the fact that, for most users, operating systems are only a means to an end—it is the application software that was designed to work with the operating system that users want. Once they have purchased an operating system, users are naturally reluctant to consider a different operating system. Unless their current operating system product prevents them from using new applications or hardware, they are likely to continue to use that operating system; for operating systems, unlike other goods, do not wear out.[6]

And the trial judge, Thomas Penfield Jackson, found that Microsoft has "market power" that, as the government lawyers and witnesses had argued, was founded on switching costs that emanated in part from the existence of seventy-thousand Windows applications, which formed the "applications barrier to entry."[7] More specifically, the judge argued:

> Since only Intel-compatible PC operating systems will work with Intel-compatible PCs, a consumer cannot opt for a non-Intel-compatible PC operating system without obtaining a non-Intel-compatible PC. Thus, for consumers who already own an Intel-compatible PC system, the cost of switching to a non-Intel compatible PC operating system includes the price of not only a new operating system, but also a new PC and new peripheral devices. It also includes the effort of learning to use the new system, the cost of acquiring a new set of compatible applications, and the work of replacing files and documents that were associated with the old applications. Very few consumers would incur these costs in response to the trivial increase in the price of an Intel-compatible PC system that would result from even a substantial increase in the price of an Intel-compatible PC operating system. For example, users of Intel-compatible PC operating systems would not switch in large numbers to the Mac OS in response to even a substantial, sustained increase in the price of an Intel-compatible PC operating system.[8]

Because of existing switching costs and the applications barrier to entry, the judge concluded that Microsoft's anticompetitive practices (mainly its predatory pricing of Internet Explorer at zero) "created a dangerous probability of achieving the objective of monopoly power in the relevant market."[9]

In such legal discussions of switching costs, there is the underlying presumption that switching costs are always and everywhere bad. The greater the switching costs, the lower the elasticity of the demand that the producer faces (or the lower the responsiveness of consumers to an increase in price), which means that the greater the switching costs, the greater the monopoly power and the further removed the price of the product will be from the (efficiency-maximizing) competitive level. Hence, the greater the switching costs, the greater the market inefficiency.

But is the impact of switching costs so simple? Not really. As it turns out, such conclusions may be warranted only when the products are developed (not before development costs are incurred), when the marginal cost of production is positive (not when the marginal cost is zero), and when buyers and sellers are not able to adjust to the prospects that switching costs make for monopoly pricing currently and in the future—and not when buyers and sellers can expect the continuance of monopoly pricing and can adjust their behavior in anticipation of switching costs leading to monopoly prices.

In this chapter, I review points relating to switching costs made by others assuming that there is some positive marginal cost of production for firms that produce goods subject to switching costs. Contrary to what might be expected, these authors have found that under certain plausible circumstances, switching costs can be expected to encourage, not discourage, entry into markets. Indeed, paradoxically, switching costs can, at times, lead to too much market entry.

I then extend the work of others to consider the case of markets for digital goods, meaning goods like software, that are produced electronically with 1's and 0's. In a market for a digital good, as widely recognized, the marginal cost each producer faces is normally assumed to be constant at zero (or very close to zero), given that such goods can be copied electronically with little in the way of material resources involved. As noted before, Dell can use its master copy of Windows to reproduce Windows on every computer it sells in a matter of two minutes.

I conclude that when there are no "natural" switching costs in markets where the marginal cost of production is zero, buyers and sellers will solve the problem of getting digital goods produced by the creation of "unnatural" switching costs through contracts (as long as the costs of contracting are not as high as the switching costs). Hence, it follows that for two reasons natural switching costs do not, under market conditions of zero marginal cost, necessarily add to market inefficiency. First, as others have found, switching costs can, within limits, drive down prices and increase output over and above what it would be in the absence of entry and switching costs. Second, if there were no switching costs, then switching costs would be created to get the products produced. Indeed, I argue that at times switching costs, like those that grow out of network effects, can be positively productive in the sense that they make possible the production of some goods, like many digital goods, that would not otherwise be produced.

MONOPOLY PRICING WITH SWITCHING COSTS

If there is only one firm in the market selling to all consumers, with no likelihood of additional consumers joining the market, and if there are prohibitive entry costs for producers and switching costs for consumers, then a single existing seller would be a full-fledged monopolist that could and would be expected to raise its price to the monopoly level. There is absolutely no reason to expect the firm to do otherwise. Its consumers are locked in. There is nothing for consumers to do other than to pay the price charged. There is no alternative source of supply inside the market, and the entry costs will prevent another supply source from entering the market when the sole seller in the market decides to restrict sales to raise its prices and profits.

Even if other firms could enter, the consumers would be prevented from switching to the new entrants by the prohibitive switching costs. The existing consumers are basically locked in completely. And assuming there are no new consumers who are not yet locked in coming into the market that the existing producer or new entrants could attract and, because of the prohibitive switching costs, could trap into continued sales, the monopolist has the consumers cornered on all scores. As explained earlier, the monopolist's restricted sales would result in market inefficiency in the sense that consumers would be willing to buy additional units of the good at prices above the firm's marginal cost of production, but consumers will not be given a chance to buy those additional units because the monopolist would not find selling the additional units profitable, given that the monopolist would have to lower its price on all units sold (which means that the monopolist would only sell the additional units if it could engage in price discrimination).

If the incumbent firm, the monopolist, were inclined to pursue some goal other than profit maximization—for example, sales maximization just to be known as a large (and possibly a benevolent or socially responsible) firm, which would require it to charge below-monopoly prices—it would not likely pursue its goal for long. This is because the firm's stock price would be suppressed by the absence of monopoly profits (and possibly losses), which means that investors could buy the stock at the low price, return the firm's policy back to monopoly pricing, and then sell the stock for a capital gain.

Nature of Market Conditions

However, it must be noted that I draw these conclusions about the market power of the incumbent producer from several very strong assumptions about the plight of consumers and possible entrants into the market. Are the market conditions specified—that consumers are totally locked in and entrants are locked out—likely? The answer is probably not.

First, note that in my example, the consumers are locked in from the start, and markets normally evolve from a more primitive setting, one in which a product is introduced and then the producer must work to attract consumers who can be expected to evaluate as best they can the immediate and long-term costs and benefits of buying the product. Granted, consumers' ability to make such evaluations is not perfect; mistakes are likely. The world is imperfect (which is the main reason they can be expected to engage in cost–benefit calculations in the first place). But that is no reason to assume that the only price consumers consider is the initial price, or just the benefits from their initial purchases. This is especially true when consumers know they will be locked in, or can expect to be locked in, or may have to incur high switching costs later to move away from the product. As are producers (monopolists?), consumers are quite capable, to one degree or another, of seeing the potential for being locked in, projecting forward, and seeing the potential for future monopoly pricing. After all, many consumers of products are not hapless individuals but are firms that are no less savvy, and have no less incentive to make profit-maximizing decisions, than the monopolists themselves. Indeed, many consumers are firms that act as surrogates for their own buyers. Hence, you can expect the more serious the threat of lock-in, the more careful consumers can expect to be in determining what they buy. The potential losses from mistakes can be long-standing in cases of lock-ins.

Second, note that in the earlier example, the producer has already obtained the sole-producer position. Again, monopolies do not normally just appear out of nowhere. They very likely emerge from an initial competitive process. This can be especially true for markets that harbor the potential for consumers being locked in. This potential translates into later monopoly prices and profits.

As several economists have recognized, the prospects of the consumers' supplier charging monopoly prices in the future that they, the consumers, cannot avoid paying will affect their initial demand for the good and the initial price they are willing to pay, since those expected higher-than-competitive prices in the future will be a part of the good's calculated cost.[10] And their assessed cost from consuming the good over time will be in terms of their present discounted value. This means that their assessed cost will be a function of the timing of the future higher prices, the consumers' discount rate, and the likelihood that the anticipated switching costs will hold into the future.

The more immediate the expected monopoly prices, the greater the assessed costs of staying with the product (which I call "staying costs") and the lower consumers' current demand for the product. Also, the lower the consumer discount rate, the lower the assessed staying cost and the greater their initial demand in spite of the prospects of later monopoly prices. If people adjust their internal discount rates, which they use to develop present values for future costs, to market interest rates, then a fall in market interest rates can give rise to a decrease in the present value of the staying cost relative to the switching costs. Hence, a decline in interest rates generally can give rise to a greater current demand for the product.

If consumers can expect to be trapped by their switching costs with 100 percent certainty, nothing more need be said about their assessed cost of being exploited in the future. However, the future is always uncertain to one extent or another. Unknown new entrants might develop means of easing consumers' future switching costs. To the extent that the probability of switching costs going down in the future goes up, consumers' initial demand will be greater than if the switching costs are expected to remain constant over time. The reason is that the expected present value of the future monopoly prices goes down with the likelihood that future switching costs will be going down.

Similarly, the prospects of later monopoly prices and profits will motivate producers to enter the initial competitive fray to become the monopolist selling to the locked-in consumers. In short, the options from which consumers can choose at the start will be affected by their prospects of being exploited later, and there is every reason to expect the consumers to pick and choose among their initial options carefully, listening to the deals the potential monopolists propose. The initial competitive fray for the later monopoly profits will likely lead to the producers offering low upfront prices, even prices that are below their costs. As explained earlier in this book, producers can figure that if they can achieve initial sales at below-cost prices, they can recoup their initial losses with later "monopoly profits."

The greater the potential for later "monopoly prices," the greater likelihood of initial price wars and of upfront losses from initial below-cost prices, as Paul Klemperer has shown.[11] This is because the initial competition would be intensified by the potential for later and greater "monopoly profits." It follows that the higher the switching costs, the greater the later "monopoly profits," which, in turn, leads to the conclusion that the greater the switching costs, the more intense the upfront competition for the monopoly position, the lower the upfront prices, and the lower the upfront profits (or greater the upfront losses) for those firms initially vying to become the "monopolist." Of course, to the extent that network effects affect future demand, as well as the extent of the lock-in of consumers, the more compelling it is for the potential "monopolists" to initially lower their prices and profits (or incur losses).

Monopoly Prices and Profits Reconsidered

I have begun to put monopoly profits, monopoly prices, and monopolist in quotes for a reason that has become more transparent as the analysis has unfolded. Those terms do not, in the context presented, carry their usual meaning, that consumers are necessarily harmed by the firm that becomes the sole producer, charging what appear to be "monopoly prices" and garnering what appear to be "monopoly profits"—or meaning the eventual sole producer earns over time a higher-than-competitive rate of return on its investment. In actuality, the eventual sole producer may not, over time, earn a rate of return that is above the competitive level. This is because it can effectively dissipate its expected, future "monopoly profits" in the upfront competition to become the sole producer that caters to consumers who can expect to become locked in.

In total dollar terms, the sole producer's later "monopoly profits" might be greater than the firm's initial losses due to below-cost pricing. However, the difference should be attributable in part to the interest payments incurred on loans that must be taken out to incur the upfront losses. In addition, when the sole producer was initially competing with other producers to become the sole producer, there was some probability that it would not be the winner, which means it would not be able to recoup its upfront losses, and that its customers would not be forever locked in. In short, some of the later "monopoly profits" recorded on the firm's books would not be profits at all, but the recovering of risk costs that were incurred earlier. This means that when both interest and risk costs are added into the equation, the sole producer may be expected to earn close to a competitive rate of return on its investment (allowing for imperfections in calculations). If the expected rate of return were substantially removed from the competitive rate of return, then it would follow that the upfront competition to be the sole producer would be heightened, and would drive up the upfront losses and drive down the upfront expected rate of return.

It follows that firms that expect to price their products to exploit their locked-in consumers with later "monopoly prices" are not necessarily doing anything that, on balance, would be deemed objectionable by their consumers. Granted, consumers might prefer to not be confronted with future high switching costs and "monopoly prices," but if high switching costs are a part of the nature of the market, then what they get in terms of initial below-cost prices, followed by later "monopoly prices," may be as good as it gets in the real world. As good as it gets as a standard for judging the attractiveness of market outcomes may not measure up well with some notion of efficiency under conditions of perfect competition. At the same time, perfect competition is hardly a realistic standard for judging markets (especially when talking about presumed market failures), given that such a market standard implies perfection, which is not achievable. Markets necessarily operate in imperfect worlds; they are designed to help consumers and producers overcome some of the observed imperfections. No one can start an analysis of a market by assuming the existence of switching costs (or the potential for lock-ins), forms of market imperfection, and then assume that market outcomes must meet an efficiency standard that can only be achieved by perfect market conditions.

THE CREDIBILITY PROBLEM

It might be thought that consumer and producer welfare can be enhanced if the firms that initially compete to become the sole producer for the locked-in consumers could commit themselves to never charging above-competitive prices in the future. However, a part of the expected gains from such commitments, if they could be made credible, will be dissipated. If firms could make the required commitments credible, consumers' initial demand would be expected to rise. Moreover, given that the producers would be committing themselves to lower future profits, producers would be less willing to offer upfront price concessions. Consumers might get lower future prices, but that gain can be expected to be offset, at least partially, by higher-than-otherwise upfront prices.

Besides, many firms will have a tough time making their commitments credible. This will be especially true for startups in new industries like high-tech/Internet-based industries. Because they are new, startups do not have a track record of holding to their commitments, and, accordingly, few might give their commitments the requisite credibility. The startups could simply be lying. Consumers will understand that the firms have good reason to lie: The firms' lies, if believed, can lead to higher initial prices than they would otherwise be able to charge and, hence, to higher upfront profits (or lower upfront losses). Consumers can also figure that if the firms held to their commitments in the future, as I have explained, the firms' future stock value would suffer on the exchanges, given that they would not then be earning the monopoly profits that are achievable. Investors could buy the stock and renege on past commitments by charging higher prices, and then the investors could sell out for a capital gain.

Firms might be expected to overcome their credibility problems with contracts that specify exactly what the firms will charge initially and in the future. However, contracts are themselves imperfect, with the firm's credibility being undermined to the extent of the imperfections. But it should be recognized that contracts are likely to be given greater credibility for very simple goods, like bolts, than more complex goods, like operating systems. With bolts, there is not much the firm can do to change the effective price of the product other than to change its stated price, which could be easily construed as a violation of the contract, enforceable by the courts.

However, for operating systems, or other products that are sophisticated and complex, and that are constantly improved, the effective price can be changed in a multitude of ways. The ticket price might be held constant while service is withdrawn or features are changed. Indeed, if the contract specifies the price but cannot specify the quality of the good produced, and if during the contract period the price ever becomes binding on the seller, which would be the case when the forces of supply and demand dictate a higher market price, the contracted price can press the seller to undercut the quality of the good.[12] Also, the courts might not hold all such changes as violations of the contract, mainly because quality is so hard to define in legally defensible terms, thereby undermining the contract's credibility. And to the extent that the credibility of the contract is undermined, the firms vying to become the sole monopoly supplier have to resort to cutting their upfront prices to once again achieve market dominance.

HIGH SWITCHING COSTS

To this point, I have assumed that the consumers who are in the market for the good with switching costs remain in the market, forever locked in because of prohibitive switching costs, and that no new consumers ever enter the market. Under such conditions, switching costs amount to a prohibitive barrier to entry, given that new producers cannot enter the market and attract away a portion of the consumers, even when the sole producer charges monopoly prices.

These starting assumptions are unrealistic, of course. Switching costs are never likely to be prohibitive, meaning consumers will not switch no matter what price is charged. Even in the case of computer platforms, switching costs might be high, but they are hardly prohibitive. The cost of moving from the Wintel platform to the Apple platform might be several thousand dollars, given the need for new equipment, software, and retraining. However, the costs might not be as high as might be initially imagined, given that consumers can minimize the costs incurred by switching when they schedule an upgrade in their computer systems. The fact that switching costs in computer platforms are less than prohibitive is evident by the fact that at least some computer users switch all the time among alternative computer platforms, and there might be even more switching than if both platform sponsors did not consider the prospects of consumers switching in establishing their pricing policies. Indeed, when switching costs are less than prohibitive, the monopoly price that the sole producer might charge can be limited by the switching costs. This is the case because monopolies, as noted, impose staying costs through their monopoly pricing. Even monopolies cannot charge their consumers so much that the staying costs are greater than the switching costs. If they did, consumers would then switch.

It follows that if switching costs are prohibitive, the sole producer will engage in clear-cut monopoly pricing, because the switching costs will then be higher than the staying costs embedded in the firm's monopoly price. Besides, there is no alternative producer to which consumers can switch. If switching costs are just high, making the staying costs embedded in the monopoly price higher than the switching costs, the firm will engage in what is called "limit pricing." That is to say, the firm will choose a price that ensures that consumers' staying costs are just below the switching costs, hence, ensuring that their consumers do not switch.

Recognizing the importance of switching costs, which are not high enough to prevent possible new entrants from entering the market, possible new entrants might start paying consumers to make the switch to them, which is one indirect way new entrants can reduce consumers' (net) switching costs. For example:

- In 1998, to help potential customers defray the switching cost of shifting their banking from tellers to online banking, Chase Bank offered its customers $25 for each of the first five online transactions they made.

- Another way to encourage switching is to give new customer discounts or some in-kind benefit. In the early 1990s, when Microsoft was seeking to dethrone WordPerfect from its dominance of the word-processing market, Microsoft gave WordPerfect users deep discounts on their purchases of Word. In 1995, Microsoft gave the deepest of all discounts when it lowered the price of Internet Explorer to zero in its efforts to get Netscape Navigator users to switch to Internet Explorer.
- In 1999, after it set up its auction Web site to compete with eBay.com, Amazon.com offered book customers a $10 gift certificate on their first auction purchase. In 2001, when it wanted to encourage software buyers to download their purchased programs, Amazon offered $10 off their advertised price for first-time downloaders. Similarly, Drugstore.com offered its first-time customers a $20 discount on any order (even for products that cost $20, meaning that customers only had to pay the shipping cost).
- Most major airlines do what American Airlines does: They offer people who open new frequent-flyer accounts a starting balance of five thousand miles, which have some economic value, given that the miles can be used toward free trips or ticket upgrades.

Of course, entrenched producers will try to counter such switching deals with competitive offers of their own, which can give rise to potential new entrants sweetening their switching offers. If all else fails, many existing businesses, protected by switching costs of one degree or another, can be expected to turn to government for laws and regulations that make switching to competitors' products costly, an approach that has a dishonorable tradition going back, perhaps, to when government was invented. Electric generating plants, which have had to face the problem of high upfront investments with low marginal costs of production, have been given exclusive franchises by state governments and then regulated to, supposedly, prevent the development of monopoly prices. Back in the 1920s, the Horse and Mule Association of America lobbied to prevent trucks from using public roads and was successful for a time in preventing cars from being parked on major city streets. With the advent of the Internet, car dealerships and their trade associations have prevented consumers in all fifty states from customizing and ordering cars from strictly online dealers (or dealers who can buy the cars they sell directly from the automobile manufacturers). Optometrists in Maine have gotten their state legislature to prevent consumers from reordering contact lenses online.[13]

The upfront payments and discounts are normally modest because new entrants do not have to cover all switching costs. This is because of the incumbent's limit pricing. All the new entrants have to do is make up the difference between consumers' switching costs and their staying costs, given the incumbent's limit pricing, plus a little extra to make sure the customers gain from making the switch. Of course, the threat of new entrants making the payments to consumers who switch will further limit the entrenched sole producer's pricing, given its expectation that its more restrictive limit pricing will discourage entry by hiking the entrants' costs.

THE IMPACT OF NEW CUSTOMERS

To this point the stock of customers has been assumed to be unchanging. Markets are generally much more fluid than that, given that consumers are always coming and going (through deaths and births, if nothing else) from most markets. Nevertheless, my initial (unrealistic) assumption of no change in the consumer base has allowed me to make several important points, not the least of which is that even when a given body of consumers are locked in, it does not follow, necessarily, that they will not feel the pain of full monopoly exploitation, meaning that consumers will not necessarily have to pay prices that ensure that producers will earn full monopoly profits (given that future monopoly prices can be offset by early low prices). Indeed, in the long run, consumers and producers might be better off with a combination of low upfront prices, followed by later monopoly prices. This would be the case when the initial low prices would help speed the development of the network effects and the greater long-run consumer demand, which means that, in spite of the monopoly prices charged in the future, consumers would have more consumer surplus.

If we, again, change our assumption and allow switching costs but, at the same time, allow for new consumers to enter the market—a far more realistic assumption—does it follow that entry will be barred or even discouraged by the switching costs? I have noted that the Justice Department and judge in the Microsoft case have concluded that in the operating system market switching costs amount to a barrier to entry. Similarly, in the IBM antitrust case, which lasted for thirteen years, from 1969 until it was dropped in 1982, the government contended, according to economists who watched the trial closely, that "the lack of transferability of software from machines of one manufacturer to those of another has constituted a substantial barrier to entry."[14]

Is that really the case? Princeton economists Joseph Farrell and Carl Shapiro say no, at least not in a market with new consumers coming in all the time, where price discrimination between new and old consumers is not practical, and where there are no scale economies.[15] They reason that if there is a sole producer in such a market that initially has the market locked up because its consumers are locked in, that sole producer is on the horns of an interesting pricing dilemma with the advent of new consumers. To bring those new consumers into its fold and to, so to speak, lock them up also, the monopolist would have to lower its price for all of the reasons given earlier, to offset the firm's future monopoly prices that would be charged the new consumers. However, unless the firm has the power to price discriminate among new and old consumers (and that might be very difficult to do, given the potential for resale of many goods), it will have to lower its price to its old consumers when it offers new consumers a lower price, and it would gain no cost advantage in expanding its sales (assuming the absence of scale economies, an assumption that will be dropped shortly). If the flow of new consumers into the market is ongoing and the firm always tries to maintain its market dominance, then the firm can always be charging a low initial price, and never reaping the monopoly profits that would inspire the initial low prices, which would negate the firm's incentive to lower its price in the first place.

Accordingly, the incumbent firm can understandably reason that it is best for it to hold its price high for its initial customers, who would have to endure switching costs, thereby making at least some monopoly profits off of them. In doing that, the firm would be forsaking the opportunity to maintain its total dominance of its market. This means, of course, that in choosing to hold its price high for its existing customer base, it encourages the entry of new firms who can sell to the new consumers. It follows that in fluid markets, in which consumers are both entering and leaving, the most profitable pricing strategy can lead to a shrinking market share for the once monopoly producer.

However, it should be noted these conclusions necessarily depend on how rapidly consumers are entering the market. The more rapid the increase in new consumers, the greater the potential gains to the incumbent from lowering its price and selling to the new customers, and the greater the likelihood that the incumbent will lower its price to attract new customers. In short, when markets are rapidly expanding, such as what happened in the Internet browser market in the 1990s and into the 2000s, you would expect firms to charge highly competitive prices in spite of switching costs.

Also, it needs to be stressed that the foregoing conclusions depend on an assumption of no scale economies from expanded sales. If there are scale economies, then the incumbent firm might try to attract the new consumers with a lower price. This would be true, however, only as long as its cost savings from greater sales were greater than the price reduction. If the price reduction required to attract the new consumers were greater than the cost savings from expanded sales, then the incumbent would stick with its old customers, charging them a higher price. This means that an entrant with higher production costs than the incumbent could enter the market and survive. Farrell and Shapiro conclude, surprisingly, that there can be too much entry, or that such entry is inefficient, since the incumbent could better serve the market at lower cost, if the switching costs allowed the incumbent to do that. The inefficiency of entry, spurred as it is in part by switching costs, is compounded when there are network effects. The new entrant can, with lower prices, break up the established network, reducing the value of the network to consumers. (However, I have put inefficient in quotes above because the outcome envisioned by Farrell and Shapiro might not be a practical option, given real-world switching-cost constraints.)

In addition, it is possible that the new entrant might have lower costs than the incumbent, but still create an inefficiency by moving into the market.[16] This is because the reduction in consumer welfare due to the breakup of the network can be greater than the lower cost of the new entrant. In a world of no switching costs, the new lower-cost entrant would be able to supplant the higher-cost incumbent. However, the switching costs will prevent the incumbent's consumers from moving to the new entrant. For the new entrant to add to market efficiency, its cost advantage over the incumbent would have to be greater than the incumbent consumers' switching costs, which would enable the entrant to lower its price sufficiently to make the consumers' staying costs greater than their switching costs.

FIRMS' SWITCHING COSTS

Consumers' switching costs are often discussed as if they are an unmitigated blessing to incumbent firms because switching costs, to one degree or another, lock in consumers. However, that is not always the case. Switching costs can also lock in firms to given technologies, which can undermine their market position.[17] I have noted that the switching costs can curb firms' efforts to attract new consumers. Switching costs can also cause the firm to curb its innovations. This is because the incumbent firm that develops a new, innovative, even superior product will, like new entrants, have to face the prospect that its customers will incur costs in switching to its new, innovative, and superior product. The firm will, like new entrants, have to lower its price to get its consumers to make the switch. This problem is real for dominant producers like Microsoft, and it has shown up in what is an amazing statistic: In 2000, only 16 percent of Windows users had made the switch to Windows 98, the then latest version of Windows. This means that 84 percent of Windows users were using earlier versions. A fifth of all Windows users were using

Windows 3.1 or earlier versions (which Microsoft no longer supported in 2000), and some users had not upgraded from MS-DOS. Why? A plausible reason is that the switching costs were greater than the added benefits.

It follows that if a firm engages in the required R&D to get a new product developed, it must be assured that either the enhancement in the value of the new product must be greater than its customers' switching costs, and/or the reduction in the cost of production must be greater than its customers' switching costs. A rule follows: The greater the switching costs, the greater must be the value added of the new product and/or the greater the cost savings, which implies that the greater the switching costs, the greater will be the curb on innovation by the incumbent firm and the greater the opportunity for entry of new firms interested in selling to new consumers who have not yet been locked in by switching costs.

Microsoft (or any other software company, such as Sun or Oracle, with a broad customer base) faces many of these problems, given its high market share in the operating system market (and, for that matter, in the office suite market). The company executives realize that their customer base must incur switching costs every time it introduces new versions of Windows (or Office). The greater the switching costs to the new version, the greater the customer resistance to moving to the new version. If switching costs rise with customer enhancements, Microsoft must be assured that its enhancements' value to its customers is greater than the added switching costs. At some point, the rise in switching costs as enhancements are added will be greater than the added value, which means that the innovativeness of new versions will be choked off not so much by the company's ability to provide additional innovations, but by the added switching costs. If Microsoft does not develop versions of Windows with the added switching costs in mind, it will find it will have to lower the price it charges (to compensate for its customers' higher switching costs).

Microsoft's problems extend far beyond the direct concerns of its consumers. Applications developers must incur their own switching costs when they upgrade their applications for new versions of Windows. Higher switching costs for developers can lead to fewer applications for Windows, as well as lower network effects and a lower price and consumer benefits for Windows when there are fewer applications. If Microsoft enhances Windows too much, it can create switching costs that are so great that the company can create a market opening for new competitors.

Understandably, Microsoft will be forced (by market forces) to hesitate adding upgrades to Windows that it may know how to add until it can be assured that the upgrades add more to the product's value than they add to the switching costs the upgrades impose on its consumers and developers. Moreover, Microsoft's customers and developers would want Microsoft to, at times, not take the lead in its product development and redevelopment and wait until there is a critical mass (Bill Gates's wording) of consumers and developers interested in the enhancement. This is because taking the lead can add to customers' and developers' switching costs, at times unnecessarily, given that not all the leads the company takes for unproven enhancements can be expected to be successful, given switching and other costs.

Of course, if Microsoft does not take the lead on many potential operating system enhancements, it will likely be required to at times play the market game of catch-up, which means it may have to respond super aggressively to competitive threats that could make Windows appear dated.

Microsoft has been severely criticized for not being innovative and for stalling innovations in the operating systems market (as well as the office suite market). For example, Jim Clark, cofounder of Netscape, has tagged Microsoft for being the "master copier" for not only aping Netscape in the development of browsers, but also for adopting the "look and feel" of the Mac operating system and for including any number of other applets (for faxing, calculating, printing, drawing, and word processing) in Windows.[18] Perhaps Microsoft should have been the one to develop the first Web browser, but there is a plausible explanation for why the company may have waited until Mosaic, followed by Navigator, demonstrated the broad demand for a browser: switching costs. Had Microsoft built the first browser and integrated it into Windows in the early 1990s, before many people were browsing the Web, it would have added switching costs for its customers and developers at a time when the added benefits were uncertain and several years in the future. Understandably, Gates advocates an "embrace-and-extend" strategy on the inclusion of new applets in Windows, but, again, only after their demonstrated market has reached critical mass.[19]

In his book on the founding and development of Netscape, Jim Clark acknowledges that in developing Navigator, he understood that "Gates was like the evil Lord Sauron in J. R. R. Tolkien's Hobbit fable *The Fellowship of the Ring*, whose all-seeing eye searched ceaselessly for any threat to his tyranny."[20] He also acknowledged that he realized that when Gates and company decided to react to the Netscape threat, it would be with "with ferocity."[21] There is a plausible, albeit partial, two-word explanation for Clark's fears: switching costs. Microsoft might be expected to compensate for its enhancement delays by retaining corporate flexibility and by being willing to respond to competitive threats aggressively, meaning it could make up for lost time by pricing its products, like Internet Explorer (or other Windows enhancements), at very competitive levels, like zero or below.

Then again, in following such a strategy, dictated partially by market pressures such as switching costs, Microsoft has to risk suffering the potential cost of being hauled into court, as it was, for anticompetitive business tactics. However, such tactics can be viewed, not so much as those of a monopolist, but as those of a producer of a digital good in a market with significant switching costs that make more preemptive business tactics not only not profitable, but also not beneficial to its locked-in consumers and applications developers.

Dominant firms like Microsoft might face a much more fundamental long-term dilemma in the maintenance of their current market prominence that goes beyond mere enhancements. Microsoft might now know of a way to reconstruct the personal computer operating system that is truly revolutionary. However, the company might never develop the system for the same reason other developers might not develop it: It is too revolutionary. That is, it adds more switching costs than it adds value for its customer and developer base. This can mean that with fluid markets Microsoft's own reluctance to introduce revolutionary new versions of Windows can leave open a hole in the operating system market through which other firms can enter and take a slice of the market. In fact, because of switching costs, Microsoft might be caught asleep at the R&D wheel, missing altogether revolutionary changes in operating system technology (as it almost did in Web browsing), which means its technology and market position can be leapfrogged by some firm that is now unknown.

Given the rapid pace of technological development in computers, it should be no wonder that Gates professes to worry about how many times he can reinvent the company to thwart the erosion of his company's market position. When switching costs are a factor in determining market position, perhaps Andrew Grove is right to argue that "only the paranoid can survive" in the long run.[22]

THE VALUE ADDED OF SWITCHING COSTS

All too often switching costs are viewed in negative terms, understandably, given that any cost is something most people want to avoid incurring. The presumption is that the lower the switching costs, the better. However, to see how switching costs can add to consumer welfare, I need to return to the natural monopoly discussion in Chapter 3 on digital costs, and then see what would happen in such a market if there were no switching costs. To do this, reconsider a market for a digital good like an operating system for which there are high development costs, constant zero marginal costs of reproduction, and zero switching costs for consumers. As in the earlier discussion of natural monopoly, average cost will decline continuously as sales are expanded (given that average cost will equal the fixed development costs divided by the growing quantity).

Problems of Zero Marginal Cost and Network Effects

If two or more producers already have developed their operating systems, their average cost is of no consequence to their pricing strategies. Their development costs are what economists call "sunk cost," that is, already incurred and nonrecoverable. Given that the cost of reproduction is zero, the goal of each producer is to get as much revenue as possible. If two producers are dividing the market and there are no switching costs, it is in the interest of each to cut its price a little and take a larger share of the market, thus increasing its revenues, and its profits (or reducing its losses).

Even if they each were dividing the market and charging a price that allowed them to recover their upfront and fixed development costs, they each would have an incentive to cut the price they charged. Each could calculate that a price reduction would allow it to more than recover its development costs. Of course, each can figure that the other operating system producer would have the same price-cutting incentive, which means that each has an incentive to reduce its price to avoid having the other producer take its market share.

Network effects would intensify each firm's price-cutting incentive. As the price falls and sales rise currently, future demand will rise, increasing the long-run potential gains from achieving a greater market share. To the extent that network effects give rise to switching costs (as Judge Jackson thinks is the case with Windows, given the development, supposedly, of seventy thousand Windows applications), the initial price-cutting incentive of the firms would be heightened again, given that the switching costs would enable the winning firm to charge higher prices in the future.

The price might fall to where each operating system firm cannot possibly recover its development costs. Still, with zero marginal cost, each has an incentive to cut its price, as noted earlier in this book. The reason? Again, each firm's costs do not rise when more units are sold, and each firm can sell more and get more revenues than it would get by not cutting its price. If either firm drops out of the market, the remaining firm can then be certain that its losses equal its development costs. By staying in the market, no matter how low the price goes, it will get some revenue and reduce its losses from what they would be on withdrawal. This kind of reasoning, and the resulting competition, can lead to a price of practically zero. Again, the revenue received by a price just above zero will lead to a lower loss for the producer than dropping out of the market, meaning that both firms could be worse off than if one dropped out. The problem is that each has an incentive to stay in the market, with the resulting competition leading the firms to lose nearly all of their development costs.

The Danger of Reentry

The prospects of the price being forever pressed downward toward zero is very likely more acute for producers of digital goods than for many producers of nondigital goods. I can imagine that, for example, the market in a given local discount office supply retailer, such as Office Depot or Staples, has many of the properties of a natural monopoly. The market can be served most cost effectively by one retailer, say, Office Depot. Accordingly, Office Depot might be willing to engage in heavy upfront price-cutting as a way of beating out Staples for the most cost-effective market share. Office Depot can reason that once Staples withdraws from the market, it, Staples, will close up shop, sell off its retail property, and move elsewhere. The maintenance of unused retail outlets can be very expensive. Office Depot can figure it will then be somewhat protected from Staples's reentry, given that Staples will once again have to rebuild its base of operations, including the building of its store.

Markets for digital goods are far more fraught with the danger of reentry. This is because digital goods need never go away. Once they are produced, they can exist in digital form on a disk, forever ready to be copied again. Their storage costs are trivial. This means that if a digital firm ever beats a rival to become the sole producer, it will still have to worry about the beaten firm reentering the market at the slightest increase in its price. Again, the defeated firm (or firms) can figure the development costs are sunk. The firm's goal should remain to garner as much revenue as possible, which it can do if the surviving firm ever tries to raise its price high enough, for instance, to recover its development costs.

Then there are some digital markets, like the one for operating systems, in which the good in question—say, Windows—is sold with complementary products—say, Word, Excel, Access, or PowerPoint. In such markets, the company—Microsoft—can have an incentive to push its price of Windows below zero when challenged by a takeover firm. That is, Microsoft might propose, if pressed by competition to do so, to pay buyers to take its product, yielding negative prices, as explained earlier in this book. This is because it can recover some of its losses from negative prices on Windows from sales of its productivity applications that either increase or do not go down because of the negative prices.

Furthermore, the producer of a digital good must recognize that all copies of digital goods are potential masters, which means that every buyer is a potential supplier who does not even have development costs to recover. If the surviving digital firm seeks to recover its development costs, its higher prices can change potential suppliers into actual suppliers, putting additional downward pressure on the price.

Of course, if the firms understand their cost structures and the threat of perpetual zero (or close-to-zero) pricing, they can see ahead the losses they will incur from the price competition. They simply will be better off by not incurring the development costs without some guarantee that they will not have to face price competition that ends up with the price equal to practically zero, or any other price that does not allow the firm to recover its development costs. Each firm will try to make sure that if it incurs the development costs, its customers cannot easily move to some new entrant. If their customers can move to some new entrant with ease, the firm can figure that the resulting competition can result in prices close to zero, if not zero (with the product being commoditized), and in the firm not being able to recover its development costs.

In short, firms will try to make sure that before they develop their products, they will be able to at least recover their development costs. In most nondigital markets, a positive and rising marginal cost of production can be all the protection the firms need, given that the rising cost would put a floor on price competition. However, barring a positive and rising marginal cost of production, which is absent in the production of digital goods, the firms will understandably look to entry costs (the counterpart of barriers to entry) for the needed protection against an eventual zero (or close-to-zero) price. Barring barriers to entry, the firms will look to switching costs for the needed protection, which suggests that even entry barriers can serve a beneficial economic function in digital (or zero marginal cost) goods markets. They will also look for goods for which there are network effects, given that the network effects can add to their consumers' potential switching costs. Accordingly, these goods have an improved chance of being produced, which, as I have noted, can enhance the evolution of the network effects and can be a self-realizing expectation. In short, the common presumption (held by the Justice Department lawyers and the judge in the Microsoft case) is that network effects give rise to switching costs, but I posit here that the reverse can be the case, switching costs can give rise to network effects (or at least, their scope and the speed with which they are realized).

Product Development

From what I have said, it follows that the greater the development costs and the closer the marginal cost of production is to zero, the greater the need for entry and switching costs and the more likely firms will seek to create switching costs if switching costs do not exist as part of the "state of nature" in the market. These are points that the Justice Department and the judge in the Microsoft case do not seem to appreciate.

Brand Loyalty and Customer Relationship Management

Without sufficient entry and/or switching costs in some products, which will allow for the recovery of development costs in the face of zero marginal product costs, a form of market inefficiency will emerge: There will be too much development of products that have entry and switching costs, and too little development of products that do not have entry and/or switching costs. That is to say, the marginal value of the goods that are developed will be lower than the marginal value of the goods left undeveloped. But it should not be forgotten that the profit motive induces firms to find ways of constructing artificial entry and switching costs when they do not exist "naturally," that is, as a part of the nature of the market. One classic means of constructing entry and switching costs is for the firm to work hard at creating brand loyalty. The creation of brand loyalty may be costly to firms such as Microsoft, Amazon, and Intel, but it can also make the recovery of development costs (and then some) possible.

Another indirect way of creating entry and switching costs that has grown in use with the development of the Internet, and business-to-business E-commerce, has been dubbed "customer relationship management," or CRM, under which firms seek to create so-called customer intimacy.[23] Customer intimacy can be created in any number of ways, not the least of which is good old-fashioned schmoozing of buyers, making sure they are entertained and rewarded with gifts. Such schmoozing amounts to giving the buyers continuing payoffs from using their discretion over their firms' resources to stay with their suppliers (accordingly, it is in the interest of the supplying firms to make sure, with appropriate incentives and disincentives, that their employees do not abuse their discretionary authority). Airlines have used their frequent-traveler programs to create a form of "customer intimacy," ensuring that frequent travelers have private incentives—payoffs in the form of free trips—to not switch airlines.

Other suppliers can increase their customer intimacy by bringing their customers in on the firms' product development and production decisions, and by getting their customers to invest in those processes with ongoing payments that effectively increase their costs of shifting to other suppliers. Suppliers can also integrate their customers' "data gleaned from every distribution channel and customer touch point across the enterprise," a way of reducing their customers' ordering costs and thereby increasing their switching costs.[24]

Other Forms of Switching Costs

Another form of switching costs is to enter into contracts with buyers before they incur the development costs. Cellular phone companies, like Verizon, often give their new customers deep discounts on the cell phone—provided the customers sign a service contract for two or more years and agree to repay the discount on the phone they are allowed to keep, a concocted form of switching costs. They also make sure that their cell phone numbers are not portable, which means that customers contemplating a switch of service providers will have to incur the costs of telling their business contacts and friends their new number with their new service provider.

An incumbent firm might also increase the risk cost new entrants can expect to incur by simply building up a large cash reserve that can be used as a (price) war chest, meaning the cash reserves can signal potential entrants that the incumbent can outlast them in any price competition they choose to start. This can be one reason that, at this writing (early 2001), Microsoft has cash reserves of more than $27 billion.[25] That bankroll can be useful in buying up promising new technology, but it can also serve as a warning: Don't tread on this company's market turf.

Microsoft's Methods

Yet another way is through a more complex pricing strategy that might be interpreted as an antitrust violation. Indeed, in 1994, Microsoft was taken to court for its pricing of Windows. It gave computer makers deep discounts on the price of Windows if they agreed to pay Microsoft a royalty on every computer—not every copy of Windows—the computer makers sold. The Justice Department saw the pricing strategy as a way Microsoft could prevent entry, given that it increased the cost of computer makers switching from Windows to some other operating system, and thereby discouraged entry into the operating system market. Presumably, the Justice Department saw a form of market inefficiency in the pricing mechanism.

However, from the switching-cost perspective being developed here, it is not necessarily clear that the pricing strategy was anticompetitive in the sense that it was actually anticonsumer. Microsoft's pricing strategy could have been a way of reducing its risk costs of not being able to recover its development costs, by raising computer makers' switching costs. When Microsoft was prevented through a 1994 consent decree from using its per-computer pricing strategy in 1995 and thereafter, it is not at all clear that consumers gained. This is because the price Microsoft was forced to charge for each copy of Windows was very likely higher than before the consent decree, given that computer makers could no longer receive the discount they once enjoyed. In addition, it is not altogether clear that consumer switching costs were, on balance, lowered as much as the Justice Department and the judge might have expected. This is because the pricing strategy may have already had its intended effect, too early on in the development of the market for Windows to play on network effects that would lead to thousands of applications being written for Windows, which could have created all the switching costs Microsoft needed to justify incurring its substantial subsequent development costs.

Microsoft's incentive to maintain its market dominance, at that point in time, by maintaining the requisite entry and switching costs remained intact; only its permissible form was changed. To compensate for any lost advantage it did suffer through the 1994 consent decree, Microsoft could have redoubled its efforts to resurrect the then required entry switching costs through other methods. One such method may have been to pay even more attention to the development of brand loyalty and its applications network, as well as to add to its cash balance. Yet another method may have been to compete even more aggressively in fending off potential computer platform entrants. Its greater aggressiveness could have included the integration of its browser into Windows, thereby reducing the switching benefits (the mirror image of increasing switching costs) of computer users who may have contemplated moving to the Netscape/Java platform.

A digital firm that is the sole incumbent in its market can also deter entry, and thereby increase switching costs, by appropriately pricing its product. The hard question is how it should price its product, whether high or low? Both strategies can be used. A low price can signal potential entrants that the incumbent has low costs and suggest to them that there are no profits to be made from entry. On the other hand, a high price can indicate that the firm has room to lower its price with the threat of entry, nullifying the value of the entry costs incurred by the entrants. In addition, high prices can signal that the firm is intent on building up its cash reserves that can be used to cover future losses that can be incurred in price wars with entrants.

CONCLUDING COMMENTS

The costs of switching are endemic not only to digital goods like Microsoft's Windows, but also to a host of other nondigital goods, from banking accounts to medical care to VCRs. Depositors who switch banks must take some time not only to transfer their deposits, but also to learn their new banks' rules, fee structures, and the particulars of the services offered. Switching doctors can entail a transfer of medical records and then informing the new physician of old medical problems not fully evident in the records. Even the purchase of a new VCR can entail switching costs, given that different VCRs have different sets of functions and buttons that must be learned.

Nevertheless, interest in switching costs among economists and management experts has understandably been heightened with the growth in the digital economy. The reasons are threefold. First, technologies require learning, and the (new) digital economy is largely defined by new technologies. Learning new technologies to make switches among them is costly, whether from one producer to the next or from one version of a given technology to the next. Indeed, switching costs are likely a key cost in the adoption of any given technology, whether old or new, and producers must plot their pricing and product development strategies with switching costs in mind. Second, network effects, strongly associated with digital goods like operating systems, can enhance consumer benefits from using any given technology, but they can also fortify switching costs. Third, given that the marginal cost of producing digital goods is zero, or close to it, switching costs will likely be seen as a key source of constraint on price competition, making the production of many goods profitable. This means we should not be surprised if many digital goods that do survive the market tests have significant switching costs

However, I should be careful not to exaggerate the role of switching costs as a force for monopoly power that is, on balance, exploitive. All costs—from materials to labor—are constraints on competition. It is the task of markets to minimize costs of all kind—including switching costs—and then achieve as much consumer welfare as is practical, given the minimized costs. To do that, policy makers and judges must understand all aspects of switching costs, both their pluses and minuses, for consumer welfare.

NOTES

1. Alan W. Beggs and Paul Klemperer, "Multi-Period Competition with Switching Costs," *Econometrica* 60 (May 1992): 651.

2. Michael Porter, *Competitive Strategies* (New York: Free Press, 1980), 10.

3. Joseph Farrell and Carl Shapiro, "Dynamic Competition with Switching Costs," *Rand Journal of Economics* 19 (Spring 1998): 123.

4. According to one study undertaken in the Norwegian banking industry, bank customers stay with their banks an average of thirteen and one-half years, and 25 percent of the additional profit made on banks' additional borrowers could be attributed to switching costs that customers must endure to switch banks. See Moshe Kim, Donou Kliger, and Bent Vale, "Estimating Switching Costs and Oligopolistic Behavior," Working Paper 1999/4 (Oslo, Norway: Norges Bank, Research Department, 1999).

5. Joel I. Klein, et al., *United States v. Microsoft Corporation*, Complaint, First District Court, Civil Action No. 98-1232, May 20, 1998, ¶108, as found at http://www.usdoj.gov/atr/cases/f1700/1763.htm.

6. Direct testimony of Frederick Warren-Boulton, *United States v. Microsoft Corporation*, Civil Action No. 98-1232, November 18, 1998, ¶49, ¶50, as found at http://www.usdoj.gov/atr/cases/f1700/1763.htm.

7. Judge Jackson found:

What for Microsoft is a positive feedback loop is for would-be competitors a vicious cycle. For just as Microsoft's large market share creates incentives for ISVs to develop applications first and foremost for Windows, the small or non-existent market share of an aspiring competitor makes it prohibitively expensive for the aspirant to develop its PC operating system into an acceptable substitute for Windows. To provide a viable substitute for Windows, another PC operating system would need a large and varied enough base of compatible applications to reassure consumers that their interests in variety, choice, and currency would be met to more or less the same extent as if they chose Windows. Even if the contender attracted several thousand compatible applications, it would still look like a gamble from the consumer's perspective next to Windows, which supports over 70,000 applications. The amount it would cost an operating system vendor to create that many applications is prohibitively large. Therefore, in order to ensure the availability of a set of applications comparable to that available for Windows, a potential rival would need to induce a very large number of ISVs to write to its operating system.

See Thomas Penfield Jackson, *United States v. Microsoft Corporation*, Findings of Fact, First District Court, civil Action No. 98-1232, November 5, 1999, ¶40, as found at http://www.usdoj.gov/atr/cases/f3800/msjudgex.htm. The judge later adds, "The applications barrier to entry does not prevent non-Microsoft, Intel-compatible PC operating systems from attracting enough consumer demand and ISV support to survive. It does not even prevent vendors of those products from making a profit. The barrier does, however, prevent the products from drawing a significant percentage of consumers away from Windows" (¶48).

8. Ibid., ¶20.

9. Thomas Penfield Jackson, *United States v. Microsoft Corporation*, Conclusions of Law, First District Court, Civil Action No. 98-1232, IB April 3, 2000, 15, as found at http://www.usdoj.gov/atr/cases/f4400/4469.htm.

10. For discussions of how the future price can play into current demand, without reference to switching costs per se, see Gary S. Becker and Kevin Murphy, "A Theory of Rational Addiction," *Journal of Political Economy* 96 (August 1988): 675–700; and Dwight R. Lee and David Kreutzer, "Lagged Demand and a 'Perverse' Response to Threatened Property Rights," *Economic Inquiry* 20 (October 1982): 579–588. For discussions of the interplay of the future price and current demand with switching costs in mind, see A. Banerjee and L. H. Summers, "On Frequent Flyer Programs and Other Loyalty Inducing Arrangements," Harvard Discussion Paper 1337 (Cambridge: Harvard University Press, 1987); Alan W. Beggs, "A Note on Switching Costs and Technology Choice," *Journal of Industrial Economics* 37 (1989): 437–444; Ramon Caminal and Carmen Matutes, "Endogenous Switching Costs in a Duopoly Model," *International Journal of Industrial Organization* 8 (1990): 353–374; Kenneth A. Froot and Paul D. Klemperer, "Exchange Rate Pass-Through When Market Share Matters," *American Economic Review* 79 (1989): 637–654; Paul D. Klemperer, "Markets with Switching Costs," *Quarterly Journal of Economics* 102 (1987): 375–394; and Paul D. Klemperer, "The Competitiveness of Markets with Switching Costs," *Rand Journal of Economics* 18 (Spring 1987): 138–150.

11. See Paul D. Klemperer, "Price Wars Caused by Switching Costs," *Review of Economic Studies* 56 (1989): 405–420.

12. See Joseph Farrell and Carl Shapiro, "Optimal Contracts with Lock-In," Discussion Paper 130 (Princeton, N.J.: Woodrow Wilson School, Princeton University, 1987).

13. Senator John F. Kerry (D-Mass.) and Robert Atkinson (Progressive Policy Institute), "Left in the Buggy: E-Commerce Is Seen as Threat to Slow Middlemen," *Investor's Business Daily*, March 1, 2001, A12.

14. Franklin Fisher, John McGowan, and Joen Greenwood, *Folded, Spindled, and Mutilated: Economic Analysis and U.S. v. I.B.M.* (Cambridge: MIT Press, 1983), 196.

15. Farrell and Shapiro, "Dynamic Competition with Switching Costs."

16. Paul D. Klemperer, "Welfare Effects of Entry into Markets with Switching Costs," *Journal of Industrial Economics* 37 (December 1988): 159–165.

17. See Paul D. Klemperer, "Entry Deterrence in Markets with Consumer Switching Costs," *Economics Journal* 97 (1987, supp.): 99–117.

18. Jim Clark, with Owen Edwards, *Netscape Time: The Making of the Billion-Dollar Start-Up That Took on Microsoft* (New York: St. Martin's, 1999), 110.

19. Bill Gates, "Internet Strategy Workshop Keynote" (Seattle, Wash.: Microsoft Corporation, December 7, 1995).

20. Clark, with Edwards, *Netscape Time*, 79.

21. Ibid.

22. Andrew S. Grove, *Only the Paranoid Survive: How to Exploit the Crises That Challenge Every Company* (New York: Doubleday, 1996).

23. Jeff Moad, "Ingrained Business Behaviors Work against CRM," *e-Business Strategies*, 1 (March 2001) (e-mailed).

24. Ibid.

25. As reported by Rebecca Buckman and John R. Wilke, "Appeals Proceedings Could Embolden Microsoft," *Wall Street Journal*, 2 March 2001, p. B1.

8

E-mailing and Surfing in the Workplace

At the time this book was being written (2001), one-fourth of American workers—or 33 million—had an Internet connection at their workplace. Three times as many Americans (workers and nonworkers) had Internet connections at home.[1] Millions more will have such connections by the time this book is published. Nevertheless, E-mailing and surfing the Web at home and work have begun to fuse. Every few months, journalists from national newspapers and magazines report, with an underlying sense of disapproval that is not always well disguised, how many workers have been wasting time at work by "Windows shopping," or surfing the Web, and, supposedly, are increasing their employers' costs and reducing their profits.

According to news reports of worker surveys, 25 percent of the time workers spend online is related to personal business.[2] The peak count of online orders for personal goods and services occurs during the nine-to-five workday, not in the evening hours when workers presumably should be doing personal chores. Online orders begin to stream into E-tailers around nine o'clock in the morning, peaking around noon, according to the *Wall Street Journal*.[3] One leisure-time E-tailer, Gamedealer.com, figures that 65 percent of its games are ordered during the workday. Indeed, its orders fall off substantially over the weekends. Other E-tailers report that a few of their online orders come with the request that the order confirmations should not be sent to the work E-mail address of the person placing the order. Moreover, one-third of the visits to pornography Web sites, according to one report, occur during the workday,[4] and some companies apparently now receive deliveries of more UPS packages for personal use than business use.[5]

To hide what they are doing from their employers, some workers apparently set up E-mail accounts at sites such as Yahoo! and MSN. Others make sure that they have a work-related window on their office computers open but minimized, so that they are only one click away from having work on their screens when their bosses drop by.

No one needs journalists to confirm that a nontrivial share of workers' E-mails, both those sent and received during the workday, have nothing to do with most workers' job descriptions. Nevertheless, one report made it official: 30 percent of E-mails that employees send during work hours are not related to work, and that is probably an underestimate.[6] As anyone who has worked in an office knows, these E-mails may take the form of back-and-forth conversations, much like instant messaging, but they can also include the distribution of jokes, family pictures, and greeting cards.

Do these reports indicate something is wrong in the workplace? That is the central question addressed in this chapter. No one should be surprised by the conclusion that some on-the-job Web surfing, E-mailing, and instant messaging (the latter of which is growing dramatically in the workplace[7]) by workers for personal ends should be expected in most organizations, mainly because it is simply cost effective for firms to permit the surfing and E-mailing to go on. All organizations should seek their "optimum level" of personal Web surfing, E-mailing, and instant messaging, meaning they should look at personal surfing and E-mailing in the same way they look at everything else that goes on in the workplace, as a means of maximizing firm profits. It should also be no surprise that the optimum level will vary by business circumstances and the firms' legal liability. As I will argue, because public bureaucracies are not constrained by the need to make a profit, more personal Web surfing and electronic forms of communications should be expected in public bureaucracies than in private firms.

LEISURE–WORK TRADE-OFFS IN THE WORKPLACE

Clearly, in some instances Web surfing by workers has been, and will remain, excessive, given what their employers expect of them and what the workers agreed to do and not do when accepting their jobs. Having said that, however, it does not follow that the reported survey evidence uncovers, necessarily, a systemic problem that anyone would necessarily want to correct, at least not for all firms. The surveys report what people do at work, not what they are expected to do or should do. Indeed, instead of being read as indicating a workplace problem, the reports could just as easily be interpreted as suggesting that labor markets are working reasonably well.

In recognizing that workers waste time at work through their personal Internet use, nothing new is being acknowledged. Some segment of workers has always shirked their duties on the job. As argued earlier in this book and at greater length in another book, shirking is endemic and a fundamental problem facing businesses, the so-called principal/agent problem.[8] To do the work of any sizable business, principals (employers) must hire agents (employees) and delegate to the agents some discretion in the use of firm resources. The problem emerges because both principals and agents have the same goal: to maximize their well-being with the resources at their disposal. The principals would like nothing better than for all agents to do exactly what they were hired to do, which is to use the resources at their disposal to maximize the principal's profits and, therefore, wealth. However, with the delegated discretion over firm resources, the agents—managers and line workers—can misuse their firms' resources to the detriment of the principals. Understanding this prospect, the principals will likely try to guard themselves against the agents' misuse of firm resources by paying them less than otherwise, which is all the more justification for the agent's (systemic) misuse of firm resources, and the expected misuse is built into the wage structure.

Of course, principals will also seek to control, by way of monitoring, agents' behavior, at least up to a point, mainly because the agents themselves might want to be monitored because of the potential for greater wages. However, the principals must also be concerned that the financial markets will punish the company for missteps on agent monitoring, both for too much and too little.

When workers violate their contractual agreements, whether in the form of Internet surfing or showing up late for work, there is a case for employers to at least consider their termination—but only if the surfing or tardiness actually means that the (offending) workers are, on balance, abusing their positions more than others in the firm (or were shirking more than they were before the advent of computers with Web connections), and only if the workers can be replaced by new recruits who produce more for the same pay.

The reported personal Web surfing and E-mailing at work might represent a net increase in worker shirking, mainly because their firms' digital nervous system might facilitate—that is, lower the employees' costs of—shirking in a new form. Then again, it might not. The reported surfing might mean, at least partially, that the workers are now substituting Web-based orders of personal products for telephone orders placed in the past. The Web orders could be so much more efficiently made—that is, less time-consuming for the workers—that the workers actually increase the amount of time spent working. This means that many workers who are surfing the Web could be more productive than the workers who are not (and who continue to place their orders via phone). No wonder a manager, cited in one of the news reports on Web surfing taking up a big chunk of the workday, quipped, "You can't characterize the people doing this stuff as goof-offs. People would perform the same stuff at work using other methods. The Internet has just given them a more effective way of doing it."[9] Finally, it simply does not make business sense to fire any worker if that worker can only be replaced by someone who demands the same (or higher) salary and is no more productive.

What news reports on personal Web surfing and E-mailing fail to indicate is that many employees use work time to surf the Web or E-mail because it is often profitable for their companies to allow them to do so, at least to some extent. How can that be? No modern executive would ever dream of trying to choke off all nonbusiness-related use of workers' office computers and Internet connections. The reason is simple: The only way that could be done is to deny workers those technologies, and not many employers whose workers need those technologies to do the firms' business would be willing to take such a drastic control option. To do so would really be a case of throwing the baby out with the bathwater.

Many employers intuitively understand that modern office technologies have always been a double-edged sword. One of the sword's edges is that the technologies offer the prospects of improving worker productivity and firm profitability, despite their misuse, which is the main explanation for why firms invest in any new technology. Computers with Internet connections allow workers to more efficiently keep records, undertake research, develop and share reports, place orders, and so forth, all of which can improve the companies' bottom lines.

The impact of a new office technology like the personal computer (or the telephone or the fax machine) on work output can be explained in terms of Figure 8.1. The horizontal axis covers how much work the workers do (measured in whatever the worker produces, for example, accounting reports). The vertical axis covers the worker's leisure-time activities, among which Web surfing can be included. With only so many hours in the day, the worker can only do so much. For example, with a given (but old) workplace technology—that is, without an office computer with an Internet connection—if the worker spent all of his or her waking hours doing the bidding of his or her employer, he or she can produce an output of ten, indicated by point *a* on the horizontal axis. Alternately, the individual can spend all of his or her waking hours on nonwork activities and produce *b* on the vertical axis. The typical worker is not likely to take either of these extremes but rather, if initially at *b*, will trade off some leisure-time activities for work output, along the line that indicates the available combinations of the two types of activities and that runs between *a* and *b* in Figure 8.1. Just for illustration, let us suppose that the worker picks combination *c* on *ab* when he does not have an office computer. This means he produces *f* at work and *e* at home.

Now, let us suppose that the worker's employer gives him an office computer and provides an Internet connection. This means that the worker can now produce more at work, for example, *d* on the horizontal axis, that is, if he again devotes all of his waking hours to work. It also means that, starting from the more reasonable combination *c*, the worker can devote the same number of hours to both work and leisure activities and move to combination *g* on the new and expanded set of available combinations on line *bd*. The increase in production measured by *c* to *g* is what might be expected from the known productivity of computers with Internet connections. However, a movement from *c* to *g* assumes that workers have the requisite incentive to do

Figure 8.1. The Leisure–Work Trade-Off

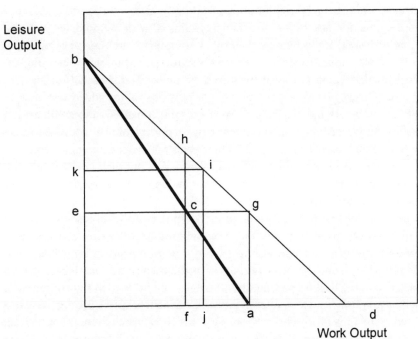

exactly what they are supposed to do: use improvements in office technologies only for work-related ends. It assumes that the principal/agent problem has been solved perfectly, which is not likely, especially with a new technology like computers and the Internet that can be so easily used on the sly, or without the principals ever knowing.

Also, principals—or owners and their supervising managers—face the very real problem that they do not always know very well the details of the jobs of their employees, including exactly what and how much the employees can do with the resources at hand. This is especially true of complicated technologies like computers; and the employers' problems are compounded when the technologies are new, can be used for many purposes (some of which are for work and others for personal ends), and are rapidly being enhanced. The newer and more complicated the technologies are, and the more varied the uses, the less likely the supervising managers and owners will know how the technologies will actually be used.

There has probably never been a new technology in the early stages of development at least, that has more bewildered technophobic managers and owners than the computer and the Internet, and as apparent from data scattered throughout this book, there probably never has been a technology (except, perhaps, for the telegraph) that has developed more rapidly. Accordingly, given the owners' and managers' lack of understanding (which at times and places may border on ignorance) of just what can be produced with technologies, it should be no surprise that workers see their office computers and Internet connections as not only adding to their workplace productivity, but also increasing the work-related resources available for their personal disposal. Workers can choose to use a portion—perhaps a major portion—of the added resources to give their owners and managers what they want: enhanced output and greater profits. However, they can also choose to use a portion of their added resources to pursue their own personal goals. These goals can include the enhancement of their job performance, which can lead to more pay, but their goals can also include more time for daydreaming or shopping on the Web (and increasing the real value of any given pay).

In terms of Figure 8.1, it is tempting to think that the represented worker will volunteer to convert all of the potential productivity gains from his office computer with an Internet connection into work output and move, as indicated earlier, from c to g. However, with the owners and managers at least partially in the dark regarding how much can be done with the computer, it will be tempting for them to convert some of the workplace productivity improvement into more personal output, which can include making contact with friends via E-mail and placing orders over the Web. In doing those things, the worker moves up to the left along line bd to, for example, combination i. The firm and the worker can observe that the worker's output still rises (from f to j), which might please the owners, but the worker's output does not rise by as much as the worker knows it could be expected to rise (from f to a), given the potential for the new technology.

By curbing work output below the potential, the worker is able to increase his or her own nonwork-related output from e to k. How does he do that? If the worker can produce more per hour because of his office computer with an Internet connection, the worker can work fewer hours, transferring some of the released time to personal activities.

Of course, the worker could conceivably transfer all the productivity gains from work output to personal output, or move from c to h in Figure 8.1. However, if that option is chosen, the worker would eliminate any incentive the firm would have to provide the computer in the first place, which means the worker would not then be able to increase his or her personal output. Hence, he or she (and most other workers) would likely settle for some combination between h and g. How close the worker comes to selecting g depends on a number of factors, not the least of which are how much the worker's supervisor knows about the productivity enhancement an office computer can potentially provide, how easily it is for the supervisor to monitor work, how much of a pay incentive the worker has to give up personal output for work output, and how shielded the supervisor and worker are from competition from alternative sources of supply (from both inside and outside the firm) of what the worker produces.

Supervisors may know very little about computers per se, but they do not necessarily need to know very much. All supervisors have to do is observe the output of several workers doing the same thing. By comparing output of various workers, they can call to task those workers who choose to move up and to the left from g in Figure 8.1, reducing their work output in the process, or they can reward workers based on their relative outputs. They can reduce the amount of personal on-the-job Web surfing and E-mailing by, effectively, having workers compete with one another.

That solution, however, is bound to be a partial solution in some cases and no solution at all in others. Having workers compete might work well when they are doing the exact same thing at work. Their outputs are then fully comparable. Unfortunately, many workers, especially those who work with sophisticated computers, are not likely going to be doing the exact same things at work, which will limit the extent to which the supervisors can tell who is and is not making the best use of the office technology. In such cases, the supervisors will likely have to resign themselves to permitting workers to absorb for personal use some of the productivity improvement the new technology provides.

INTERACTION BETWEEN COMPUTERS AND WORKERS

Many companies allow—implicitly, if not explicitly—some personal use of company computers and Internet connections for the same reason they allow gabbing at the proverbial office watercooler. To thwart totally, or just in large measure, use of the new technologies for personal ends could undermine the workers' incentives to make effective use of the new technology (or to advocate the introduction of the new technology). In drawing the new line *bd* in Figure 8.1, attributing the outward expansion to the introduction of an "office computer with an Internet connection," I simplified the analysis by implicitly assuming that the additional productivity that could be obtained by the computer was inherent in the machine itself, and had nothing to do with how the worker approached the use of the machine. But that is hardly a realistic description of the way productivity is enhanced with the introduction of office computers. How productive computers are depends on how much the users actually know about using them in various and creative ways. And the users must learn how to use them—and must have an incentive to do so. Without any incentive to learn how to use the computers, the computers can remain "dumb," expensive machines that will gather dust on people's desks, or be used to do tasks that are far below their capability. It seems altogether reasonable to conclude that the greater the incentive workers have to learn how to do more with their computers (and how to perform computer tasks in less complicated and time-consuming ways), the more they will learn.

In short, it is a gross oversimplification to assume that with the introduction of an office computer, line *ba* in Figure 8.1 pivots outward to *bd* based on what the machine can do and independent of what the worker does. There are two reasons personal Web surfing can cause the line to pivot outward: First, personal surfing experience can improve workers' proficiency at surfing, which can make work-related surfing more productive. Second, the personal surfing can provide the requisite incentive for the worker to learn how to use the office computer and the Internet.

All of this means that it is altogether plausible to argue that the more personal work—Web surfing—workers are permitted to do, the further out the *ba* line will pivot. Thus, if employers allow their workers the opportunity to engage in Web surfing and E-mailing for personal ends, their computer investments can result in not only more Web surfing (and E-mailing), but also more firm output than there would otherwise be, not necessarily always the reverse, which is the implicit assumption behind the news reports of wasted time at the office.

Granted, there can always be abuse of any technology, but misuse of firm resources did not start with the introduction of personal computers and then the addition of Internet connections. As noted, personal surfing and E-mailing can take the place of gabbing around the office watercooler. The surfing and E-mailing can inspire workers to work harder and with greater efficiency, just so they can free up time not only to surf and E-mail more, but also to work more. The prospect of Web surfing giving rise to more firm output is very likely one reason so many firms turn a blind eye to how much Web surfing goes on in their offices. As one executive stresses, "We have a philosophy around here that people should be comfortable at work and if they're comfortable, they'll work harder. I'm totally fine with these areas where business life and personal life mix."[10]

MONITORING COSTS

Even if much personal Web surfing were considered by the owners and managers to be a waste to their companies, the elimination of the waste could require a monitoring system that might be productive in terms of reducing the waste, but it would also be costly. Therein lies the potential for another trade-off that firms need to appraise with care.

It is altogether reasonable to assume that monitoring systems are subject to diminishing returns. That is, as more and more of employees' work-time activities are monitored, the cost incurred by the firm escalates, for three reasons. First, the monitor–boss will start by observing those worker activities that are relatively easy to observe, meaning little cost is incurred. For example, the monitor might look at workers' computer screens as she walks past their offices. After doing that, she might have to start looking at the histories of their Web surfing as recorded on their office computers (or the office servers), or buy software programs that prevent her employees from going to identified sites (or that record efforts to go to explicitly forbidden sites). To extend her monitoring further, she might increase the marginal cost incurred by hiring computer experts to manage banks of servers designed to store all employee work-time computer activities.

Second, as the monitor–boss extends her monitoring efforts, she will be taking time away from doing other things that could add to the efficiency of her area. She can be expected to start her monitoring by giving up other activities that are of little consequence to the firm, like responding as quickly to her employees' E-mails. But then she might have to give up on closely scrutinizing the costs incurred on various product projects, perhaps leading to more cost overruns on the projects.

Third, there is also the technical problem of diminishing returns that is built into almost any technology, whether it has to do with producing products or monitoring projects, as noted much earlier in this book: Beyond some point the addition of resources can be expected to have less and less of an impact. This is mainly because some fixed resource is being more and more thinly used with a larger and larger amount of another resource. More resources devoted to monitoring a fixed number of workers can be expected, beyond some point, to yield progressively smaller improvements in work-related productivity, meaning the marginal cost of extending employee monitoring will rise.

On the other hand, the firm surely has a demand for monitoring and eliminating personal surfing and E-mailing (even when it might decide not to do anything about it). Its demand can be affected by a number of factors. For example, some firms have to worry that their employees will reveal trade secrets or will use the Web to conduct illegal activities. Others might worry that worker productivity will suffer. And yet other firms may have to worry about lawsuits. A reasonable presumption is that the value of the monitoring and elimination of additional units of Web surfing at work is likely to decline as additional units of Web surfing are eliminated. In its monitoring efforts, the firm is likely to start by eliminating the most costly forms of surfing, meaning the monitoring has the greatest value to the firm. It will then be stuck with eliminating the second-least costly form of personal surfing, then the third-least, and so on. It follows that the value of eliminating additional forms of surfing declines.

Consequently, we can conclude that the firm is willing to eliminate more and more surfing as the price of doing so is lowered. Another way of saying the same thing is how much actual monitoring of employees the firm demands will be inversely related to the price of monitoring. The lower the price, the greater the amount of monitoring demanded, and vice versa. This is nothing more than a repeat of the now-familiar law of demand.

How much personal surfing should a firm allow? There is no point in addressing that question for a particular firm, given the variation in firms' cost and demand conditions. The general economic rule for firm profit maximization applies: The firm should extend its monitoring of employees as long as the additional cost of monitoring is less than the additional value, or up to the optimal level of surfing, where the value of the last unit of monitoring equals the marginal cost of that unit of monitoring.

Why does the firm allow as much personal surfing at work as it does? It simply pays for the firm to allow what it does. Put another way, its profitability and perhaps competitive position in its product markets would fall if it allowed less. If it allowed less, the firm's lower profits would translate into a lower stock price, which means that if the firm persisted in its efforts to strictly curb personal surfing at work, someone would be able to buy the firm's stock at a deflated price, take over the firm, change the amount of monitoring of employees, enhance the firm's bottom line, and sell the stock for a capital gain. I make these points fully cognizant of the fact that stock prices have their limits in finely reflecting all firm policies, such as monitoring, which might result in excessive costs. At the same time, the point is that firms cannot choose their policies—Internet or otherwise—without an eye toward market pressures on their stock. In addition, markets have ways of correcting the behavior of firms that are not concerned with optimizing their employee policies, including how lenient they are with regard to their workers' E-mail and Internet rights or privileges.

It follows that if a computerized surveillance program—for example, IM Inspector or IM Message Inspector from Elron Software, Inc.—is developed that makes monitoring easier and less intrusive, meaning less costly, more monitoring and less surfing would be expected. The firm will extend its monitoring for both offensive and defensive reasons. The offensive reason is that it can justify trying to eliminate additional forms of personal surfing that are less valuable to the firm, because the cost of doing so has been lowered. Furthermore, if the new program is available to other similarly situated firms, our firm will feel the competitive pressure to more tightly monitor its employee surfing costs, just so its cost structure is no higher than its competitors.

In short, how much personal surfing goes on at work depends on factors such as the availability of software programs, like Little Brother (a program that can control what Web sites workers can visit), that can be used for monitoring. The cheaper and more effective the programs, the less personal surfing there will tend to be in the workplace.

The amount of personal surfing can also be affected by the nature of the work. Where work is routine and done in-house—for example, by workers who input data from claims at insurance companies, or who make calls for telemarketers—it may be easy and cost effective for firms to monitor what their workers do with their Internet connections. Where work is creative and can be done via telecommuting—for example, research done by professors or stock analysts—the cost of monitoring can be very high. This is because it is difficult to distinguish work-related surfing and E-mailing from personal surfing and E-mailing. Moreover, the personal surfing and E-mailing can often complement work activities. Thus, two different levels of monitoring should be expected for the different types of workers. Put another way, with the shift in employment from routine to creative work, we should expect a reduction in monitoring and, perhaps, an increase in personal surfing.

I say perhaps for a good reason. When work is creative in nature and/or is done in remote locations, or away from the office, we might expect pay to be tied to some overall measure of firm output, such as sales or profits. The incentive built into such a pay scheme not to surf can be used to offset the absence of direct monitoring of what the workers do on an hour-by-hour basis. Relating executive pay to company performance or stock price should have different results for different settings. It all depends on whether personal surfing and E-mailing net cost savings or greater profits.

SURFING AND E-MAILING IN
PUBLIC BUREAUCRACIES AND PRIVATE FIRMS

The amount of personal Web surfing and E-mailing that goes on in any organization depends on a number of factors, not the least of which are whether the organization is private or public, and the laws and regulations that must be followed. Such considerations can affect the cost and value of monitoring employees, and, hence, can affect how much personal Web surfing and E-mailing that the organizations choose. I leave a discussion of the legal constraints on Web surfing and E-mailing, both for personal and work-related purposes, for a later section in this chapter.

Here, I can note briefly the logic of why we would expect more personal Web surfing and E-mailing in public bureaucracies, like my own university or, for example, the Social Security Administration, than in private firms that undertake much the same kind of work. The main governing difference is that private firms are controlled by the need to make a profit, where public bureaucracies are not. This is important for two reasons: First, the goal of the private firm is well defined and relatively easy to measure. All people have to do is look to a private firm's bottom line on its accounting books. Public bureaucracies do not have such a focused and easily monitored goal. Indeed, they, like my university, often have a constellation of goals they pursue, none of which are evaluated by transparent, readily available statistics.

I cite my university because it may, at any time, be seeking to achieve dozens of goals, grouped under three main categories: the education of undergraduate and graduate students, cutting-edge research in a multitude of disciplines and subdisciplines, and service to the citizens of the surrounding communities and state. You can probably surmise that there are a large number of subgoals that capture the kinds of education, research, and service the professors and staff provide. Oftentimes, the professors and staff members define their own (and their universities') subgoals in the process of pursuing them. You can imagine how the imprecision of the goals gives professors and staff members wide latitude to do more or less what they want at work. This means they have more latitude to consider their Web surfing and E-mailing undertaken at work to be work-related than do employees of private firms.

This brings us to the second reason for expecting more personal Web surfing and E-mailing in public bureaucracies than in private firms. Public bureaucracies do not have to face the discipline of the financial markets that private firms do. If the amount of personal Web surfing and E-mailing is excessive, the workers do not have to worry about the impact on their bottom line or their stock prices, because they do not have bottom lines (in the same sense that private firms have). They can come up with a multitude of explanations for why the bureaucracy has not been operating as efficiently as might have been expected, citing any one of a number of their goals, real or concocted, for the purpose at hand. Moreover, their supervising agencies at higher governmental levels might be too far removed in spacial and bureaucratic distance to understand the extent to which they are being misled. Bureaucracies certainly do not have to fear failure (few bureaucracies have ever been closed down for inefficient operations[11]).

Private firms, on the other hand, can expect any excessive Web surfing and E-mailing to show up in a loss (albeit small) in their market shares as their costs and prices are inflated above levels of their competitors that better control personal Web surfing and E-mailing. Their loss in market positions can show up in the firms' profit-and-loss statements, with the cuts in profits or hikes in losses translated into declines in their stock prices. As noted in several places in this book, when stock prices deteriorate with inefficient firm policies, savvy investors can be expected to buy the offending firms' stocks and replace the management team that, in turn, can be expected to correct the inefficient policies. The result can be a hike in the stock prices, and a capital gain for those investors who made the takeover.

We might anticipate that the cost of making corrections to a public bureaucracy would also be higher (if for no other reason than public bureaucracies often do not face the threat of their markets being subject to takeover by new, more cost-effective competitors, and because the costs of public bureaucracies are typically subsidized with treasury funds). Granted, voters and their agents—politicians—have oversight roles to play in the running of bureaucracies. However, voters face the temptations of proverbial free riders to remain largely ignorant of what bureaucracies do, or do not do. Voters' political agents, hence, have impaired incentives to monitor bureaucracies carefully.[12] Both voters and politicians do not have the direct financial incentives to engage in monitoring that takeover artists have. This is because voters and politicians cannot buy out public bureaucracies and reform their errant policies for a profit in a sell-off.

Okay, personal Web surfing and E-mailing might not have the kind of earth-shattering impact on firms' profitability that might be implied in the foregoing analysis. However, my point remains sound: The financial markets impose a form of pressure, no matter how small, to correct inefficient policies that are unmatched, and cannot be matched, in the public sector. Hence, public bureaucrats should not be expected to seek out and adopt the same kind of optimum policies, no matter what the issue, that are expected of private managers.

WORKERS' DEMAND FOR WORKPLACE SURFING

To this point, I have adopted the perspective of the employer, but there is obviously a worker point of view. This is because a monitoring system that conceivably could radically curb much misuse of company computer and telecommunication resources would likely be very intrusive and offensive to many workers who rarely, if ever, use the Web, as well as the true offenders. The resulting hostile work environment would, without much question, encourage some very productive workers to quit and, as the word got out in labor markets, to discourage other workers from joining the company. The curb in the company's supply of workers could be expected to result in an increase in the company's wage bill.

Again, personal surfing and E-mailing at work can be profitable for the company. The lost work time can be more than offset by the reduction in the firm's wage bill from what it otherwise would be, making the firm more profitable than otherwise. (Alternatively, the lost work time could be offset by an increase in the skilled level of workers that would be available to the company because it allows personal use of office computers and Internet connections.)

Workers can also demand some flexibility on the job with firm technologies for the same reason that they demand company-provided health insurance: It is cheaper for the workers to cover the cost of their insurance needs by enrolling in their company's group policy and paying for the insurance through paycheck deductions than for them to buy their own individual insurance policies. Similarly, it is also cheaper for many workers (especially those whose pay is tied to performance) to use their high-speed Internet connections at work than to waste even more time at home with far slower connections. Workers should be willing to give up some wages for this fringe benefit of work-based Web surfing and E-mailing. The result can be a win–win outcome for both workers and their employers.

To see this point more clearly, consider Figure 8.2, which provides standard labor market supply and demand curves. I can start by assuming that the employers are carefully monitoring their workers with the initial curves labeled S_1 and D_1. The market-clearing wage is accordingly W_1 when Q_1 workers are hired. Now, suppose that workers really value workplace Web surfing and E-mailing. Suppose further that the employers relax their efforts to curb Web surfing and E-mailing. With more work time being spent on surfing and E-mailing, the workers might, in fact, be less valuable, causing the employers to be willing to pay their workers less and causing their demand curve to shift downward from D_1 to D_2.

If the workers truly value the policy shift, their supply curve should shift outward from S_1 to S_2, reflecting the fact that they should be willing to accept a lower wage for the relaxed demands at work. After all, they may see the workplace monitoring as an intrusion on their lives and/or see some gain in time to be had from shifting their surfing from their home computers to their office computers.

The result of the shifts in the two curves is that the new market equilibrium moves to the intersection of curves D_2 and S_2. Accordingly, the wage rate falls from W_1 to W_2. The employers incur workplace cost, which is why their demand falls. However, notice that the drop in the wage they have to pay, $W_1 - W_2$, is greater than the reduction in the wage that they had to have to incur the greater costs of more personal surfing and E-mailing, which equals the vertical drop in the demand curve or ac. The employers are better off by the difference: $(W_1 - W_2) - (c - a)$. In addition, they can justify hiring more workers, which means their collective output must be rising.

Similarly, the workers benefit on balance from the change in monitoring. Their wage rate falls from W_1 to W_2, but notice that they value the more relaxed monitoring equal to the wage reduction they were willing to accept, or the vertical difference between the two supply curves, ab, which is greater than $W_1 - W_2$. Workers receive a wage equal to W_2, but they also gain the benefits of the relaxed monitoring, equal to ab. If you add the wage to the benefits, they get an effective wage equal to W_3, which means the workers' effective pay does not fall. It rises from W_1 to W_3.

Careful readers may suspect that I have rigged the way the curves shift in Figure 8.2 so that the major point—that both workers and employers gain, on balance—is made by assumption. Those readers might be thinking that it is

Figure 8.2. The Supply and Demand of Labor

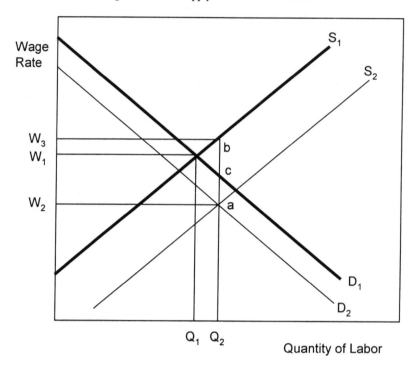

possible for the vertical downward shift in the demand curve to be greater than the vertical downward shift in the supply curve, which would make either employers or workers worse off, or perhaps both. That, of course, is possible and would imply no shift away from the initial equilibrium, meaning no personal surfing and E-mailing at work. However, I have drawn the graph the way I have because "no personal surfing and E-mailing at work" would probably mean that the marginal cost to employers and lost value to employees of wiping out the last remnants of personal surfing and E-mailing at work would likely be very steep. This implies that it would be possible for employers to initially relax their monitoring a little and not only increase the supply of workers but also increase their demand for workers, given that they could save the cost of monitoring and thereby could pay their workers more.

As the employers continue to relax their monitoring, we might expect that at some point, they begin to suffer net costs (the lost time at work adds more to firm cost than the reduction in cost from the monitoring). This is the interesting case I have tried to illustrate in Figure 8.2. I actually believe that for the reasons illustrated in Figure 8.2, it is likely that employers would not stop relaxing their monitoring at the point implied by the shift in the supply and demand to S_2 and D_2. This is because as long as the increase in worker supply is greater than the decrease in employer demand from a relaxation of monitoring—meaning in terms of Figure 8.2 the vertical drop in the demand curve is less than the vertical drop in the supply—there are gains to be had by both workers and employers. In short, as in all things economic, the monitoring should be relaxed up to the point that the vertical downward shifts in the two curves are identical. That would be the point of maximum gains for both sides of the labor market.

While I cannot show it in the graph, there is an added potential benefit from the relaxed monitoring at work. There is the prospect of workers staying at work longer, simply because they do not have to waste time on their home computers. If their home Internet connections are slower than their work connections, there can be a time gain for everyone involved. For example, suppose that workers would have to spend an hour at home to place online orders that would take them twenty minutes at work to complete. There are forty minutes of time that are not spent in what has come to be called the "world wide wait." That time released by the shift of the surfing can be divided between the workers and their employers. The workers can spend, say, thirty-five additional minutes at work, partially to compensate for the twenty minutes spent on personal surfing, but gain twenty-five minutes to do things other than work. The employer gains fifteen extra minutes of real work time.

CONTROLLING E-MAIL

E-mail has done what the post office has not been able to do, make sending a letter excessively cheap. Indeed, for many E-mailers, the price of sending an additional message across town or across the country is virtually zero (above the value of the time involved). Therein lies the cause of a mounting problem for American managers: controlling the volume of E-mails not only from external junk E-mail distributors, but also from E-mail abusers internal to the firm. The growing volume of E-mails from intra-firm sources means workers are spending an escalating amount of company time composing the E-mails they send and, perhaps more cumbersome, sorting through and reading the E-mails they receive.

The growing problem of junk E-mail from external sources can be partially solved by the installation of E-mail filters that, in a rough-and-ready way, weed out spam (unsolicited commercial messages sent to a large number of recipients) from legitimate and important correspondence. However, the growing problem of junk E-mail from internal sources should have managerial solutions. An unheralded solution to the burgeoning internal E-mail problem is for managers to reintroduce some sanity into the process by charging for the E-mails sent. Indeed, raising E-mail charges above the current level of zero can, paradoxically, lower the growing cost of E-mailing to businesses.

Sending a letter by way of the U.S. Postal Service (now, widely regarded as "snail mail") has one unheralded advantage: It remains tolerably expensive. To send a letter, the writer must apply a 37-cent stamp, as well as go to the trouble and expense of writing and printing the letter and addressing the envelope. In the case of internally distributed hard-copy memorandums, the messages have to be printed, often enclosed in envelopes, and then stuffed in mailboxes. While there are some economies of scale for external mailings, each letter requires an individual address and stamp. The total expense of mailings no doubt causes businesspeople to often pause before they send out large volumes of mail. Therein lies the unheralded advantage: The recipients are not bombarded daily with mailed letters and can normally (but certainly not always) count on the letters they receive having some (at least small) marginal value. The recipients' sorting problem is partially controlled by the people doing the mailing.

Such is not likely to be nearly as common with e-mailed messages. Any given message can be e-mailed to five, ten, or one hundred people with a couple of clicks of the mouse, and without the cost of the paper or stamps. While some E-mail services charge for messages sent or time spent connected to the service, many E-mail systems, especially within firms, do not increase the monthly fee with the count and sizes of messages sent. Such pricing schemes effectively make the additional cost of sending additional E-mails zero (or very close to it).

For example, the president of the entire University of California system (which has several thousand employees) can send an E-mail to the faculty and staff on all nine campuses scattered across the state with little more effort and time than anyone else devotes to sending a single letter by regular mail. All the president has to do is click the button for a mailing group entitled "all university employees." His computer automatically includes the addresses, and another click sends the thousands of E-mails on their way.

The problem businesses face is that the volume of E-mails received by many employees is now quite large and growing rapidly. How large is the problem? Large enough that no one can actually count the total number of E-mails at the University of California–Irvine, much less for the entire university system or all businesses in the country combined. However, businesspeople will readily complain that they get too many E-mails, many of which are worthless and a waste of time.

The problem is that for many businesses E-mailing has gotten out of hand, and shows no promise of correction anytime soon. There is no way that a productive business professional can wade through a couple of hundred E-mails a day, discarding the obviously worthless ones, much less read them all. As Roger Ebert, television and movie critic, observes, "Although it is simple enough to 'delete' one example of spam, it is a nuisance to delete a dozen, and torture to delete 50."[13] To save time, many people do what is most cost effective in terms of time saved: delete all of the E-mails at once, with little or no attention to distinguishing the important from the worthless E-mails. The sorting process would itself take too much time, given the expected value of the E-mails that have accumulated over, say, a week. No doubt, many important ones are discarded, but that is simply an expected cost of reducing the much greater and certain cost of wading through the E-mails trying to figure out which should be read with care and which should be trashed. The handwriting now appears to be on the wall (or should it be Web?): If E-mail is not yet a problem for some businesses, it will soon be one as more and more people become comfortable E-mailing and find more and more creative ways of passing around their golden words.

To some limited extent, the E-mail problem will solve itself. Many of the E-mailers who send worthless E-mails will learn of the trouble they are causing others (by recognizing the trouble others are causing them). If not, they can expect to be ignored, eventually (maybe). If ignored, those who misuse and abuse the system might partially correct their ways, reserving E-mails more and more for important communications—but, again, this sort of correction will likely be slow in coming and imperfect, not likely to be a full solution to the growing problem of excessive E-mails. With some success AOL has blocked the E-mailing from junk E-mail distributors.

By the mid-1990s, Ebert reported that participants at a conference on world affairs held in Boulder, Colorado, recognized the then so-called Spam Plague and decided to give allegiance to the "Boulder Pledge": "Under no circumstances will I ever purchase anything offered to me as the result of an unsolicited email message. Nor will I forward chain letters, petitions, mass mailings, or virus warnings to large numbers of others. This is my contribution to the survival of the online community."[14]

While such pledges have honorable intentions, they are unlikely to have a major impact on the size of the overall problem. The impact of the Boulder Pledge has certainly been very limited over the years, if it had any impact at all. Each person (or E-mail marketer) can reason that his or her E-mails represent a very minor, if not trivial or inconsequential, fraction of the overall problem. This is true of mass markets or large societal settings. Again, the

E-mail problem is much like the familiar pollution problem: Many people do not pick up trash on the streets because they know their limited efforts to clean up will have precious little impact on the beauty of the streets. We should not expect people to behave any differently with regard to E-mail than they do with respect to the trash in their communities. A core reason for the growing spam problem is the growth of the Internet community. Not only are there more people online, all too eager to contribute their own E-mail trash, but each person's E-mails are rapidly becoming a smaller portion of the overall problem.

Even in most large organizations, one person's efforts to curb his or her E-mails will not materially solve the sorting problem faced by E-mail recipients. Each employee, acting separately, can easily justify doing nothing on his or her own. Granted, if everyone were to cut back, the problem could be solved, but the core problem facing managers remains: How to motivate everyone to do what is in the interest of all others. If simple managerial appeals to everyone to cut back would work, there would be no problem; managers could simply send out (by E-mail) their appeals. Voila! The problem would evaporate. However, even if appeals had an initial impact, their value would likely dissipate with time, as people started violating the spirit of the appeals because everyone else had started to do so. Indeed, if some people did cut back, others could see the cutback as an opportunity to distribute more E-mails, given that their E-mails would likely then be given more consideration by the recipients. In large groups of employees—which is where the problem of excessive E-mails is likely to be most severe—the logic underlying the problem is compelling, ensuring that it remains a challenge worthy of managerial attention.

Then, how can businesses cope with the growing problem of E-mail overload? Managers can encourage their workers to take their names off discussion groups. They can threaten suit, given laws against using computers to distribute unsolicited advertisements. Another obvious solution is technological. Workers can use one of the several available E-mail programs that allow recipients to automatically screen out E-mails from sources generating what are deemed to be worthless messages.

Technology also allows people to be even more aggressive in responding to writers of worthless E-mails. Employees can have their computer send an automatic response to identified E-mailers, brashly saying something to the effect, "I have concluded that because you have sent E-mails that have been a waste of time in the past, I have instructed my computer to no longer accept E-mails from you." However, few people in business can afford to be so brash and, maybe, rude. Again, a major part of the problem, especially in large organizations, is that the individual recipient is put in the position of trying to police the system for the good of the whole. While some personal benefits are garnered, all of the costs are incurred by the person doing the policing, while most of the benefits are received by all others in the organization who do nothing. In other words, this solution is beset with virtually the same problem that is at the core of the E-mail problem.

What then can a manager do? Start treating E-mailing as a scarce resource, which it is, and then give workers an incentive to do the same. This can be done by giving employees an E-mail budget and then charging them for the E-mails sent. For example, employees can be allocated some budgeted amount—say, $100 per month (or any other amount deemed appropriate)—that can be used strictly for E-mails or can be used more broadly for any other purpose (from telephone calls to trips to office equipment). These accounts can then be charged so much—for example, $.20—for each E-mail sent to each identified address.

The allocated budget and charge should not be viewed as totally arbitrary. They should be chosen with an aim toward making the E-mail process more thoughtful and efficient. If sending messages is to be made more efficient, the charge chosen for each E-mail should probably be below the cost of a stamp ($.37), given E-mailing is likely to be less costly for firms than mailing. By way of the charge, employees should be encouraged to use E-mailing over mailing. The allocated budget should probably enable employees to use the E-mail system without curbing their expenditures on other important activities, like taking business trips and making business calls. After all, E-mails and trips do have value to the employees and the firm. The problem managers face is trying to make sure that their workers view trips and E-mails with the same thoughtful question in mind: Do the expected benefits more than cover the expected cost? If yes, the firm's profits rise. If no, the activity should be curbed.

Theoretically, the addition to the budget and the price charged for each E-mail can be so configured that the employees could be no worse off than they were before the new budget-and-charge system was installed. That is, with some given budget, the employee could send as many E-mails as he or she had previously sent at no charge. For example, suppose that a typical employee has previously sent two hundred E-mails over an average month. If the price of E-mails is set at $.20, then the employee can be allocated a budget of $40 a month, which would allow him or her to continue to send two hundred E-mails per month.

However, we would expect that under this budget-and-charge system, E-mailing would be curbed voluntarily. The demand for E-mailing is no different than the demand for any other good or service: The quantity bought will be inversely related to the price. The higher the charge, the lower the number of E-mails that will be effectively "purchased" by the employee, and vice versa. Given that this system raises the price of E-mailing by $.20 (from $.00 to $.20), the volume of E-mailing should fall. How much? Unfortunately, I cannot say. The quantity response depends on a host of factors, and the drop is likely to vary from business to business, depending on the nature of the business and the urgency and value of the E-mails to the particular business (which is likely to depend on how many other firms in the industry use E-mails). The actual drop will simply have to be determined from experience.

At the same time, we should expect a drop in E-mailing because, if for no other reason, the explicit charge per E-mail will force workers to consider the worth of any given E-mail when sending it to additional people. Adding one more person to the address list for an E-mail must be worth at least $.20 (or whatever the charge is). The charge for sending an E-mail to one hundred people will then cost $20 (half of the budget in my example). Sending out jokes or diets or love notes will also incur a charge.

If the allocated E-mail budget ($40 in my example) is restricted in use to only E-mailing, then the worker will have to decide whether an E-mail sent now will be worth more or less than some E-mail that can be sent later. The efficiency improvement will, accordingly, be limited. On the other hand, if the addition to the worker's budget can be used more broadly, the worker will have to decide whether the E-mails will be more valuable than, say, a more expensive meal with additional clients on the next trip. The firm's resources can be allocated to the most valuable uses, which is what any pricing system is supposed to do. Now, with no charge on E-mails, there should be no wonder that employee time is devoted to uses the value of which is next to nothing, if not a total drain on the firm's resources.

Charging for E-mails can improve the efficiency of a business in another unheralded way: By curbing the number of E-mails sent, the charge reduces the time the recipients must spend sorting through and reading E-mails, again, many of which would have been worth close to nothing (because of the prior zero charge). The employee time saved can translate into more real work getting done and more profits. The employees are also more likely to treat the E-mails received from intra-firm sources with greater respect and attention, adding to the cost effectiveness of the organization. The recipients can reason that the people sending the E-mails were willing to put a part of their budget literally on the line. Now, they need not do that. E-mailing is essentially free.

Granted, $.20 is not a high price, and such a charge may represent only a minor fraction of the total cost of composing and sending an E-mail. But $.20 is still higher than $.00, the current charge. If, after the charge, there are still too many E-mails sent, then the price can be raised, and/or the budget allocated each employee can be lowered.[15] The point is that the volume of E-mails, and the business costs associated with E-mailing, can be lowered by manager discretion. All managers need to do is stop complaining and use the levers at their disposal. An E-mail charge is not likely to be a total solution, but it can at least be a partial one.

Legal Constraints

The foregoing analysis assumes that employers and workers can develop their own policies without legal constraints. That is hardly the case. Companies have to worry about getting sued on any number of grounds. A growing number of major firms—for example, Dow Chemical, Xerox, the *New York Times*, Edward Jones, and First Union Bank—have fired workers for misuse of company Internet and E-mail systems, if for no other reason than to protect their legal backsides and their bottom lines, given that suits against them can be expensive.

Understandably, the threat of legal penalties for lenient policies on workplace surfing and E-mailing can also affect the amount of surfing and E-mailing in the workplace, both work related and personal. A number of firms around the country have been sued because their employees used the firm's E-mail system to make unkind, if not hateful, comments about other workers or to distribute inappropriate jokes that contribute, according to the lawyers pressing the suits, to a hostile work environment. For example, in 1995, Chevron agreed to pay four female workers $2.2 million to settle their legal claim that they were harassed by sexually explicit messages sent over the company's E-mail system, including an E-mail that listed "25 reasons beer is better than women."[16]

Continental Airlines' first female pilot filed suit against Continental on the grounds that male pilots made, in the words of one report, "derogatory and insulting gender-based comments" on the Crew Member Forum, an employee bulletin board that CompuServe had set up for the company's pilots.[17] The New Jersey state court that heard the case dismissed it on the grounds that use of the forum was not required and that the employees, not Continental, bore the cost of its use. The court of appeals agreed. However, in June 2000, the New Jersey Supreme Court reversed the decision and found that while employers do not have a duty to monitor their employees' private communications, they do have a duty to stop employee harassment when, according to the court decision, "the employer knows or has reason to know that such harassment is part of a pattern of harassment that is taking place in the workplace and in settings that are related to the workplace."[18]

As a consequence of these and other widely reported cases, company surveillance of worker E-mails and Internet surfing behavior has been on the rise. In 2000, 27 percent of companies snooped on their workers' E-mails. In 1993, only 15 percent undertook E-mail snooping.[19]

Visits to pornography Web sites—so-called dirty surfing—are common in the workplace. According to one report, 70 percent of visits to such sites occur during the nine-to-five workday.[20] Sixty-two percent of the firms surveyed had caught their workers visiting pornography Web sites while at work, and 27 percent had issued reprimands to the offending workers, and they did so for good reason: Firms have also been sued because their workers have visited pornography sites and have had nude pictures on their screens that have been seen, if only in passing, by workers who find the pictures offensive, leading to the creation of a hostile work environment.[21]

At the Dow Chemical plant in Midland, Michigan, thirty-nine employees were dismissed and two hundred others were suspended from work from one to five days for sending sexually explicit pictures over the company's E-mail system. For years, the workers had used the E-mail system for such purposes. However, in early 2000 the company established a "respect and responsibility" policy that stated that it would not tolerate "utilizing email . . . to view or pass along inappropriate material (particularly relative to race, ethnicity, gender, disability, religious, or of a sexual nature)."[22] Two months later, one worker complained of having seen offensive material on a monitor. As a consequence, and based on a surveillance of the company's E-mail records for one day, one male worker was fired for sending an E-mail containing a picture of a nude man and a nude female dwarf. Another male worker was fired for forwarding a picture of a woman having sex with a horse. Yet another worker—a woman—was fired for sending an E-mail of a man cutting his finger off. The company says it did not discipline anyone for just receiving materials. Dow fired another 22 employees and disciplined 240 others at its Freeport, Texas, plant, again because of the complaint of a single employee.[23]

Enron Corporation, which made headlines when it suddenly filed for bankruptcy in the fall of 2001 and thereafter for apparent problematic, if not corrupt, accounting practices, fired one worker for posting on the Internet that the company had paid top managers and executives $55 million in retention bonuses just before it announced its financial collapse. According to a *New York Times* report, Enron may have fired another worker for posting coarse critical comments about the company's chief executive officer under an alias, which was traced back to the worker's company computer.[24]

The moral of the firings is that firms face nontrivial growing legal constraints, not the least of which are harassment charges that workers can file against one another and the company. These constraints have tightened for three reasons:

- Congress and state legislatures have passed stricter laws on various forms of workplace harassment.
- Offensive material in the workplace is nothing new to the digital age. Copies of pictures from erotic magazines and dirty jokes have always circulated in many workplaces. However, the advent of the Internet has reduced the cost of finding and getting all kinds of materials into the workplace, especially sexually explicit materials. Some of the material available for free or little cost is likely to test the limits of most people's sense of propriety. (In a half-second search of Google.com at the time of this writing, there were 182,000 sites listed with the phrase *sexually explicit* typed in. In less time, even more sites were found for *bestiality*.) With E-mail, material of all kinds has become easier—that is, less costly—for employees to distribute widely, increasing the odds that some employees will deem the material offensive.
- With the ongoing shift of work to computers and the development of new software programs, firms can more easily monitor their workers, and the ability to monitor can mean that the monitoring can be done at lower cost, but also can carry with it a legal obligation for firms to do exactly that, monitor their workers' surfing and E-mail activities.

As the Microsoft antitrust case has shown, firms must now also be mindful that if they are ever suspected of violating the nation's antitrust laws, their computer records, including all Web sites visited and all personal and work-related E-mails sent by all employees, are subject to being subpoenaed and used against the firm. In Microsoft's case, the E-mails of top executives were introduced in court to prove (according to the Justice Department) that Microsoft intended to destroy Netscape in Microsoft's drive to take over the browser market.[25]

The threat of penalties from workplace surfing and E-mailing that firms feel adds to the firms' estimated value of instituting policies and monitoring systems discourage inappropriate and offensive, not to mention illegal, surfing and E-mailing. Given that firms cannot always know exactly what forms of surfing and E-mailing will be subject to prosecution in the future, their monitoring efforts might curb more than inappropriate and offensive E-mails. They might discourage frank and open discussions of firm business that could possibly later be reinterpreted for legal ends that, when the E-mails were written, were never imagined. No one should be surprised if Dow's line workers and Microsoft's executives are now far more guarded in their E-mails. The legal threats the workers feel from their personal surfing and

E-mailing at work can increase their estimated personal costs from doing such, causing them to cut back. Firms would then find monitoring their employees less costly.

Of course, the legal threats are probably felt most by large firms, those with deep pockets that can be tapped, via court rulings, by the lawyers and their clients. We might anticipate that the deeper the financial pockets of firms (large or small), the greater the legal threat of misuse of company computers and Internet connections and the greater the firm demand for the elimination of the misuse of those technologies. This does not mean that less misuse should be expected in larger firms than smaller firms. Workers in larger firms can often get by with more misuse of firm resources because monitoring a larger number of workers is more difficult in larger firms than smaller firms. In a two-person firm, the misuse can be easily detected and attributed to one or the other person. In a firm with thousands of employees, the misuse can be far more difficult to detect. All I can say is that the legal threats firms face will tend to lead to more monitoring than would otherwise exist. Larger firms will likely have a greater incentive to curb the misuse, whatever the level, than smaller firms.

Firms of all sizes are currently in something of a legal quandary. On the one hand, they can be sued for employees who use their office computers in various ways to create, intentionally or inadvertently, what a court might describe as a hostile work environment. On the other hand, the law surrounding their right to monitor their workers with or without telling them remains somewhat uncertain. The federal Electronic Communications Privacy Act of 1986 (ECPA) makes it a federal felony for an employer to intercept and disclose employee E-mails. This means that they can be sued by workers who are disciplined for misusing their office computers for invasion of privacy. Needless to say, this uncertainty must temper employers' eagerness to monitor their workers.[26]

However, as attorneys James Garrity and Eoghan Casey point out, the ECPA allows the provider of a computer system to "intercept, disclose, or use that communication in the normal course of his employment while engaged in any activity which is a necessary incident to the rendition of his service or to the protection of the rights or property of the provider of that service,"[27] which would appear to allow employers to investigate, in the event of network misconduct, security breaches, especially if the employer has employees acknowledge the company's Internet/E-mail policies. However, this "provider exception" will ultimately depend on the nature of the monitoring and the content of the communications intercepted.

The University of California goes to great length to assure employees of the privacy of their electronic communications. Before anyone on campus can intercept another employee's electronic message or boot up another employee's computer, written consent must be obtained from the executive vice president for administration.[28] Like so many other employers, the University of California system is bound by other laws, most notably the California Public Records Act that "declares that access to information concerning the conduct of the people's business is a fundamental and necessary right of every person in this state," which can mean that the privacy rights of state employees to their electronic communications can be abridged, given requests from outside the university.[29]

Given the uncertainties in the law, employers—especially ones with deep pockets—would be well advised to clearly articulate the company's surfing and E-mail policies to their employees and then make a good faith effort to enforce them. As for workers, they need to recognize that:

- Workplace computers, and the work done on them, are considered the property of the firm, and not the workers.
- Most E-mails (and instant messages) can be easily read by many people, including supervisors, as they make their way to the designated recipients. In this regard, E-mails are much more like postcards than sealed letters.
- Almost all E-mails can be traced back to their senders.
- Most people's Web surfing can be easily tracked in a variety of ways.
- Workers can be disciplined—even fired—for violating their companies' announced Web surfing and E-mailing policies.
- Computers used to engaged in Internet-based crimes are treated in the law much as guns are treated, as weapons, which can add to the charges and, if convicted, to the severity of the punishment.[30]

CONCLUDING COMMENTS

This chapter has made one central point: The steady stream of reports on the supposed misuse of workplace technologies is interesting but not very instructive. The reports fail to recognize that many workers effectively pay for the time they waste and that many firms do little to heed implied advice in such reports because they understand their goal is a very complex one, not easily resolved by simple-minded general rules on employee Web surfing. A firm's most fundamental goal is to make money for their stockholders, not play nanny to the adults they hire. In pursuit of profits, more, not less, personal Web surfing and E-mailing at work might be the way to go.

Does the analysis of this chapter mean that workers would want themselves and their coworkers to do what they wish at work? Of course, each worker might want a workplace in which he or she were free to do as he or she wished while everyone else, because of the monitoring, had to strictly follow company rules on the use of work time for work only. But that is not to say that they would like to work in an environment in which anything goes. The reason is that little would likely get done as many, if not most or all, workers shirk on the job at will. As a consequence, the firm's survival would be in jeopardy and the workers' jobs and incomes would be at risk.

Accordingly, workers have a demand for workplace rules and restrictions that encourage everyone to work with the interest of the firm in mind. Indeed, up to a point, such restrictions can reduce the firm's wage bill because workers in greater numbers want to work for firms with such restrictions. The workers might get lower wages as a result but they would also incur lower risks of losing their jobs, meaning the expected value of their earnings might be higher even when their actual wages, along with the risk cost of losing their wages, are lower. At the same time, employers must understand that they can be too restrictive on their workplace rules and monitoring, forcing them to pay higher wages than their competitors.

The basic point of this chapter is straightforward: In setting firm policies regarding personal Web surfing and E-mailing at work, or anything else, firms have to optimize their way through a complex web of interconnected market pressures. The journalists who write about wasted time at work on the Web do not seem to appreciate just how complex the problems facing managers are, and how delicate the balance struck must inevitably be.

NOTES

1. Greg Farell, "Online Time at Office Soars," *USA Today*, 18 February 2000, p. 1A.

2. Diane Duvall, "Many Factors Drive 'Business Only' Computer-Use Policy," *Kansas City Business Journal*, February 25, 2000, 23.

3. Eleena de Lisser, "Windows Shopping—One-Click Commerce: What People Do Now to Goof Off at Work," *Wall Street Journal*, 24 September 1999, p. A1.

4. Farell, "Online Time."

5. Lisser, "Windows Shopping."

6. Duvall, "Many Factors Drive 'Business Only' Computer-Use Policy."

7. Instant messaging in the workplace more than doubled between September 2000 (2.3 billion minutes) to September 2001 (4.9 billion minutes), according to Jupiter Media Metrix. See Dan Costa, "IM Watching: Like E-Mail, Instant Messages Can Be Monitored," *PC Magazine*, April 9, 2002, 25.

8. See Richard B. McKenzie and Dwight R. Lee, *Managing through Incentives: How to Develop a More Collaborative, Productive, and Profitable Organization* (New York: Oxford University Press, 1998), chap. 2.

9. Farell, "Online Time."

10. Lisser, "Windows Shopping."

11. See Jonathan Rauch, *Demosclerosis: The Silent Killer of American Government* (New York: Times Books, 1994).

12. For a lucid discussion of voter ignorance, see Gordon Tullock, *The Mathematics of Politics* (Ann Arbor: University of Michigan Press, 1972).

13. Roger Ebert, "Enough! A Modest Proposal to End the Junk Mail Plague," *Yahoo Internet Life*, December 1996, 26.

14. Ibid.

15. Of course, managers may want to vary the E-mail charge, letting it depend on whether the E-mail is sent to someone within the firm or someone outside. And the charge might very well be greater for E-mails sent inside, especially when the inside recipients have no administrative control over the senders. Employees who send E-mail messages to other far-removed inside employees may feel little cost from their E-mailing. The burden of sorting through and reading the E-mails is imposed on someone else in another department or division who can impose little in the way of reciprocal cost (which may help explain why so much of the E-mail I—and others— receive is of little value; the senders know they bear little cost other than being ignored). Employees of one firm who must E-mail employees in other firms understand that a real and abiding threat—cost—looms from their excessive E-mailing. They understand that they can lose potential business or, what amounts to the same thing, that their prices for goods and services bought or sold will be less favorable than they would otherwise have been (had E-mails been controlled).

16. Torsten Ove, "Caught in the Web Watch: Some Companies Spy on Your Surfing Activities, But Others Couldn't Care Less, If You Are Getting Work Done," *Orange County Register*, 17 April 2000, p. C12.

17. Carla Feldman and Jill Westmoreland, "Minimizing Employer Liability for Employee Internet Use," *Los Angeles Business Journal*, July 31, 2000, 30.

18. Ibid.

19. Ibid.

20. Dana E. Corbin, "Keeping a Virtual Eye on Employees," *Occupational Health and Safety*, November 1, 2000, 24–28.

21. Timothy Burn, "Employers Find Internet Misuse, Use Software to Block 'Dirty Surfing,'" *Washington Times*, 15 February 1999, p. D8.

22. As quoted by Greg Miller, "Fired by Big Brother," *Los Angeles Times Magazine*, January 28, 2001, 36.

23. Ibid., 11–13.

24. Alex Bergenson, "Enron Fired Workers for Complaining Online," *New York Times*, 21 January 2002, p. C1.

25. For example, in its complaint against Microsoft, the Justice Department concluded that "Microsoft purposefully set out to do whatever it took to make sure significant market participants distributed and used Internet Explorer instead of Netscape's browser—including paying some customers to take IE and using its unique control over Windows to induce others to do so." The government then used Bill

Gates's internal E-mail written in July 1996, two years before the complaint was filed, to support its contention: "I was quite frank with him [Scott Cook, chief executive officer of Intuit] that if he had a favor we could do for him that would cost us something like $1M to do that in return for switching browsers in the next few months I would be open to doing that." See Joel I. Klein et al., *United States v. Microsoft Corporation*, Complaint, First District Court, Civil Action No. 98-1232, May 20, 1998, 5, as found at http://www.usdj.gov/at/cases/f1700/1763.htm. Judge Thomas Penfield Jackson used the Gates E-mail quote, along with other Microsoft E-mails, in November 1999 to find that Gates had used Microsoft's market power to thwart competition. See Thomas Penfield Jackson, *United States v. Microsoft Corporation*, Findings of Fact, First District Court, Civil Action No. 98-1232, November 5, 1999, 16, as found at http://www.usdoj.gov/atr/cases/f3800/msjudgex.htm. That finding resulted in the judge ruling in 2000 that Microsoft had violated the antitrust laws and needed to be broken into two firms. See Thomas Penfield Jackson, *United States v. Microsoft Corporation*, Conclusions of Law, First District Court, Civil Action No. 98-1232, April 13, 2000, 2–3, as found at http://www.usdoj.gov/atr/cases/f4400/4469.htm.

26. See James Garrity and Eoghan Casey, "Internet Misuse in the Workplace, A Lawyer's Primer," *Florida Law Journal*, n.d., as found at http://www.flabar.org/newflabar/publicmediainfo/TFBJournal/nov98-2.html.

27. Ibid.

28. "Electronic Mail Policy," Office of the President, University of California, reissued March 23, 1998, as found at http://www.ucop.edu/ucophome/policies/E-mail/E-mail.html.

29. Government Code, Sec. 6250-7270, as found at http://www.leginfo.ca.gov/cgi-bin/displaycode?section=gov&group=06001-07000&file=6250-6270.

30. Ibid., 5.

9

Intellectual Property Rights

At one time, maybe no more than thirty years ago, an entire university-level introductory course in economics could be completed with no mention of the role of private property rights—and certainly no mention of private intellectual property rights. Property rights were subsumed in discussions of markets. There was then little overt professional appreciation for just how critical respect for and enforcement of property rights are to well functioning markets, digital or otherwise.

Over the past three decades, a lot of professional ink in economic and legal journals has been spilled to make a simple but crucial economic point: To work well, markets need respected and enforced property rights, a point fully pertinent to digital markets, as we will see.[1] Without property rights, there would be nothing to trade in market settings, because trades are, fundamentally, exchanges of specified rights to things, or, to be more precise, rights to use things in certain highly prescribed ways. If you buy a computer, you really buy a set of rights to use the computer in certain ways, which necessarily implies that the computer cannot be used in other ways. You can use your computer to run a multitude of applications, but you cannot use it to reproduce those applications for sale to others, at least not legally, and you cannot use it to send out anonymous hate E-mails to targeted groups. You can buy a lot of goods on the Internet, but in most advanced countries around the world, it is illegal for you to buy or sell child pornography. (In some places, it is even illegal for you to intentionally use your computer to view pictures of naked children.) If you live in France or Germany, you cannot use your computer to buy Nazi memorabilia because, again, it is illegal to do so.

It stands to reason that the more rights that come with your computer, the more valuable it is to you. The more restricted the rights, the less valuable. Of course, this means that the price you are willing to pay for a computer can be expected to rise and fall with the rights that are bought. It also means that property rights provide people with the requisite incentives to use the resources available to them judiciously and to produce what others want. But as we will also see, if carried too far, the unchecked spread of property rights harbors the potential for disincentives to produce efficiently and with creativity. Both the potential boon and bane of property rights are captured in what have been called "tragedies"—the "tragedy of the commons" and the "tragedy of the anticommons"—both of which are made more problematic for intellectual property (which will be defined later) and aggravated even more in the digital sector of the economy.

THE REASONS FOR PROPERTY RIGHTS

Property rights are important in the American way of life for any number of reasons, most prominently because they afford people—as distinct from governments—a measure of power over things, and, therefore, a measure of freedom to do as they please (within bounds). And in giving people control over things, private property rights restrict the power of governments, which for the country's Founding Fathers' was seen as one of the more attractive attributes of these rights.[2] From the Founding Fathers' philosophical perspective, the assignment of private property rights would keep resources out of the hands of kings and queens and national political leaders who would, if given the chance, misuse and abuse the resources at hand to suppress others, those outside of the power elite. The Founding Fathers' presumption was that private property rights, along with constitutional precepts and the rules of democratic decision making, enhanced people's welfare by limiting the mischief that the ruling class could do with the country's resources. If politicians could be further constrained in taxing people's property, or the income property could yield, the citizenry's welfare would be further enhanced, or so the Founding Fathers reasoned.[3]

Property rights also allow a multitude of individuals to use the local information that is at their disposal. Hence, private property rights tap into the intelligence of many people who are interested in doing things they consider productive and useful. As the late Friedrich Hayek, a Nobel laureate in economics, argued at length over much of his career, central control of property (through some sort of Soviet-style central planning authority) would inevitably fail because centralization invariably means that the intelligence of decisions that are made would be circumscribed by the intelligence of those relatively few people who were a part of the ruling class (or the polity or planning bureaucracy). The quality, if not efficiency, of their decisions would necessarily be impaired by the limited amount of information available to them, and the even more limited amount of information they could absorb and manage intelligently. People in power can only know so much, and they simply cannot get the required information on what the great mass of people want, need, and are willing and able to spend their own money on, given what they know about their local situations.

The essential problem of rational economic order is that, Hayek wrote, "the knowledge of circumstances of which we must make use never exists in concentrated or integrated form, but solely as the dispersed bits of incomplete and frequently contradicted knowledge which all the separate individuals [in a society] possess."[4] If central authorities cannot get access to the information that is dispersed everywhere, how does society make use of the information available to only individuals? Hayek's answer is straightforward: Assign rights to property and then ensure that people's activities, founded on their local information, are coordinated through market exchanges. Through such exchanges, and the prices that markets spawn, individuals learn much about what others want to do with their property and about how they must adjust their own activities. Of course, the digitization of business processes and goods, along with the advent of the Internet, harbors the potential of greatly expanding the number of people who can interact, as well as the array of ways they can interact, all at lower costs of production.

As I will argue, the social problems of both digital piracy and privacy emanate from much the same source, an absence of clearly defined and effectively enforced property rights. The development of the digital sector of the economy will depend critically on respect for and enforcement of property rights to what is commonly referred to as "intellectual property." Intellectual property includes the legal rights associated with the following:

- *Patents*, or inventions that are new, nonobvious, and applicable to commerce;
- *Trademarks*, such as words, letters, drawings, emblems, or signatures that distinguish a particular good or service from others;
- *Industrial designs*, or original or novel ornamental aspects of useful articles, such as shapes, lines, and colors;

- *Copyrights*, or the expression of ideas, not the ideas themselves, in the form of, for example, books, music, photographs, and movies.

A key characteristic of these forms of property, for the purposes of this book, is that almost all of them can be produced in digital form, and that they can also be stored, sold, and distributed in the form of 1's and 0's, or a series of electrons. As I will argue, we should not be surprised if some digital firms encourage the pirating of their products, at least up to some point. Because the cost of copying digital goods is so low (and falling year by year), relative to the cost of copying nondigital goods, we should not be surprised if the digital sector of the economy is plagued with too much copying, or piracy, or unauthorized copying of electronic goods, whether software, E-books, E-music, or E-movies. In the software industry, piracy can take the form of the following:

- *Softlifting*, or software shoplifting, which occurs when someone buys a single copy of a program and, without authorization from the software producer, loads the program onto more than one of his or her computers or shares the program with friends, family members, and/or coworkers;
- *Software counterfeiting*, which occurs when someone duplicates and distributes a copyrighted program and makes the program appear to be produced and distributed by the legitimate producer;
- *Original equipment manufacturer (OEM) unbundling of software*, which occurs when an OEM sells bundled programs (for example, those programs included in Microsoft Office) separately (and usually for a higher combined price than the bundled software).

Software piracy can also include unauthorized renting of software and unauthorized downloading of software from Internet sites. Piracy of other forms of electronic goods—E-books, E-music, or E-movies—would include all unauthorized copying that, unlike the copying of the printed word, electronic law (at this writing) does not provide for fair use.[5] The prospect of digital piracy raises a whole new set of economic and legal issues, not the least of which is whether goods and services—such as newspaper and magazine articles and books and songs—produced digitally are covered by prior contracts and what constitutes fair use. Then there is the nontrivial issue of whether the fair-use doctrine should be sacrificed because unfair use of digital technology cannot be avoided if fair use is permitted at all and whether some piracy might, in fact, be beneficial in markets beset with network effects. But before we tackle such issues, we need a firm understanding of the social role private property rights, whether relating to physical or intellectual property, play in the economy.

THE TRAGEDY OF THE COMMONS

To many, the ideal state of affairs may appear to be one in which everyone has the right to use all resources, goods, and services and in which no one (not even the state) has the right to exclude anyone else from their use. We may designate such rights as "common property rights" or just "communal rights." Many rights to scarce property have been and still are allocated in this way. Rights to the use of a university's facilities are held communally by the students. No one admitted to the university has the right to keep you off campus paths or lawns or from using the library according to certain rules and regulations. (Such rules and regulations form the boundaries, much as if they were natural, within which the rights are truly communal.)

The rights to city parks, sidewalks, and streets are held communally. Before our country was settled, many Indian tribes held communal rights to hunting grounds, that is, at least within the tribe's territory, no one had the right to exclude anyone else from hunting on the land. During most of the first half of the nineteenth century, the rights to graze cattle on the prairies of the western United States were held communally; anyone who wanted to let cattle loose on the plains could do so.

Under communal ownership, no one can be excluded from the use of the resource. Consequently, once in use, the resource becomes, for that period of time, the private property of the user. The people who drive their cars onto the freeway take up space on the road that is not in use; no one else (hopefully!) can then use that space at the same time. Unless the drivers violate the rules of the road, they cannot be excluded from that space; and if they are rational, they will continue to use the resource until the marginal cost of doing so equals the marginal benefits to them. They may consider most of the costs involved in their use of the road, but one they may overlook, especially as it applies to themselves personally, is that their space may have had some alternative use, that is, by others. Their presence also increases highway congestion and the discomfort of the other drivers. As a result, they may overextend the use of their resource, meaning they continue to drive as long as the additional benefits they, themselves, get from driving additional miles is greater than the additional cost. However, they can overlook the costs they impose on others, which can mean that the total cost for everyone driving additional miles is greater than the total benefits. We have now considered the distinction between private and communal property. Several examples will enable us to amplify that distinction and to understand more clearly the limitations of communal property rights and the pervasive use of private property.

Pollution can be described as a logical consequence of communal property rights to streams, rivers, air, and so forth. The state and federal governments, by right of eminent domain, have always held rights to these resources; but until very recently they have inadequately asserted their right to exclude people and firms from their use. As a result, the resources have been subject to communal use and to overuse, in the same sense discussed previously.

By dumping waste into the rivers, people, firms, and local governments have been able to acquire ownership to portions of the communal resource—they use it and pollute it. Furthermore, because of the absence of exclusion, those people doing the polluting do not have to pay to draw the resource away from its alternative uses (like pretty scenery) or to reimburse the people harmed by the pollution for the damage done. Under communal ownership, in which government does not exercise its control, the firm with smoke billowing from its stacks does not have to compensate the people who live around the plant for the eye irritation they experience or the extra number of times they have to paint their homes.

Pollution is often thought to be the product of antisocial behavior, as indeed it often is. Many who pollute simply do not care about what they do to others. However, much pollution results from the behavior of people who do not have devious motives. People may view their behavior as having an inconsequential effect on the environment. The person who throws a cigarette butt on the ground may reason that if this cigarette butt is the only one on the ground, it will not materially affect anyone's sensibilities, and in fact it may not. However, if everyone follows the same line of reasoning, the cigarette butts will accumulate and an eyesore will develop. Even then, there may be little incentive for people to stop throwing their butts on the ground. Again, a person may reason on the basis of the effects of his own individual action, If I do not throw my butt on the ground here with all the others, will my behavior materially affect the environment quality, given the fact that other butts are already there?

Biologist Garrett Hardin argues that cattlemen will ask much the same question when contemplating adding to their stock of cattle on pastures that are held in "common," meaning not owned privately by anyone. The more important right that is missing is the ability of anyone to stop others from adding to their stock of cattle on the entire pasture, or parts of it. In deciding how many cattle to add, each cattleman will likely be compelled to reason, as does the smoker, that the addition of his cattle—and his cattle alone—to the pasture will make no difference to the amount of feed available to the cattle of other herdsmen. One person's cattle just do not eat that much, given the size of the pasture. The result is that the cattlemen will collectively face an out-come—what Hardin dubs the tragedy of the commons—that none of them would want: "Therein is the tragedy. Each man is locked into a system that compels him to increase his herd without limit—in a world that is limited. Ruin is the destination toward which all men rush, each pursuing his own best interest in a society that believes in the freedom of the commons. Freedom in the commons brings ruin to all."[6] Note that under a communal-property arrangement, people have rights to use the property (or usage rights), but they do not have the right to exclude anyone (or exclusion rights). The prospect of the emergence of a tragedy under communal ownership has been a very pow-erful argument for conversion of communal rights to private rights, which is an institutional setting under which the owners simultaneously have both usage and exclusion rights.[7]

According to Harold Demsetz, the hunting grounds of the Indian tribes of the Labrador Peninsula were held in common until the emergence of the fur trade there.[8] The Indians had full usage rights, meaning they each could hunt as they wished without being excluded by other members of their tribe. Pre-sumably, given the cost of hunting and the limited demand for meat, there was no inclination to overhunt, that is, continue to hunt until there was an adverse effect on the stock of animals in the area.[9]

However, when fur trading commenced and the Indians hunted animals for their skins, the demand and, therefore, the price of animal skins in-creased. This provided an incentive for the Indians to hunt beyond their de-mand for meat. Under communal ownership, when a beaver was killed, an Indian hunter did not have to consider the effects that his action had on the ability of the other hunters to trap and hunt. Each hunter, through his own efforts, imposed a cost on the others; when a beaver was killed by one hunter, the task of finding beavers was made more difficult for the other hunters. The cost may be construed as a social cost, much like the congestion a driver can impose on other drivers. Furthermore, under a communal rights structure, there was little incentive for hunters to avoid trapping or incurring the costs of increasing the stock of animals. If a hunter refrained from killing a beaver, perhaps someone else would kill it. In addition, if one person tried to increase the stock of animals, perhaps many others would benefit from his efforts in terms of more animals for them to kill. There was, in other words, no assurance that the Indian who built up the stock of animals would reap the benefits. The Indians' solution to the problem of overkill was to assign private property rights to portions of the hunting grounds. Each individual, by virtue of his right to exclude others, had an incentive to control his own take from the land and to take measures, much as ranchers do, to increase the potential stock of animals.

Today, we rarely hear talk about an overkill of cattle or pigs or chickens that are being raised for food by farmers, but we read news reports all the time about how people are overfishing the oceans, lakes, and streams, a fate that is showing up in decreases in fishermen's daily catches of a variety of sea creatures of all kinds, not the least of which are tuna, salmon, and whales.[10] The difference in the reports can be chalked up to the fact that cattle, pigs, and chickens are owned, whereas the fish and whales are not. Cattlemen, for example, give up future profits when they overkill their stock. That is, they lose the opportunity to sell their cattle later, perhaps at a higher price, which provides an incentive for cattlemen to conserve their herd. Individual fishermen lose nothing by overfishing the oceans. Each fisherman's fishing does little or nothing to exacerbate the overfishing problem. Similarly, each fisherman's restraint on fishing does little or nothing to correct the problem. One fisherman's restraint only increases the ease, albeit in a minor way, with which other fishermen can increase their catch.

Indeed, following on the work of University of Chicago law and economics professor Ronald Coase, economists have often come to the conclusion that to make markets work well, property rights need to be assigned and respected and/or enforced. When markets do not work well (that is, there is a degree of inefficiency) or do not work at all (as happens in war-ravaged areas where theft is rampant), economists have learned to look at how property rights are, or are not, assigned, respected, and enforced as a source of the problem. And as far as the efficiency of the system goes, when transaction costs are not material, it does not much matter who gets the property right initially. Property rights can be assigned randomly, or they can even be distributed by dumping ownership rights out of an airplane. If the rights are picked up by people who can use them most productively, all to the good. No trades need be made. If, on the other hand, the rights are picked up by people who cannot use the rights most productively, then the initial rights holders will sell their rights to those who can use them more productively. This is because the people who can use the rights most productively can offer those who have the rights a payment that is higher than what the initial rights holders can earn if they are not traded.

For example, if one of the initial rights holders—who happened to pick up the property certificates that were dumped from the plane—can earn only $1,000 (in present value terms) from use of the property, while someone else can earn $2,000 from using the property, then the latter person should be able to buy the property rights for something over $1,000—say, $1,500. The trade will make both parties better off.

PROPERTY RIGHTS ENFORCEMENT

What do property rights have to do with digital economics? A whole lot, but the main reason is because of the inherent difficulty of enforcing property rights to digital goods.

A key lesson learned from property rights theory is that when the rights for any good are not assigned and protected, then the firm producing the good has an impaired incentive to produce it. Granted, when rights are not protected, some people might buy the good out of respect for the firm's rights to what it produces (just as some people resist the temptation to pollute when they could go undetected). At the same time, if people can claim and consume units of a good that are produced without having to pay for the units, then we should expect some unknown number of consumers—at times, perhaps all—to do exactly what they can do, claim and use the good without paying for it.

The firm producing the good will not be able to charge as much as it could otherwise. This is because the demand for the good will be undercut by the number of people who use the good without paying. The lower price will mean that the firm cannot justify producing as many units as it would produce if it could charge a higher price. This is because the marginal cost of producing additional units can be expected to rise. The firm would be reducing its profits by producing and selling units on which the marginal cost is greater than the price, which is suppressed by the lowered demand that, in turn, is suppressed by the absence of property rights enforcement.

The laws against theft and their enforcement by police departments, backed up by the threat of fines and incarceration, are an important way property rights are protected. It stands to reason that the greater the enforcement—meaning the greater the chance (or probability) that thieves will be caught, prosecuted, convicted, and penalized—the greater the expected cost thieves must incur from stealing other people's property, the greater the price of stolen goods, and the greater the demand for the legal alternatives. Hence, the greater the enforcement, the greater the incentive a firm may have to produce the good legally and the more that will be produced.

More formally, it is altogether reasonable to suggest that theft will occur when the payoff from theft is positive, or when the expected gains from theft are greater than the expected costs, or

$$\text{Expected Gains} > \text{Expected Costs}$$

and where

$$\text{Payoff} = \text{Expected Gains} - \text{Expected Costs}$$

The expected gains from theft are a function of when the gains are received (the further out in the future the gains are received, when they are received, the lower their expected value) and the probability that the gains will actually be received (the higher the probability that the gains will be realized, the greater the expected gains from theft). The expected costs of theft, on the other hand, are related to the out-of-pocket expenditures (E) the thief must make; the thief's opportunity cost (O); and the assessment of the losses the thief will incur when caught (C), prosecuted (P), convicted (V), and then penalized (L). The last cost is the one most problematic for the prospective thief, because of the serial probabilities involved, which imply that

$$\text{Expected Costs} = E + O + (C*P*V*L*\text{Penalty})$$

The probability that most thieves will be caught for most property theft is far from certain. The same can be said of the thief's chance of being prosecuted if caught, of being convicted if prosecuted, and of being penalized if convicted. With low probabilities for being caught, prosecuted, convicted, and penalized, the prospective thief might figure that his or her expected cost from the law enforcement is quite low, despite a heavy penalty if he or she is actually forced to incur the heavy penalty.

To see this point, assume that the penalty imposed when a thief is convicted is $10,000. Suppose also that the thief can reasonably expect to be caught only 3 percent of the time (which is high for shoplifting and could be high for software piracy), prosecuted only 25 percent of the time he or she is caught, convicted 50 percent of the time he or she is prosecuted, and penalized only 60 percent of the time he or she is convicted. The thief can reason that he or she will incur the penalty of $10,000, only .225 percent of the time, which means that the thief can expect, on average, to incur a penalty cost of only $22.50 on each theft. Put another way, the thief can be expected to steal as long as the theft can be expected to yield more than $22.50 plus his or her out-of-pocket expenditures and the opportunity cost.

Granted, some people are not inclined to steal, for all kinds of good reasons, not the least of which is that they consider theft wrong. However, the theft calculus that I have laid out allows us to make several key points:

- The frequency of theft can be expected to be positively related to the payoff. The greater the payoff, the greater the expected frequency of theft. This means that the greater the value of the stolen property, the greater the expected frequency of theft, everything else constant.

- The frequency of theft can be expected to be negatively related to the probabilities of being caught, prosecuted, convicted, and penalized. The higher their probabilities, the greater the expected cost of theft, the lower the payoff, and the lower the frequency of theft.
- The frequency of theft can be expected to be negatively related to the penalty imposed when the thief is caught, prosecuted, and convicted. The higher the penalty, everything held constant, the greater the expected cost, and the lower the expected payment from theft.
- Up and down movements in the various factors that affect the expected frequency of theft—the gains and the probabilities of being caught, prosecuted, convicted, and penalized—can be offsetting or reinforcing in affecting thefts. For example, if the probabilities of being caught, prosecuted, convicted, and penalized go down, the penalty would have to be increased to prevent the frequency of theft from rising.

The police cannot be everywhere at all times, mainly because there are costs to ensuring that they are everywhere. If enforcement of property rights is extended, the costs of enforcement can be expected to rise at the same time that the gains in terms of improved production incentives can be expected to go down. Beyond some point, it does not make economic sense for the enforcement to be extended. The expected economic gains from extended enforcement will, beyond some point, be less than the expected economic costs of the extended enforcement.

This means that there is always and everywhere some optimum amount of enforcement. This also means that property rights can only be expected to be protected up to a point. It follows that if the cost of enforcement rises, then we can expect a curb in police presence, and a reduction in the probability that the thieves will be caught and eventually penalized. However, the implied reduction in the thief's expected cost can be offset with a rise in the penalty that is imposed when the thief is caught, prosecuted, and convicted. If the optimum level of public enforcement of property is not enough for property holders, then the property holders will have to use private enforcement means. These supplemental means of private enforcement of private property rights can include chain-link fences topped with razor wire, safes, guards and guard dogs, security cameras, and electronic tags.

Such enforcement mechanisms may be costly to property holders, but having public enforcement totally protect all property rights has built-in incentive problems. Knowing that they stand little to lose (because of the public enforcement) by making theft easy, firms can be expected to make theft easy, which means they can shift their cost of property protection to the government. Each firm might like to do that—but only if other firms are not allowed to do the same. If all firms are allowed to shift their protection costs to public enforcers, there can be a form of government-inspired "pollution," given that people can impose costs on each other through their greater governmental enforcement demands and higher taxes. In short, the optimum level of enforcement would presume some private enforcement efforts. Otherwise, there could easily be too much public enforcement, meaning a loss of welfare for everyone concerned.

The property rights for nondigital goods have a natural built-in form of self-enforcement, which reduces the need for public enforcement: Nondigital goods are typically costly to produce. Not only that, production typically runs up against the law of diminishing returns, which means that the marginal cost of production rises, sometimes rapidly. People clearly have an interest in stealing goods that are costly to produce by simply ripping off a firm's output, as they do millions of times a year in the United States. Thieves can sell their stolen property, albeit at a substantial discount, but they do not have to incur the production costs. Thieves also have an interest in pirating goods, that is, making copies of goods—for example, Levi jeans and Rolex watches—that have established markets, and then selling their copies as originals. The pirates might have to sell their goods at a discount, but they do not have to incur the heavy development costs. The pirates effectively steal the rights of the owners of the goods they copy, and their theft shows up in the form of lower prices that the owners can charge for their goods, which, in turn, can be reflected in the owners' lowered stock values.

Still, the pirates' ability to erode the owner's market, and stock values, is limited by the pirates' own production costs. They have to replicate the good from scratch and incur material costs, as well as establish and maintain distribution channels and sales forces, which can be expensive, perhaps made even more expensive by the fact that the pirates' goods are typically visible and weighty, and, accordingly, subject to detection by law enforcement. Their marginal production costs are also likely to rise, beyond some point, because of the law of diminishing returns, and rising marginal production costs limit the ability of pirates to take an ever-larger share of the owner's markets. Moreover, the number of potential pirates normally would exclude the count of young people in the general population, mainly because the production of pirated nondigital goods often requires a level of sophistication and skills not yet acquired by many (but not all) young people. Because the pirates' operations are illegal, subject to penalties, pirates are likely to operate on a much smaller scale than the owners of the pirated goods. As a consequence, the owners of the firms that produce goods subject to being copied usually have a cost advantage over the pirates, which lowers the pirates' expected returns from their illegal work. Indeed, some goods such as airplanes and automobiles are rarely pirated, mainly because the pirates cannot hope to compete with the producers of the goods they want to pirate.

Digital goods are in a totally different class when it comes to the potential for them to be pirated. This is because digital goods are made of nothing more than electrons and can be easily copied. Indeed, every copy that the owner of the digital good produces harbors the potential to be a master, which means that every buyer can become a seller. Moreover, each buyer can reproduce copies at little more, and perhaps less, cost than can the owner of the original, and there is nothing stopping the buyers of the pirated copies from becoming pirates themselves.

Digital goods piracy often requires minimum skills and computer sophistication, given that all the pirate has to know how to do is turn on a computer and be able to install computer software on the hard drive, or to be able to use a program like Easy CD Maker that more or less automates the burning of counterfeit CDs—software, E-music, E-books, or any other copyrighted electronic good—and requires no more than a few clicks of the mouse. The required limited skill set, which is now being taught in many elementary schools, means that a sizable percentage of young people are potential, if not actual, pirates of digital goods.

Even when each pirate produces few copies, the number of copies produced by all pirates can escalate geometrically. Suppose four pirates each buy a copy of a digital good—for example, a song—and each produces four copies that are sold to pirates who do the same, and so on. After only eight iterations, more than 87,000 copies will have been pirated. After two more iterations, nearly 1.4 million will have been produced, and three iterations later, there will be nearly 90 million pirated copies in existence.

Moreover, the originals of many pirated goods, such as many software applications, sell for several thousands of dollars, which means even after discounting by the standard fencing rate of 80 percent, pirated goods can carry market prices of several hundred dollars, far more than the cost of copying them. The copies of the digital goods can be distributed at minimum cost, via E-mail and the Internet, and can be sold through online auctions or even downloaded from Web sites that can be anywhere in the world. The economies of scale can be on the side of the pirates, not the owners of the digital goods, given that the pirates do not have the owners' development costs.

Granted, the threat of being caught can contain the pirates' individual operating scale. However, as noted, electronic distribution of digital goods means that what is lost in the scale of operations can easily be made up in terms of the multitude of potential pirates, all operating on scales that make detection difficult and prosecution uneconomical. Pirates who are caught and put away can easily be supplanted by other pirates willing to enter the market. Cracking down on the pirating of digital goods is made difficult by the fact that the copies can be made, literally, in the privacy of the pirates' homes, all with computer equipment that is now fairly inexpensive. In addition, there need be no inventory of the copies: They can be made one by one on demand.

THE TRAGEDY OF THE ANTICOMMONS

The tragedy of the commons is a powerful justification for the establishment of private property rights (or at least a case for managing any resource so that the resource is not overused, meaning its full value is somehow not realized). But the argument for the establishment of property rights must be understood in its proper context. For the tragedy of the commons to be a potential threat, the resource itself must have a characteristic that land has, subject to use by different people for the same or different purposes. This means that the resource is subject to rivalry and must be exhaustible, much like the pasture in Garrett Hardin's common's problem.[11] There is no reason for establishing property rights when the resource is inexhaustible, because there can be no rivalry and the resource cannot be subject to overuse. In such cases, there is no reason to exclude people from the use of the resource, which is a key element of property rights.

Numbers (1, 2, 3, and so on), letters (A, B, C, and so on), and musical notes (or marks on sheet music or sounds from instruments) need not be subject to property rights assignment because they are inexhaustible in supply—anyone can create them at any time—and they are nonrivalrous. When these words were typed into a computer, the supply of letters available to everyone else in the world was not diminished. Granted, there is a case to be made for assigning property rights to a book, given that the published copies will be limited by the cost of their production, but the letters themselves from which the words (and paragraphs and arguments) were constructed remain as available as they ever were. Hence, there can be no potential for a "tragedy of overuse of letters."

Granted, one might argue that, for example, there is too much information with letters and words freely available, suggesting that the costless letters and words cause people to use real resources to print and transmit the resulting excessive information and to sort through the information clutter to find what is needed. However, even if we accept this argument as valid (which I do not), the argument for privatizing letters and words loses its force when it is recognized that privatization can lead to a greater tragedy, a monopoly of letters and words, which in turn can lead to the under use of letters and words, which is another form of waste, recently dubbed the "tragedy of the anticommons."[12]

This tragedy of the anticommons would be especially tragic if all letters and words were privately owned by one person or firm. The tragedy might even be more severe if individual letters or words were owned by different people or firms, because there could be enormous transaction costs that would have to be incurred by many people to secure the rights to letters and words they need to produce any given piece of information. The assignment of private rights could, in other words, substitute one tragedy—overuse—for another—under use— with no convincing argument that the rights assignment had improved welfare on balance.

Sources of the Anticommons Tragedy

The tragedy of the anticommons can also be encouraged by the require- ment that users seek agreement on usage rights from several (or many) agents who control access to the resource. For example, Michael Heller noticed the anticommons tragedy as it played out in the streets of Moscow after the fall of the Soviet Union. As it was, the streets were lined with carts of goods out- side of perfectly good buildings that stood empty. The buildings remained unused because vendors had to get permission to use the buildings from sev- eral agencies, each of which had exclusion rights but not usage rights. The vendors obviously found it less costly to set up their carts and kiosks than to incur the transactions costs involved in obtaining the required use rights.[13] James Buchanan observed a similar case of the anticommons tragedy in Italy. An entrepreneur in Sardinia was unable to develop a seaside hunting preserve and resort because he was required to get permits from the tourist board, the hotel–restaurant agency, and the public wildlife protection agency.[14]

Heller also points to the problems faced in Moscow with *komunalkas*, or apartments in the center of the city that were shared by several families.[15] Each family might have a bedroom to themselves, but the other rooms of the house—bathrooms, kitchens, and living rooms—would be shared. When these apartments were privatized after the 1989 revolution, all tenants in each apart- ment were separately given property rights to the apartment, meaning each family had the right to block the sale of the apartment. Because the multiple ownership arrangement increased the transaction costs incurred by potential buyers (because of the need to deal with multiple owners) and because each owner could bargain strategically, hoping to extract an undue share of the profits to be made from the sale by holding out, komunalkas often went un-sold, even when they were more highly valued by potential buyers than by the owners. In the sense that the full value of the property could not be realized, the komunalkas were, in a sense, underutilized, an anticommons tragedy.

Buchanan and his George Mason University colleague Yong Yoon are able to show (with a formal mathematical model) that with more than one person with exclusion rights, the resource will be less utilized than would be the case under a single owner/monopoly. They found this to be the case as long as each person with exclusion rights seeks to maximize his or her gain, subject to what the other person does. That is, multiple exclusion rights result in under-utilization of the resource as long as the excluders do not work together with their joint welfare in mind.[16]

What these examples highlight is a point that has been stressed indepen-dently by Stanford Law School professor Lawrence Lessig and University of Wisconsin–Madison information professor Siva Vaidhyanathan, who argue for balance in the privatization process especially relating to intellectual prop-erty, as in all other things.[17] Their point would not be worth mentioning if they did not take their analysis several steps further. Both professors start by point-ing out that copyright and patent law, which is grounded in the Constitution, was never meant to give property rights to copyright holders in the same sense that people have rights to, say, real estate. Instead, copyright and patent hold-ers were given a temporary "monopoly" over what they had created for a lim-ited amount of time.[18] The premise of this constitutional provision was that any implied gains were more of a privilege than a right, and a limited one at that. In Vaidhyanathan's words, the Constitution advocated "thin copyright" protection for authors, leaving much created work in the commons. The Con-stitution did not envision the kind of "thick copyright" body of law, which is a perpetual form of omnipresent market protection, that we now have.

On the other hand, Lessig argues that the seductive logic underlying the tragedy of the commons has been so widely accepted by policy makers and the courts that analysts might not harbor the requisite appreciation for hav-ing at least some resources—especially those that are digital in nature—remain under common ownership, to be exploited with a high degree of free-dom by all without the need to get the permission of the property owners (es-pecially multiple owners). As a consequence, we may be suffering in several key ways through a growing tragedy of the anticommons, without noticing the damage of under usage that is developing, especially in the growth of ideas and technology.

Since the early part of the twentieth century, the radio spectrum (within a range of 3 kilohertz and 300 gigahertz) has been regulated, mainly to prevent the clutter in frequency use that prevented a ship within twenty miles of the sinking *Titanic* from picking up its distress calls after it hit the iceberg. Following Ronald Coase, who argued that government regulation of the radio spectrum is no more justified than government regulation of any other scarce resource, we have auctioned off the radio spectrum, assigning segments, or bands of frequencies, to various owners.[19] The presumption behind the sell-off is that the property rights will tend to reside, ultimately, with those who can use the spectrum frequencies to the greatest value. However, according to Lessig, radio technology has now developed to the point that frequencies can be shared. That is to say, signals can be sent in much the same way that messages are sent over the Internet, with the signals being broken down into packets and the packets routed across bands of frequencies in various ways, using whatever frequencies are not in use at the time, only to be reassembled on reaching their destinations. This technology greatly increases the capacity of the radio spectrum, potentially making its use nonrivalrous (within limits set by government regulations).[20] However, with the frequencies broken up among different owners, such a method would require agreement across a number of owners and would require a dramatic shift in government policy, with the radio spectrum being returned to the commons. But maintenance of the status quo in spectrum use is being supported by powerful political interest groups. Hence, exploitation of the spectrum's full capacity and the development of technology that can increase the spectrum's carrying capacity is being throttled, according to Lessig: "Innovation moves too slowly when it must constantly ask permission from politically controlled agencies."[21]

Patents (and copyrights) can have much the same effect, especially when products incorporate any number of patented parts held by different owners. The owners can hike development costs as they each bargain strategically or just seek monopoly profits. Moreover, patents on parts can increase transaction costs, or they can require an increased scope of operations, with more parts held in one firm than otherwise, without the fragmented patents.

Indeed, Gordon Tullock has pointed out another form of resource misallocation through patents: The existence of patents can give rise to either overemployment or underemployment of resources in research and development activities (depending how the odds of success in securing the patent are appraised). Excessive research expenditures can occur because several firms might simultaneously seek to obtain the patent, with only one firm's development expenditures (those of the firm that applies for the patent first) paying off with the patent. Underemployment of R&D resources can occur when no firm seeks to develop the products because all firms conclude that their prospects of winning the patent race, and the expected return (discounted for time and risk) from their efforts to secure the patent, are not sufficient to justify the R&D expenditures, which is to suggest that the property rights paradigm needs amending for these problems.[22]

The Need for Balance in Control and Freedom

Lessig and Vaidhyanathan, of course, recognize that copyrights and patents are devices that have been developed to provide economic incentives for creativity. However, the incentive for creativity does not need to be unlimited, a fact that has historically been recognized in patent (and copyright) law by the limited life of patents. Lessig and Vaidhyanathan point out that the life of patents (and copyrights) have been extended greatly in the last half century. These extensions might indeed be required, given the growth in development costs for many products and given the reduction in costs of duplicating unprotected goods as the world has moved relentlessly into the digital era. At the same time, the extensions may have been grounded in special-interest politics, not economics, which can imply that the extensions have unnecessarily increased the monopoly rents patent holders have realized, meaning that the economic reward for many patents exceeds the reward required for creating the products and processes. The extensions, Lessig and Vaidhyanathan argue, have given rise to an extended tragedy of the anticommons in the form of too few technological developments in the commons available for exploitation at no cost by other creative people.

Since patents (and copyrights) embody ideas that are by their nature nonrivalrous, Lessig, especially, is concerned about how the continued privatization of ideas will stifle future intellectual developments. He points out that Thomas Jefferson appears to have understood fully the crux of the anticommons problem in the case of ideas:

> If nature has med any one thing less susceptible than all others of exclusive property, it is the action of the thinking power called an idea, which an individual may exclusively express as long as he keeps it to himself; but the moment it is divulged, it forces itself into the possession of everyone, and the receiver cannot dispossess himself of it. Its peculiar character, too, is that no one possesses the less, because every other possesses the whole of it. He who receives an idea from me, receives instructions himself without lessening mine; as he who lites his taper at mine, receives light without darkening me. That ideas would freely spread from one another all over the globe, for the moral and mutual instruction of man, and improvement of his condition, seems to have been peculiarly and benevolently designed by nature, when she made

them, like fire, expansible over all space, without lessening their density at any point, and like air in which we breathe, move, and have our physical being, incapable of confinement, or exclusive appropriation. Inventions then cannot, in nature, be a subject of property.[23]

Lessig and Vaidhyanathan stress that the Founding Fathers envisioned the public domain being constantly fed by works losing their limited copyright protection. They also suggest that something is inherently unreasonable, if not unfair, about copyright law when firms like Disney are able to use works in the public domain—for example, Victor Hugo's *The Hunchback of Notre Dame* and Hans Christian Andersen's *Little Mermaid*—to produce films that perpetually have copyright protection.

Sources of Growing Control

We do need some "system of control to *assure the resource is created*" (emphasis in original), Lessig writes, which explains the patent (and copyright) system that enables developers to recover their development costs but that also is imperfect, assuring that not all of the value of any development is appropriated by the developer: "Intellectual property does this by giving the producers a limited exclusive right over their intellectual property. . . . A 'sufficient return,' however, is not perfect control. . . . Instead some of the benefits ought to be reserved for the public, in common."[24] He concludes:

> In essence, the changes in the environment of the Internet that we are observing now alter the balance between control and freedom on the Net. The tilt of these changes is pronounced: control is increasing. And while one cannot say in the abstract that increased control is a mistake, it is clear that we are expanding this control with no sense of what is lost. The shift is not occurring with the idea of a balance in mind. Instead, the shift proceeds as if control were the only value.[25]

And Lessig argues that control has increased because of the passing of the tragedy of the commons from an intellectual argument that has recognized limitations into a form of policy ideology that is presumed to be unbounded in its application. For example, Jack Valenti, longtime head of the Motion Picture Association of America, argued in his congressional testimony on the proposed extension of the copyright term, "A public domain work is an orphan. No one is responsible for its life. But everyone exploits its use, until that time certain when it becomes soiled and haggard, barren of its previous virtues. Who, then, will invest the funds to renovate and nourish its future life when no one owns it? How does the consumer benefit from the scenario. The answers is, there is no benefit."[26]

The means by which control is increasing are several:

- In the early years of this country, most works were not copyrighted because the protection was, presumably, not worth the trouble and expense. Of the 13,000 book titles published between 1790 and 1799, only 556 were copyrighted. This means that the overwhelming majority of new works remained in the commons and could be freely reproduced without permission and cost. Now, almost everything published is copyrighted: "There is no registration requirement—every creative act reduced to a tangible medium is now subject to copyright protection. Your email to your child or your child's finger painting: both are automatically protected."[27] Lessig obviously fears that the current trend in copyright law will one day allow Vanna White, the hostess on the long-running and widely viewed television show *Wheel of Fortune*, to control not only all images of her, but even those that only "evoke the celebrity's image in the public's mind."[28]
- Before 1891, all foreign printed works were, effectively, in the commons, available for free reproduction by Americans, because they were not protected by U.S. copyright laws. Now, of course, they are protected.[29]
- The first copyright law gave authors fourteen years of protection, with the prospects of renewal for another fourteen years if the author were still alive. Now, through a series of eleven extensions of the copyright term in the past four decades of the twentieth century, authors are protected from the date of copyright until seventy years after their deaths, with extensions of the protected period coming ever more frequently.[30]
- At one time, composers could charge for the first recording of their songs, but not for subsequent recordings, a provision in the law that ensured that original owners of music "would not acquire too much control over subsequent innovation" with their original works.[31] People who made subsequent recordings were required to pay a fee to the copyright owner, but the fee was fixed by statute, not by market forces. Now, the fees for subsequent recordings are negotiated.
- Musical traditions—for example, jazz, blues, and rap—have flourished because artists have been able to borrow from one another, build on, and mix and match components of songs that have been recorded.[32] Digital sampling has held out the prospects of even greater developments in these musical traditions. However, court cases—notably a case involving George Harrison, a former Beatle—have effectively given artists progressively greater control over the components of their music. A judge ruled in the Harrison case that "'My Sweet Lord' is the very same song as 'He's So Fine' with different words." The judge further ruled that Harrison infringed the copyrights of the author of "He's So Fine" even though the sequence of notes was not the same and that

the copying was "subconsciously accomplished."[33] Accordingly, while older songwriters may have been relatively free to borrow from earlier works, newer songwriters have a greater burden of clearing influences and must tread carefully in how they make their music, both on paper and in performances.

- Cable television was born in an environment in which television signals of the networks were, in effect, free for the taking. When the networks acquired copyright protection for their signals, the protection they were afforded meant only that they could receive fees that the cable companies were required to pay by law. The networks did not have the right to deny cable companies the use of their signals. Now, this is no longer the case.[34]

- Napster, a company that permitted file sharing among computer users, has been vilified for enabling tens of millions of people from around the world to steal music. As a consequence (and as I will cover in the next chapter), Napster has been forced by court decision to change its business model to one that requires users to pay, via Napster, royalties to record companies for music downloads. What has not been so widely understood is that Napster was foremost a means of locating music that was wanted. "The important fact is not that a user can get Madonna's latest songs for free; it is that one can find a recording of New Orleans jazz drummer Jason Marsalis's band playing 'There's a Thing Called Rhythm.'"[35] The legal constraints now in place on Napster have taken one whale of a lot of music out of the Internet commons, perhaps constraining the development of new musical (and other intellectual) ideas via Internet downloads.

- The Internet developed on the backs of the telephone wires owned by telephone companies. The telephone companies could charge people for the use of their wires, but they could not prevent Internet service providers (ISPs) from setting up shop and tapping into the wires. However, the wires of cable companies have not been left in the commons to the extent that telephone wires have been. Cable companies themselves have been able to restrict other firms from tapping into their wires. Given that there has been a growing shift from telephone wires to cable wires in Internet services, there has been a growing tightening of constraints on the evolution of the Internet in several forms:

  - Limits on the extent of allowable streaming video.
  - "Acceptable use" restrictions that can prevent customers from developing Web sites.
  - Restrictions on what can be sent through cable wires to the Internet (for example, some cable companies prohibit file sharing).
  - Restrictions on Web searches that can result in search results favoring the sites of the cable companies' partners.[36]

- ISPs like AOL/Time Warner have begun to restrict the code used with their networks to code that they control on the argument that their systems—for example, servers—are their property.[37]

- "Spiders" and "bots" that crawl constantly around the Web are notorious for the problems they can inflict on servers, but they are also used to provide valuable services, not the least of which is to develop indexes for all of the Internet search engines like Google. Bots can also be used, as they are being used, to search auction sites for prices on various goods, which, of course, means that bidders can place their bids where they can most likely get the best prices (with the effect of prices equalizing across auction sites). However, eBay has established a no-bot policy on the grounds that the bot searches of its site are a form of digital trespassing. Although eBay's bot restriction is a legal issue yet to be resolved, Lessig sees an anticommons tragedy forming: "[T]o the extent that individual sites begin to impose their own rules for exclusion, the value of the network as a network declines. If machines must negotiate before entering any individual site, then the costs of using the network climb."[38]
- In "real space" (that is, in the world of real tangible objects), control of the use of copyrighted material is strictly limited by the cost of enforcement to the copyright holder. Displaying a picture of Bart Simpson, Lessig notes, in a dorm room might technically violate Fox's rights. However, Fox is not likely to pursue potential real-space violators because of the costs it would have to incur to root out the culprits. In the digital world, copyright enforcement is far easier, given the availability of copyright bots that can constantly survey the Internet landscape for sites that have not obtained permission to use copyrighted materials in digital form, thus reducing, because of the greater threat of being caught and prosecuted for violations, the use of copyrighted material. Hence, a student who can freely display a picture of Bart Simpson, which he may have purchased, in his dorm room cannot display as freely the same image on his personal homepage. Individuals and their homepage hosts (Yahoo!, MSN, and so on might be reluctant to post copyrighted material because of the threat of copyright penalties.[39]
- "Censorware" has emerged as a boon to parents and public libraries that want to protect children from objectionable materials, mainly pornography, on Web sites. The problem is that the programs often impose blocks on sites that are not objectionable. For example, with one censorware program, Amnesty International's Web site was blocked.[40]
- Copyrighted materials are normally subject to the fair-use doctrine, meaning, generally, that the materials can be copied at least once for personal use. However, the Digital Millennium Copyright Act (DMCA) of 1998, which was declared constitutional in 2002 by a federal judge,[41] forbids the development and use of code that cracks code designed to protect copyrighted code. This means that use of DeCSS, a computer program that disables the encryption of DVD disks and prevents the disks from being copied, is illegal. In a court test of the constitutionality, a court has ruled that the fair-use doctrine applies to copyrighted material but not to code. Code is covered by

the dictates of the DMCA.[42] The ongoing shift of creative material to digital form will gradually constrict the relative scope of the fair-use doctrine.

There has been a creeping spread of copyright protection through any number of adverse court decisions, from both Lessig's and Vaidhyanathan's perspective. At one time the courts drew a reasonably sharp distinction between an idea, which was not copyrightable, and the expression of an idea, which is copyrightable.[43] That distinction has been blurred with a sequence of court cases, as is evident in these examples (of the many) that Lessig and Vaidhyanathan cite:

- Art Buchwald submitted a two-page treatment for a proposed movie to Paramount in the 1980s. When Eddie Murphy's *Coming to America* was released in 1989, Buchwald claimed that the movie plot resembled the plot in his treatment. Buchwald's suit was not founded on copyright law (given that he had little chance of invoking copyright law in the protection of his movie idea), but his suit, which was founded on a breach of contract claim and which he won, had the effect of extending Buchwald's copyright protection to his movie idea.[44]

- One of the more successful children's Saturday morning television programs of the early 1970s was *H. R. Pufnstuf*, which was set on a fantasy island and had talking trees. McDonald's, which unsuccessfully sought to license the rights to "Pufnstuf" for an advertising campaign, went on to develop its own fantasy, "McDonald's Play Place," using characters that it freely admitted were founded on, but were still different in expression from, the character ideas in *H. R. Pufnstuf*, but that it assumed could not be copyrighted. However, the Ninth Circuit Court of Appeals ruled against McDonald's.[45]

- But, as Vaidhyanathan notes, perhaps the McDonald's ruling should be construed as only one more extension of copyright protection by the Ninth Circuit Court of Appeals. Years earlier, it had considered the case of two greeting card companies that had developed, one after the other, cards with the phrase *I wuv you*, but with different artwork. The Ninth Circuit Court of Appeals ruled in favor of the plaintiff, the first company to market with the greetings cards at issue, noting that the defendant had infringed the plaintiff's copyright on the grounds that the former's cards shared the same "total concept and feel" of the latter's cards.[46]

- In movie scenes, copyright law has developed to the point that, say, almost everything that is used in the scenes—pictures on walls, distinctive chairs and couches, computers, place settings, and images of identifiable bystanders, not to mention the images and voices of the actors and actresses in lead and supporting roles—is owned by someone, which means usage rights from all the various owners must be secured before the movie can be shot. If permission is not secured before the scene is shot, each owner can bargain strategically, trying to secure a price for his or her agreement that extracts the full value of the scene. This means, of course, that the scene might not be used, even though it is in the can. For example, in 1995, a visual design artist charged that a chair used incidentally in one scene of the two-hour drama *12 Monkeys* looked like one he had designed and, accordingly, was able to charge the production company with copyright infringement and sought an injunction that ultimately delayed the release of the film.[47]

- *i*CraveTV is a Canadian firm that sought to distribute captured U.S. and Canadian broadcasted television signals to Canadians via the Internet, a venture that is perfectly legal in Canada but not the United States. If the programs are on the Internet, they are available everywhere, including the United States, which made the Canadian-based venture illegal in the United States.[48] Lessig sees restrictions to new ventures in the U.S. court decision, which required *i*CraveTV to block out all Americans in order to continue operating:

  > [I]magine a German court telling Amazon.com that it must stop selling *Mein Kampf* until it can guarantee that no German citizen will be able to get access to that book—since the book is illegal in Germany. Or imagine a French court telling Yahoo! that it has to block French citizens from purchasing Nazi paraphernalia, since that is illegal in France. (Oops, no need to imagine. A French court did just that.)[49]

- MyMP3.com is a Web business that allows users to transmit their music collections to a Web site for storage, enabling the users to play their music from anywhere without their CDs. As Lessig notes, users could upload their friends' CDs to the site, thus engaging in a form of music theft. However, users could copy their friends' CDs without MyMP3's service, meaning that MyMP3 did not add to the theft potential (according to Lessig).[50] However, the court found that MyMP3's service was a violation of copyright laws and imposed $110 million in damages on the Internet firm, which Lessig suggests will chill "experimenting with a different way to give consumers access to their music."[51]

- Eric Eldred has been building a Web-based library of books that have fallen into the public domain. However, in 1998, Congress extended (again) the copyright term for materials still under copyright by twenty years, meaning that the works due to fall into the public domain in 1999 will not do so until 2019. The term extension, which was found to be constitutional by both a district court and a court of appeals, meant that Eldred would be restricted from adding many books to his Web commons that, in turn, could have fed the creativity of many people who could freely download the books on the Internet library.[52] Of course, with so many recent extensions of the copyright term, people might come to expect the copyright term to be, in effect, for perpetuity. Indeed, in ruling on the Eldred case in early 2003, the Supreme Court approved the extension in a seven-to-two vote, arguing that Congress abided by its constitutional duty to impose a limit on the copyright term, and it was not within the "province" of the court to second-guess the "wisdom" of the length of the term Congress selected.[53]

CONCLUDING COMMENTS

Ronald Coase and other economic and legal theorists make a powerful point: Property rights matter. All too often, when resources are misused or overused, the problem is that the resources are a commons. That is to say, everyone has usage rights without anyone having exclusion rights. The assignment of private property rights, meaning rights of owners to exclude others, can improve resource allocation, and prevent classic tragedies of the commons.

However, Lawrence Lessig and Siva Vaidhyanathan also have a point: We have to be mindful of the fact that not all resources held in common lead inextricably to the form of ruin that Garrett Hardin envisioned. Some resources are nonrivalrous and need not be subjected to exclusion rights. We also have to be mindful of the potential for a symmetrical source of allocation problems: The tragedy of the anticommons, in which resources are underused because of the extant rights of exclusion that come with the assignment of multiple property rights.

As is true in all matters of institutional design, Lessig and Vaidhyanathan implicitly, if not explicitly, make a plea for a sense of balance in matters of control (property rights) and freedom (commons). We need to use rights assignments to properly organize incentives for people to be creative. This may be especially true when goods and services are made from digits, which means that their replication can be made at little or near-zero cost and that recovery of development costs may be difficult.

At the same time, we must acknowledge that ideas, once created, are also nonrivalrous. Moreover, these ideas are requisites for growth in technology and human welfare. Ideas are crucially important in digital markets where many products and services are nothing but ideas reduced to code that is everywhere abundant, and where ideas incorporated in some products and services can spawn a multitude of other goods and services, if the ideas are themselves protected as property for which payments can easily and everywhere be extracted.

NOTES

1. Ronald Coase highlighted the importance of property rights in "The Federal Communications Commission," *Journal of Law and Economics* 2 (October 1959):

1–40; and "The Problem of Social Costs," *Journal of Law and Economics* 3 (October 1960): 1–45. See also Armen A. Alchian and Harold Demsetz, "The Property Rights Paradigm," *Journal of Economic History* 33 (March 1973): 17.

2. It is true that governments retain the power of eminent domain, which is, effectively, the power to reclaim property, but governments' taking power is delimited. To reclaim private property, governments in the United States must go to court and must provide just compensation. See Richard A. Epstein, *Takings: Private Property and the Power of Eminent Domain* (Cambridge: Harvard University Press, 1985).

3. For extended discussions of how property increases efficiency in the use of resources, see James M. Buchanan, *The Limits of Liberty* (Chicago: University of Chicago Press, 1975): 20; James M. Buchanan and Yong J. Yoon, "Symmetric Tragedies: Commons and Anticommons," *Journal of Law and Economics* 43 (April 2000): 1–13; and Winston C. Bush, "Individual Welfare in Anarchy," in *Explorations in the Theory of Anarchy*, ed. Gordon Tullock (Blacksburg, Va.: University Publications, 1972): 5–18.

4. Friedrich A. Hayek, "The Use of Information in Society," *American Economic Review* 35 (September 1945): 519.

5. Fair use under the U.S. Copyright Act (sec. 170) provides that copying for "purposes such as criticism, comment, news reporting, teaching (including multiple copies for classroom use), scholarship, or research is not an infringement of copyright." The Computer Software Copyright Act does not provide for any form of fair use.

6. Garrett Hardin, "The Tragedy of the Commons," *Science* 162 (1968): 1243–1254.

7. For extended discussions of how the tragedy of the commons has formed the foundation of the property rights literature, see Tom Bethel, *The Noblest Triumph: Property and Prosperity through the Ages* (New York: St. Martin's, 1998). The important point in the tragedy of the commons is that the externalities of individual actions have to be managed, or have to be internalized in some way, and private property is only one way to do the managing, as recognized by H. Scott Gordon, "The Economic Theory of a Common Property Resource: The Fishery," *Journal of Political Economy* 62, no. 2 (1954): 124–142; and Anthony Scott, "The Fishery: The Objective of Sole Ownership," *Journal of Political Economy* 63, no. 2 (1955): 116–124.

8. Harold Demsetz, "Toward a Theory of Property Rights," *American Economic Review* 57 (May 1964): 347–359.

9. For additional examples of how the absence of well-assigned property rights have affected people's behavior throughout history, see Alchian and Demsetz, "The Property Rights Paradigm," 20.

10. Whales, for example, have been hunted for centuries, but there has never been a problem with their possible extinction until the last two centuries. Whales have always been more or less communal property; however, because people in bygone centuries did not have the technology we now have to kill and slaughter whales far at sea, the sheer cost of hunting them prevented men from exceeding the whales' reproductive capacity. Theoretically, the problem could be solved by applying the same solution to the whale

overkill as the Indians applied in their hunting grounds: establish private property rights. However, whales present a special problem. The annual migrations of whales can take them through six thousand miles of ocean. Establishing and enforcing private property rights to such an expanse of ocean is an ominous task, even without the complications involved in securing agreement among several governments to respect those rights. Without doubt, these costs have been a major reason why whales remain communal property and are threatened still with extinction.

11. Hardin, "The Tragedy of the Commons," in which he writes, "Therein is the tragedy. Each man is locked into a system that compels him to increase his herd without limit—in a world that is limited. Ruin is the destination toward which all men rush, each pursuing his own best interest in a society that believes in the freedom of the commons. Freedom in the commons brings ruin to all" (p. 1245).

12. See Michael A. Heller, "The Tragedy of the Anticommons: Property in Transition," *Harvard Law Review* 111 (1998): 621–688.

13. Ibid.

14. Buchanan and Yoon, "Symmetric Tragedies," 11.

15. Heller, "The Tragedy of the Anticommons," 650–660.

16. Buchanan and Yoon, "Symmetric Tragedies."

17. Lawrence Lessig, *The Future of Ideas: The Fate of the Commons in a Connected World* (New York: Random House, 2001); and Siva Vaidhyanathan, *Copyrights and Copywrongs: The Rise of Intellectual Property and How It Threatens Creativity* (New York: New York University Press, 2001).

18. In art. 1, sec. 8 of the Constitution, Congress is given the authority to "promote the Progress of Science and useful Arts, by securing for limited times to Authors and Inventors the exclusive Right to their respective Writings and Discoveries."

19. Coase, "The Federal Communications Commission," 1–38.

20. Lessig, *The Future of Ideas*, chap. 5.

21. Ibid., 84.

22. Gordon Tullock, *The Logic of the Law* (New York: Basic Books, 1971).

23. Letter from Thomas Jefferson to Isaac McPerson (August 13, 1813), as quoted in Lessig, *The Future of Ideas*, 94.

24. Lessig, *The Future of Ideas*, 97.

25. Ibid., 99.

26. *Copyright Term Extension Act: Hearings on H.R. 989 before the Subcommittee on Courts and Intellectual Property of the House Committee of the Judiciary*, 104th Cong., 1st Sess. (June 1, 1995), as quoted in Jessica Litman, *Digital Copyright* (Amherst, N.Y.: Prometheus Books, 2001), 77.

27. Lessig, *The Future of Ideas*, 106–107.

28. Ibid., 203. The quote is from *Vanna White v. Samsung Elecs. Am., Inc.; David Deutsch Assocs.*, 898 F. 2d 1512, 1514 (1993).

29. Ibid., 106.

30. Ibid., 107. The copyright term was increased to twenty-eight years, with renewal for another fourteen years in 1983. In 1909, the copyright term was increased to

twenty-eight years with renewal for another twenty-eight years. In 1976, the copyright term was expanded to the author's life, plus fifty years. In 1998, the copyright term was increased to the life of the author, plus seventy years. At that time, the terms of all existing copyrights in existence were extended to 2019.

31. Ibid.,109.

32. Vaidhyanathan, *Copyrights and Copywrongs*, chap. 4.

33. Ibid., 129.

34. Lessig, *The Future of Ideas*, 109–110.

35. Ibid., 131.

36. Ibid., 151–155.

37. Ibid., 168.

38. Ibid., 171.

39. Ibid., 180–183.

40. Ibid., 184–187.

41. Jon Healey, "Judge Allows Electronic Copyright Case to Proceed," *Los Angeles Times*, 9 May 2002, p. C1.

42. Lessig, *The Future of Ideas*, 190.

43. The idea/expression dichotomy was embedded in federal law in 1976: "In no case does copyright protection for an original work of authorship extend to any idea, procedure, process, system, method of operation, concept, principle, or discovery, regardless of the form in which it is described, explained, illustrated, or embedded in such work." See Vaidhyanathan, *Copyrights and Copywrongs*, 29.

44. Ibid., 33–34, 115–116.

45. Ibid., 112–114.

46. Ibid., 114.

47. As related by Vaidhyanathan in *Copyrights and Copywrongs*, 115. If moviemakers do not get permission to use items in scenes, they can have claims made against them that are disproportionate to the value of the items. The rights' owners can each bargain strategically, that is, each claiming something close to the full value of the scene (given their individual veto power over the use of the scene), with the total value of all claims easily exceeding by severalfold the value of the scene. To prevent such strategic bargaining, and wastage, the producers can bargain for the rights prior to filming. However, the potential for an anticommons tragedy in the form of fewer films produced still exists, given the multiple resource owners who must give their consent. Again, the transaction costs involved can result in too few films being produced.

48. Ibid., 190–192.

49. Lessig, *The Future of Ideas*, 193.

50. Ibid., 192–194.

51. Ibid., 194.

52. Ibid., 196–199.

53. *Eldred et al. v. Ashcroft, Attorney General*, Opinion, No. 01-618, decided January 15, 2003, as found January 22, 2003 at FindLaw.com.

10

Piracy and Privacy

I t should surprise no one that piracy, or a failure to protect intellectual property rights, is much more of a problem in the digital goods sector of the economy than in the nondigital goods sector. Indeed, piracy in music and software, which have long been digitized, is rampant around the country and the world. Piracy in E-books and E-movies has not yet become a major problem, mainly because the markets for digital books and movies remain in their infancy. However, piracy in those markets can be expected to grow with those markets, while, perhaps, never being as pervasive as music and software piracy has been. This is because, as we will see, many legal issues surrounding piracy are being settled in lawsuits being brought over music and software piracy.

MUSIC PIRACY, NAPSTER STYLE

Napster, a Web site based in San Mateo, California, and set up in 1999, developed software that allowed people to swap music (and any other digitized) files that remain housed on the downloaders' own computers. From its start, Napster did not actually perform the swaps of files from those who had the songs on their hard drives to those who wanted the songs. Napster users did the swapping "peer-to-peer," or "P2P." While Napster did not store the songs on its servers—possibly out of concern for the cost of the required storage space as well as the fear that such a service would clearly violate copyright laws—it did facilitate the P2P swapping by maintaining directories of which users had which songs. In short, Napster enabled users to quickly and efficiently find the songs they wanted and then go P2P for the downloading. Accordingly, Napster provided a hybrid file-sharing system. The directories of songs were centralized, but the actual file storing and sharing was decentralized. Napster effectively increased all users' storage capacity as well as increased the size of the database users could tap.

Napster quickly became a household name, given that the use of Napster software spread more rapidly than any other single program in the history of computing. All a user had to do was go to the Napster site, type in the name of a desired song, and the Napster software would find it on some personal computer. With a couple of clicks, virtually any song could be burned to a downloader's writable CD and played. Indeed, a savvy Napster user could burn a standard album-length CD in about twenty minutes' worth of computer time—all without charge. Even the person allowing his or her files to be downloaded did not incur a cost because, in true digital manner, the files downloaded remained intact; they were only replicated, an economic fact that explains why so many Napster users allowed their files to be downloaded by other anonymous users. Moreover, every time someone downloaded songs, network effects emerged. This is because there was then one more Napster user with music files. Hence, the probability that users would be able to find desired songs from those people who were connected to the Napster system at the time went up, increasing the collective value of the system.

By early 2001, Napster had 40–50 million users around the globe who were making hundreds of millions of downloads a year. Between 1999 and 2000, the Recording Industry Association of America estimated that sales of single records fell 39 percent, which they attributed mainly, if not fully, to Napster and other similar file-swapping Web sites.[1] Accordingly, Sony, Warner, BMG, Universal, and EMI—all major record companies—filed suit against Napster in 1999 when Napster started giving away the software that allowed users to copy music files in MP3 format.

While Napster might have been partially to blame for the 2000 fall-off in album sales, the fall-off in single sales that year could also be attributable to a drop in the willingness of record stores to carry singles, given that the market share of sales of singles (in terms of units, not dollars) dropped from 70 percent of store sales in 1990 to 45 percent in 1999.[2] Also, the annual per capita music expenditures of young people, 15–19 years old, who tend to buy singles, dropped in real (1999) dollars by 36 percent from 1995 ($127) to 1999 ($93). Finally, the ending year (2000) for the sales report for singles may have been a particularly bad year for new material by artists that caught the attention of the buying public, but then major record companies might have started holding up releasing their "good stuff" that year because of the Napster threat and the prospects of a court ruling favorable to the record industry on lawsuits that had already been filed by 1999.[3]

For the first half of 2001, album sales remained 5–10 percent (depending on the data source) below the level achieved for the same period during the previous year. However, the exact "Napster effect" remains, again, uncertain (at the time of this writings). This is because the count of Napster users dropped from 17 million in February 2001 (the month before the court ruling against Napster, which will be considered later in the chapter) to 11 million in May, or by more than one-third. What is even more confounding is that album sales rose between January 1, 2001, and March 5, 2001 (the date of the copyright infringement ruling against Napster), and fell from March 5 through the middle of June that year by nearly 1 percent.[4] Moreover, 2000 may have been a very good year for albums, given the major releases from stars such as Britney Spears and 'N Sync, while the first half of 2001 may have been a not-so-good half year for album releases.

NAPSTER COPYRIGHT VIOLATIONS

Was Napster guilty of copyright infringement? Before Napster, that was an unanswered legal question, given that the courts had never before had to consider a file-sharing, P2P operation. The Ninth U.S. Circuit Court of Appeals in San Francisco ruled in 2001 that Napster was indeed guilty of a new form of copyright infringement, "vicarious copyright infringement," and that Napster "knowingly encourages and assists" in the exchange of copyrighted works, and that "repeated and exploitative unauthorized copies of copyrighted works were made to save the expense of purchasing authorized copies."[5] The court of appeals also reasoned that unlike in the case of the VCR, which was declared legal on the grounds that such recorders had a "substantial non[copyright]infringing use," the Napster file-sharing system had no "substantial noninfringing use."[6] Unlike VCR producers, Napster does not simply sell equipment to its users, it maintains an ongoing relationship with them, exerts ongoing control of them, and plays a crucial role in the users' infringement.

As a consequence, the court of appeals enjoined Napster from further assisting users with exchanging files without payment, but it also required the record companies to provide Napster with lists of copyrighted works that required payment. Nevertheless, as Napster's court-ordered restrictions on song downloads took effect, the number of Napster users dropped by 80 percent by mid-2001, and the number of songs offered for sharing through Napster plunged by more than 99 percent, or from 220 songs per person in February to 1.5 songs per person in late June 2001.[7]

The legal issues surrounding file sharing were hardly settled in the Napster decision. Software pirates, and their collaborators, immediately began developing software that used code names for song titles, which would allow Napster users to continue sharing music files, mainly because Napster began blocking file sharing by way of the song's legitimate titles.

In addition, other file-sharing systems remained unaffected by the Napster decision. For example, Gnutella (or Freenet, Aimster, Audiogalaxy, and Bit-Bop) is a software-based technology that allows users to swap files without going through a Napster-like central computing system. One open-source Gnutella programmer has noted:

> Unlike the Internet that we are familiar with, with all its signs, dots, and slashes, Gnutella does not give meaningful and persistent identification to its nodes. In fact, the underlying structure of the Internet on which Gnutella lives is almost entirely hidden from the end user. . . . Gnutella creates an application-level network in which the infrastructure itself is constantly changing. Sure, the wires stay in the ground and the routers don't move from place to place, but which wires and which routers participate in the Gnutella network changes by the second. The Gnutella network comprises a dynamic virtual infrastructure built on a fixed physical infrastructure.[8]

With Gnutella software (for example, Gnotella, Furi, and Toadnode), a user can send out a query through any host to other users, asking for a particular song, all anonymously. The request could be relayed from those who received the initial message to others with whom they have links (with the potential links in the system reaching ten thousand). The person making the query would receive back from the network that develops for that particular inquiry information on where the files might be downloaded. The route the query takes could change every time the query is sent out. There are several features that might enable Gnutella to withstand the type of legal challenges that Napster faced:

- Under Gnutella, there is no centralized organization that is responsible for the actual file sharing and, hence, can be sued as Napster was.
- Since the technology is pure P2P, with no directories being developed by a single firm, the copying that is done by the peers might be construed as fair use.

- It is very difficult (but not impossible) for the downloads to be traced to the people involved in the file sharing. (No one may even be able to count the amount of file sharing.)

It might be some time before the legal entanglements surrounding file sharing are sorted out, mainly because of the prospect of Napster clones being established so rapidly that law enforcement cannot keep up with them (and the clones might be established in countries friendly to free file sharing). By May 2001, seven Napster clones (Music City Morpheus, Audiogalaxy, ICQ 2000b, Kazaa Media desktop, iMesh, WinZip, and BearShare), which did not exist when the court ruling against Napster came down in the previous February, were up and operating. The seven clones had between 500,000 and 1.1 million users each, as reported by Jupiter Media Matrix.[9] A year after the Napster decision was handed down, CNN reported that there were thirty-eight thousand Web sites worldwide that provided strictly P2P downloads, with the CNN reporter indicating that the downloading of a piece of music he played in part on the air was done with little more trouble than was done under Napster.[10] In the spring of 2002 (when this book was being finalized), Napster clones had an estimated 2.6 million worldwide users connected at any time of the day. With a number of the sites actually making a profit.[11]

Will such Napster clones, and their many variations, especially those in foreign countries, be constrained by U.S. court decisions? Will the clones multiply more quickly than the music industry (and other E-industries) can shut them down through legal actions? At this writing, no one knows. All that is clear is that file sharing through Napster, and similar organizations in the United States, has been made marginally more costly, at least temporarily. However, it looks as if E-industries might end up much like the dog chasing its tail, which explains why in 2002 Senator Fritz Hollings introduced a bill—the Consumer Broadband and Digital Television Act—that, if enacted, would require devices that are capable of playing and/or transmitting digitized video or audio products and services to have an industry-agreed-upon piracy detection device that prevents pirated copies from being played. Deleting or tampering with the piracy detection system would also be made illegal.[12] Understandably, firms like Intel and Dell have opposed the Hollings legislation because it would impair the demand for their products (given that the ability of computers to play and copy works adds to the market value of computers and the microprocessors they use, and that such a law would increase the tendency of computer users to stay with their old computers).[13]

All the while, the recording companies that won the case against Napster have encountered legal problems of their own with their artists. When artists' works are used in television programs, movies, or commercials, they are normally paid a licensing fee, which is split evenly between the artists and the recording companies. However, when the music has been licensed by Internet companies like MusicNet, which charges for downloads, the recording companies have received a licensing fee but have only been paying the artists a standard royalty, which can be less than 15 percent of the fee received.[14] The issue the courts will have to resolve is whether Internet downloads should be treated as music sales under the recording contracts.

SOFTWARE PIRACY

The piracy in computer software is so widespread around the world that the pirates have their own vocabulary: all copied computer programs, *warez*; copied software applications, *appz*; and copied computer games, *gamez*. Pirates also have several other terms that denote operations that are critical to their trade, for example, *crackz*, broken software codes that allow pirates to convert a software firm's demonstration software version into a full-blown program, and *serialz*, which denotes serial numbers for copied software programs.

The International Planning and Research Corporation (in a study for the Business Software Alliance) has estimated the software piracy rates for only business applications (or percent of business software packages in use that have been illegally copied) and software revenue losses for eighty-seven countries (or small country groupings) for 1995 through 2000.[15] Two observations stand out in this report. First, in 2000, despite some decline since 1995, the piracy rates for the countries covered remained strikingly high. In 2000, only six of the eighty-seven countries had piracy rates of one-third or less, with the United States having the lowest piracy rate, 24 percent (which is, incidentally, in line with the percent of American adults who believed "copying software not licensed for personal use is okay"[16]). That is to say, practically one out of every four software programs in use in the United States in 2000 was being used illegally. Nearly half of the countries (forty-one) had piracy rates greater than 60 percent. Vietnam had the highest piracy rate of 97 percent, followed by China, 94 percent; Indonesia, 89 percent; and Russia, 88 percent. The overall world piracy rate was 37 percent (lower than might be expected from a perusal of the piracy rates for individual countries, mainly because of the dominance of the United States and Western Europe in legal software sales and their relatively low piracy rates).

Second, there were slight declines in the piracy rates for almost all countries between 1995 and 2000, with the piracy rate for all countries dropping from 46 percent in 1995 to 37 percent in 2000. Zimbabwe is the only country where the piracy rate did not fall. Overall, during the period 1995–2000, the piracy rate declined in Western Europe from 49 to 34 percent; Eastern Europe, from 83 to 63 percent; Latin America, from 76 to 58 percent; the United States and Canada combined, from 27 to 25 percent; Asia/Pacific, from 64 to 51 percent; the Middle East, from 83 to 57 percent; and Africa, from 74 to 52 percent. The loss to software firms from world piracy fell from $13.3 billion in 1995 to $11.8 billion in 2000. The revenue lost from piracy for 1999 represented 56 percent of software firms' total sales of $21.6 billion.

The decline in the piracy rates can be chalked up to several factors, not the least of which are

- a reduction in the real, if not nominal, price of software, which has reduced the profitability of piracy and reduced the incentive of consumers to buy pirated copies;
- an expanded effort on the part of software companies to convince the public that piracy is a crime;
- improved technological means of preventing software copying;
- an increase in the penalties for software piracy (in the United States, the Digital Theft Deterrence and Copyright Damages Improvement Act of 1999 raised the penalty range for each copyrighted work infringed by 50 percent, from $500–$20,000 to $750–$30,000; in cases of willful infringement, the top penalty was raised from $100,000 to $150,000);
- an increase in enforcement of antipiracy laws (the U.S. Justice Department has set up the Computer Crime and Intellectual Property Section, and the FBI has computer crime offices in several major cities);
- a growth in media reports on penalties being imposed on pirates, which likely increased the perceived or expected costs of piracy.

In short, the fall in piracy rates around the world may be due in part to a decline in the gains from using and selling pirated copies, and an increase in the expected cost of producing pirated copies. The expected cost pirates must incur may have risen because of an increase in the imposed penalty along with an increase in the probability of pirates being caught, prosecuted, and convicted. Nevertheless, I hasten to add that in spite of the fall in piracy rates, the rapid rise in software usage between 1997 and 1999 has meant that the actual count of pirated software programs in use still rose by 34 percent between 1998 and 1999, according to the Software Information Industry Association.[17]

THE CONSEQUENCES OF PIRACY

Microsoft is so concerned about software piracy that it has a whole Web site devoted to the subject (http://microsoft.com/piracy/), and with the release of Windows XP, the company has sought to crack down on piracy by requiring Windows home buyers to purchase a separate copy of Windows for each computer.[18] On its Web site, Microsoft tries to educate visitors on what piracy is and then reports key statistics, such as those I have reported. It then adds that in the United States alone software piracy costs 107,000 jobs, $5.3 billion in annual lost wages, and $1.8 billion in lost tax revenues. There is no mention on the Web site of Microsoft's own economic losses, although its own losses no doubt go further in explaining Microsoft's interest in curbing software piracy than the more aggregate losses to the national and the world economies.

However, if Microsoft were to estimate its own piracy losses, its estimates would likely suffer in two ways (as do the estimates of losses for the whole industry):

- The estimates would likely assume that software prices are the same with piracy as they would be without piracy. However, if it were not for the pirates, it is very likely that all legitimate copies of the computer programs would have been sold at higher prices. This is because the legitimate producers would have had one less source of competition. Put another way, there would have been a reduced overall supply of the programs in the world market, which would have increased the demand for legitimate copies of the programs and driven prices upward.
- Absent piracy, the increase in the sale of legitimate copies would be less than the curb in sales of pirated copies.

OPTIMUM PIRACY

With greater antipiracy efforts and a concomitant reduction in the sales of pirated copies, the market demand that legitimate producers face might not rise as much as they might imagine. That is, there might not be a one-for-one substitution of legitimate sales for pirated sales for several reasons. First, preventing pirates from copying digital works will likely prevent legitimate users from copying those same works for their limited, personal (fair-use) purposes, which, in turn, can reduce the value legitimate users place on the legitimate copies and, hence, can reduce their market demand for the protected works. The lower demand can be expected to lower the price—from what it would be otherwise—that the producers could extract for their works. The prospect of an impaired market value for protected works is especially problematic when the protection technology has flaws that appear unavoidable. For example, when record companies began releasing CDs in early 2002 with copying protection developed by Macrovision, users found that the protection technology impaired the quality of the sound. With the protection in place, the CDs also could not be played on computer CD drives, and could not be transferred to MP3 players, with all three of these factors undercutting the potential market demand for the CDs. Understandably, some record companies did not use the available technology, reasoning that sales would likely be higher with piracy than with the protection.[19]

Second, producers have to face the prospects of the reinforcing power of network effects on market demand. When network effects exist, then a spread of the use of a given form of software can give rise to greater benefits for all buyers, those who buy from legitimate producers and those who buy from pirates. When piracy is curbed and overall sales go down, some of the network benefits will be lost, resulting in the legitimate producers' sales not rising by as much as the pirates' sales fall.

The potential for network effects suggests that not all legitimate producers of the digital goods can be expected to favor eliminating piracy, at least up to a point. Again, this is because the potential for piracy can add value to consumers, increasing their willingness to pay higher prices for the original product. Furthermore, piracy can add to the network benefits associated with the product and create what has been called "marketing buzz." The buzz can convince consumers that the pirated software will be widely used, raising the demand for legitimate copies. Indeed, some consumers might reason that if the good is not subject to at least some piracy, then it is not likely to be sufficiently popular to become the industry standard. Others might actually buy legitimate copies of the software just so they can be compatible with people who use pirated copies.[20] One explanation given for the rise of WordPerfect's domination of the word-processing market in the 1980s was that the program was more easily copied, illegally as well as legally, than other word-processing programs. Back then, when most word-processing programs could not read the files of other word-processing programs, having a lot of pirated copies of WordPerfect around could have stimulated the demand for legitimate copies.

The evidence on the tie between pirated copies and legitimate sales is limited. Nevertheless, it is worth noting that one study did find that with the elimination of copy protection for spreadsheet and word-processing software programs in England there was, between 1987 and 1992, a growth in the ratio of pirated copies to bought copies up to six to one. However, the researchers also found that the pirated copies of the software stimulated legitimate sales. They also concluded that when the software was introduced pirating was very limited (as expected, given that there were few copies to pirate); that 80 percent of the copies actually bought was very likely attributable to the network effects of the growing pirated copies; and that over time the count of pirated copies decreased to 15 percent of all available copies.[21] Similarly, other researchers have found that copying of printed publications has actually increased publishers' profits, mainly because the publications are more valuable and because the publishers can price discriminately between individual users, who might have limited needs for copying and therefore are charged a low price, and libraries, which have a demand for allowing their patrons to copy their holdings.[22]

Finally, and more recently, the Consumer Electronics Association (CEA) found that 59 percent of people who downloaded music said that free downloads had no impact on their music purchases (with another 6 percent uncertain of the impact). CEA did find that 15 percent of the downloaders agreed that their downloads lowered their music purchases. However, a higher percent of the downloaders—20 percent—said that their downloads increased their purchases.[23]

One of the problems the courts face in fashioning a remedy for Napster's copyright violations is that, according to reports, Napster provides a very valuable service to the 99.97 percent of musicians who are not sufficiently established to have a major record company behind them and who make little or nothing from the private sales of their work.[24] Many of these artists would like nothing better than to be able to sell their work, but barring sufficient demand, many may want, and actively encourage, people to pirate their work, mainly in the hope that the free exchange of their work will create a sufficient buzz to stimulate demand for their live appearances at small local bars, coffeehouses, and theaters, which is where they can expect to make most, if not all, of their income from music. In short, appearances are the artists' complimentary good, and they offer one good free of charge—downloaded music—to increase the demand for the other—appearances.

The question that artists and record companies will ultimately have to address is whether piracy actually lowers profits. Piracy can, however, lower marketing costs. What Napster has demonstrated is that millions of music lovers are willing to download a lot of songs at a zero price. Music lovers might not be willing to download as many at a positive price, but if there are (practically) no costs for the digital downloads, the price charged per download could possibly be closer to zero than to the going price of CDs, which ranged generally in 2002 from $13 to $20, and may need to be closer to zero just to discourage piracy.

In short, firms should not seek to stamp out all piracy of their products. Instead, they should be expected to seek optimum piracy, or that rate of digital property theft that maximizes their revenues and, hence, given their zero marginal cost of production, maximizes their profits. In digital markets with network effects, zero piracy is not necessarily the optimum piracy rate. Indeed, flagrant piracy might be closer to optimum piracy for some firms than zero piracy. This means that firms, and their trade associations, will not necessarily seek technological fixes and enforcement of the antipiracy laws that would make piracy prohibitively expensive to undertake, even if doing that were possible (which it is not). Digital firms might want to press law enforcement to enforce the laws with greater diligence, and they might want to raise the piracy penalties—all because there is too much piracy. But there are limits to what they would be willing to do, both because of the costs they would have to incur in their political efforts and because of the damage the greater enforcement and penalties might do, beyond some point, to their sales and profits. Antipiracy fixes, including penalties for copying, can reduce the value of the products to legitimate users, since they will be restricted in copying the products for their own personal use. In addition, antipiracy fixes can reduce the extent of the products' networks, which can, in turn, reduce the value of the product to individual users, the net effect of which can be a reduction in the prices consumers are willing to pay, now and/or in the future, for the products. From this perspective, it is altogether understandable why the penalties under the Digital Theft Deterrence and Copyright Damages Improvement Act of 1999 were raised by only 50 percent, and not much more.[25]

PIRACY SOLUTIONS

It is easy to presume that the piracy fixes will be legal or technological in nature. New laws with higher penalties and greater enforcement can certainly help to curb piracy, mainly through deterrence, which amounts to making piracy a poor business model for many firms. However, it is doubtful that legal solutions can accomplish as much as legitimate producers would want from law enforcement, given the ease with which piracy can be practiced by so many individuals in so many places around the globe.

Legitimate producers can be expected to look for improved technical solutions, not the least of which will involve the encoding and encrypting of digital goods and services. For example, music and software producers are already embedding "watermarks" (or embedded code) in their digital goods. Supposedly, without the watermarks, the digital goods cannot be used (although computer experts have, according to reports, already broken several watermarks).

Microsoft has degraded the quality of the sound that computer users can get from CDs that can be recorded using the MP3 file format and the recording applet built into Windows XP. Music recorded via Windows XP will have the quality of listening to a radio through a telephone.[26] The software giant will be making the shift for several reasons:

- Microsoft might be intent on helping the computer industry curb software piracy, in part by making widely pirated goods inferior to legitimate versions.
- Microsoft might be making the change to enable the company to avoid paying Thompson Multimedia SA and Fraunhofer a $2.50 royalty for use of any recording applet that is based on MP3 technology.
- Microsoft might be counting on the degradation in sound quality to cause computer users to buy Windows Media Audio, which will not only sound clearer and require less storage space, but also has built-in protections against piracy. However, we can easily imagine skilled software programmers reengineering any and all technological fixes.

Whatever its motive, Microsoft will continue to face stiff competition from the likes of RealNetworks, Inc., which has developed its own so-called rights-management software that it plans to use in its own music distribution service, organized in conjunction with major record producers BMG, Warner Music Group, and EMI. Instead of trying to prevent copying altogether, RealNetworks' software will allow all labels and studios to set the rules for how their products are used, including copying.

Fortunately for the digital industry not all fixes need be legal and technical. Legitimate digital producers can take pages from the history of the book and movie industries. For centuries libraries have provided free access to books, yet book publishers have been able to compete, mainly by providing products that serve ends that libraries cannot serve. They also pushed the price of books down so much that it is actually cheaper for many readers to buy books than to go to the trouble of checking them out at their local libraries. When free television became widely available, there were pessimists who predicted the downfall of movie producers and theaters. However, movie producers and theaters began introducing visual effects that could not be fully duplicated on television.

E-businesses can be expected to find a variety of ways to adjust to piracy, which cannot now be identified, that will make buying E-goods preferable to getting them free or at cut-rate prices from pirates (and few goods that are touted as being free are really that, when all costs, including the opportunity costs of people's time, are considered).[27] One potential (albeit partial) solution for the software piracy problem that is now on the horizon is the rental of software over the Internet, and one reason firms like Microsoft are considering software rentals is they can better control piracy. They think that they can substantially lower the prices for rentals, choke off a lot of software piracy, and raise their revenues. Whether such solutions will be anything more than a partial solution is not yet known, mainly because so little is known about the elasticity of demand for rented application services.

PROTECTION BREAKING

When firms try to protect their products by technical or electronic means, others interested in piracy can be expected to try to break the protection, leading to more piracy than expected. To discourage pirates, Congress passed the Digital Millennium Copyright Act (DMCA) in 1998, which is intended to make illegal any efforts to defeat methods to protect digital copyrights.[28] However, the act has had what appears to be unexpected consequences.

In the spring of 2001, the music industry threatened to sue Edward Felten, a prominent computer-science professor and encryption researcher at Princeton University, if he presented the results of his academic research on the breaking of watermarks embedded in computer programs to a professional group. The industry claimed that Professor Felten and his research team had violated the DMCA. Whether the music industry will prevail in the case, if they actually file suit, is uncertain at this writing. Critics of the law, including Felten, argue that the law is unconstitutional precisely because it threatens to violate free-speech protections and to stifle legitimate academic research, which it has, given that Felten decided not to present his paper.[29]

The basic problem with the DMCA appears to be that it overrides long-standing copyright rules. As I have noted, copyright law protects copyrighted material for a limited period of time and allows for fair use of copyrighted material. This means that, for example, library patrons can make personal copies of journal or newspaper articles. However, the DMCA makes illegal all efforts to break the code that protects digital goods and does not have a set time limit on the protection. This means that the fair-use doctrine of copyright law is overridden by the DCMA. "Thus," writes Lawrence Lessig, the Stanford law professor introduced in the previous chapter, "when the DMCA protects technology that in turn protects copyrighted material, it often protects much more broadly than copyright law does. It makes criminal what copyright law would forgive."[30]

To illustrate the potential mischief of this new digital law, Lessig points to the case of Dimitri Sklyarov, a Russian programmer for a firm called Elcom-Soft who wrote a program that allows users of Adobe eBook Reader to override publisher-imposed electronic restrictions on how books developed for eBook Reader are used. For example, a publisher might prevent its E-books from being read aloud. The Sklyarov program allows blind users to bypass the publisher's restriction and have the book read aloud. The problem with the program, as far as Adobe is concerned, is that it also allows eBook Reader users to copy and disseminate E-books by breaking the copy protection code in the Adobe reader. As a consequence, and because Adobe was able to purchase a copy of the program via the Internet, Sklyarov was arrested and jailed by the FBI when he went to Las Vegas, Nevada, to give a lecture on encryption weaknesses—even though his efforts to break the Adobe code were perfectly legal in his own country and, for that matter, in much of the rest of the world. Policy makers now have a difficult problem on their hands: How does a country protect the legitimate interests of copyright holders when copying and distributing digital material is so cheap and where fair use is extraordinarily difficult to monitor?

In addition, the Supreme Court will likely have to take up the issue of whether fair use is a fundamental constitutional right of citizens that requires producers to allow users to copy works for personal use. If users do have a fair-use right, producers might not be allowed to use available technology that precludes copying altogether. Already, the U.S. Court of Appeals has ruled that consumers of CDs have a right to "space shift" music, which means they can copy music from CDs to Rio MP3 players.[31] This suggests that the provision in the DMCA that prohibits the breaking of copy protection code may, eventually, be declared unconstitutional. Ditto for the Hollings bill, if it is ever passed.

As this book was being finalized in the spring of 2002, U.S. District Court judge Ronald Whyte ruled in the Sklyarov/Adobe Systems case that the DMCA was constitutional on the grounds that "the DMCA does not 'eliminate' fair use. Although certain fair uses may become more difficult, no fair use has been prohibited."[32] The judge reasoned that the fair-use doctrine does not guarantee consumers "the right to the most technologically convenient way to engage in a fair use." Furthermore, raising the difficulty of copying materials was, according to the judge's ruling, a "sacrifice Congress was willing to make in order to protect against unlawful piracy and promote the development of electronic commerce and the availability of copyrighted material on the Internet."[33]

PRIVACY

According to one privacy scholar, privacy is the ability of people to determine "when, how, and to what extent information about them is communicated to others."[34] Another privacy researcher offers a half dozen definitions of privacy, probably the best of which is that privacy "is the ability to live a life unobserved, or to have a zone where we can develop intimate relations, blow off steam, relax and be ourselves in a way that is impossible in public."[35]

Most people have always valued some degree of privacy and have resented unauthorized invasions of their privacy. This may be because they have thought of their personal space as a form of personal property, which we can allow others to invade to varying degrees. That is, we might think nothing of spouses knowing virtually everything about us (perhaps denying them only access to our correspondence with select others). We might allow our children and siblings to know much less about us than our spouses. Then, we might want our ex-spouses and enemies to know little or nothing about us, because they might use what they learn against us.[36]

In the past, most people's private space has been relatively secure for a simple, but solid, economic reason: Their personal information—for example, telephone and fax numbers, addresses, medical and tax records, employment histories and addresses, and histories of purchases—had minimal value to others, given what little could be done with the information. Other forms of personal information we now take for granted—for example, E-mail addresses and cell phone numbers—did not exist

Moreover, collecting information was typically very costly, requiring many man-hours in one form of spying or another, which is why the collection of personal information was highly targeted on those individuals whose personal information was worth something. Storing the information also usually required a lot of paper and file space. Retrieving the stored information, and then using and distributing it, was also costly, given that the information was often available from varied, decentralized sources and could only be duplicated in paper form and distributed at best at the speed of the U.S. Postal Service. In this earlier era, many people may not have thought much about having formal legal protections of their personal space because such protections would have added little to their privacy, which was fairly well protected by the high cost of invasion of their space by others.

Granted, even before the advent of the digital age, the collection, storage, and distribution of personal information gradually got cheaper with reductions in the price of paper and phone calls and with the advent of the ability to convert paper documents to film files, along with the development of large firms set up to achieve scale economies in the collection and distribution of marketing and credit information. However, the digital era has resulted in new forms of communicating and in a quantum drop in the cost of information collection, storage, and distribution. Since E-mails are born digital, their collection and storage by firms is simply a matter of copying them to a tape or a hard drive. Some documents still have to be transcribed into digital form, but a growing number of documents—relating to medical, legal, tax, or educational matters—are filled out on computers, which means they can be stored, retrieved, replicated, and distributed with ease—that is, at little cost.

In addition, unlike letters, which postal employees are prohibited by law from opening and reading (without judicial oversight), the law is fairly clear that E-mails (and instant messages) can be read by the senders' employers, Internet service providers, and E-mail services (while the government still cannot read E-mails without judicial oversight). E-mailers (and instant messengers) must also understand that their E-mails are much more like postcards than letters sealed in envelopes, given that E-mails sent out over the Internet can be intercepted as they speed along and read (albeit illegally) by hackers via so-called sniffer devices. Also, each E-mail has in its header every server it has passed through on its way to the recipient. As a consequence, any determined privacy invader can trace an intercepted E-mail (and instant message) back to its sender. Web browsing and purchasing habits can easily be tracked with so-called spyware, involving encrypted code called "cookies." I have noted how the characteristics of Web browsers and channel surfers might be deduced more indirectly from their "clickstreams."

The digitization of information has resulted in a nontrivial threat to people's privacy, partially because much personal information that once served businesses only as a means of producing and selling other business goods and services has been transformed into a business asset that has economic value in itself, apart from how the business might use the information to produce and market other goods and services. This is another way of saying that businesses—or more generally, all collectors of information—have a greater interest in using the personal information at their disposal, regardless of whether they have paid for the right to use the information in expanded ways. In short, the reduction in the cost of personal information collection, storage, and use has led to more information being demanded.

Understandably, as this chapter was being written, matters of personal privacy were being given growing attention in the press. Indeed, in the Dow Jones Publication Library (covering more than five thousand news publications) during the eighteen months prior to when this chapter was finalized in 2002, the word *privacy* was in news reports nearly two hundred thousand times, double the count in the previous eighteen months. Many of these reports on privacy have to do with very narrow and technical legal matters, involving numerous recently passed laws and considered court cases, that, if we considered them fully, would in themselves require book-length discussions.[37] Suffice it to say here (in order to contain the discussion to reasonable limits), many of these reports at their foundation revolved around the issue of who has rights to personal information made available in digitized form on the Web—the individuals involved or the businesses using the information—and how can and should people's personal information be protected. In other words, the issues reduce to such questions as Who owns telephone numbers, E-mail addresses, medical records, and purchasing histories? Such questions have had to be addressed in part because the conditions, or contracts, under which much of the information was collected did not anticipate the emergence of the digital technology that would permit the information to be used in a variety of new ways and more intensely in old ways.

For example, when many telephone numbers were originally collected decades ago, few people may have anticipated that the numbers would one day be used by telemarketers to pepper people with sales calls (just as they sit down for dinner), many of which are automated. When people contracted for their telephone service, did they give to their phone companies the right to sell their numbers to telemarketers? For that matter, who owns the numbers as a form of information, the subscribers or the telephone companies? DoubleClick, the country's largest Web-based advertising firm, was severely criticized in 2000 when it merged its Web-surfing databases with the databases of Abacus Direct, a firm that tracks the purchases of consumers from mail-order catalogues. Did DoubleClick's or Abacus's customers ever give, implicitly if not explicitly, either firm the right to merge the two separate sets of personal information? Who has rights to available information when new uses are created? These are the sorts of legal questions that ultimately will force the courts to play catch up (again) with the technology and, in essence, redefine property rights. These are also the kinds of legal questions that cannot be settled here. What we can do here is note the economic and legal pressures on firms that use, or rather misuse, the personal information at their disposal.

When a firm has personal information that it uses in ways that have not been authorized by way of prior contract by the people involved, the firm has to fear that the demand for its services can be undercut, thus reducing the prices that it can charge its customer base. From this perspective, it is understandable why RealNetworks apologized when its customers learned and complained that the company's RealJukeBox was recording users' musical selections. When Microsoft included code that identified users of Windows 98, the company was forced by criticism to eliminate the identifier (because of the potential demand consequences). When Microsoft started requiring buyers of Windows XP to register their copies by way of taking out a Passport account, strong concerns were raised that Microsoft would sell the information, a charge that caused the company to issue a pledge that its Passport database would never be so used.[38]

Of course, when they misuse the information, businesses have to worry that the courts will rule that they did not have the (property) right to do what they have done with the information and must therefore compensate the established owners. U.S. Bancorp paid out $3 million to settle a suit in Minnesota brought because the company had sold its customer information to a direct-marketing firm.[39]

Again, some of these legal issues, which obviously involve privacy concerns, are now being debated only because the digital age is relatively new. Many privacy issues—especially who has control over digitized personal information—have just been recognized, and there has not been time to resolve all of the issues. There is not really much economists can add to many firm and public policy discussions other than point out that many of these debates are fundamentally concerned with either the assignment or the clarification of already existing assignment of rights to digitized information. Where the assignment is unclear, Congress, state legislatures, or the courts will have to decide who has rights to the personal information property. Once the assignments have been made, then people can trade based on those rights, an important point that was at the heart of earlier analysis.

Ronald Coase, who devised what has come to be known as the "Coase Theorem," introduced in an earlier chapter, argued that it does not really make a lot of difference who is initially assigned the rights to the digitized information (as long as the transaction costs are minimal). The way the information is used will end up being pretty much the same. If individuals who use the Web are assigned rights to their own personal information, and that information is valuable to the businesses, because they want to use it for marketing or other purposes, then the businesses can buy access to the information from the individuals. They can do that either by making explicit payments to people for their personal information or by lowering the prices of the products they sell. This will happen, of course, only as long as the businesses value the information more than the individuals do. If that is not the case, then the firms cannot buy the information from the individuals.

This is how the Coasian theory has played out in business practice. Predictive Networks, Inc., a marketing firm based in Cambridge, Massachusetts, is in the business of tailoring Web and television ads to meet the buying interests of television viewers and Web browsers. Predictive Networks customizes its ads based on people's "clickstreams," or the sequences of clicks people make on their mouse as they browse Web sites or on their remote controls as they surf television channels. From its research, Predictive has found that it can distinguish, with some statistical confidence, between, for example, male and female channel surfers, mainly because men click more often than women. On the other hand, women tend to choose a single channel—frequently with music videos—and stay there even through commercials. Children can be distinguished from adults because children tend to make more sweeping movements with the computer mouse than do adults. Predictive also has concluded that clickstreams are sufficiently influenced by the personal characteristics of the people involved, so that it can tell when a man is watching television or surfing the Web with a woman.[40]

With its clickstream identifiers, Predictive can match ads with the likely shopping interests of the users and watchers. For example, a teenager who goes to an MTV site might be shown ads for albums or clothes, while the teenager's parents who browse online automobile dealers might be shown ads for cars and vacation getaways. To develop its clickstream models and customize its ads, Predictive has had to effectively "buy" the cooperation of computer users and television watchers by giving them cut-rate prices on Internet and cable services. For instance, Predictive and AT&T joined forces to offer customers unlimited Internet access through AT&T's WorldNet online service at $4.95 per month (down from AT&T's usual $19.95 monthly charge) if the customers would agree to download Predictive's software and to accept customized ads as frequently as every two minutes.[41]

If the rights to the information are assigned to the businesses, then we should expect businesses to use the rights to the information they have at their disposal as long as they, the businesses, value the rights more than the individuals. If, on the other hand, the individuals value the rights more highly than do the businesses, then we should expect that the individuals will buy the rights from the businesses. The individuals can make explicit payments to the businesses to not use personal information they divulge, or they can simply pay higher prices to those firms that agree not to use the information they collect. The higher prices can compensate the firms for not exploiting the information rights they own. And the higher prices will be an incentive for other firms, which might be inclined to exploit the information at their disposal, to follow suit and not use their information improperly.

Where the individuals' actions that result in the accumulation of information are voluntary, individuals always have the upper hand in these negotiations—as long as they have not given out the information. This is the case because individuals do not have to give out the information. That is to say, they do not have to surf the Web, or make purchases that leave a digital trail. In these cases, if individuals know they will have to buy the information back to avoid its exploitation by firms, then we should expect individuals to demand some form of upfront payment to release the information, and if firms can use or sell the information in undesirable ways for the users, then they, the firms, should be willing to make the payments.

In short, if individuals really value their privacy more than the firms value the personal information, then firms should be willing to take measures to assure individuals that their privacy will be protected. Of course, once again, this assumes that the information has not yet been given out. If the information has been given out, and new uses emerge, then we have a classic legal dispute over who owns the rights to use the information in the new ways. And the resolution of such legal disputes can be expected to hang on such matters as whether the individuals who gave out the information should have expected the emergence of the new information uses, and whether such expectations were computed into the prices they paid for the services involved. If individuals could have anticipated that their divulged information would have new uses that have negative consequences for them, then such expectations should have been expected to feed into a lower market demand for the services and, hence, lower prices, which then means they have been "paid" indirectly for their information. If the courts rule after the new uses emerge that the individuals still retain rights to their information, then the service vendors will be required to pay double for the information they have.

OPTIMAL PRIVACY, INFORMATION MISUSE, AND PRIVACY PROTECTION

In accepting payments for their information, we should expect most people to seek not so much complete privacy, that is, never release any personal information (after all, some personal information, for example, one's exact height, is not worth very much to most people, given that height can be observed), but to only release that information which is more valuable to others than it is to the individuals themselves. In this regard, individuals will be seeking optimal privacy (just as they can be expected to seek an optimum consumption or sales of anything else).

In other words, individuals typically can be expected to divulge only information that is less valuable than the price firms are willing to pay for the information. Without much question, different individuals value information differently, which means their optimums on privacy will differ, an important reason that laws which make blanket prohibitions against the use (or sale or dissemination) of personal information collected on the Web should be resisted. Such laws may benefit some individuals, but damage others.

This is not to say that all privacy problems can be resolved with contract negotiations. Once the negotiations have been completed, as in all other business relationships, there remain incentives for the parties to violate the contracts they have accepted. And as has long been the case, there will be disputes over what the negotiated contracts—reduced to disputes over the definitions of words in the contract—mean for the parties involved. Because contracts are fragile, subject to breakdown, individuals will try, as best they can, to make the contracts self-enforcing. That is, if individuals are concerned that the Web firms they deal with will, at a later date, misuse the information collected, they will tend to deal with firms that base their reputations on clearly worded public affirmations that they will not misuse the information they collect. If the firms violate their privacy protection policies, they can not only be sued for breach of contract, but they can also undercut their reputations among consumers and can suffer a loss of sales. Firm reputations can be seen as the equivalent of bonds that the firms hand over to their customers and others who deal with them. If firms renege on their agreements, their customers can destroy the value of the bonds, meaning that the contracts are at least in part self-enforcing.

When the prospect of privacy invasion emerges, we should expect firms to establish privacy policies that clearly state what they will and will not do with collected information, and then to appoint internal and external monitors of the firms' privacy policies and practices. Indeed, as this chapter was being written, major firms in the country—such as Kodak, IBM, and AT&T—were falling over themselves to establish privacy policies and then appoint vice presidents for privacy.[42]

At the same time, other firms—most notably Yahoo! and Excite—that had established privacy policies which tightly restricted what they would do with collected information began announcing changes in their privacy policies, putting their users on notice that their contact information (for example, E-mail addresses, phone numbers, and so forth) would be sold or rented—unless the users go to their sites within sixty days and explicitly request that their information not be divulged. In Yahoo!'s case, this meant that users had to know not only about the change in the policy, distributed by E-mail, but also had to go to a particular site (www.subscribe.yahoo.com/showaccount), click on the "Sign—Yahoo!" link (among a dozen links on the page), and then click "no" up to fifteen times. The justification was straightforward; the companies needed the added sources of revenues. Plus, according to one Excite executive, "They [their users] are getting free content and utility that is unparalleled, and in return we will be marketing products to them."[43]

These turns of privacy policies are likely to give rise to additional lawsuits over the rights that companies retain to make changes in their privacy policies once they have initially given their users the right to opt out of being bothered by marketers. The turns, which can fuel expectations of instability in firms' privacy policies, will no doubt have feedback effects on the willingness of new users to join and of old users to stay with the firms. These changes will likely inspire other firms to firm up their commitments to stick with established privacy policies, mainly because, to the extent users do not want to be bothered with changes, they will be willing to pay higher prices for such services.

At the dawn of the digital era, many brick-and-mortar businesses had two strong advantages over purely digital firms in giving customers assurances that their privacy would not be unduly invaded. First, brick-and-mortar businesses already had established reputations that they could carry with them into their Web-based endeavors. Digital firms had to build their reputations from scratch, overcoming people's fears of many unknowns about how the Web might be used and misused. Second, at the time they entered Web commerce, the established market values of the investment in brick-and-mortar stores served as an additional bond for customers, given that the value of those real-world firm assets would be diminished if the firms violated any of their contracts, not the least of which may be to hold its customer information private. Other Web-based firms that had not yet been able to establish reputations for holding to their contracts, and did not have the required brick-and-mortar bonds to support their contracts, were paying firms like Verisign to monitor them and then to put the Verisign insignia of its approval on their marketing and privacy policies—a new digital-era form of the "Good Housekeeping Seal of Approval."

Some privacy protection can be expected to come from technology, simply because technological fixes may be not only more complete but also cheaper for individuals. In E-mails, encryption/decryption programs such as Publius or NetPost.Certified (an encryption service for certifying E-mails provided by the U.S. Postal Service) afford users a degree of anonymity by first converting plaintext (original) E-mails into "cyphertext" (or encrypted code), and then reconverting cyphertext back into plaintext that can be read by the recipient.[44] Other firms such as Authentica.com or Disappearing, Inc. allow E-mail senders not only to encrypt E-mails but also to set a time limit on their E-mails' existence (whether five minutes or forty-five days, after which the E-mails will be expunged from the recipients' in boxes) and to determine whether the E-mails can be copied, printed, or forwarded.[45] Other programs, called "remailers," for example, Mixmaster, can add to the security of E-mails by first sending the E-mail to a remailer that might hold the cyphertext message for some time, say, an hour, to throw off anyone who might be interested in intercepting messages, and then by routing the message through additional remailers that are permitted to know only the next address to which the E-mail will be routed, not the final destination. The remailing process does not make backtracking of the E-mail to the sender impossible, but it certainly makes it much more difficult.[46]

INVOLUNTARY INFORMATION DISCLOSURE

The comments to this point have been founded on the presumption that the personal information at stake is subject to voluntary disclosure by the people involved. Accordingly, they can decide whether the deal proposed by firms to buy their information is beneficial on balance. Clearly, there is personal information that is not subject to voluntary disclosure, for example, the information reported on tax returns, census questionnaires, and legal records. Other forms of information may, in a sense, be voluntarily disclosed, but also is disclosed as a necessary condition of a service being provided, for example, medical care. In these cases, there are good arguments for government-backed prohibitions on information disclosure by the firms and organizations collecting the information. This is because it is hard to see how deals could be made that would compensate individuals for the disclosure of their personal information and loss of privacy when the information was obtained through forced disclosure. In addition, since those government agencies and other organizations collecting the information do not have to pay anyone for their information disclosures, there is a likelihood that the information will be excessively disclosed, that is, be disclosed when the marginal cost to the individuals of the information disclosures is greater than any benefits they could possibly reap.

Having said that, however, policy makers still need to tread carefully on instituting blanket prohibitions on what businesses can and cannot do with the information they gather. Such prohibitions can leave many people, who are the object of the protection, worse off. They will not be able to make deals with businesses that give them payments that are worth more than the value of the personal information they disclose.

CONCLUDING COMMENTS

Private property rights are crucial for the efficient function of markets. The policy debate surrounding property rights is really a debate over how extensive, complete, and secure the rights should be. This has been especially true of private intellectual property rights in the form of patents and copyrights. Property rights are costly to enforce, and stamping out all piracy of intellectual property rights makes about as much economic sense as stamping out all theft. It cannot be done. And even if the elimination of all piracy could be achieved, it would be too costly to do so. Even then, if property rights were fully protected by public policing means, firms would be given the wrong incentive; that is, they might become slack in their own efforts to thwart piracy.

Moreover, the rights embodied in patents and copyrights always afford the holders a degree of market power, more or less. In this regard, the public policy concern always involves the potential trade-offs between giving people an incentive to be creative by virtue of giving them rights to the product of their efforts, and giving them monopoly power to exploit their rights ultimately to the detriment of consumers. One of the problems in automatically conceding to the demands of the music establishment to shut down P2P music exchanges like Napster is that the established music houses may have more than the protection of the copyrights at stake. As noted earlier, they may want to shut down Napster because it shuts out competition from artists who do not have labels behind them. The established labels, and the artists they represent, may be thinking that if Napster is shut down, or just has to block copyrighted material, which forces it also to restrict file sharing of noncopyrighted material, the established labels can sell more of their own recordings at higher prices.

The debate over what to do with Napster-like, Web-based services will rage on in the digital age. Piracy problems are evident everywhere in the music and software industries, and they are becoming progressively more evident in E-book and E-movie industries as they grow in popularity. Indeed, before *Spider-Man* and *Star Wars: Episode II Attack of the Clones* hit theaters in the spring of 2002, pirated copies of the movies were already on the Internet. At the time, movie industry analysts were predicting that 1 million people saw the movie before its theater premier.[47]

The law will have to develop quickly to keep pace with digital developments, but the law has always played catch-up to technology. Copyright law was of no consequence until the printing press was invented, and the law evolved through legislation and court cases to accommodate the particular reproduction costs of printing. In the late nineteenth century, copyrights became a growing concern because the price of printing books was dropping precipitously, which means that publishers and writers were losing some of their natural market protection from the cost of printing.[48] Now, the law will likely have to evolve to accommodate the dramatically different cost structure underlying digital industries.

No doubt, many new legal issues will emerge as digital goods and services become ever more popular and a greater share of the economy, and some of these issues will seem to be out of left field, as we have already seen. For example, the software code known as "DeCSS" can decrypt encoded movies. In August 2000, a federal judge used federal copyright law to ban the posting of the DeCSS on a hacker Web site known as "2600.com." However, that judgment did not stop the debate over how else the code could be used. In early 2000, the code started showing up on the Web as a part of elaborate poetry and was incorporated into a movie as symbols that scroll off into space.[49] Eventually, the courts will have to decide whether blocking the code in such forms would be a violation of free speech.

In 2001, the U.S. Supreme Court considered a case that had been brought back in 1993 by six freelance writers (led by the head of the New York–based National Writers Union, Jonathan Tasini) who argued that those news organizations—for example, the New York Times Company, the Tribune Company, AOL Time-Warner, Time Magazine, Reed Elsevier, and University Microfilms International—that made available their article databases, including articles written by the freelancers, for electronic downloads for fees from organizations such as LexisNexis and Dow Jones were violating the freelancers' copyrights.[50]

Since 1996, most publishers have made explicit allowances for electronic reproductions of works. The representatives of the freelancers argued that in the contracts they had negotiated prior to 1996, they had not signed away the digital rights to their works and that, consequently, they deserved to be paid for electronically viewed or downloaded articles. (The freelancers also pointed out that several of the organizations that were violating their copyrights were, ironically, parties in the copyright infringement case against Napster.[51]) Given that the penalty for copyright violation could range up to

$30,000 in damages per violation, and given that Nexis alone had one hundred thousand freelance articles in its database, the penalties could be huge (especially if "per violation" were interpreted to mean "per download").

Naturally, the defendants argued that they had already paid for the rights to the freelanced work and that the fee Web users paid was payment for the time Web users spent searching the databases, not for the particular articles that were downloaded. But those claims are disputable, which is one reason the case made it to the Supreme Court.[52] When the publications contracted with the freelancers for articles (say, back in the 1980s and before), few could have anticipated the emergence of digital distribution of articles. Many of the freelance contracts likely included provisions for reproduction in paper and video forms, but not digital. The central question confronting the Supreme Court was whether the freelancers gave up their rights to payment for reproductions in forms that did not exist at the time they signed their contracts, and could not have been anticipated. If the publications got an adverse ruling, the publications might have to clean their databases of numerous publications of freelancers, many of whom are now dead. The cost of tracking down the freelancers or their heirs might be prohibitively expensive. Then, the consequences of the case might be more problematic because many freelance writers might want their work to be kept in the databases because they understand that the payment they would receive would be trivial, and they would prefer to have continued inclusion in the databases to any payment they might receive.

The Supreme Court ruled in late June 2001, "The crucial fact is that the Databases . . . store and retrieve articles separately within a vast domain of diverse texts. Such a storage and retrieval system effectively overrides the Authors' exclusive right to control the individual reproduction and distribution of each," which stands in conflict with copyright law that specifies that the author retains rights to his or her works as long as he or she has not expressly transferred the right.[53]

Accordingly, the Court ruled in a seven-to-two decision for the freelancers. In the process, it recognized that the publishers had warned the Court that an adverse ruling for them would have "devastating consequences." However, the Court argued that the "dire predictions" need not come true:

> The parties (Authors and Publishers) may enter into an agreement allowing continued electronic reproduction of the Authors' works; they, and if necessary the courts and Congress, may draw on numerous models for distributing copyrighted works and remunerating authors for their distribution. . . . In any

event, speculation about future harms is no basis for this Court to shrink au-
thorial rights Congress established in 201(c). Agreeing with the Court of Appeals that the Publishers are liable for infringement, we leave remedial issues
open for initial airing and decision in the District Court.[54]

Similarly, the courts will have to revise the legal definition of a *book* for
the digital age. Before books could be sold in digital forms, either through
CDs or the Web, many book contracts negotiated before the mid-1990s gave
publishers rights to the work of authors—for example, Kurt Vonnegut,
William Styron, and Robert Parker—in "book form." When books could be
sold digitally, Rosetta Books, a startup electronic publisher, bought the electronic rights to Vonnegut's, Styron's, and Parker's books published before
their contracts explicitly gave the electronic publication rights to their publisher, Random House. Random House sued, claiming that their prior contracts that used the words "in book form" meant "any means of presentation
that faithfully reproduces the author's full text in a fashion that allows the
text to be read."[55]

Rosetta, of course, uses a far more restrictive definition: A book is something made of paper and is printed. Rosetta argues that when publishers
began including clauses in their contracts with authors to cover electronic
publication in the mid-1990s, they were inadvertently admitting that "in
book form" did not cover electronic means of publication. Random House
claims that the new contractual words were intended only to clarify the
meaning of "in book form." Interestingly, as implied in the arguments of this
chapter, the outcome of the case will hang largely on whether electronic publication could have reasonably been anticipated by publishers and authors. If
electronic publication could have been anticipated when the authors signed
their publishers' contracts, then following earlier court precedents, the publishers would get the rights unless they were explicitly held back by the authors.[56] This is because in anticipation of electronic publications, the authors
would have required a fee (equal to some portion of the expected value of
those rights) before turning over those expected rights to the publishers.

These are the kinds of legal issues that are new to the digital age. As a consequence, the law will have to play catch-up again, given the dramatically
lower costs of reproducing digital goods. We should not be surprised that a
new body of law develops under the rubric of "digital copyright law" and
that that body of law takes a decade or more to solve, albeit partially, the
piracy and privacy problems. In the meantime, firms will continue their
search for technological, market, and management fixes. Hopefully, economics will not be far behind in facilitating our understanding of the likely impact

of this new body of law. Perhaps economics might even guide lawmakers and judges in the development of the law.

NOTES

1. Jeff Leeds, "Record Industry Says Napster Hurt Music Sales: Data Show a 38.8% Drop-Off in CD Singles Last Year," *Los Angeles Times*, 24 February 2001, p. C1.

2. In addition, sales of singles accounted for only 7 percent of record store revenues in 2000 and are not nearly as profitable as albums. See Richard Siklos and Steven V. Brull, " Download This! Free Music on the Web Has Let the Genie Out of the Bottle," *Business Week*, May 29, 2000, 120.

3. David Lieberman, "So Long, Singles; CD Sales Sinking Napster, Costs Blamed in Decline of One-Song Format," *USA Today*, 19 February 2001, p. 4B.

4. Jeff Leeds, "Album Sales Test the Napster Effect," *Los Angeles Times*, 20 June 2001, p. C1.

5. As reported by Matt Richtel, "The Napster Decision: The Overview: The Appellate Judges Back Limitations on Copying Music," *New York Times*, 13 February 2001, p. A1.

6. In the VCR case, the Supreme Court articulated the staple article of commerce doctrine under which any product that could be used to infringe another copyright could be deemed lawful for as long as it had a "substantial noninfringing use." See *Sony Corp. of Am. v. Universal City Studios, Inc.*, 464 U.S. 417, 442 (1984), at 441–442. See also Stacey L. Dogan, "Is Napster a VCR? The Implications of *Sony* for Napster and Other Internet Technologies," *Hastings Law Journal* 52 (April 2002): 939–959.

7. "Napster Numbers Are Falling, Study Says," *Los Angeles Times*, 28 June 2001, p. C5.

8. Gene Kan, "Gnutella," in *Peer-to-Peer: Harnessing the Power of Disruptive Technologies*, ed. Andy Oram (Cambridge, Mass.: O'Reilly and Associates, 2001), 96–97.

9. Matt Richtel, "With Napster Down, Its Audience Fans Out," *New York Times*, 20 July 2001, p. A1.

10. As reported on *CNN Headline News*, April 29, 2002.

11. Jon Healey, "File-Sharing Finds Perfect Pitch," *Los Angeles Times*, 16 May 2002, p. A1.

12. U.S. Senate, 107th Cong., 2d Sess., Consumer Broadband and Digital Television Act, March 21, 2002.

13. See James Lardner, "Hollywood versus High-Tech," *Business 2.0*, May 2002, 40–48.

14. Neil Strauss, "Record Labels' Answer to Napster Still Has Artist Feeling Bypassed," *New York Times*, 18 February 2002, p. A1.

15. *Sixth Annual BSA Global Software Piracy Study* (West Chester, Penn.: International Planning and Research Corporation, May 2001), as found at http://www.bsa.org/

resources/2001-05-21.55.pdf. Software packages in the following categories were not covered by the survey: recreation, home creativity, home education, integrated, personal finance, reference software, and tax programs.

16. As determined by TNS Intersearch in a survey of 1,056 U.S. adults in February 2001 and reported in "Copy It? No Problem," *PC Magazine*, April 24, 2001, 68.

17. *SIIA's Report on Global Software Piracy: 2000* (Washington, D.C.: Software Information Industry Association, 2000, 3), as found at http://www.siia.net/sharedcontent/press/2000/5-24-00.html.

18. Microsoft limits family sharing of any copy of Windows purchased by requiring buyers to "activate" their copies of Windows. In the process of activation, a "profile" of the computer on which the computer is installed is sent to Microsoft, which it uses to effectively "lock" the copy of Windows to that particular computer. If a copy of Windows XP is not activated, then it will stop working after thirty days, a feature that caused *Wall Street Journal* technology columnist Walter Mossberg to worry in print that Microsoft might use the collected information to the company's advantage ("Microsoft Cracks Down on Sharing Windows among Home Users," *Wall Street Journal*, 5 July 2001, p. B1).

19. Amy Harmon, "CD Technology Stops Copies, but It Starts a Controversy," *New York Times*, 1 March 2002, p. C1.

20. Kathleen Reaves Conner and Richard P. Rumelt, "Software Piracy: An Analysis of Protection Strategies," *Management Science* 37 (1991): 125–139.

21. See Moshe Givon, Vijay Mahajan, and Eitan Muller, "Software Piracy: Estimation of Lost Sales and the Impact of Software Diffusion," *Journal of Marketing* 59 (1999): 29–37.

22. See Stanley M. Besen, "Private Copying, Reproduction Costs, and the Supply of Intellectual Capital," *Information Economics and Policy* 2 (1986): 2–52; Stanley M. Besen and Nataraj Kirby, "Private Copying, Appropriability, and Optimal Copying Royalties," *Journal of Law and Economics* 32 (1989): 255–280; William R. Johnson, "The Economics of Copying," *Journal of Political Economy* 93, no. 1 (1985):158–174; and Ian E. Novos and Michael Waldman, "The Effect of Increased Copyright Protection," *Journal of Political Economy* 92 (1984): 236–246.

23. As reported by sBrain Market Research at http://www.ebrain.org/crs/crs_head.asp?headID={68B2E5AF-0046-11D5-A204-00508B44E4E6}.

24. As reported by Tyler Cowen, "Music Industry Needs Napster," *National Post*, 13 February 2001, p. A18.

25. How much piracy producers will try to prevent, either by penalties or technological fixes, will actually depend on the elasticity of demand for the product. The greater the elasticity of demand for a product, the smaller the penalty needed to achieve the optimum level of piracy.

26. Teb Bridis, "Tech Industry Aims to Render MP3 Obsolete," *Wall Street Journal*, 12 April 2001, p. A3.

27. See Don Clark and Martin Peers, "Can the Record Industry Beat Free Web Music?" *Wall Street Journal*, 20 June 2000, p. B1.

28. Digital Millennium Copyright Act, Public Law 105-304 (1998).

29. As reported by David P. Hamilton, "Music-Industry Group Moves to Quash Professor's Study of Antipiracy Methods," *Wall Street Journal*, 24 April 2001, p. A2.

30. Lawrence Lessig, "Jail Time in the Digital Age," *New York Times*, 30 July 2001, p. A21. See also Amy Harmon, "New Economy: New Visibility for 1998 Copyright Protection Law, with Online Enthusiasts Confused and Frustrated," *New York Times*, 13 August 2001, p. C4.

31. Harmon, "CD Technology Stops Copies," p. C1.

32. As reported in Jon Healey, "Judge Allows Electronic Copyright Case to Proceed," *Los Angeles Times*, 9 May 2002, p. C1.

33. Ibid.

34. Alan Westin, *Privacy and Freedom* (New York: Atheneum, 1967), 3.

35. Charles J. Sykes, *The End of Privacy* (New York: St. Martin's, 1999), 13.

36. Charles Sykes writes about a "ladder of privacy" within our "zone of privacy" that allows people to have access to information about us depending on our closeness to them in terms of intimacy. In descending order of closeness (and ascending order of the damage others might do with personal information), one such ladder might have these privacy steps: spouse, priest or rabbi, parents, children, friends, in-laws, coworkers, neighbors, marketers, employers, government, news media, ex-spouses, and potential rivals/enemies (ibid., p. 14).

37. For more details on the legislative and court details of information law, see Sykes, *The End of Privacy*; Anne Wells Branscomb, *Who Owns Information: From Privacy to Public Access* (New York: Basic Books, 1994); and Amitai Etzioni, *The Limits of Privacy* (New York: Basic Books, 1999).

38. David Berlind, "Microsoft's Sohn: ' We Won't Sell Passport Data,'" *ZD Tech Update*, February 21, 2002, as found at http://techupdate.zdnet.com/techupdate/stories/main/0,14179,2849411,00.html.

39. John Schwartz, "First Line of Defense, Chief Privacy Officers Forge Evolving Corporate Roles," *New York Times*, 12 February 2001, p. A1.

40. The software is hardly foolproof, which means that it is possible that children, who have clicking patterns similar to adults, might be shown age-inappropriate ads. See William M. Buckley, "Software Uses Clicking Pattern to Customize Ads," *Wall Street Journal*, 25 May 2001, p. B1.

41. Ibid.

42. Ibid.

43. Saul Hansell, "Seeking Profits, Internet Alters Privacy Policy," *New York Times*, 11 April 2002, p. A1.

44. See Marc Waldman, "Publius," in *Peer-to-Peer: Harnessing the Power of Disruptive Technologies*, ed. Andy Oram (Cambridge, Mass.: O'Reilly and Associates, 2001), 145–158.

45. Thomas E. Weber, "How to Keep Control of Your Digital Data after It Gets to the Net," *Wall Street Journal*, 7 May 2001, p. B1.

46. See Adam Langley, "Mixmaster Remailers," in *Peer-to-Peer: Harnessing the Power of Disruptive Technologies*, ed. Andy Oram (Cambridge, Mass.: O'Reilly and Associates, 2001), 89–93.

47. Jon Healey and Richard Verrier, "Latest Plot Twist for 'Star Wars': Attack of the Cloners," *Los Angeles Times*, 10 May 2002, p. A1.

48. See Siva Vaidhyanathan, *Copyrights and Copywrongs: The Rise of Intellectual Property and How It Threatens Creativity* (New York: New York University Press, 2001): 50–55.

49. See *Tasini, et al v. New York Times, et al*, U.S. District Court, Southern District of New York, December 1993, downloaded from http://www.nwu.org/tvt/tvtcomp1.htm on April 17, 2001. See also David P. Hamilton, "Banned Code Lives in Poetry and Song," *Wall Street Journal*, 12 April 2001, p. B1.

50. James Vicini, "USA: US High Court Reviews Free-Lancers' Online Rights," *Reuters English News Service*, March 28, 2001, as found at the Dow Jones Publications Library, April 16, 2001.

51. One of the principals in the freelance writers' suit against the *New York Times*, Jonathan Tasini, president of the National Writers Union, chided the *Times* for its hypocrisy:

> Here is the real truth: *The New York Times*, and for that matter, broad segments of the entire media industry, wants everyone to respect copyright laws and pay for information—but they themselves do not respect those laws, nor do they want to allow the people who actually create information to make a fair living from the exploitation of their copyright. And, if you consider *The Times*' illegal behavior, I cannot imagine why any person in this country would listen to their pleas for copyright protection as long as they steal from authors (nor should anyone listen to other media companies such as Time Warner, the parent corporation of Time Inc., which was also caught stealing from writers).

See "The Hypocrisy of the *New York Times*," as found at http://www.nwu.org/tvt/schypoc.htm and downloaded April 17, 2001.

52. The other major reason the court took up the case is that federal district ruled for the defendants, dismissing the case (the publishers) (see *Tasini, et al v. New York Times, et al*, U.S. District Court, Southern District of New York, 93 Civ. 8678 (SS), August 13, 1997, as found at http://www.nwu.org/tvt/tvtrule.htm, while the court of appeals ruled for the writers (*Tasini, et al v. New York Times, et al*, U.S. Court of Appeals, Second Circuit, September 24, 1999, as found at http://www.tourolaw.edu/2ndCircuit/September99/97-9181.html on April 17, 2001).

53. *New York Times Co., Inc., etal. v. TASINI etal.*, No. 00201. Argued March 28, 2001. Decided June 25, 2001, sec. III, as found at http://caselaw.lp.findlaw.com/cgi-in/getcase.pl?court=US&navby=case&vol=000&invol=00-201). The relevant section of the Copyright Act is sec. 201(c):

Copyright in each separate contribution to a collective work is distinct from copyright in the collective work as a whole, and vests initially in the author of the contribution. In the absence of an express transfer of the copyright or of any rights under it, the owner of copyright in the collective work is presumed to have acquired only the privilege of reproducing and distributing the contribution as part of that particular collective work, any revision of that collective work, and any later collective work in the same series.

54. Ibid., sec. 4.
55. As reported by Matthew Rose, "Definitions Are Key in Publishers' Dispute over Electronic-Book Rights," *Wall Street Journal*, 7 May 2001, p. B1.
56. Ibid.

11

Antitrust

Antitrust thinking and enforcement have traditionally been firmly grounded in conventional economic models of monopoly and oligopoly market structures, all fully and inevitably constrained by the laws of demand and decreasing returns. In this chapter, I explore various ways digital economics should give rise to revisions in the way antitrust cases against digital firms should be appraised, and how antitrust prosecution of digital firms will be restrained. I use the experience with the Microsoft antitrust case to show how errors can be made in antitrust prosecutions when underlying monopoly models are not revised to accommodate these digital economic postulates. Although the thrust of the arguments advises restraint in antitrust prosecution, I also argue that the prospects of effective, anti-monopoly, antitrust prosecution can, under some conditions, be seen as having beneficial effects for those firms, like Microsoft, that are subject to digital and network forces and that become dominant, if not monopoly, producers in their markets.

KEY ISSUES IN THE MICROSOFT CASE

I focus on the Microsoft antitrust case partially because the case involves a major American and international company, but also because the case has been a "laboratory" for how digital economics can play out in court. In its original antitrust complaint against Microsoft filed in May 1998, the Justice Department grounded its case in the relatively new digital economics:

> Microsoft has maintained a monopoly share (in excess of 80%) of the PC operating system market over an extended period of time. The durability of Microsoft's market power in part reflects the fact that the PC operating system market is characterized by certain economies of scale in production and by significant "network effects." In other words, the PC operating system for which there are the greatest number, variety, and quality of applications will be selected by the large majority of PC users, and in turn writers of applications will write their programs to work with the most commonly used operating system, in order to appeal to as many potential customers as possible. Economies of scale and network effects, which reinforce one another, result in high barriers to entry.[1]

District Court judge Thomas Penfield Jackson affirmed both the Justice Department's and his own view of scale economies for software developers (which he developed as the trial proceeded) when he found, "What is more, once a firm had written the necessary software code, it could produce millions of copies of its operating system at relatively low cost."[2] The judge concurred with the Justice Department that Microsoft had a dominant market position, well within the requirements for an antitrust trial to proceed: Microsoft possesses a dominant, persistent, and increasing share of the worldwide market for Intel-compatible PC operating systems. Every year for the past decade, Microsoft's share of the market for Intel-compatible PC operating systems has stood above 90 percent. For the last couple of years, the figure has been at least 95 percent, and analysts project that the share will climb even higher over the next few years. Even if Apple's Mac OS were included in the relevant market, Microsoft's share would still stand well above 80 percent.[3]

The reason for the existence of the high barriers to entry is, according to the Justice Department (and the trial judge), the self-perpetuating nature of sales to build on sales:

> One of the most important barriers to entry is the barrier created by the number of software applications that must run on an operating system in order to make the operating system attractive to end users. Because end users want a large number of applications available, because most applications today are written to run on Windows, and because it would be prohibitively difficult, time-consuming, and expensive to create an alternative operating system that would run the programs that run on Windows, a potential new operating system entrant faces a high barrier to successful entry.[4]

Moreover, the Justice Department found that key Microsoft executives appear to have understood key digital economic concepts and used them in designing the company's monopoly maintenance through winning the browser battle. According to the Justice Department, two Microsoft executives reasoned that "the 'key factors to keep in mind' were, first, the need to increase browser share and, second, that the way to do that was: 'Leveraging our strong share on the desktop will make switching costs high (if they get our technology by default on every desk then they'll be less inclined to purchase a competitive solution).'"[5]

Hence, the Justice Department concludes:

> Indeed, because of the extraordinary growth and importance of the Internet, the Internet browser market is itself a substantial source of potential profits to any company that might achieve a durable dominant position and be able to charge monopoly prices for the efficient use of the Internet or the web. The importance of the Internet and the significant public benefits resulting from its use, make the potential benefit to a monopolist and the potential economic and social cost of monopolization in this market very high.[6]

Again, according to the Justice Department, the emergence of Netscape's Navigator, used in conjunction with Sun Microsystem's Java programming language that would make for a cross-platform Web-based operating environment, threatened "to reduce or eliminate one of the key barriers to entry [the array of seventy thousand Windows applications] protecting Microsoft's operating system monopoly."[7]

THE ROLE OF MARKET DOMINANCE

Historically, in antitrust matters, a firm's market dominance, measured by its share of industry sales (as the "industry" is defined for the particular case), has been an important surrogate for the firm's market power, or ability to raise its prices to monopoly levels (or above the marginal cost of production). As antitrust scholar and University of Iowa law professor Herbert Hovenkamp notes, courts have relied "on the fact that there is a positive correlation between market share and market power,"[8] with market power defined earlier as the ability of a firm "to deviate profitably from marginal cost pricing."[9] The courts have reasoned that the ability of a firm to deviate from marginal cost pricing is functionally related to its ability to reduce the market supply of the product below competitive levels. With the curbed supply, the market price will rise, and so will the firm's profits. Of course, if there are no other producers in the market, and none can enter because of prohibitive barriers to entry, the firm is in total control of industry output, which it alone can manipulate to maximize profits.

If the firm is merely the dominant producer, not the sole producer, then the dominant producer's ability to restrict aggregate industry supply is itself restricted by the ability of the other firms in the industry (and those who can enter) to make up for sales not made by the dominant producer. For nondigital goods (those that are material in nature and cannot be reduced to 1's and 0's), the smaller the share of the market supplied by firms other than the dominant producer, the greater the ability of the dominant producer to restrict aggregate industry supply and the greater its market power, ceteris paribus. The market power of the dominant producer in markets for nondigital goods stems in part from the fact that the existing nondominant producers face positive and increasing marginal costs of production. This means that as the nondominant producers try to expand sales in response to the dominant producer's curb in sales, the nondominant producers' expansion in sales is choked off, eventually, by their rising marginal costs. The result can then be an aggregate net reduction in sales equal to the difference between the dominant producer's curb in sales minus the nondominant producers' total expansion in sales. The market (monopoly) price charged will be set by the net reduction in industry supply and, presumably, constant demand.[10]

Market share and market power should not have the same correlation in markets for digital goods, like operating systems, as in nondigital goods, for example, cereal or microprocessors. The reason is simple, as the Justice Department has found is the case in operating systems: The marginal cost of production is virtually zero, if not zero, and is practically constant for what is likely to be the full scope of the expected market (even when that market might be quite large). If the dominant producer tries to restrict production, then the nondominant producers can expand output without their marginal production costs ever rising much above zero. If the Justice Department starts an antitrust case with the presumption that, for example, Microsoft's marginal cost is practically zero, it would have to assume, for the sake of consistency, that IBM's marginal cost is also practically zero. Accordingly, if Microsoft were to restrict sales of Windows, IBM could easily, with no added costs, expand its output of OS/2 by duplicating Microsoft's license with computer manufacturers, making the computer manufacturers responsible for transferring OS/2 to the computers sold. Hence, the collective expansion of nondominant producers' output will fully offset the supply curb of the dominant producer, meaning that in such limited cases there would be no correlation between market share and market power. The supply response of the non-dominant producers can be fully offsetting no matter whether the dominant producer's market share is 50 percent, 80 percent, or even 99 percent.

This is to say, in the case of digital goods, the relationship between market share and monopoly power would at best be discontinuous. That is, the dominant producer might have monopoly power if it had 100 percent of market sales, provided there were no alternative digital products available and the firm with 100 percent market share was protected by prohibitive barriers to entry. It would have no such monopoly power if its market share were lower than 100 percent, regardless of whether it was protected by prohibitive barriers to entry.

Hovenkamp effectively recognizes this point by citing a formula original with William Landes and Richard Posner that includes the elasticity of supply, as well as the elasticity of demand, as a determinant of a dominant producer's market power.[11] In that formula, as the supply (or demand) elasticity goes to infinity, the firm's market power goes to zero. With constant and virtually zero marginal cost of digital goods, the dominant producer's market evaporates, no matter what its level of dominance is, mainly because the elasticity of supply of the nondominant producers is infinity when their marginal cost is constant and zero.

The practical consequence of this revised thinking can be seen in the Microsoft case. In developing its case, the Justice Department does not seem to appreciate that its declaration that the marginal cost of production of operating systems is practically nil and constant, and that the operating system market is beset with network effects, belies its argument that Microsoft has market power simply because of its more than 80 percent (really upward of 95 percent) market share.[12] The two lines of argument are inconsistent. The existence of one other operating system producer—for example, IBM with OS/2—can totally undermine Microsoft's market power even if IBM has a trivial portion of market sales, simply because, as indicated, the nondominant producer could supplant any reduction in sales of the dominant producer. (Frankly, Windows might even have 100 percent of the market and still have no more monopoly power than it has with 90 percent. The reason is that OS/2 still exists on IBM's digital storage systems, meaning additional copies can be produced at virtually the same marginal cost, practically zero, that would be incurred if OS/2 had some positive share of the market.)

Perhaps nondominant producers of a digital good eventually do face, within the bounds of total market sales, somewhat escalating marginal production costs (after all, someone may have to provide customer service, which might only be provided with nondigitized resources that are subject to increasing marginal cost[13]). Still, the point is that dominance per se in markets does not mean nearly as much in digital markets as in nondigital markets (say, markets for industrial goods, such as cereal or cars). Put another way, to achieve any given level of monopoly power, a dominant producer in a digital market would have to have a greater market share than a dominant producer in a nondigital market. Hence, there should be less need for antitrust enforcement in digital markets, or fewer antitrust cases should be expected in digital markets, ceteris paribus.

THE MEASURE OF MARKET SHARE

Stripping market share as used in antitrust analysis of all its complexities, real-world calculations of market sales are basically made by dividing the annual sales of a firm by total annual sales within the relevant market.[14] All sales that are normally considered are legal sales. If Kellogg has $5 billion in annual sales of cereal with the relevant cereal market defined as $10 billion of legal sales, then Kellogg has a 50 percent market share. There is no reason to consider Kellogg's past cereal sales because cereal is perishable. There is a good reason for not including illegal sales: Cereal pirates very likely would operate on a smaller scale than Kellogg and likely would face production costs per box that are much higher than Kellogg's and perhaps would rise at a faster rate. As a consequence, it may reasonably be argued that Kellogg's market share, as computed, can say something about Kellogg's ability to restrict sales within the cereal market and raise the prices it charges.

Digital goods are far from perishable. Indeed, there is no reason that they should ever deteriorate physically, mainly because, at their core, they are not physical. Hence, past sales of digital goods cannot be summarily dismissed as being irrelevant when calculating market share.

Microsoft might indeed have 90+ percent of the operating system market, when the relevant market is restricted to those operating systems sold each year through retail stores and computer makers for computers that employ Intel-compatible microprocessors. However, does that mean that Microsoft has 90+ percent of all operating system "sales"? The answer is clearly no, as Cato Institute economist Alan Reynolds has pointed out, given that the relevant market was so narrowly defined in the Microsoft antitrust case that it does not include the Apple Mac (because Apple computers are not Intel-compatible) or Linux (because Linux is not generally installed on computers to be used by single users).[15]

However, the answer remains no, even when the relevant market remains restricted to Intel-compatible computers. The reason is that past sales of Windows cannot be dismissed because they have not perished.[16] When buyers do not upgrade their computers, they effectively "buy" their old operating system from themselves, and the price is very attractive—nothing. Their ability to effectively buy their old operating system from themselves is relevant because it is an additional check on the monopoly pricing of a dominant firm like Microsoft. In 1998, when the Justice Department computed Microsoft's market share at 95 percent for trial purposes (albeit incorrectly[17]), only 16 percent of personal computer owners had upgraded to Windows 98 (the then latest version of Windows). Consider also that in 1999, there were nearly 113 million desktop computers in the United States. Microsoft sold slightly under 11 million copies of Windows 98 in 1998, which means there were approximately 102 million U.S. Windows users in 1999 that could have upgraded to Windows 98. These users in effect elected that year to "buy" the old version of Windows they already had installed on their personal computers from themselves at, of course, a zero price; or they bought (or stayed with) some other operating system, like IBM's OS/2. Hence, Microsoft's sales of Windows 98 in 1999 of under 11 million copies represented a remarkably low share of all operating system "sales" (broadly defined) in the United States, just over 10 percent.

In other words, Microsoft is in competition with its previous sales, for reasons that Ronald Coase explained in a celebrated article on market power and durable goods.[18] Digital goods have one very important characteristic not fully appreciated in conventional antitrust thinking: they are highly durable. The Justice Department convinced the trial court (but not the court of appeals) that Microsoft had no good business reason to integrate Internet Explorer into Windows 98—other than to predate against Netscape. Yet there is one very good reason Microsoft must do something like integrate an important new feature—for example, an Internet browser—every time it comes out with a new version of Windows: It must give its customer base—its network—a good reason to spend even a modest sum of money for the new version. When Microsoft was contemplating the construction of Windows 98, it was obvious to just about everyone in the computer industry, including people at Netscape and Microsoft, that the Internet would play an important role in the future of computing. Microsoft had to move aggressively toward making Windows useful in the emerging Internet world and thereby giving its customer base, and applications developers, a reason to move to Windows 98. Microsoft also had to give its customers a good reason not to move toward rival operating systems that could easily emerge.

In addition to their durability, digital goods are capable of being copied by pirates at small cost. Pirates can also distribute their easily replicated copies electronically. Accordingly, pirated copies of digital goods cannot be dismissed from computing market share as easily as they can be dismissed in computing the market shares of nondigital goods. Pirating can be pervasive in digital goods, and is very pervasive in software markets, as I showed in Chapter 10. If a digital goods producer, for example, Microsoft, increases its price, it gives pirates an incentive to expand their market sales. Put another way, the pirates add to the elasticity of supply that, when considered in the context of the Hovenkamp equation, lower the market power of firms computed for antitrust purposes. The potential for piracy, therefore, lowers the firm's ability to deviate profitably from marginal cost pricing, no matter what its dominance is.

DEMAND-SIDE SCALE ECONOMIES

My discussions in earlier chapters lead to key understandings that are relevant to antitrust enforcement:

- Within a market with network effects, the larger the sales, the greater the value of the product to consumers, and the greater the demand. The link between current and future demand creates an incentive for the producer of network goods (or addictive and lagged-demand goods) to push its price downward. When future demand is positively linked to current consumption, any revenue foregone currently can be made up, possibly, with greater sales and higher prices in the future.
- To the extent that all production costs are upfront, once the competitive process begins, it is likely to play out with few, if any, competitive holds barred, given that the spoils of the market competition will go to the one that achieves market dominance. In the search for developing dominance through network effects and zero marginal production costs, below-zero prices are not unreasonable, or necessarily predatory, contrary to what is so often presumed in conventional antitrust thinking.[19]
- Regardless of exactly how the competitive process develops, network effects imply that the long-run demand elasticity of network goods will be increased by two factors. The first factor is one that affects the demand for nonnetwork goods as well as network goods: time. The long run provides consumers with more time (or just opportunities) for them to seek out and switch to substitutes, which implies they can be more responsive to a price change of either a digital or a nondigital good in the long run than in the short run. The second factor is unique to network goods. The short-run demand for network goods can build as consumption increases, or as the value of the good for consumers also increases, implying that the quantity response to a price change will be much greater in the long run than in the short run.[20] There is no such presumption of demand building on sales for nonnetwork goods. Again, using the formula Hovenkamp cites for determining the market power of a firm, the

long-run market power of firms with a given market share (and given elasticity of supply) should be less for a producer of a network good than a nonnetwork good. The greater the network effects, the greater the elasticity of demand. This means that the gap between the price a dominant network firm would choose and the competitive price would be smaller. The deadweight loss for network goods should also be smaller, implying a reduced interest in the prosecution of a dominant producer of a network good (with any given market share).

- Network effects, combined with the prospects of market tipping, can also affect the expectations of both consumers and producers. Consumers will want to buy the good that is expected to be dominant, because it will be the good that yields the most consumer value over time. The greater the expectations of a particular's firm's dominance in the future, the greater the current demand and consumption, and the greater the likelihood of that firm's eventual market dominance.

- The prospects of expected future dominance and greater market demand can add to the firm's incentive to suppress its current price in two ways: First, the lower price can lead to greater current consumption and greater future demand. Second, the lower current price can be considered a signal of how much the firm understands the interconnectedness of current price with future demand and dominance. It can also signal its interest in achieving future dominance and its willingness to forego current revenues and profits for future revenues and profits. As a consequence, consumers can be expected to move to network firms that offer relatively lower current prices because of their expectation that that firm will achieve market dominance. Their expectations, encouraged by the firm's pricing strategy, can be self-fulfilling.

The demand-side scale economies embodied in network effects require some revision of antitrust thinking mainly because, conventionally, "'predatory pricing' refers to a practice of driving rivals out of business by selling at a price 'below cost'" when the "intent—and the only intent that can make predatory pricing rational, profit-maximizing behavior—is to charge monopoly prices after rivals have been dispatched or disciplined."[21] With network effects, a firm's upfront suppressed prices can only have one intent, which is to respond to the nature of the market and price its network good so that other firms are driven out of the market (or to prevent other firms from driving it out of the market). The intent is to make consumers expect that the lower-than-marginal-cost upfront price will contribute to its eventual dominance. The price charged upfront can rationally be zero or, for that matter, negative. The firm's goal should be to maximize revenues, given that the achievement of that goal will also maximize profits.[22]

If the upfront pricing strategy leads to a current loss, that loss has to be offset by an improvement in its future profits, which implies rising future prices that are, eventually, above cost. However, for two reasons, it does not follow that any rise in the future price to points above cost is necessarily a monopoly price, implying the collection of monopoly rents over time. First, any excess of the future revenue stream above production costs must be set against the upfront losses from below-cost pricing. Over the course of time, the firm may not make more than a competitive rate of return. Indeed, the firm's upfront pricing strategy, and its upfront losses, can be viewed by the firm not so much as a loss, but rather as a necessary upfront investment, which implies that its true cost of production must incorporate that fixed investment to determine whether the future price is above the true production cost, considering all upfront investments, including the upfront loss.

Second, the future price might be rising, but so is demand along with the buildup of network effects. As a consequence, it does not follow that a rising future price is further removed from the competitive price, or closer to the monopoly price, than the lower (perhaps zero or negative) upfront price that is charged. Indeed, net consumer surplus available to buyers (graphically, the area under the demand curve and above the price that is charged) can be greater at higher future prices (that might give the appearance of monopoly prices, because of the suppressed upfront prices) than at the lower upfront prices. Although the firm may appear to be charging above-cost monopoly prices, buyers can benefit from the higher future prices because the future profits encourage the network firm to suppress its upfront price and build the network. The greater the potential for future profits, the greater the upfront investment the network firm would be willing to make in the form of upfront losses. Future profits will also affect the speed with which the network will develop. The greater the speed of network development, the greater the net consumer surplus over time, and the closer the link between suppressed upfront prices and higher future prices.

Conventional antitrust thinking requires that proof of an offense of attempted monopolization contain three elements: "1) specific intent to control prices or destroy competition in some part of commerce; 2) predatory or anticompetitive conduct directed to accomplishing the unlawful purpose; and 3) a dangerous probability of success."[23] The problem with using these criteria in network markets is that a single firm will very likely dominate such markets, given the underlying postulates about the market. In addition, there is a reasonable expectation that the winning dominant firm will achieve its dominant position (with a greater likelihood than in markets for nonnetwork goods) by lowering its price to below-cost levels for the specific purpose of building the network that, given conventional antitrust wisdom, can be misconstrued as "predatory" in the sense that the pricing strategy is used to achieve monopoly power, not just mere market dominance.

Given the implied upfront losses from the adopted initial pricing strategy, there is not just a dangerous probability that the dominant producer will raise its price in the future, there is the virtual certainty that the dominant firm will do so to achieve the anticipated rate of return on its investment in the long run. Furthermore, the firm that achieves dominance will very likely have had the intent of achieving its dominance by eliminating existing competitors with the upfront low prices. Otherwise, the firm could be supplanted by some other firm that also had the intent of wiping out its competitors.

Does that mean that the emerging dominant firm has somehow constricted, by the combination of the low early price and the higher later price, the size of the market for its network good as a monopolist might try to do? Not necessarily. In fact, the pricing combination could enhance market efficiency because the market is actually larger than it would otherwise be, and the average price charged to consumers could be lower than it otherwise would be. The reason is that with the early price reduction and the expansion of the demand, the elasticity of the long-run demand can be higher than it would have been if some other more reserved upfront pricing strategy had been used, leading to the long-run price being lower than it would be if the elasticity of the long-run demand were lower. However, given conventional thinking about the correlation of market dominance and market power, there is definitely a dangerous probability that a dominant network firm will be prosecuted for antitrust violations unjustly, that is to say, the dominant network firm may not have acted any more monopolistically (and may have acted more competitively) than other nonnetwork firms with much lower market shares.

In conventional markets for conventional goods, a finding that a firm was capable of raising its price was sufficient to conclude that the firm presented a dangerous probability of raising its price in the future. After all, if a firm could raise its price but did not do so, it would be losing collectible profits, causing the price of its stock to suffer, with the result that savvy investors could snap up the stock and revise the firm's pricing strategy.[24]

However, the theory of networks requires that a distinction be made between the ability of a dominant producer to exploit the inelasticity of its short-run demand for greater profits and the incentive to do so, given the much higher elasticity of its long-run demand under which the network effects can build—and unravel. A firm producing a network good must fear that an increase in the current price might lead to greater current profits, but also to an unraveling of the network in the long run, causing the firm to gain short-run profits at the expense of profits later on. The net effect of the firm seeking to exploit its current ability to raise its price could be a reduction in the market value of its stock. In short, the dominant firm might have the ability to raise its price, which could be equated with a dangerous probability of the firm raising its price; yet such a conclusion could be misguided because the dominant firm, beset with network effects, would not have the requisite incentive to raise its price to monopoly levels.

Microsoft has been charged with violating both sections of the Sherman Act mainly because of its predatory pricing of Internet Explorer. It charged nothing for Internet Explorer despite having "spent something approaching the $100 million it has devoted each year to developing Internet Explorer and some part of the $30 million it has spent annually marketing it," as Judge Jackson found.[25] According to Jackson, Microsoft incurred the substantial browser development costs and potential revenue loss from giving away the browser (and then bartering away space on the Windows desktop with Internet service providers in exchange for their willingness to distribute Internet Explorer) for one overriding reason: the protection of the applications barrier to entry.[26] The array of other complaints against Microsoft, including exclusionary agreements with computer makers and Internet service providers, as well as its pricing of Internet Explorer, "lacked pro-competitive justifications."[27]

Indeed, the only justification the judge found was to protect the applications barrier to entry by rapidly gaining a substantial market share for Internet Explorer at Netscape Navigator's expense, making Microsoft's business tactics necessarily predatory.[28] Hence, the judge concluded that Microsoft posed the dangerous probability of achieving monopoly in the browser market.[29] What is important to note is that Judge Jackson never once indicated that the legal standard for making the dangerous probability assessment is affected in the least by the nature of the market for digital goods on which the case is founded. Indeed, the judge does nothing more than cite the relevant cases that lay out the conventional legal standard for market share and dangerous probability.[30]

While it is difficult to take issue with aspects of the judge's ruling against Microsoft (for example, his finding that Microsoft did seek to divide the operating system and browser markets in a meeting that was held on June 21, 1995), it is equally clear that using the prism of the two central postulates of digital economics, Microsoft's business tactics could indeed be construed as having a "pro-competitive justification," as well as effect. The effect of Microsoft's tactics appears straightforward: a reduction in the price of the two leading browsers—Navigator and Explorer—to zero. The intent of the zero pricing of the browser may have been to destroy Netscape, as the Justice Department and trial judge claimed, but it could also be construed as a natural competitive response to the advent of a competitive threat—Netscape—in the form of a new computer platform market that, like Windows, is presumably subject to network effects and zero marginal cost.

After all, when marginal cost is zero, competitive, marginal cost pricing would dictate a zero price. Moreover, when a network is threatened, one would expect the ensuing competition to be intense because current and future profits, as well as market dominance, are at stake.[31] Microsoft might have an incentive to lower its price to zero (and beyond) just to ensure that its network does not unravel as the market tips toward Netscape's platform. The tipping could be the consequence of both applications developers and computer users moving to a new lower priced and superior standard.

Furthermore, Microsoft did not preclude a superior platform from establishing itself as the standard. It could not do so. If Microsoft were restricting sales and pricing its products like a monopolist, the task of a standard takeover by Netscape would be relatively easy, especially if Netscape were truly a superior platform and were being sold at a competitive price. Even if Microsoft had not charged a monopoly price for Windows, but threatened to do so in the future with a dangerous probability, consumers could be expected to move to the Netscape standard (or some other standard). There might be switching costs for shifting, but there would also be expected staying costs, or consumer surplus that would be surrendered to Microsoft for not making the switch to another operating system. In addition, there is no problem of the network effects being network externalities. The gains from the switching would be received by Netscape, which could be expected to cover many of the switching costs with the added long-run profits that could be received (especially if Microsoft were to produce and price like a monopolist).

Microsoft may have responded to the Netscape threat "with ferocity" (to use Netscape's founder Jim Clark's phrase[32]), but that is not unexpected in a world of network and digital goods. In fact, it is indeed expected because of the magnitude of the "prize," which is not simply for more current sales, but for very possibly most, if not all, of the market that will tip toward the standard setter. Moreover, the additional sales are likely to be lucrative, given that they add nothing (or very little) to cost.[33] To keep the network together, a network sponsor for software like Microsoft has to assure applications developers that it, Microsoft (not Netscape), will continue to be the standard computer platform, thus giving them reasons to continue to refine and upgrade their applications for Windows. The advent of other potentially successful platforms can unsettle their expectations, which may only be resettled by the network sponsor (Microsoft) proving that it will remain very competitive. Such proof can take the form of zero prices for product upgrades and strong reactions to competitive threats.

Do such reactions by Microsoft lack pro-competitive justification? They could easily be seen as the essence of pro-competitiveness, maybe not in markets for industrial, nondigital goods, but certainly in digital goods markets.

THE BENEFITS OF SWITCHING COSTS AND LOCK-INS

In the Microsoft case, switching costs and lock-ins are treated by both the Justice Department and Judge Jackson as sources of monopoly power and, hence, market inefficiency. For example, Judge Jackson found:

> Unfortunately for firms whose products do not fit that bill, the porting of applications from one operating system to another is a costly process. Consequently, software developers generally write applications first, and often exclusively, for the operating system that is already used by a dominant share of all PC users. Users do not want to invest in an operating system until it is clear that the system will support generations of applications that will meet their needs, and developers do not want to invest in writing or quickly porting applications for an operating system until it is clear that there will be a sizeable and stable market for it. What is more, consumers who already use one Intel-compatible PC operating system are even less likely than first-time buyers to choose a newcomer to the field, for switching to a new system would require these users to scrap the investment they have made in applications, training, and certain hardware.[34]

Such a view of switching costs might be appropriate for nondigital goods, because their marginal costs are positive and generally rising within the relevant range of the market. However, again, when the marginal cost is zero and the products exist, perspectives must adjust. This is because the price competition among competitors can drive the price to zero, at which, of course, all existing competitors will incur losses equal to their upfront development costs. Even with only two producers in the market with the same cost structures that equally divide the market, the price would not stop falling at their average costs (which is equal to the development costs divided by the quantity, since there are no reproduction costs). The reason is that their products exist, and it would be beneficial for each producer to lower its price and try for a larger share of the market. With a larger scale, their average cost would fall and some revenues will always reduce their losses. In short, selling some units at any price above zero results in losses that are less than would be incurred if one or both producers dropped out, at which point their losses would equal their development costs.

Potential producers of digital goods like Microsoft and applications developers would want to see some protection against such intense competitive incentives that can result in prices close to zero, if not zero, before they incur upfront development costs. Switching costs—and, at the limit, lock-ins—can be the type of restraint producers need for them to incur the necessary upfront development costs. Hence, consumers need not be worse off because of the switching costs, even when they are later exploited. The reason is that they get the products they need at levels of development that are greater than they would be otherwise, and their upfront prices would be lower than otherwise (because of the prospects of higher prices later).[35] Here, we can extend the point by noting that if the prospect of zero pricing is not muted by natural switching costs (the kind that Judge Jackson is concerned about), then we would expect the digital producers to seek out unnatural forms of protections that come in the form of short- and long-term contracts. We might anticipate that the greater the development costs, the closer the marginal cost is to zero, and the lower the natural switching costs, the longer the contract that the digital producers would seek with consumers. Hence, antitrust enforcers must tread very carefully in equating switching costs, or long-term contracts, with monopoly power or market inefficiency. Each can be seen as a substitute for the other, and each can give rise to market activity that would not otherwise occur and, as such, could be construed as efficiency enhancing.

THE DOMINANT PRODUCER'S DEMAND FOR ANTITRUST ENFORCEMENT

Textbook models of monopolies suggest that monopolies—and their legal counterparts, dominant producers—would be opposed to antitrust laws that are effectively enforced. After all, effective antitrust enforcement would mean lower firm prices, monopoly profits, and stock values.

However, such a line of analysis is narrowly conceived, and not necessarily fully applicable to network markets. The line of analysis starts, it needs to be stressed, with the existence of the monopoly, but does not consider the circumstances under which the monopoly (or just dominant producer) might emerge. Firms that produce digital goods with the potential for network effects that might cover almost all, if not all, of the market have at least one potentially good reason for wanting effective enforcement of antitrust laws. Such firms can reason that their network members can see the potential for the firm's market dominance that can give them the power, when switching costs come into play, to raise their prices and garner monopoly rents in the future. To build their networks, such firms would have to lower their upfront prices to encourage the building of the network effects; they would have to lower their upfront prices even more to offset the expectation of the later monopoly pricing threat.

In the case of the operating system market, the likely dominant producer would have to temper the fears of both applications developers and their software buyers, as well as their own buyers of the operating system. The operating system buyers would fear that they would have to pay monopoly prices for upgrades. Applications developers would fear that the future curb in sales for the operating system caused by monopoly pricing would undermine their application sales, and undermine the market value of their upfront development investments. Their fear would be even stronger if the market for the operating system is subject to tipping (which also could mean "untipping," or unraveling) as buyers and applications developers moved to lower-priced computer platforms. Buyers of applications would fear that the network effects they garner by joining a particular computer platform would dissipate as applications developers withdrew their support. The reduced demand for the platform would mean that the operating system firm that threatens to be a monopoly would have to lower its upfront price by more than would be the case if the operating systems buyers, applications developers, and applications buyers did not fear being subject to future monopoly pricing. Through lower upfront prices, these developers and buyers would effectively demand prepayment of the monopoly rents that they fear will be extracted later.

A firm that has the potential to be a monopoly might try to handle the extant fears by committing itself to competitive, or nonmonopoly, prices in the future. However, the developers and buyers have good reasons to doubt the commitment. When a network is in the early stages of development, the verbal or written commitment may not be credible, simply because of the newness of the firms and network. In addition, the developers and buyers can reason that if the commitment to price competitively into the future is honored by the parties making the agreement, then in the future, monopoly rents will be foregone and the company's stock will then be less than it could be if the monopoly rents were then extracted. Savvy investors may be able to buy controlling interest in the firm, institute monopoly prices (in overt or covert ways), generate monopoly rents, and then sell their stock for a capital gain. Realizing the lack of credibility of its commitments not to act monopolistically, the firm would naturally be interested in having third-party enforcement of its commitments, which may take the form of contracts. However, contracts are difficult to make foolproof, especially when substantial monopoly rents may be at stake in finding legal ways of skirting the contractual language.[36]

In the incompleteness and other flaws of contracts lie a firm's potential interest in antitrust laws and their effective enforcement. The enforcement of antitrust laws can, in effect, add credibility to a firm's commitment that in the future it will not charge monopoly prices. The firm can say, in effect, to developers and buyers, "You may not believe me when I commit to competitive, nonmonopoly prices (and other business practices), but you can take comfort from the fact that antitrust officials are standing watch and will prosecute when you or others complain." Such a statement can carry even greater weight if there is more than one source of antitrust enforcement. The monopoly practices missed by one source of enforcement (for example, the Federal Trade Commission) can be caught by another (for example, the Antitrust Division of the Department of Justice), and the competitiveness of the enforcement sources can add credibility to the firm's commitment not to act monopolistically in the future.

Naturally, if the antitrust laws are never enforced, they may add little to the credibility of the firm's commitment not to act monopolistically. Hence, firms that might become monopolies, or just dominant producers who threaten to achieve monopoly power, can have an interest in active enforcement, especially when the enforcement is against others.[37]

An array of economic and legal critics has argued that the problem with antitrust laws is that their enforcement has been perverse.[38] With the encouragement of less aggressive competitors, antitrust enforcers have all too frequently used the laws to thwart competition, rather than monopoly.[39] If, or when, antitrust enforcement thwarts (contrary to the presumed intent of antitrust law) the emergence of lower future prices from competition among rivals for the network standard, the conventional model of competition would suggest that antitrust enforcement would lead to higher current prices. However, that would not be the case for producers of network/digital goods. Developers and consumers would anticipate smaller networks in the future, as the market shares of competitors are prevented from shrinking with the emergence of a dominant (more competitive) producer. To overcome the resistance of developers and buyers, network firms would have to charge, over time, lower prices than they otherwise would. Consumers would be getting lower prices, but it does not follow that they would be better off. This is because their demand for the networks that are achieved would be lower, leaving them a smaller consumer surplus.

COMPLEMENTARY GOODS

Conventional models of monopoly that undergird antitrust enforcement start with the presumption that the monopoly good is sold in isolation from all other goods. Indeed, for a pure monopoly, all substitutes are ruled out by assumption. The typical presumption is that the monopoly (or just dominant producer) does not produce complementary products, nor does it have an incentive to produce complementary products that other firms do not have— unless such products can be used to fortify the monopoly. As noted, the trial judge in the Microsoft case has found that Microsoft's development of its browser, which can only be construed as a complementary software product to Windows (given that the browser can be integrated into Windows), had one overriding purpose: to protect the applications barrier to entry into the operating system market. Accordingly, the browser's zero price was declared to be predatory.

Nothing in the trial was ever said about Microsoft's other, largely complementary products, for instance, Office (Microsoft's suite of productivity applications), which means that the Justice Department did not link the pricing of Windows with the pricing of Office (or any other Microsoft software or hardware product), and vice versa. However, the absence of evidence presented at trial on the market linkages between Windows and Office did not stop the Justice Department from proposing a breakup of Microsoft into two firms, one that would get Microsoft's operating systems and another that would get everything else, including Internet Explorer. By not raising the complementarity of Windows with Microsoft's various other products, the Justice Department and outside supporters of the breakup made the argument that the breakup would lead to more competitive operating systems and applications markets, which, in turn, could potentially lower the price of the products more or less across the board and improve market efficiency. By splitting off Office from Windows, Microsoft would no longer, so the Justice Department argued, release the application program interfaces early to Office program developers, giving Microsoft a market advantage in the suites market. By leveling the playing field, there supposedly would be more effective market competition to Office and lower suite prices. If Office is made the core of a firm that is independent from Windows, then the Office firm could, possibly, form the basis of a new computer platform, given that Office has as high a share of the suites market as Windows has of the operating system market. The owners of Office would be more inclined to develop its applications for alternative operating systems, for example, Linux, or so it has been argued.

My purpose here is not to contest the theories underlying the proposed breakup that was adopted by the trial judge, rather, it is to introduce two points about complementary products that were sidestepped in the Justice Department's case against Microsoft, perhaps because the lawyers and economists at the Justice Department hold to conventional antitrust lines of thinking about why firms do what they do.

First, it must be noted that a monopoly (or just dominant producer) in conventional analysis will always produce and price where marginal cost equals marginal revenue, thus extracting monopoly rents. However, that is not necessarily true for a monopoly with complementary products, especially one that dominates the market for complementary products, as does Microsoft.

Granted, the monopoly owner of a digital good will seek to maximize revenues, which in itself will lead to maximum profits, mainly because marginal cost is zero, but this is only when it does not have complementary products. By lowering the price of the monopolized products to some point below the monopoly price, the firm might lose revenues in the market for the monopoly products. However, it will increase the demand for the complementary digital product that can then be sold in greater numbers at a higher revenue-maximizing price. The stronger the complementarity of the products, the lower the price of the monopoly good. The greater the number of complementary products, the greater the incentive the monopoly has to lower the price of its product. Moreover, the greater the concentration of the complementary products market, the greater the incentive the monopoly firm has to lower its monopoly price. (If the market for the complementary products is highly fragmented among a number of producers, the increased sales of the monopoly product will lead to few sales of the monopoly's complementary products.) This means that the greater the monopoly's share of the complementary products market, the greater the increase in demand and price of the complementary products from a price reduction in the monopoly good.

In all of the testimony in the Microsoft case, no one on the Justice Department's side thought to suggest that a plausible explanation for why the price of Windows is so low is its complementary products, perhaps most importantly Office, given its 90 percent or higher share of the suites market. The Justice Department could have made the point that Microsoft was extracting a monopoly price, not through Windows, but rather through the sales and price of Office (if in fact that was the case).

There is a second, perhaps more important, reason Microsoft has complementary products like Office: network effects. When Windows was first introduced in 1983, there were few Windows applications, and it was unclear that Windows would achieve the market dominance that it now enjoys. Applications developers were understandably leery of joining the Windows network. One practical reason Microsoft had for developing Office (or, rather, its component applications) was to start the network effects rolling. That alone could encourage applications developers to write for Windows. In addition, by developing Office, Microsoft was alerting developers of its own confidence in Windows' market potential and was willing to put its own upfront investment funds at risk, which could also encourage developers to write for Windows.

Moreover, applications developers then had an understandable fear that a dominant producer of an operating system like Microsoft will exploit its monopoly power at some point in the future. The applications developers would have to worry that an increase in the price of Windows in the future will lower the demand for their complementary products that are necessarily complements to the operating system (given that the applications are technologically tied to the operating system). This means that the value of their upfront investment in the development of their applications would be lost. The greater the incentive Microsoft has to charge the monopoly price, the greater the risk that the applications developers incur. This means, as I have explained, that the developers' risk costs of writing for the operating system–dominant producer are functionally related to how many complements the dominant producer has, how strong the complementary relationship is, and the concentration of segments of the applications market controlled by the dominant producer in the operating system.

In other words, by Microsoft having market dominance in a major software market like productivity suites, the company provides a form of self-enforcing contract to applications developers. Put another way, Microsoft gives applications developers some assurance that it will not exploit any monopoly power it achieves in the operating system market, which is to say that Microsoft's own complementary products reduce the risk cost incurred by applications developers that, in turn, can give rise to more developers being willing to write for Windows and that, in turn again, can translate into a greater demand for Windows. Consumers may pay higher prices (although this is not certain) for software products, but that does not mean they are worse off. The size of the network can expand with the reduction in the developers' risk cost, as can consumer surplus value. Contrary to conventional antitrust thinking, no monopoly pricing need be involved.

Indeed, the elimination of Microsoft's complementary products through a breakup can have consequences that could be construed as contrary to the purpose of antitrust enforcement. The breakup along the lines that Judge

Jackson has ordered could take away Microsoft's incentive to lower the price of Windows below the monopoly price, which is to say that a higher price for Windows would be encouraged. Moreover, the breakup could increase the risk costs incurred by applications developers, reducing their willingness to write for Windows and curbing the network effects and consumer benefits.

Network sponsors like Microsoft must stand ready to defend the network, not only because of their direct interest in retaining control over the standard for, say, operating systems, but also because they must defend the interests of the applications developers who also have an economic interest in a stable standard. The applications developers do not want their investments undercut by destabilizing threats to the network. Seeing the network shrink with the advent of a new entrant (or just the threat of a new entrant), developers will understandably consider redeploying their applications for what looks to be the next new "big thing," or standard. Developers must also be concerned that other developers are thinking the same way and that the cumulative effects of such thinking across applications developers—especially when the number of developers is large (as is true for Microsoft's Windows[40])—can give rise to an accelerating decline in the network, which can feed on itself. Accordingly, the network sponsor has a strong incentive to defend the network with efforts that are not only in proportion to the threat of entrance but also disproportionately to it. In other words, the network sponsor has an incentive to meet the lighting of a competitive "match" with the lighting of its own "welding torch," just to maintain confidence that it, the network sponsor, will defend the interests of the applications developers.

This line of argument can be used to reinterpret events at the heart of the Microsoft antitrust case. As the trial evidence shows, Microsoft did not recognize the Internet threat in the form of Netscape's Navigator to its operating system market until late 1994 or early 1995.[41] In a long May 1995 memorandum to his executive staff ominously titled, "The Internet Tidal Wave" that was then marked "confidential," Bill Gates radically upgraded companywide interest in and commitment to the Internet, outlining both the threats and the opportunities the Internet presented Microsoft. He insisted that his executive staff give the Internet the "highest level of importance." Indeed, in that memo, as in his 1995 book, Gates equated the importance of the Internet to Microsoft with the development of the first IBM PC and asked all company divisions to rethink and redesign their products with the Internet in mind, indicating with force the problems Microsoft would face in playing catch-up to existing Internet players and noting that the proposed network computer was a "scary possibility."[42] Because Navigator, along with Sun's Java programming language, was at the heart of the

Internet threat, Microsoft undertook an intense campaign to develop its own browser with the obvious intent of making sure that Internet Explorer would be technologically superior to Navigator, the purpose of which was, naturally, to gain market share from Navigator. The company then bundled Internet Explorer with Windows, eventually integrating Internet Explorer into Windows. Moreover, it gave away the browsing technology and tried to tie up an array of distribution outlets (computer manufacturers and Internet service providers, for example) to maximize Internet Explorer's market share.[43]

Were these actions predatory, the natural response of a monopoly trying to protect its market dominance, or were they merely competitive? The Justice Department and the trial judge obviously concluded they were predatory and anticompetitive. However, the perspective developed here offers a contrary, and more charitable, view of Microsoft's actions: They were pro-competitive, the type of actions that a dominant producer would take to respond to a competitive threat in a market beset with network effects and a minuscule marginal cost of production. Microsoft's tactics were, without question, aggressive, but perhaps also necessary to assure network members, consumers, and applications developers that Microsoft, the network sponsor, stood ready to protect the operating system standard and their interests. The ferocity of Microsoft's response was attributable in part to the existence of the twenty thousand applications developers (not so much to the count of applications per se). Had Microsoft had far fewer developers, like so many other software firms have, then the competitive response would have been more tempered. However, that would have meant that the price charged would have been higher.

ROLE OF CARTELS

Conventional cartel models hold that the colluding firms form cartels to restrict production and raise their prices and collective profits. The presumption is that cartels have an interest in hiking prices in both the short run and the long run. However, according to conventional analysis, cartels have a difficult time holding to their production agreements, as evident in the history of the unstable OPEC cartel agreements. The greater the number of colluding firms, ceteris paribus, the greater the incentive cartel members have to cheat on their production agreements, and the less likely the colluding firms will charge monopoly prices and earn monopoly rents, or the more likely the cartel agreement will break down into competitive pricing.[44]

Network/digital economics forces revisions in the way cartels are expected to behave. Most prominent, with network effects, competitors initially have an incentive to collude with the intent of lowering, not raising, prices in order that the development of the network will be encouraged and the future demand for the product will rise, perhaps along with the price. If there is cheating in this initial period, it will come in the form of members breaking with the cartel and raising their prices, not lowering them. By raising its price, each member will increase its current revenue at the greater expense of reducing market demand and cartel revenue in the future. But the additional current revenue is captured entirely by the member that raises prices, and the future loss is spread over all members of the cartel. If such cheating is insufficient to prevent the cartel from eventually establishing a valuable network, the members will then have the standard cartel incentive to restrict sales. However, because the market will have expanded between the short run and the long run, the incentive to enter the market in the long run will be greater than it was in the short run, especially if the cartel members do restrict sales. In effect, by colluding initially to lower prices and expand the market, the cartel members encourage entry and, hence, encourage price-cutting in the long run. Their collusive efforts undermine, as in conventional cartel thinking, their incentive to form the cartel in the first place.

In conventional markets, cartels are unambiguously harmful to consumers. That is not necessarily the case in markets for digital/network goods. In spite of higher anticipated prices in the future, consumers could want cartel agreements to stick, mainly because of the lower initial prices and the benefits from a larger network. And because of the problems of cartels holding to their agreements, consumers could prefer the emergence at the start of a single (if only dominant) producer of the network product. With the emergence of such a producer, the more likely the initial price will be lowered and the faster and more complete will be the development of the network, market demand, and consumer surplus. Indeed, the more aggressive a firm is in developing its dominance (say, by charging nothing for its product or paying consumers to take the product), the greater the development of the network, demand, and consumer surplus. However, given the way antitrust enforcers interpret business tactics (as was true in the Microsoft case), the more aggressive the actions of the dominant producer initially, the more likely the dominant firm would be charged with predation.

MULTIPLE OUTCOMES

Brian Arthur, whose pioneering work has led to renewed interest in network effects, argues that economists have traditionally founded their economic models on an assumption of diminishing returns for one overriding reason, the theoretical attractiveness of the models: "Diminishing returns imply a single equilibrium point for the economy, but positive feedback—increasing returns—makes for many possible equilibrium points."[45] He has also argued with elaborate mathematical models, "There is no guarantee that the particular economic outcome selected from the many alternatives will be the 'best' one. Furthermore, once random economic events select a particular path, the choice may become locked-in regardless of the advantages of the alternatives" (p. 92).

The feedback effects that can give rise to increasing returns, and multiple outcomes, include anything that can lead to a reduction in production costs, such as learning by doing and network effects. And Arthur sees network effects that extend well beyond the interdependency of operating system sales and applications that has been central to the examples I have used. He also sees feedback effects in the markets for typewriter keyboards, which I have considered, and VCR recording formats. According to Arthur, the VCR market started with the VHS and Beta formats. A large number of recorders that used one or the other format would lead to video stores carrying more of those kinds of tapes, which would then feed the demand for recorders for that kind of format. Hence, "a small gain in market share would improve the competitive position of one system and help it further increase its lead" (p. 116). He concludes that the early market gains for the VHS format tipped the market toward the VHS format, making it the ultimate dominant format. Not only was it impossible for anyone to know when the competition began which format would ultimately win, it is possible that the "superior" format did not win the struggle for market dominance. Indeed, Arthur surmises that "if the claim that Beta was technically superior is true, then the market's choice did not represent the best economic outcome" (p. 116). Instead of the outcome depending on product superiority, there is a good chance that the outcome will be dependent on chance events that favor one product or the other; or the outcome favors, as Arthur quotes Alfred Marshall's *Principles of Economics* approvingly, "whatever firm gets a good start" (p. 116).

Because I dealt with the arguments earlier in this book, I do not need to take up the issue of whether Arthur is correct in theory or practice. At the same time, I note here, as I have argued earlier in this book, that other economists have found serious flaws in the reported history of the two major examples of markets that Arthur and others use: the keyboard and the VCR format.[46] It does not now appear that the products that came to dominate their respective markets, QWERTY in keyboards and the VHS in recording formats, are indeed the inferior products they have been thought to be. For purposes of argument, we accept the contention that increasing returns can yield multiple outcomes and that, from time to time, the competitive process might result in inferior products being selected that have some durability.

The issue of concern for this section is how those prospects might affect antitrust thinking and enforcement. This issue is of some concern because antitrust enforcement is grounded in the fear that firms with market dominance will exert their monopoly power on production and prices, and the increasing returns/feedback literature is replete with arguments that those firms which get the better starts will come to dominate their markets. Should antitrust enforcement be used to attack dominant firms with the intent of increasing the frequency with which "superior" outcomes are chosen, or decrease the frequency with which "inferior" outcomes result? Can it be used for that purpose with some probability of success, on balance? To understand the problem, we must first note that while an inferior product might become dominant, there is nothing in the feedback/network effects literature that says how frequently inferior outcomes will occur. It might be very infrequent. We must also note that even Arthur starts with a humbling acknowledgement, "Yet it would be impossible at the outset of the competition to say which system would win, which of the two possible equilibria [in the VCR market] would be selected."[47]

The problem of picking the winner in other markets with far more than two possible outcomes would be even more problematic. Then there is the prospect that if an inferior outcome were selected—meaning that the present value of the benefits of switching to a new outcome were greater than the switching costs, properly discounted, for years to come—there are at least some grounds for believing that in some, if not all, of the inferior outcomes, a correction is likely, given that there would be net gains that could be garnered by entrepreneurs who have the foresight to engineer the switchover.[48]

Still, we might concede the prospects of true market failure, in which the network effects are true network externalities. Problems remain with using antitrust enforcement, or any other form of regulation, to improve on market outcomes, given that antitrust enforcers will have to sort through all the various possible outcomes to select the one outcome that would be superior to the one chosen by market forces. It is doubtful that the enforcers would have the required information to make the assessment of relative merits of outcomes after the fact, but less so before the fact. Equally difficult is knowing how the enforcers would be able to determine the costs and benefits of outcomes that never occurred. It would appear that any contemplated antitrust attack on a dominant producer because of its dominant winning market position would also have repercussions on how the competitive process would work itself out.

Such antitrust prosecutions might in fact deter inferior outcomes from occurring, but given the prospects of antitrust mistakes, they could also discourage superior outcomes from occurring. The firm that expects to be the eventual winner in the competitive process may temper its competitiveness, fearing antitrust prosecution, thus giving an "inferior" firm a better start than it would otherwise have—and a greater prospect of being the winner. If, as Arthur postulates, we cannot know the outcome of a freewheeling competitive process, can we know better the net effect—whether there is, on balance, an improvement or degradation in outcomes—of antitrust enforcement intended to "improve" outcomes?

The Justice Department clearly adopted the theory of feedback effects in its antitrust case against Microsoft. It showed signs in its case that it also accepted Arthur's extension, that a market like the operating systems market, if left alone, could lead to an inferior outcome, especially if a firm like Microsoft with an already good start used its market muscle to discourage entry by a competitor like Netscape that might have had a superior product.[49] Throughout its complaint, the Justice Department argued strongly in favor of antitrust remedies to ensure that people have choices among alternative computer platforms.[50] Judge Jackson seems to have concurred that absent antitrust action and penalties there could be no guarantee that the superior computer platform would win, given Microsoft's starting advantages and its aggressive competitiveness.[51] The judge dismissed the possibility that if the Netscape/Sun combination had truly been superior, then Netscape/Sun would not have withdrawn from the market. Seeing its superiority, applications developers would switch to the new Netscape/Sun platform—especially if Microsoft were actually producing and pricing like a monopoly. If the company were not producing and pricing like a monopoly, then the antitrust actions against Microsoft could definitely choke off its competitiveness; but there is no guarantee that under those circumstances the "superior" outcome would then emerge.

CONCLUDING COMMENTS

The advent of network and digital economics poses no threat to conventional microeconomic models of markets. As recognized, demand curves in the network and digital portions of the economy still slope downward with the demand elasticity remaining a function of the number of existing competitors and the openness of markets to entry. The distinction between fixed and variable costs remains valid, implying that profit-maximizing pricing still requires consideration of marginal cost. At the same time, network and digital economics does elevate the theoretical prevalence and importance of increasing returns, self-reinforcing market development, tipping, and lock-ins in economic models. This means that expectations are of greater importance in network/digital economic analysis than in conventional economic analysis. What I have done here is show how these changes in emphasis of concepts play out in economic theory and how they force revisions in antitrust thinking and enforcement. If antitrust enforcement was often on shaky ground under conventional market analysis, as critics have maintained, then surely the enforcers will want to tread even more carefully in the network/digital sector of the economy.

NOTES

1. Joel I. Klein et al., *United States v. Microsoft Corporation,* Complaint, First District Court, Civil Action No. 98-1232, May 20, 1998, ¶58, as found at http://www.usdoj.gov/atr/cases/f1700/1763.htm.

2. Thomas Penfield Jackson, *United States v. Microsoft Corporation*, Findings of Fact, First District Court, Civil Action No. 98-1232, November 5, 1999, ¶30, as found at http://www.usdoj.gov/atr/cases/f3800/msjudgex.htm. Judge Jackson also found that network effects pose what he called a "chicken-and-egg" problem for software developers:

The ability to meet a large demand [because of scale economies in supply] is useless, however, if the demand for the product is small, and signs do not indicate large demand for a new Intel-compatible PC operating system. To the contrary, they indicate that the demand for a new Intel-compatible PC operating system would be severely constrained by an intractable "chicken-and-egg" problem: The overwhelming majority of consumers will only use a PC operating system for which there already exists a large and varied set of high-quality, full-featured applications, and for which it seems relatively certain that new types of applications and new versions of existing applications will continue to be marketed at pace with those written for other operating systems. Unfortunately for firms whose products do not fit that bill, the porting of applications from one operating system to another is a costly process. Consequently, software developers generally write applications first, and often exclusively, for the operating system that is already used by a dominant share of all PC users. Users do not want to invest in an operating system until it is clear that the system will support generations of applications that will meet their needs, and developers do not want to invest in writing or quickly porting applications for an operating system until it is clear that there will be a sizeable and stable market for it.

What is more, consumers who already use one Intel-compatible PC operating system are even less likely than first-time buyers to choose a newcomer to the field, for switching to a new system would require these users to scrap the investment they have made in applications, training, and certain hardware. (ibid.)

3. Ibid., ¶35.

4. Klein et al., *United States v. Microsoft Corporation*, ¶3.

5. Ibid., ¶108.

6. Ibid., ¶65.

7. Ibid., ¶7.

8. Herbert Hovenkamp, *Federal Antitrust Policy: The Law of Competition and Its Practice*, 2d ed. (St. Paul, Minn.: Westlaw, 1999), 80.

9. Ibid., 79. Hovenkamp reports how the Fourth Circuit Court specified the market share requirements in cases involving an attempted monopolization of a market: "(1) claims of less than 30% market shares should presumptively be rejected; (2) claims involving between 30% and 50% shares should usually be rejected, except when conduct is very likely to achieve monopoly or when conduct is invidious, but not so much so as to make the defendant per se liable; (3) claims involving greater than 50% share should be treated as attempts at monopolization are also satisfied" (*M&M Medical Supplies and Service v. Pleasant Valley Hospital* as cited in ibid., 285). Hovenkamp then cites a number of cases in which "most other courts use numbers in the same range, with a few indicating that a rising market share is a stronger indicator of sufficient market power" (p. 285, nn. 35, 26).

10. A graph-based presentation of these points can be found in most any standard microeconomics textbook, for example, Edgar K. Browning and Mark A. Zupan, *Microeconomics: Theory and Applications* (New York: Wiley, 2002), 365–367.

11. Hovenkamp, *Federal Antitrust Policy*, 80, with citation to p. 945. The Landes/Posner formula for monopoly power is:

$$(Pm - Pc) = Si/(e^d_m + e^s_j(1 - S_j))$$

where: Pm = monopoly price; Pc = competitive price (marginal cost); e^d_m = market elasticity of demand; e^s_j = elasticity of supply of competing or fringe firms; and S_j = firm's market share.

12. The Justice Department actually represents Microsoft's market share at 95 percent for 1997 through 2000 with the introduction of its exhibit 1, a table entitled "Microsoft's Actual and Projected Share of the (Intel-Based) PC Operating System Market" (Klein et al., *United States v. Microsoft Corporation*, as found at (http://www.usdoj.gov/atr/cases/exhibits/1.pdf). A firm's market share is normally viewed as its sales divided by industry sales (as the industry is defined for purposes of the case at hand). In the case of exhibit 1, Microsoft's market share is something quite different: the percent of existing personal computers (not annual sales) that have Windows installed on them.

13. Even if Dell provides service support for Windows, any decreasing returns it faces in service can feed into Microsoft's decision making, given the highly competitive nature of the computer manufacturing industry and how Dell's added support costs can reduce the price Dell is willing to pay for Windows.

14. Hovenkamp defines the "relevant market" as "the smallest grouping of sales for which the elasticity of demand and supply are sufficiently low that a firm with 100% of that grouping could profitably reduce output and increase price substantially above marginal cost" (*Federal Antitrust Policy*, 82).

15. Alan Reynolds, "U.S. vs Microsoft: The Monopoly Myth," *Wall Street Journal*, 9 April 1999, p. A12.

16. This may be the unstated reason the Justice Department chose to define Microsoft's market dominance with reference to the percentage of Intel-compatible computers that use Windows. However, it did not draw out the implications of its definition.

17. As noted, the Justice Department's computed market share for Microsoft is the ratio of the existing personal computers with Intel-compatible processors and with Windows installed on them to the total number of personal computers with Intel-compatible microprocessors.

18. Coase wrote a celebrated article years ago in which he pointed out that even a monopolistic producer of a durable good would charge a competitive price for its product. Why? Because no sane person would buy all or any portion of the durable good at a price above the competitive level. He used the example of a monopoly owner of a plot of land. If the owner tried to sell the land piecemeal, he would have to lower the price on each parcel until all the land was bought, which means the owner would have to charge the competitive price: the price where the demand for the land and the supply of the land come together. It might be thought that the sole owner of land would be able to restrict sales and get more than the competitive price. However, buyers would reason that if the monopoly owner eventually wanted to sell the remaining land, it could only be sold at less than the price of land already sold, which means the buyers who bought the land at the high price would suffer a loss in the market value of their land. This means that the buyers would wait to buy until the price came down, but then the owner would sell nothing at the monopoly price, and would only be able to sell the land at the competitive price. See Ronald H. Coase, "Durability and Monopoly," *Journal of Law and Economics* 15 (April 1972): 143–149.

19. See Benjamin Klein, "Microsoft's Use of Zero Price Bundling to Fight the 'Browser Wars,'" in *Competition, Innovation, and the Microsoft Monopoly: Antitrust in the Digital Marketplace* (Boston: Kluwer Academic Publishers, 1999), 217–254.

20. For more details on the pricing pattern for network goods over time, see Dwight R. Lee and Richard B. McKenzie, "A Case for Letting a Firm Take Advantage of 'Locked-In' Customers," *Hastings Law Journal* 52 (April 2001): 795–812.

21. Hovenkamp, *Federal Antitrust Policy*, 335.

22. With marginal cost constant at zero, maximum revenue necessarily implies maximum profits, given that the difference between total revenues and total costs

(meaning fixed costs) is as great as can be. This line of argument also implies that the firm should price where the elasticity of demand equals 1.

23. Hovenkamp, *Federal Antitrust Policy*, 280. In *Spectrum Sports Inc. v. McQuillan*, the Supreme Court ruled, "We hold that petitioners may not be liable for attempted monopolization . . . absent proof of a dangerous probability that they would monopolize a particular market and specific intent to monopolize" (note 8 at 506 U.S. at 459 113 S, Ct. 884, at 892).

24. If the dominant firm did not raise the price for its good, then savvy investors could buy up controlling interest in the company, change the firm's pricing policy, and sell the stock at a capital gain.

25. Jackson, Findings of Fact, ¶140.

26. Ibid., ¶141.

27. Ibid., ¶410.

28. In the judge's words:

> Microsoft also gave other firms things of value (at substantial cost to Microsoft) in exchange for their commitment to distribute and promote Internet Explorer, sometimes explicitly at Navigator's expense. While Microsoft might have bundled Internet Explorer with Windows at no additional charge even absent its determination to preserve the applications barrier to entry, that determination was the main force driving its decision to price the product at zero. (ibid., ¶136)

The judge concluded, "Microsoft's campaign must be termed predatory," given that "the Court has already found that Microsoft possesses monopoly power," as reflected in its substantial market share. See Thomas Penfield Jackson, *United States v. Microsoft Corporation*, Conclusions of Law, First District Court, Civil Action No. 98-1232, April 3, 2000, p. 18, as found at http://www.usdoj.gov/atr/cases/f4400/4469.htm. More generally, the judge concluded:

> While the evidence does not prove that they would have succeeded absent Microsoft's actions, it does reveal that Microsoft placed an oppressive thumb on the scale of competitive fortune, thereby effectively guaranteeing its continued dominance in the relevant market. More broadly, Microsoft's anticompetitive actions trammeled the competitive process through which the computer software industry generally stimulates innovation and conduces to the optimum benefit of consumers. (ibid., 18)

29. Judge Jackson wrote, "The Court is nonetheless compelled to express its further conclusion that the predatory course of conduct Microsoft has pursued since June of 1995 has revived the dangerous probability that Microsoft will attain monopoly power in a second market. Internet Explorer's share of browser usage has already risen above fifty percent, will exceed sixty percent by January 2001, and the trend continues unabated" (ibid., 22).

30. Judge Jackson quotes approvingly *M&M Medical Supplies & Serv., Inc. v. Pleasant Valley Hosp., Inc.*, 981 F.2d 160, 168 (4th Cir. 1992) (en banc), "A rising share may show more probability of success than a falling share. . . . [C]laims involving greater than 50% share should be treated as attempts at monopolization when the other elements for attempted monopolization are also satisfied") (citations omitted). Also see Phillip E. Areeda and Herbert Hovenkamp, *Antitrust Law* (New York: Aspen Law and Business, 1996), 354–355 (acknowledging the significance of a large, rising market share to the dangerous probability element).

31. See W. Brian Arthur, "Competing Technologies, Increasing Returns, and Lock-In by Historical Events," *Economic Journal* 99 (1989): 116–131; "Positive Feedbacks in the Economy," *Scientific American* 262 (1990): 92–99; and "Increasing Returns and the New World of Business," *Harvard Business Review* (July–August 1996): 100–109. Also see Michael L. Katz and Carl Shapiro, "Network Externalities, Competition, and Compatibility," *American Economic Review* 75 (1985): 424–440.

32. Jim Clark, with Owen Edwards, *Netscape Time: The Making of a Billion-Dollar Start-Up That Took on Microsoft* (New York: St. Martin's, 1999), 49.

33. Stanley Besen and Joseph Farrell note, "Because the prize (becoming the 'standard') is so tempting, sponsors may compete *fiercely* to have their technologies become the standard, and this competition will generally dissipate part—perhaps a large part—of the potential gains." See Stanley M. Besen and Joseph Farrell, "Choosing How to Compete: Strategies and Tactics in Standardization," *Journal of Economic Perspective* 8 (Spring 1994): 119.

34. Jackson, Findings of Fact, ¶30.

35. See Lee and McKenzie, "A Case for Letting a Firm Take Advantage of 'Locked-In' Customers."

36. For a discussion of the problem of incompleteness of contracts, see Paul Milgrom and John Roberts, *Economics, Organization, and Management* (Englewood Cliffs, N.J.: Prentice Hall, 1992), 127–129.

37. However, that is not to say that they would not want the laws enforced against them (at least at some point). Such enforcement could add significant credibility to the firm's commitment to not act monopolistically (at least not for long). As a consequence, a firm that is prosecuted could gain from antitrust actions being taken against it, at least up to some undefined point. The firm might incur legal costs in being prosecuted, and convicted, but it could gain by a greater demand by developers and buyers to join its network, meaning its upfront prices could be higher than they would otherwise be. The result could be that the net revenue gains upfront more than offset its legal costs. Of course, too many actions (or any one action being too severe) can undermine the credibility of its commitment, causing its network to unravel. As in all things, firms would see optimal antitrust enforcement (which could be predicated on a host of factors that cannot be considered here).

This does not mean that Microsoft should relish its ongoing antitrust troubles with the Justice Department. The penalties could be severe, even a breakup of the company (Thomas Penfield Jackson, *United States v. Microsoft Corporation*, Final

Judgment, First District Court, Civil Action No. 98-1232, June 7, 2000). However, this line of argument suggests that the company's troubles do have some potential hidden benefits, a reactivation of the government's commitment to prevent dominant producers like Microsoft to act monopolistically. Such an outcome could increase (at least marginally) the willingness of applications developers to write for Windows, and operating system and applications buyers to stay with the Wintel computer platform, thus allowing Microsoft to charge (marginally) higher prices than it otherwise would be capable of doing.

38. Once a critic of antitrust enforcement in the 1970s and before, Robert Bork concludes that "modern antitrust has so decayed that the policy is no longer intellectually respectable. Some of it is not respectable as law; more of it is not respectable as economics; and now I wish to suggest that, because it pretends to one objective while frequently accomplishing its opposite, and because it too often forwards trends dangerous to our form of government and society, a great deal of antitrust is not even respectable as politics." See Robert H. Bork, *The Antitrust Paradox: A Policy at War with Itself* (New York: Basic Books, 1978), 63.

39. William Baumol and Janusz Ordover have observed, "There is a specter that haunts our antitrust institutions. Its threat is that, far from serving as the bulwark of competition, these institutions will become the most powerful instrument in the hands of those who wish to subvert it. . . . We ignore it at our peril and would do well to take steps to exorcise it" (William Baumol and Janusz Ordover, "Use of Antitrust to Subvert Competition." *Journal of Law and Economics* 28 [May 1985]: 247). Later, they add, "Paradoxically, then and only then, when the joint venture [or other market action] is beneficial [to consumers], can those rivals be relied upon to denounce the undertaking as 'anticompetitive'" (p. 257).

40. Microsoft estimates that there are twenty thousand developers writing for Windows, the source of the seventy thousand applications that make up the judge's so-called applications barrier to entry (according to Scott Fallon, Microsoft Corporation, as reported to Richard McKenzie in an E-mail exchange from September 13, 2000, through October 5, 2000). McKenzie has questioned the existence of seventy thousand applications (2000). Both he and Fallon agree that many of the applications counted in the so-called applications barrier to entry have minimal sales and, thereby, are of no consequence to a firm that seeks to take over a portion of the operating system market, especially if Microsoft restricts its sales in order to charge above competitive prices. See Richard B. McKenzie, *Trust on Trial: How the Microsoft Case Is Reframing the Rules of Competition* (Boston: Perseus Books, 2001), epilogue (paperback edition).

41. Jackson, Findings of Fact, ¶17, ¶71, ¶72.

42. Bill Gates, "The Internet Tidal Wave," memorandum, May 26, 1995, Department of Justice exhibit 20, p. 1, as found at http://www.usdoj.gov/atr/cases/ms_exhibits.htm.

43. Judge Jackson found:

As soon as Netscape released Navigator on December 15, 1994, the product began to enjoy dramatic acceptance by the public; shortly after its release, consumers were already using Navigator far more than any other browser product. This alarmed Microsoft, which feared that Navigator's enthusiastic reception could embolden Netscape to develop Navigator into an alternative platform for applications development. In late May 1995, Bill Gates, the chairman and CEO of Microsoft, sent a memorandum entitled "The Internet Tidal Wave" to Microsoft's executives describing Netscape as a "new competitor 'born' on the Internet." He warned his colleagues within Microsoft that Netscape was "pursuing a multi-platform strategy where they move the key API into the client to commoditize the underlying operating system." By the late spring of 1995, the executives responsible for setting Microsoft's corporate strategy were deeply concerned that Netscape was moving its business in a direction that could diminish the applications barrier to entry. (Findings of Fact, ¶72)

44. See Richard A. Posner, *Antitrust Law: An Economic Perspective* (Chicago: University of Chicago Press, 1976), chap. 4.

45. Arthur, "Positive Feedbacks in the Economy," 92.

46. See Stan J. Liebowitz and Stephen E. Margolis, "The Fable of the Keys," *Journal of Law and Economics* 33 (April 1990): 1–26; and "Path Dependence, Lock-In, and History," *Journal of Law, Economics, and Organization* 11 (1995): 205–226.

47. Arthur, "Positive Feedbacks in the Economy," 116.

48. Liebowitz and Margolis, "Path Dependence, Lock-In, and History."

49. In its original complaint, the Justice Department argued:

Because of its resources and programming technology, Microsoft was well positioned to develop and market a browser in competition with Netscape. Indeed, continued competition on the merits between Netscape's Navigator and Microsoft's Internet Explorer would have resulted in greater innovation and the development of better products at lower prices. Moreover, in the absence of Microsoft's anticompetitive conduct, the offsetting advantages of Microsoft's size and dominant position in desktop software and Netscape's position as the browser innovator and the leading browser supplier, and the benefit to consumers of product differentiation, could have been expected to sustain competition on the merits between these companies, and perhaps others that have entered and might enter the browser market. (Klein et al., Complaint, ¶11)

50. For example, consider these two passages: (1) "Thus, Microsoft began, and continues today, a pattern of anticompetitive practices designed to thwart browser competition on the merits, to deprive customers of a choice between alternative browsers, and to exclude Microsoft's Internet browser competitors" (ibid., ¶12). (2) "Microsoft intends now unlawfully to tie its Internet browser software to its new

Windows 98 operating system, the successor to Windows 95. Microsoft has made clear that, unless restrained, it will continue to misuse its operating system monopoly to artificially exclude browser competition and deprive customers of a free choice between browsers" (¶19).

51. Judge Jackson found:

> Many of the tactics that Microsoft has employed have also harmed consumers indirectly by unjustifiably distorting competition. The actions that Microsoft took against Navigator hobbled a form of innovation that had shown the potential to depress the applications barrier to entry sufficiently to enable other firms to compete effectively against Microsoft in the market for Intel-compatible PC operating systems. That competition would have conduced to consumer choice and nurtured innovation. The campaign against Navigator also retarded widespread acceptance of Sun's Java implementation. This campaign, together with actions that Microsoft took with the sole purpose of making it difficult for developers to write Java applications with technologies that would allow them to be ported between Windows and other platforms, impeded another form of innovation that bore the potential to diminish the applications barrier to entry. There is insufficient evidence to find that, absent Microsoft's actions, Navigator and Java already would have ignited genuine competition in the market for Intel-compatible PC operating systems. It is clear, however, that Microsoft has retarded, and perhaps altogether extinguished, the process by which these two middleware technologies could have facilitated the introduction of competition into an important market. (Jackson, Findings of Fact, ¶411)

Selected Bibliography

Alchian, A. A., and H. Demsetz. "The Property Rights Paradigm." *Journal of Economic History* 33 (March 1973): 16–27.

Arthur, W. B. "Competing Technologies, Increasing Returns, and Lock-In by Historical Events." *Economic Journal* 99 (1989): 116–131.

———. "Positive Feedbacks in the Economy." *Scientific American* 262 (1990): 92–99.

———. *Increasing Returns and Path Dependence in the Economy.* Ann Arbor, Mich.: University of Michigan Press, 1994.

———. "Increasing Returns and the New World of Business." *Harvard Business Review* 74 (July–August 1996): 100–109.

Baily, M. N., and R. J. Gordon "The Productivity Slowdown, Measurement Issues, and the Explosion of Computer Power." *Brookings Papers on Economic Activity* 2 (1988): 347–420.

Baily, M. N., and R. Z. Lawrence, "Do We Have a New E-conomy?" Working Paper 8243. Cambridge, Mass.: National Bureau for Economic Research, April 2001.

Baily, M. N., and J. B. Quinn, "Information Technology: The Key to Service Productivity." *Brookings Review* 12 (Summer 1994): 37–41.

Bain, J. S. *Barriers to New Competition.* Cambridge: Harvard University Press, 1956.

Bass, F. M., and T. L. Pilon. "A Stochastic Brand Choice Framework for Econometric Modeling of Time Series Market Share Behavior." *Journal of Marketing Research* 17 (November 1980): 486–497.

Baumol, W. J., and J. Ordover. "Use of Antitrust to Subvert Competition." *Journal of Law and Economics* 28 (May 1985): 247–265.

Becker, G. S. *The Economic Approach to Human Behavior.* Chicago: University of Chicago Press, 1976.

Becker, G. S., and K. Murphy. "A Theory of Rational Addiction." *Journal of Political Economy* 96, (August 1988): 675–700.

Beggs, A. W. "A Note on Switching Costs and Technology Choice." *Journal of Industrial Economics* 37 (1989): 437–444.

Beggs, A. W., and P. Klemperer, "Multi-Period Competition with Switching Costs." *Econometrica* 60 (May 1992): 651–666.

Besen, S. M. "Private Copying, Reproduction Costs, and the Supply of Intellectual Capital." *Information Economics and Policy* 2 (1986): 2–52.

Besen, S. M., and J. Farrell. "Choosing How to Compete: Strategies and Tactics in Standardization." *Journal of Economic Perspective* 8 (Spring 1994): 117–131.

Besen, S. M., and S. Kirby, "Private Copying, Appropriability, and Optimal Copying Royalties." *Journal of Law and Economics* 32 (1989): 255–280.

Bethel, T. *The Noblest Triumph: Property and Prosperity through the Ages*. New York: St. Martin's, 1998.

Blinder, A. S. "The Internet and the New Economy." *Briefing the President*. Washington, D.C.: Internet Policy Institute, January 2000, as found at www.internet policyinst.org/briefing/1_00_sum.html.

Bork, R. H. *The Antitrust Paradox: A Policy at War with Itself*. New York: Basic Books, 1978.

Branscomb, A. W. *Who Owns Information: From Privacy to Public Access*. New York: Basic Books, 1994.

Brooke, G. M. "The Economics of Information Technology: Explaining the Productivity Paradox." Working Paper 238. Cambridge: Center for Information Systems Research, Sloan School of Management, MIT, April 1992.

Brynjolfsson, E. "The Contribution of Information Technology to Consumer Welfare." *Information Systems Research* 7 (September 1996): 281–300.

———. "The Productivity Paradox of Information Technology." *Communications of the Association of Computing Machinery*, December 1996, 66–77.

Brynjolfsson, E., and L. M. Hitt. "Information Technology as Factor of Production: The Role of Differences among Firms." *Economics of Innovation and New Technology* 3, no. 4 (1995): 183–200.

———. "Paradox Lost? Firm-Level Evidence on the Returns to Information Systems Spending." *Management Science* 42 (April 1996): 541–558.

———. "Beyond Computation: Information Technology, Organizational Transformation, and Business Performance." *Journal of Economic Perspectives* 14 (Fall 2000): 23–48.

Brynjolfsson, E., A. Renshaw, and M. Van Alstyne. "The Matrix of Change." *Sloan Management Review* 38 (Winter 1997): 37–54.

Brynjolfsson, E., and S. Yang. "The Intangible Benefits and Costs of Computer Investments: Evidence from Financial Markets." Working Paper. Cambridge: Sloan School of Management, MIT, December 1999.

Buchanan, J. M. "An Economic Theory of Clubs." *Economica* 32 (February 1965): 1–14.

———. *The Limits of Liberty*. Chicago: University of Chicago Press, 1975.

Buchanan, J. M., and W. C. Stubblebine. "Externalities." *Economica* 30 (November 1962): 371–384.

Buchanan, J. M., and Y. J. Yoon. *The Return to Increasing Returns*. Ann Arbor: University of Michigan Press, 1994.

———. "Symmetric Tragedies: Commons and Anticommons." *Journal of Law and Economics* 43 (April 2000): 1–13.

Bush, W. C. "Individual Welfare in Anarchy." In *Explorations in the Theory of Anarchy*, edited by Gordon Tullock, 5–18. Blacksburg, Va.: University Publications, 1972.

Caminal, R., and C. Matutes. "Endogenous Switching Costs in a Duopoly Model." *International Journal of Industrial Organization* 8 (1990): 353–374.

Carpenter, G. S., and K. Nakamoto. "Consumer Preference Formation and Pioneering Advantage." *Journal of Marketing Research* 26 (August 1989): 285–298.

Christensen, C. M. *The Innovator's Dilemma: When New Technologies Cause Great Firms to Fail*. Cambridge: Harvard Business School Press, 1997.

Clark, J., with O. Edwards. *Netscape Time: The Making of a Billion-Dollar Start-Up That Took on Microsoft*. New York: St. Martin's, 1999.

Coase, R. H. "The Federal Communications Commission." *Journal of Law and Economics* 2 (October 1959): 1–40.

———. "The Problem of Social Costs." *Journal of Law and Economics* 3 (October 1960): 1–45.

———. "Durability and Monopoly." *Journal of Law and Economics* 15 (April 1972): 143–149.

———. *The Firm, the Market, and the Law*. Chicago: University of Chicago Press, 1988.

Cole, J. I. et. al. *The UCLA Internet Report: Surveying the Digital Future*. Los Angeles: Center for Communication Policy, University of California–Los Angeles (November 2000), as found at http://ccp.ucla.edu/ucla-internet.pdf.

Conner, K., and R. Rumelt. "Software Piracy: An Analysis of Protection Strategies." *Management Science* 37 (1991): 125–139.

Corbin, D. E. "Keeping a Virtual Eye on Employees." *Occupational Health and Safety*, November 1, 2000: 24–28.

Council of Economic Advisors, Office of the President. *Economic Report of the President 2000*. Washington, D.C.: U.S. Government Printing Office, January 2000.

———. *Economic Report of the President 2001*. Washington, D.C.: U.S. Government Printing Office, January 2001.

Cowen, T. "Music Industry Needs Napster." *National Post*, 13 February 2001, p. A18.

Cusumano, M. A., Y. Mylonadis, and R. S. Rosenbloom. "Strategic Maneuvering and Mass-Market Dynamics: The Triumph of VHS over Beta." *Business History Review* 66 (Spring 1989): 51–94.

David, P. A. "Clio and the Economics of QWERTY." *American Economic Review* 75, no. 2 (1985): 332–337.

———. "The Dynamo and the Computer: An Historical Perspective on the Modern Productivity Paradox." *American Economic Review* 80, no. 2 (1990): 355–361.

———. "Computer and Dynamo: The Modern Productivity Paradox in a Not-Too-Distant Mirror." In *Technology and Productivity: The Challenge for Economic Policy*. Paris: Organisation for Economic Co-operation and Development, 1991, 315–348.

———. "Understanding Digital Technology's Evolution and the Path of Measured Productivity Growth: Present and Future in the Mirror of the Past." In *Understanding the Digital Economy: Data, Tools, and Research*. Cambridge: MIT Press, 2000, 49–95.

Demsetz, H. "Toward a Theory of Property Rights." *American Economic Review* 57 (May 1964): 347–359.

Dogan, S. L. "Is Napster a VCR? The Implications of *Sony* for Napster and Other Internet Technologies." *Hastings Law Journal* 52 (April 2002): 939–959.

Economics and Statistics Administration, Office of Policy Development, U.S. Department of Commerce. *Digital Economy 2000*. Washington, D.C.: U.S. Electronic Policy. As found at http://www.esa.doc.gov/de2000.pdf.

Eisenach, J., T. Lenard, and S. McGonegal. *The Digital Economy Fact Book: Second Edition, 2000*. Washington, D.C.: Progress and Freedom Foundation, 2000.

Epstein, R. A. *Takings: Private Property and the Power of Eminent Domain*. Cambridge: Harvard University Press, 1985.

Etzioni, A. *The Limits of Privacy* . New York: Basic Books, 1999.

Farrell, J., and G. Saloner. "Standardization, Compatibility, and Innovation." *Rand Journal* 16 (1985): 70–83.

Farrell, J., and C. Shapiro. "Optimal Contracts with Lock-In." Discussion Paper 130. Princeton, N.J.: Woodrow Wilson School, Princeton University, 1987.

———. "Dynamic Competition with Switching Costs." *Rand Journal of Economics* 19 (Spring 1998): 123–137.

Fisher, F., J. McGowan, and J. Greenwood. *Folded, Spindled, and Mutilated: Economic Analysis and U.S. v. I.B.M*. Cambridge: MIT Press, 1983.

Flamm, K. *More for Less: The Economic Impact of Semiconductors*. Washington, D.C.: Semiconductor Industry Association, December 1997.

Frank, R. H., and P. J. Cook. 1995. *The Winner-Take-All Society: Why the Few at the Top Get So Much More Than the Rest of Us*. New York: Penguin, 1995.

Froot, K. A., and P. D. Klemperer. "Exchange Rate Pass-Through When Market Share Matters." *American Economic Review* 79 (1989): 637–654.

Garrity, J., and E. Casey. "Internet Misuse in the Workplace, A Lawyer's Primer." *Florida Law Journal* (n.d.). As found at http://www.flabar.org/newflabar/publicmediainfo/TFBJournal/nov98-2.html.

Gates, B. "The Internet Tidal Wave." Memorandum, May 26, 1995. Department of Justice exhibit 20. As found at http://www.usdoj.gov/atr/cases/ms_exhibits.htm.

———. "Internet Strategy Workshop Keynote." Seattle, Wash.: Microsoft Corporation, December 7, 1995.

Gersick, C. J. "Revolutionary Change Theories: A Multilevel Exploration of the Punctuated Equilibrium Paradigm." *Academy of Management Review* 16 (1991): 10–36

Gibbs W. W. "Taking Computers to Task." *Scientific American*, July 1997, 82–90. As found at http://www.sciam.com/0797issue/0797trends.html.

Gilder, G. *Microcosm: The Quantum Revolution in Economics and Technology.* New York: Simon & Schuster, 1989.

———. *Telecosm: How Infinite Bandwidth Will Revolutionize Our World.* New York: Free Press, 2000.

Givon, M., V. Mahajan, and E. Muller. "Software Piracy: Estimation of Lost Sales and the Impact of Software Diffusion." *Journal of Marketing* 59 (1999): 29–37.

Gordon, H. S. "The Economic Theory of a Common Property Resource: The Fishery." *Journal of Political Economy* 62, no. 2 (1954): 124–142.

Gordon, R. J. "Does the 'New Economy' Measure Up to the Great Inventions of the Past?" *Journal of Economic Perspective* 14 (Fall 2000): 49–74.

Gould, S. J., and N. Eldridge. "Punctuated Equilibria: The Tempo and Mode of Evolution Reconsidered." *Paleobiologist* 3 (1977): 115–151.

Griliches, Z. "Productivity, R&D, the Data Constraints." *American Economic Review* 84 (March 1994): 1–23.

Grove, A. S. *Only the Paranoid Survive: How to Exploit the Crisis Points That Challenge Every Company.* New York: Doubleday, 1996.

Gurbaxani, V., and S. Whang. "The Impact of Information Systems on Organizations and Markets." *Communication of the ACM* 34 (January 1991): 59–73.

Hardin, G. "The Tragedy of the Commons." *Science* 162 (1968): 1243–1254.

Hayek, F. A. "The Use of Knowledge in Society." *American Economic Review* 35 (September 1945): 519–530.

Heller, M. A. "The Tragedy of the Anticommons: Property in Transition." *Harvard Law Review* 111 (1998): 621–688.

Hovenkamp, H. *Federal Antitrust Policy: The Law of Competition and Its Practice*, 2d ed. St. Paul, Minn.: Westlaw, 1999.

Jackson, T. P. *United States v. Microsoft Corporation*, Findings of Fact, First District Court, Civil Action No. 98-1232, November 5, 1999, ¶40. As found at http://www.usdoj.gov/atr/cases/f3800/msjudgex.htm.

———. *United States v. Microsoft Corporation*, Conclusions of Law, First District Court, Civil Action No. 98-1232, IB, April 13, 2000, ¶15. As found at http://www.usdoj.gov/atr/cases/f4400/4469.htm.

Johnson, W. "The Economics of Copying." *Journal of Political Economy* 93, no. 1 (1985): 158–174.

Jorgenson, D. W., and K. Stiroh. "Computers and Growth." *Economics of Innovation and New Technology* 3 (1995): 295–316.

Katz, M. L., and C. Shapiro. "Network Externalities, Competition, and Compatibility." *American Economic Review* 75 (1985): 424–440.

Kelly, K. *New Rules for the New Economy.* New York: Viking/Penguin, 1998.

Klein, B. "Microsoft's Use of Zero Price Bundling to Fight the 'Browser Wars.'" In *Competition, Innovation, and the Microsoft Monopoly: Antitrust in the Digital Marketplace.* Boston: Kluwer Academic Publishers, 1999, 217–254.

Klein, J. I., et al. *United States v. Microsoft Corporation,* Complaint, First District Court, Civil Action No. 98-1232, May 20, 1998, ¶56. As found at http://www.usdoj.gov/atr/cases/f1700/1763.htm.

Klemperer, P. D. "The Competitiveness of Markets with Switching Costs." *Rand Journal of Economics* 18 (Spring 1987): 138–150.

———. "Entry Deterrence in Markets with Consumer Switching Costs." *Economics Journal* 97 (1987; supp.): 99–117.

———. "Markets with Switching Costs." *Quarterly Journal of Economics* 102 (1987): 375–394.

———. "Welfare Effects of Entry into Markets with Switching Costs." *Journal of Industrial Economics* 37 (December 1988): 159–165.

———. "Price Wars Caused by Switching Costs." *Review of Economic Studies* 56 (1989): 405–420.

Kuhn, T. S. *The Structure of Scientific Revolution,* 2d ed. Chicago: University of Chicago Press, 1962.

Lal, R., and V. Padmanabhan. "Competitive Response and Equilibria." *Marketing Science* 14, no. 3 (1995): G101–G108.

Lee, D. R., and D. Kreutzer. "Lagged Demand and a 'Perverse' Response to Threatened Property Rights." *Economic Inquiry* 20 (October 1982): 579–588.

Lee, D. R., and R. B. McKenzie. "A Case for Letting a Firm Take Advantage of Network Effects and 'Locked-In' Customers." *Hastings Law Journal* 52 (April 2001): 795–812.

Lessig, L. *The Future of Ideas: The Fate of the Commons in a Connected World.* New York: Random House, 2001.

Liebowitz, S. J. *Rethinking the Network Economy.* New York: American Management Association, 2002.

Liebowitz, S. J., and S. E. Margolis. "The Fable of the Keys." *Journal of Law and Economics* 33 (April 1990): 1–26.

———. "Network Externality: An Uncommon Tragedy." *Journal of Economic Perspectives* 8 (Spring 1994): 133–150.

———. "Path Dependence, Lock-In, and History." *Journal of Law, Economics and Organization* 11 (1995): 205–226.

Litan, R. E., and A. M. Rivlin. "The Economy and the Internet: What Lies Ahead." *Conference Report.* Washington, D.C.: Brookings Institution, December 2000. As found at www.brook.edu/comm/conferencereport/cr4/cr4.htm.

Lyman, P., H. Varian et al. *How Much Information?* Working Paper. Berkeley, Calif.: School of Information Management and Systems, University of California, Berkeley, November 2000. As found at http://www.sims.berkeley.edu/how-much-info/.

McCarthy P. "Computer Prices: How Good Is the Quality Adjustment?" Paper presented at a conference on capital stock organized by the Organisation of Economic Co-operation and Development, March 10–14, 1997. As found at http://www.oecd.org/std/capstock97/oecd3.pdf.

McKenzie, R. B. *Trust on Trial: How the Microsoft Case Is Reframing the Rules of Competition*. Boston: Perseus Books, 2000.

———. "Microsoft's 'Applications Barrier to Entry': The Case of the Missing 70,000 Programs." *Policy Analysis* 380 (August 31, 2000).

———. "The Importance of Deviance in Intellectual Development." In *The Production and Diffusion of Public Choice Theory*, edited by D. Eckel, J. C. Pitt, and D. Salehi-Isfahani. London: Blackwell, forthcoming 2003.

McKenzie, R. B., and D. R. Lee. *Quicksilver Capital: How the Rapid Movement of Wealth Has Changed the World*. New York: Free Press, 1991.

———. *Managing through Incentives: How to Develop a More Collaborative, Productive, and Profitable Organization*. New York: Oxford University Press, 1998.

McKinsey Global Institute. *U.S. Productivity Growth, 1995–2000*. As found at http://www.mckinsey.com/knowledge/mgi/reports/productivity.asp.

Milgrom, P., and J. Roberts. *Economics, Organization, and Management*. Englewood Cliffs, N.J.: Prentice-Hall, 1992.

Miller, D., and P. H. Friesen. "Momentum and Revolution in Organizational Transition." *Academy of Management Journal* 23 (1980): 591–614.

Mokyr, J. "Are We Living in the Middle of an Industrial Revolution?" *Federal Reserve Bank of Kansas City Economic Review* 82, no. 2 (1997): 31–43.

Nordhaus, W. D. "Do Real Output and Real Wage Measures Capture Reality, The History of Lighting Suggests Not." Discussion Paper 1078. New Haven, Conn.: Cowles Foundation for Research in Economics, 1994.

Novos, I., and M. Waldman. "The Effect of Increased Copyright Protection." *Journal of Political Economy* 92 (1984): 236–246.

Oliner, S. D., and D. E. Sichel. "Computers and Output Growth Revisited, How Big Is the Puzzle?" *Brookings Papers on Economic Activity* 2 (1994): 273–317.

Olson, M. *The Logic of Collective Action: Public Goods and the Theory of Groups*. Cambridge: Harvard University Press, 1965.

Peters, Thomas, and Robert H. Waterman. *In Search of Excellence: Lessons from America's Best-Run Companies*. New York: Warner, 1982.

Posner, R. A. *Antitrust Law: An Economic Perspective*. Chicago: University of Chicago Press, 1976.

Raff, D. M. G., and M. Trajtenberg. "Quality-Adjusted Prices for the American Automobile Industry: 1906–1940." In *The Economics of New Goods*, edited by T. F. Bresnahan and R. J. Gordon, 77–108. Chicago: University of Chicago Press, 1997.

Rauch, J. *Demosclerosis: The Silent Killer of American Government*. New York: Times Books, 1994.

Rohlfs, J. H. *Bandwagon Effects in High Technology Industries.* Cambridge: MIT Press, 2001.

Rubin, P. H., and T. M. Lenard. *Privacy and the Commercial Use of Personal Information.* Boston: Kluwer Academic Publishers, 2002.

Scott, A. "The Fishery: The Objective of Sole Ownership." *Journal of Political Economy* 63, no. 2 (1955): 116–124.

Seybold, P., and R. Marshak. *Customers.com: How to Create a Profitable Business Strategy for the Internet and Beyond.* New York: Times Books, 1998.

Sichel, D. E. *The Computer Revolution: An Economic Perspective.* Washington, D.C.: Brookings Institution, 1997.

SIIA's Report on Global Software Piracy: 2000. Washington, D.C.: Software Information Industry Association, 2000, 3. As found at http://www.siia.net/shared content/press/2000/5-24-00.html.

Sixth Annual BSA Global Software Piracy Study. West Chester, Penn.: International Planning and Research Corporation, May 2001. As found at http://www.bsa.org/resources/2001-05-21.55.pdf.

Sykes, C. J. *The End of Privacy.* New York: St. Martin's, 1999.

Tellis, G. T., and P. N. Golder. *Will and Vision: How Latecomers Grow to Dominate Markets.* New York: McGraw-Hill, 2002.

Triplett, J. E. "The Solow Productivity Paradox: What Do Computers Do to Productivity?" *Canadian Journal of Economics* 32 (April 1999): 309–334.

Tullock, G. *The Logic of the Law.* New York: Basic Books, 1971.

Tushman, M. L., W. H. Newman, and E. Romanelli. "Convergence and Upheaval: Managing the Unsteady Pace of Organizational Evolution." *California Management Review* 29, no. 1 (1986): 1–16.

Tushman, M. L., and C. A. O'Reiley III. "The Ambidextrous Organization: Managing Evolutionary and Revolutionary Change." *California Management Review* 38 (Summer 1996): 1–23.

Tushman, M. L., and E. Romanelli. "Organizational Evolution: A Metamorphosis Model of Convergence and Reorientation." *Research in Organizational Behavior,* vol. 7, edited by L. L. Cummings and B. M. Staw, 171–222. Greenwich, Conn.: JAI Press, 1985.

Vaidhyanathan, S. *Copyrights and Copywrongs: The Rise of Intellectual Property and How It Threatens Creativity.* New York: New York University Press, 2001.

Young, A. "Increasing Returns and Economic Progress." *Economic Journal* 152 (December 1928): 527–540.

Index

About the Author

RICHARD B. MCKENZIE is the Walter B. Gerken Professor of Enterprise and Society in the Graduate School of Management at the University of California at Irvine, where he teaches courses for MBA students on microeconomics for managers, managing organizational incentives, and digital economics. He is also a regular columnist for *Investor's Business Daily*.